Advance Praise for

Learning Organizations

"In a rich dialogue of many voices this book explores some key ideas of an emerging new management paradigm. Community, networks, feedback, self-organization, and learning are essential aspects of understanding business organizations as living systems. For managers and entrepreneurs in the twenty-first century this perspective will be vital."
— Fritjof Capra
author, *The Turning Point*

"This book will be referenced many times because the depth of material is profound. *Learning Organizations: Developing Cultures for Tomorrow's Workplace* is a collection of essays for the serious learner involved with creating learning organizations. The essays presented by key practitioners, range from theory to models and applications, and all are thoughtful and insightful. The result for the reader is a richer understanding of what organizations may become. I strongly recommend this collection."
— Herbert Rau
total quality manager
National Semiconducto

"The authors of *Learning Organizations* capture the depth, breadth, vision, and challenges inherent in the struggle for modern corporations to 'learn together as one body.' This book is a magnificent mosaic of experience, theory, and practice."
— Kazimierz Gozdz, editor
Community Building: Renewing Spirit & Learning in Business

"This could be the definitive volume on the principles and the power of the learning organization. *Learning Organizations* is an immediately useful compendium of extraordinary ideas and tools with supporting rationale for creating exceptional possibilities. It is all the more exciting coming from so many strong new voices. This book packs a wallop."
— John Nirenberg, partner, Center for Workplace Community, Denver; author, *The Living Organization: Transforming Teams Into Workplace Communities*

"Bravo! The *Learning Organizations* collection bridges the gap from theory to practice with a compilation of reading that deepens one's understanding while broadening the bounds of application. Clearly, the authors represent an array of talented minds that combine years of practical experience with visionary thinking to enhance the already dynamic theoretical framework we call the learning organization. Its pages are a treasure chest of useful models, real world examples, and inventive thinking. This is definitely a tool that will enable and empower organizations to make the next big step forward in the journey toward becoming true learning organizations."

> — Bob Hetzel
> assistant superintendent
> Kyrene School District

"Now that knowledge drives the economies of the globe, what could be more essential than a fresh ability to learn? This kaleidoscope of 32 perspectives on learning organizations will dazzle the mind of any reader."

> — William E. Halal, author,
> *Internal Markets;* professor,
> The George Washington University

"A real treasure of information and ideas on learning organizations—should be a valuable reference for practitioners."

> — William J. Mullin, director
> Quality Assurance & Planning
> Mfg. Division, Merck & Co. Inc.

"Even for people who have been managers for years, this collection should be read and contemplated by anyone whose mind is even a little open."

> — George F. Schmitt
> executive vice president
> International Operations
> AirTouch Communications

"John Renesch and Sarita Chawla have put together a collection of thoughts and writings that provide a picture of the challenges and opportunities facing all of us as 'working individuals' in the organizations of tomorrow. The book's format is a brilliant tour guide for the reader's journey. An excellent book... well done!"

> — Dick Beckhard, director
> Richard Beckhard Associates;
> retired professor, M.I.T.
> Sloan Management School

"...a book which will create value in industry. The content is wonderful. There were sections which worked really well for me. Sarita's series of questions in the introduction is very powerful."
— Michael Munn, senior consultant
Lockheed Corporation

"This collection...is remarkable...this book will replace numerous collected articles and other references which clutter any credenza. This is a collection of relevant, insightful, and applicable writings which I will share with all my colleagues and other students of learning...everyone can gain."
— Bill Schrum, V. P. Human Resources
Lutheran Hospital - LaCrosse

"Anyone in the trenches of Corporate America knows how tough it is to live one's life with genuine compassion and with an openness and commitment to learning. The pages of this book are filled with the stories and experiences of people who have been there. As they share their questions and their vulnerabilities, I am inspired to search for my own."
— Chris Strutt, consulting engineer
Client/Server Software Engineering
Digital Equipment Corporation

"This anthology brings together the voices of many of the key players in the transformation of organizations today. The different voices, interpretations and applications provide a variety of lenses through which to view and understand learning organizations. Some essays are illuminating, others are reinforcing. They provide tools and examples to draw from. Overall, they are encouraging. They show that a learning organization is not just a theoretical ideal, but, given the right circumstances, a probability."
— Edie Heilman, vice president
Customer Relations
Working Assets

"The authors succeeded in both challenging and inspiring me! Certainly a lot of hard work is involved in times of transformation, but now I've found my traveling companions."
— Lindy Ashmore, director
Corporate Service Quality
Charles Schwab & Co., Inc.

"Through the voices of several authors, one hears the provocative insights and questions raised by the notion of seeing learning organizations as a vehicle for bringing about 'higher order wisdom' and higher order change in the world. This collection is a real contribution to the evolution of our current thinking about learning organizations."

> — Cathe Carlson
> organization development consultant

"Sarita Chawla and John Renesch have assembled an excellent resource for those who are struggling to integrate organization learning into the corporate environment. The writers cover widely diverse topics that are supportive of the goal of organization learning. I highly recommend this book both for newcomers to this endeavor and for experienced practitioners who are looking for supporting inspiration."

> — Eileen Beltran
> OD consultant, Intel Corporation

"*Learning Organizations* is rich in delectable morsels of nutritious nourishment for the brain — a book to be savored. Brain food is what we need if we are going to satisfy our appetites for learning about learning, and this book belongs on every organization's buffet table. Read it and salivate."

> — Jim Kouzes, co-author
> *The Leadership Challenge* and
> *Credibility;* chairman and CEO,
> Tom Peters Group/Learning Systems

Learning Organizations

Featured essays by:

Sarita Chawla • Fred Kofman & Peter Senge
Charles Handy • Marilynne Anderson
Rosabeth Moss Kanter • John W. Thompson • Jayme Rolls
Lisa J. Marshall, Sandy Mobley, & Gene Calvert
Diane Cory & Paula Underwood
Barbara Shipka • Judy Brown
Sherrin Bennett & Juanita Brown • Susan J. Bethanis
Kendall Murphy • W. Brian Kreutzer • David P. Kreutzer
Robert Dilworth • Joel & Michelle Levey
Stephanie Ryan • Eric Edwards Vogt
Carol Sanford • Linda E. Morris • Bob Guns
Daniel H. Kim • David R. Schwandt • Alain Gauthier
John H. Wood • Robert Weintraub • Robert L. Masten
Alan K. Graham • Frank Hoffmann & Bill Withers
Mary Byrd • Dinesh Chandra

Learning Organizations

Developing Cultures for Tomorrow's Workplace

edited by

Sarita Chawla and John Renesch

Productivity Press
Portland, Oregon

Productivity Press
P.O. Box 13390
Portland OR 97213-0390
United States of America
Telephone: 503-235-0600
Telefax: 503-235-0909
Email: staff@ppress.com

Permissions and Credits

The editors and publisher wish to acknowledge the following sources:

"Communities of Commitment: The Heart of Learning Organizations" by Fred Kofman and Peter Senge was first published in *Organizational Dynamics* (Autumn, 1993) by American Management Association, and is reprinted with permission of the publisher.

"Managing the Dream" by Charles Handy was initially published as a booklet from Gemini Consulting as "Managing the Dream: The Learning Organization," and is published with permission of the author.

"Mastering Change" by Rosabeth Moss Kanter is based on a speech to the International Management Symposium, St. Gallen, Switzerland, May, 1993; copyright 1993 by Rosabeth Moss Kanter; used by permission.

The table entitled "Modes of Being and Learning" contained in Linda E. Morris' essay "Developmental Strategies for the Knowledge Era" is published with permission of Transform, a U.K. consulting firm, and Tom Boydell, developers of this material.

Photo Credits: Photo of Charles Handy by Elizabeth Handy. Photo of W. Brian Kreutzer by Hutchins Photography, Inc.

Drawing on page 230 by Arnie Levin is published with permission of the artist.

Cover illustration by Susan Malikowski © 1994
Composition by Select Press
Printed and bound by Edwards Brothers in the United States of America

Learning Organizations: Developing Cultures for Tomorrow's Workplace.
Edited by Sarita Chawla and John Renesch.
ISBN 1-56327-110-9

00 99 98 97 96 95 10 9 8 7 6 5 4 3 2 1

*In these pages many mysteries are hinted at.
What if you came to understand one of them?*

*Words let water from an unseen, infinite ocean
Come into this place as energy for the dying and
even the dead.*

*Bored onlookers, but with such Light in our eyes!
As we read this book, the jewel-lights intensify.*

—Rumi

Table of Contents

Case Studies:

Preface

The concept of the learning organization took seed several decades ago and gained major recognition with the incredible success of Peter Senge's 1990 book *The Fifth Discipline.* Thanks to the growing popularity of this field of inquiry among organizational consultants, practitioners, and academics, thousands of people in the U.S. and abroad have been exposed to the science of systems thinking and the transformational aspects of "new thinking for new times."

This collection of essays has been compiled as part of New Leaders Press' Business Anthology Series, which began in 1991. Each book in this series focuses on some transformative aspect of business, addressing new ways of thinking about commercial enterprise and organizational life.

My co-editor, Sarita Chawla, played a primary role in compiling this collection, serving as a coach for many of the authors. As you can read in the acknowledgements that follow, her efforts were much appreciated. She has been a scholar of learning organizations and a member of this community for many years. Included among her many activities was her career with Pacific Bell, from which she retired in 1993.

It is my hope that you will read this book with an intention to learn—like Sarita points out in the Introduction—asking questions and being willing to engage in true discovery, as children do before they become conditioned (or trained) to have all the "right answers."

This collection contains many powerful essays, offering incredible wisdom, perspective, and structure for those who wish to be involved in bringing about positive change for their organizations. A meaningful role exists for them in this turbulent and chaotic environment. Some of the reading may require considerable focus and rigor, "mental tenacity" so to speak, as many of these essays are quite scholarly—only natural since M.I.T. served as one of the incubators for this discipline.

Whether you are a marketing executive, an entrepreneur, a personnel officer, or a line supervisor, I urge you to engage with this book as an adventure into a new way of being in your job, in your business, and in your industry. If you are a secretary, a strategic planner, or a plant foreman, consider this collection to be an opportunity to forever change your mind about work—as a place to learn and create, to contribute and revolutionize, to play and have fun—not just a place where you go to "make a living."

A learning organization culture represents more than an environment for personal development and continuous challenge. It represents the only type of work environment that can be competitive in the "knowledge-value" era, described by Taichi Sakaiya, former MITI economist and author of over thirty books in Japan.

As a member of any workforce in any industry or productive community, you can regain the curiosity that once thrived within you. Let the "curious you" come alive. Drop the cloak of "knowing" and take on the shawl of "not knowing"—of being curious, intrigued, and innocent.

As you and others you work with take on this attitude of inquiry, you will find new life, new "verve" living in your organization.

Read and enjoy. Inquire and allow yourself to be changed.

> — John Renesch, co-editor
> April, 1995

Acknowledgements

The compilation of this comprehensive anthology involved a significant effort by many people—those who are identified as contributing authors as well as those who are more behind the scenes. Everyone connected with this book is grateful for various contributions over the two years this book was in development. The authors and editors wish to thank several specific people for their talent, skill, and support.

Starting with the authors, Marilynne Anderson gives heartfelt thanks to Sarita Chawla and Don Anderson for their unwavering support and encouragement through the writing of her essay, and to Gayle Holmes and Mary Mahoney for the spirit, enterprise and significance of Minnesota 100, a one-to-one learning experience aimed at leveling the practice field for women in leadership.

Lisa J. Marshall, Sandy Mobley and Gene Calvert wish to acknowledge the profound influence of Chris Argyris, who models double loop learning, as well as teaches it.

Paula Underwood expresses her gratitude to everyone who went before her, passing down all the Ancient Wisdom in the tradition of her Native-American ancestors. She acknowledges members of her own family and thanks her co-author Diane Cory for her wisdom and courage in recognizing, years ago, the value of an Ancient Way. She also acknowledges "all those learning organization practitioners, beginning with Peter Senge, who have quickly recognized this value. Thank you for listening."

Barbara Shipka gratefully acknowledges Sarita Chawla for encouraging the planting of a specific seed and expresses her indebtedness and deep appreciation to Sharon Jeffrey Lehrer for support in hoeing, watering, and weeding the ground in which her essay grew.

Judy Brown expresses her appreciation to Sarita Chawla and Lorna Fitzgerald Morris for their editorial assistance and to many other colleagues for their contributions to the dialogue tradition.

Juanita Brown wishes to honor those who inspired her earliest musings about dialogue, community, and committed action. From Mildred Cowan, Billie Alban, and the years of patient community-building with Cesar Chavez she learned the importance of strategic thinking, of "great conversations about things that matter," and of the power of keeping faith and hope alive. The writings of Paulo Friere, Saul Alinsky and Fran Peavey helped her discover the bridges between action and reflection, advocacy and inquiry, and the architecture and powerful questions. She is grateful to Peter Senge, Bill Isaacs, and her community of colleagues at the MIT Organizational Learning Center for providing a rich context of challenge and creativity. Sherrin Bennett, her co-author in this collection, has brought her penetrating insights and deep understanding of interactive learning. She gives special gratitude to her partner in life and work, David Isaacs, whose trust in the transformative power of appreciative inquiry has never wavered.

Susan J. Bethanis is especially grateful to Dr. Annie Herda, Dr. Avis Stafford, and Else Tamayo. She thanks Annie for shedding light on the magic of metaphor and language as action; Avis for her support on this project and her constant encouragement; and Else for developing the drawings and her kind listening in "our many conversations." While Susan originated the illustrations in her essay, she thanks Annie, Else, and Avis as well as Sarita Chawla and David Ancel for their input. The interpretive framework that informs her work is steeped in hermeneutics, and language is central to this philosophy. Some 20th Century writers who have shaped this domain are Martin Heidegger, Hans-Georg Gadamer, Jurgen Habermas, Paul Ricoeur, and anthropologist Clifford Geertz. Ricoeur, especially, sparked her interest in the metaphorical nature of language; others influencing her work on metaphor are George Lakoff, Mark Johnson, Susan Sontag, James Dicenso, Gareth Morgan, and C.A. Bowers.

Kendall Murphy acknowledges James Flaherty of New Ventures West for his development of the approach to coaching that has so inspired him. He is indebted to Flaherty "for the impact that his work has had on me personally and for providing such an important alternative to working with people in and out of organizational settings." He also is thankful for the exceptional coaching provided by his wife and editor, Sarita Chawla, who "continues to clear new spaces for me to step into."

David P. Kreutzer would like to thank everyone at Gould-Kreutzer Associates, Inc., the MIT System Dynamic Group, IDON, Ltd., as well as all the clients and students who have helped to develop the ideas on how to best implement systems thinking and system dynamics applications in management teams. He gives special thanks to his teachers Jay Forrester, John Sterman, John Morecroft, Peter Senge, Alan Graham, Ed Schein, Barry

Richmond, Tony Hodgson and Gary Chicoine-Piper. Also special thanks to Janet Gould, Ginny Wiley, Ken Friedman, Brian Kreutzer, Julia Kilcoyne and Valerie Rossi for help on this article.

Robert Dilworth wishes to acknowledge three friends and colleagues who have been particularly important in helping him shape his views about the learning organization: Jack Mezirow and Victoria Marsick of Teachers College at Columbia University for their insights into Transformative and Workplace Learning; and Reg Evans for sharing his experience as the principal pioneer of action learning for over fifty years.

Joel and Michelle Levey would like to thank the members of project, R & D, and leadership teams they have worked with at Weyerhauser, Monsanto, DuPont, MIT, SRI International, AT&T Bell Labs, Kimberly-Clark, Hewlett-Packard, Travelers Insurance, Group Health Cooperative (HMO), NASA, US Army, and International Center for Organization Design who have contributed to evolving and validating the business value of the methods outlined in their essay. They also wish to thank their colleagues Bill Veltrop, George Por, Ruth and Chris Thorsen, Richard Moon, William C. Miller, Peter and Trudy Johnson-Lenz, Eric Vogt, Jim Channon, Suzanne Mamet, Mario Narduzzi, and Diane Robbins for their inspiration in this work. The Leveys send special thanks and heartfelt appreciation to their co-editors, Sarita Chawla and John Renesch, for modeling the qualities of higher order learning and creative flexibility that helped bring this essay to life.

Stephanie Ryan offers "namaste" to Sarita Chawla for her unconditional love and coaching as co-editor of her essay. Blessings to Craig Fleck for giving the necessary feedback she often did not want to hear, teaching her the value of living in the unknown space. She thanks Maura Ryan for her patient and humorous editing. She is grateful to her many friends—Diane, Stephen, Greg...who listened and read the countless drafts and believed in the value of what she had to say.

Eric Edwards Vogt would first like to thank all his colleagues at MicroMentor, who helped him understand more about learning by constantly experimenting with new designs and reflecting upon the results. In particular, he thanks Doug Bissonette, Mike Rubin, Cindy Steinberg, Karen Wise, Linda Koretsky, Kathleen May, Patrick Littlefield, Jeff Rand, Janet Toole, Susan Good, Kate Merritt, and Mark Nordenson.

A second source of inspiration has been his clients and colleagues at the annual MicroMentor Corporate Learning Conference. He would like to particularly thank Juanita Brown, Brian Byrne, Diane Cory, Stan Davis, Jeannie Duck, Carol Gorelick, Meg Graham, Helena Light Hadley, Brook Manville, Victoria Marsick, Rob Masten, Suzanne Merritt, Linda Morris, David Morrison, George Murray, Harrison Owen, Charlotte Pollard, Nick Rudd, Peter Senge, Harvey Shrednick, Wick Sloane, Gordon Stone, Susan Stucky, Alan Webber, and Dave Wilson.

He is additionally grateful for the continuous flow of ideas and perspectives which emanate from his associating with InterClass, the International Corporate Learning Association. Principal contributors to his thinking from that creative community include Jim Botkin, Jim Chrz, Clifford Gilpin, John Greco, Julie Greenberg, Peter Henschel, Jan Lapidoth, Kate O'Keefe, Hubert St. Onge, Rebecca Phillips, Susan Stucky, Jeri Thornsberry, Wayne Townsend, and Nancy Tuyn.

Vogt would like to specifically thank his teachers and co-learners in the field of Ontology and Ontological coaching: Fernando Flores, Julio Olalla, Rafael Echeverria, Manuel Manga, Suzanne O'Brien, Peg Joukowsky, Lesley Pollitt, David Jenkins, and Gordon Snyder.

On a more personal note, he would like to thank his remarkable father, Evon Z. Vogt, Jr., who has demonstrated throughout his life an enduring passion for ideas and people. To his continuing source of ideas and inspiration, many thanks and much love goes to his wife, Robin Grumman-Vogt.

Linda E. Morris would like to especially acknowledge two individuals whose thoughts have acted as catalysts for her chapter: Don Michael and Tom Boydell. Don, a social psychologist and urban planner wrote *On Learning to Plan and Planning to Learn* in 1973. Many of his earlier thoughts about changing toward forward-future-responsive societal learning are as applicable now as they were then, and he has extended his perspective in the interval. His exploration of the psychological needs and underpinnings of the learning society ring true for the learning organization as well, and he writes at a depth that illuminated much that was hidden. Tom, who with Michael Pedler and John Burgoyne wrote the *Learning Company* and initiated the Learning Company project, links together the concepts of individual and organizational development within a transformational context. His writings and thoughts about the "modes of being" we humans traverse provide a foundation for human resource developers to describe and actually address human development in the workplace.

Bob Guns wants to thank Arie de Geus for his inspiration and support, and Hubert St. Onge for encouraging him to write this essay. He also appreciates the great help both Sarita and John provided in his writing journey. Moreover, Bob wishes to acknowledge the FLO Executive Reading Network for their continuing commitment to enrich and refine his thinking. Finally, he appreciates and deeply values his wife and partner, Veronica, who has acted as primary sounding board, feedback provider, and head cheerleader. "Many thanks, Veronica."

David R. Schwandt acknowledges Dr. Anne-Michele Gundlack, the co-author of the Organizational Learning Model, for the research contribution she made in the area of sense-making. He also thanks Dr. Francis O'Neal for his research in the area of information movement and Chris Johnson and Somsri Siriwaiprapan for their contributions in theory-building.

Alain Gauthier wishes to thank Peter Senge for introducing him to the "Learning Organization" as well as to the healthcare field. He is also very grateful to Kathryn Johnson, Mike Guthrie, John King, Cheryl Scott, and Hank Walker, for the opportunity to help build healthcare learning organizations, and for their thoughtful editing suggestions. He acknowledges his wife and partner Dr. Joan Kenley for her constant inspiration and support on the path of personal development and self-understanding.

In addition to those teachers already acknowledged in his article, John H. Wood wishes to acknowledge the support and advice of a few others: Carol Sanford, a co-author and friend, was always there to give the right guidance at the right time; Dick Raymond, a long time friend and source of inspiration, provided the encouragement when frustration or resignation would appear; and, lastly Sarita Chawla's gentle and precise advice was greatly appreciated.

Robert Weintraub offers much thanks to Jack Mezirow, Victoria Marsick, and Stephen Brookfield of Columbia University Teacher's College for facilitating his study and critical reflection; and to Robin Sternbergh, Mark Simon, John Morris, and Ross Williams of IBM for facilitating the application of his ideas.

Alan K. Graham would like to acknowledge several contributions: the Medrad vice presidents on the Steering Committee, Ken Grob, John Friel, and Joe Havrilla for their leadership and commitment. He also thanks all the other members of the Steering Committee for their enthusiastic participation. He thanks John Carter, his partner on the Medrad work, for his support, Lyse Fontaine for her editorial help and Shoji Shiba, who "constantly teaches me TQM."

Frank Hoffmann and Bill Withers would like to offer their thanks and gratitude to Hal Rosenbluth and all of the associates of Rosenbluth International, past, present, and future. They would also like to send very special thanks to the associates in Learning and Development for "the daily inspiration you provide. Without each of you, there would be no story to tell."

Mary Byrd thanks Linda Morris, Sarita Chawla, and Valerie Truelove, who provided ideas and encouragement for her writing her essay. She also acknowledges several authors and leaders in the field who have inspired her thinking, including Peter Senge, Eric Vogt, Michael Ray, and George Por. She thanks Phil White, David Stanley, and Jim Hendrickson at Informix Software for their feedback. She offers special thanks to the employees of Informix "who taught me that learning occurs when it is nurtured in the environment."

Co-editor Sarita Chawla is deeply grateful to the community of authors for allowing her to both explore their writings and their thinking with them, and learn from them. She feels humbled by them and wiser from the experience. Of special note, her deep appreciation for Ken Murphy, who patiently took his turn as one of the thirty-nine authors, even though they were newlyweds through this process! Significant teachers, her parents, Madan and Pushpa Chawla, and her son Rahul played more of a role than they might guess. The women authors of this book brought a presence that she cannot define. She says, "It was too significant to ignore." She also thanks Sterling and Stone for the opportunity to learn with the wise.

Co-editor John Renesch wishes to acknowledge all the authors for their incredible contribution of wisdom, particularly Peter Senge who has contributed so much to the better understanding of system thinking as a tool for social transformation. He also acknowledges Charles Handy and Rosabeth Moss Kanter for their contributions, joining Senge and his colleague Fred Kofman as lead authors for this exciting collection. He also thanks Sarita Chawla, for her partnership in creating this collection, specifically for her heartfelt coaching of authors. Renesch also thanks Linda Morris and her assistant Jill Harper for their help in expanding the network of contributors, Elizabeth Handy for her contributions and support, and Wendy D'Ambrose of Good Measure, Inc., agent for Rosabeth Moss Kanter, for her help in arranging for the text of her European speech to be included in this collection. He also thanks Joel and Michelle Levey for their support, caring, and understanding.

New Leaders Press, the book's developer, thanks everyone connected with the design and production of this book. This includes production editor Rick Crandall, the composition team of Jennifer Barclay, Carolynn Crandall, and Chuck Karp, New Leaders Press staff members John Renesch, executive editor; Amy Kahn, operations manager; administrators Laura Kothavalaand Cathleen Moore; and Gretchen Andrews, research associate. For their help in recommending prospective endorsers, we thank Ken Murphy, Dan Kim, and Sheryl Erickson. The staff also thanks Paul Pederson for his computer assistance. For her help and creative ideas, we thank Sue Malikowski of Autographix, who worked with us on the jacket design and production.

The advisory board of New Leaders Press/Sterling & Stone, Inc. has been invaluable as a resource and we wish to acknowledge each of them: Pat Barrentine, David Berenson, William Halal, Willis Harman, Paul Hwoschinsky, Jim Liebig, William Miller, Shirley Nelson, Christine Oster, Steven Piersanti, Catherine Pyke, James O'Toole, Michael Ray, Stephen Roulac, Jeremy Tarcher, Peggy Umanzio, and Dennis White.

For those generous people who agreed to preview this collection in advance of its publication, the editors and authors are profoundly grateful. These people are Lindy Ashmore, Dick Beckhard, Eileen Beltran, Fritjof Capra, Cathe Carlson, Kazimierz Gozdz, William E. Halal, Edie Heilman, Bob Hetzel, Jim Kouzes, William J. Mullin, Michael Munn, John Nirenberg, Herbert Rau, George F. Schmitt, Bill Schrum, and Chris Strutt.

Finally, this book exists because of the talent, experience, and active participation of the authors. This collection has been a true collaboration—a partnership in a very real sense among the authors, editors, and publisher who worked together in creating this unique offering of diverse views about a very exciting field of inquiry. We thank you one and all.

Sarita Chawla is a partner with her husband, Ken Murphy, in MetaLens, a consulting firm which specializes in dialogue and coaching for individuals and organizations in the art and practice of creating sustainable excellence. She has comprehensive experience in generative coaching and total quality systems, after over twenty years of working within a large corporation. She is now focusing on her own "areas of passion"—primarily learning, dialogue, and diversity. To this end, she and her husband/partner have created several ongoing dialogue groups that represent the diversity so well represented by California.

She has a masters degree in anthropology from Delhi University. She is a member of the Association for Quality and Participation, and of the World Business Academy. She serves on the advisory board of the Elmwood Institute, founded by Fritjof Capra. She lives with her husband and her son Rahul Narang in Larkspur, California.

Introduction:
Beginner's Mind

Sarita Chawla

> *If your mind is empty, it is* always *ready for anything; it is open to everything. In the* beginner's *mind there are many possibilities; in the expert's mind there are few.*
> —Suzuki Roshi
> *Zen Mind, Beginner's Mind*

Is it possible that organizations will never learn much until they can create an environment in which individuals are able to learn? Is it possible that we've created organizations that systematically take most of what is living, creative, natural, and vital in individuals and turn it off? How did that happen? Is it also possible that organizations have been shooting themselves in the foot and are searching elsewhere for the sharpshooter?

The essays in these pages—explorations into the creation and sustenance of learning organizations—address these questions.

A different drumbeat:

The year is 2004. Chiang Soon walks into his MBA class. He has struggled all night, preparing a paper on the long-term implications of the AIDS epidemic in Asia for the world labor market. He is drained. He has considered the hidden time delays of the impact

1

of previously able-bodied men dying at alarming rates in some areas. He has attempted to examine the statistics of just one key city. He has reflected on the potential implications for one particular U.S. industry which has moved a majority of its operations offshore, not too far from the region with the greatest carnage from the killer disease. He has absolutely no answers. He has no idea how to predict, with any surety at all, what the consequences might be. How is he ever going to feel sure about going out and working in the corporate world?

He approaches a cluster of his classmates. They are in an animated discussion with their professor. The passionate tones of their voices indicate the dynamic flow of learning that he cherishes. Sounds of "But what if...?" "But that might lead to...," "How is that connected with...?" "What does that imply a hundred years from now?" and "I might as well pull a rune or use a Ouji board!"

Chiang's energy starts to rise. He is not alone. He joins in the exploration. More questions than answers. He has such a thirst for knowledge. It is such a relief to not be expected to have all the answers.

His mom used to tell him stories of her days at Harvard, where answers were not only expected but the terror of not knowing was to be covered up by hurling a response with an "I know it all" demeanor. Knowing was far more important than learning in those days. Now, the quality of inquiry and questions are valued as much as arriving at a sound theory. Genuine exploration of the interconnectedness of seemingly intractable problems are not only valued but required. Chiang joins in the learning adventure with the spirit if Indiana Jones, a popular movie character decades earlier.

"How different most classrooms are today," he reflects, "than ten years ago when my mother went to Harvard."

In those bygone days, both organizations and education had begun to re-examine the core assumptions upon which learning and development had been based. The behaviorist schools of management, founded in the philosophies of Skinner, Pavlov, and Taylor were being deeply questioned and, in some ways, reversed. Business schools produced what industry had wanted at the onset of the Industrial Revolution: Employees who were inputs to production. Taylor's principles of shifting responsibility to the manager, using the scientific method with a single-minded focus on efficiency, selecting the best person for the job, training for efficiency, and monitoring work performance were foundational to management theory. As Taylorism took root, employees were seen as "hands" or "headcounts" to be used like any other resource. Rewards, punishments, and monitoring work performance to hold it all in place were also embodied in the education and "production" of graduates.

How thankful Chiang was that the tide had turned over the past decade or so.

A Line of Inquiry

Science fiction? Impossible? A dream come true? You are invited to join us in a line of inquiry. What thoughts and feelings are evoked as you read the above? How did you categorize this— as fantasy, foolishness, or something else? Did you laugh it off as an impossible dream? What sort of yearnings arose in you for such an environment? What memories were recalled of your own days of education and learning on the job? Can you trace the edge of fear in your body when you do not have an answer? What does that feel like? Do you notice the impulse to quickly solve a problem by providing a seemingly intelligent response—no matter what? What are your feelings about learning? What emotions are triggered by the word "mistake" and how are those emotions different from those evoked by the word "learning?"

What image arises when you imagine a work situation where issues seem simply too complex to arrive at the answer? Where do you land on the continuum of a collective inquiry that might lead to a re-framing and deeper understanding of an issue on the one hand, to stark terror at the thought that you really have no clue about how to solve the problem, or even frame it in a comprehensive way on the other? Can we learn without experimentation? Can we learn without making mistakes? What is the relationship of trust and fear to learning? Mastery comes from practice. And yet, how safe do you feel to practice?

You could either scan through these questions one by one, or you could use this as a practice field and actually stop, reflect, try to answer, and live with the questions. You could be selective about which questions you value or not. The choice is yours. This anthology is intended to develop a line of inquiry from multiple perspectives on learning organizations. These questions are offered in that spirit.

*In oneself lies the whole world
and if you know how to look and learn,
then the door is there and the key is in your hand.
Nobody on earth can give you either the
key or the door to open
except yourself.*
—J. Krishnamurti

On A Personal Note

I've noticed a pattern in myself and others. When faced with something unknown, or when a long-held assumption is being challenged, I search frenetically for an answer, as though I am drowning, looking for a buoy or a "hook" in my mind. It feels like *nothing* or *no-thing.* There is no ground to stand on—just a sense of free fall. There is no precedent in my memory banks. I scan for "it smells like, tastes like, feels like...." At this point, I have to listen deeply. I have to pay attention with the intention of appreciative inquiry. If I feel unsafe, it is tremendously arduous to stay with it and in it. I have to search for what I do not know, while all my instincts cry for security. I want to connect with what I know—what I can count upon. This new place fits no known category. It seems both nebulous and much deeper. It escapes— like sand through my fingers. Shapes shift like a kaleidoscope. It's not the black nor the white I know. But, if I have the courage to stay with it long enough, if there is an environment in which I feel safe to hang in there, the shape shifts. Yes! I'm learning! Just like Chiang Soon in the preceding story.

During the process of co-creating this anthology with the authors, I've experienced this process many times over. The message of a fertile, safe, and authentic environment as a necessity for co-generation kept emerging. I found the ability to create this environment to be the critical skill required of me as coach and co-editor. This effort has been for me a difficult and magical journey into the structures, processes, myths, meta- phors, context, content, heart, body, mind, and soul of learning and learning organizations. It is one snowflake on the tip of the iceberg. It is also the result of gallant efforts of a collective learning as authors share their perspectives, not from the "ex- pert" model but from their own real learning in the moment.

As author Paula Underwood said, there are many ways of

learning—each of us learns in at least one of these ways. What is offered to you are thirty-two ways of learning about learning organizations—different voices speaking through the written word, offering their questions, insights, and possible answers. The poet Rumi ruminated "What if you come to understand one of them?"

This collection of essays has been organized to parallel and harmonize with the structural model described by Peter M. Senge in *The Fifth Discipline Fieldbook*. This book has been segmented similarly. You'll find Guiding Ideas, Theories/Methods/Processes, and Innovations in Infrastructure. We've added Arenas of Practice to reflect some specific applications and case studies. This model has been echoed because of the generative learning it creates. How were the essays selected for the various categories, you might ask? As the co-editor, working closely with the authors individually and as a community, I sensed the fit through conversations while maintaining a vision of the whole. It is my hope that the structure, sequence, and collective content of this book assists you in your own learning quest.

If you the reader see these essays arranged differently, I welcome your input.

Part One: Guiding Ideas

Guiding ideas for learning organizations start with vision, values, and purpose: what the organization stands for and what its members seek to create.
—The Fifth Discipline Fieldbook

What are some of the guiding ideas that can energize and focus effort to build a learning organization. This question is addressed by MIT's Fred Kofman and Peter M. Senge in their major essay on "Communities of Commitment."

What new learning theories are required for organizations to survive the transition into the 21st Century? London's Charles Handy offers his insights on this question.

How will the gender perspective make a difference? Does adding the feminine to make a whole endorse and demonstrate the way to mutuality, authenticity, and balance? Will it have a ripple effect? Marilynne Anderson addresses these questions as she examines gender perspective.

How can leaders help their organizations master change?

Harvard's Rosabeth Moss Kanter addresses this question in a presentation she originally made to a European audience.

Is organizational learning important? Why? How do you actually create a learning organization? Does investment in the learning process pay out in terms of creating economic value for shareholders? Consultant John W. Thompson responds by writing about the renaissance of learning in business.

How can we create the conditions that urge employees to make the personal changes necessary for an organization to become a learning organization? Psychologist Jayme Rolls examines the role of the transformation leader in addressing this question.

What is preventing smart people from creating and implementing learning organizations? The team of Lisa J. Marshall, Sandy Mobley, and Gene Calvert looks at why "smart organizations" find it so difficult to become learning organizations.

Part Two: Theories/Methods/Processes

Theories represent hypotheses that have been tested: "...a fundamental set of propositions about how the world works, which has been subjected to prepared tests and in which we have gained some confidence....Methods...a set of systematic procedures and techniques for dealing with particular types of issues and problems....Tools are what you make, prepare or do with."
—*The Fifth Discipline Fieldbook*

Story

How can we develop the sensitivity we need to use story for real learning? How can we begin to use story in our learning organization. Diane Cory and Paula Underwood demonstrate the power of storytelling from the perspective of two different cultures.

Given the powerful position of business in today's world, how might we learn in ways that serve the organization and beyond. Consultant Barbara Shipka shares her own experience and elaborates on her insights.

Dialogue

Who has the capacity to engage in dialogue and how do they

do it? Judy Brown examines capacities for this powerful process in her essay.

How can those responsible for making decisions of strategic importance use dialogue to improve their collective thinking about the opportunities and challenges they face? Consultants Sherrin Bennett and Juanita Brown examine strategic dialogue as a tool for organizational learning.

By understanding conversation as interpretive inquiry, how do we make distinctions that lead to different actions? Susan J. Bethanis links the use of metaphor with the transformation of organizations.

Coaching

How might we move away from behaviorism-based "human resource" systems that objectify and demean people, towards a more human way of working with people in organizations? How might we create successful organizations where groups are self-correcting, self-generating, and bring their whole beings to work? How can we create human systems in organizations so that personal mastery is possible? Kendall Murphy offers "generative coaching" as a tool for addressing these challenges.

Systems Thinking

What might a Management Flight Simulator look like? W. Brian Kreutzer offers a facilitative approach for breakthroughs in systems thinking.

How are "learning laboratories" created? What does the process look like? David P. Kreutzer shares the technology of building learning laboratories where we can practice and learn.

Tools

How can we facilitate creation of a learning organization? What approaches can be used to integrate business and learning processes? What are some of the gaps in current thinking that serve as barriers to organizational learning? How can we go about developing a genetic architecture that can perpetuate a learning organization? Robert Dilworth examines the DNA of the learning organization in his essay.

What are the core competencies that support the emergence of higher order learnings and creativity intelligence within a generative learning organization? Husband-and-wife team Joel and Michelle Levey respond to this question with their examination of "higher-order learning" and the evolution of wisdom.

Part Three: Infra-Structure

*...the means through which an organiza-
tion makes available resources to support
people in their work*
   —*The Fifth Discipline Fieldbook*

How might our conversations be different if we experience learning together? What ways of "sensing" and relating to one another support our learning together? Where can we find the practice fields to "learn in relationship" with others? What does it mean to live with the questions? Stephanie Ryan challenges the assumptions underlying the traditional "expert" model.

Why can't organizations learn new tricks? Why can't we learn enough? Executive Eric Edwards Vogt looks at a new context for learning in his essay for this collection.

Will the work design we are pursuing get us where we want to go? How might we choose between various approaches to business performance improvement? Carol Sanford proposes a new philosophy—a developmental one—as a work design context.

What development strategies can learning organizations adopt? What are the pros and cons, methods and techniques of each? And for which situations might each be appropriate? Ernst & Young's Linda E. Morris offers some strategic processes for development appropriate to the Knowledge Era.

What are the strategies for sustaining competitive advantage? How do we place the learning organization within a strategic framework in order to start and implement it? How do you create a faster learning organization? What will sell CEOs on learning organizations? Bob Guns pursues faster ways of learning organizationally in his essay.

How do we create an infrastructure in our organizations that will promote and sustain learning as an integral part of doing business? Daniel H. Kim puts forth ideas for "practice fields" for learning in his essay.

If learning is the missing counterpoint to performance in the process of change, what are the implications of treating organizational learning lightly or as a movement? If organizational learning is a complex social phenomenon of the collective, what models are required to understand it? Consultant David R. Schwandt examines chaos as one path into our collective learning for organizations.

Part Four: Arenas of Practice

How do you build a learning organization in a service industry which needs to reinvent itself amidst drastic and multi-faceted changes? Alain Gauthier examines stewardship and its role in establishing learning organizational thinking in health-care.

What effects are being taken by students in their formal learning environments that limit the evolution of the workplace and the society being served through them? What will be the nature of relationships between society's different workplaces (education, business, community, health)? John H. Wood addresses the role of education in the development of future workplaces.

Most workplace educators have not geared themselves toward transforming mental models—a fundamental requirement for learning organizations. What existing and new approaches can they use to help transform mental models? IBM's Robert Weintraub examines mental models in the world of education.

Can the U.S. Navy become a learning organization? Former Navy officer Robert L. Masten takes a close look at the naval institution as a prospective learner.

In tangible terms, what does it look like when an organization is doing organizational learning? Alan K. Graham writes about learning, using medical metaphor.

What are the critical ingredients in a corporate culture that will provide both the optimal environment for organizational learning and the degree of control desired by senior leadership? Co-authors Frank Hoffmann and Bill Withers together examine corporate cultures and their influences on learning.

Can learning organizations be created through formal programs, or are they a natural evolution of a company's culture, structure, and daily business processes? Informix's Mary Byrd applies her own experience with her software company to resolve this question.

How do we develop wisdom? Dinesh Chandra shares his own experience with the Eicher banking organization in getting beyond ego.

A few reflections on creating this collection: The intent was to create a learning community of authors in the process of putting this book together. I held a vision of the whole as a "web," connecting each author with all of the other authors and their work; working with each person in order to more fully develop his/her thoughts while maintaining a sense of coherence. When similarities or parallels became obvious, I often suggested that authors communicate with each other to share meaning. It was curious that more of the women chose to connect and solicit feedback on their work. I have wondered about that.

This book has been a practice field—both receiving and providing coaching. Learning to provide feedback in a caring, authentic, and coherent way requires practice and patience. My creativity soared when there were openings to coach these writers. I am deeply grateful to the authors for all that I have learned, both in content and in the process.

In closing—a personal story. At a particularly difficult time during this compilation, I was standing in my husband's office very early one morning and looked out to see steam arise from our hot tub just outside his office. We were planning to use it the night before and had forgotten it was still on. I invited him in. We had never taken a *sunrise* hot tub. After we were in for a while, I saw a spider swimming like crazy in the tub. I almost jumped out. Then it occurred to me that, just because I don't see spiders in the dark doesn't mean they are not there!

It is like all of that is waiting to be learned! Art, music, and story metaphor can open a different channel, revealing programmed mental models for examination and conscious shift. I chose to stay for the sunrise with the spider that was no longer concealed.

> — Sarita Chawla, co-editor
> March, 1995

*When you eventually see
through the veils to how things really are,
you will keep saying again
and again
"This is certainly not like
we thought it was."
—Rumi*

PART ONE

Guiding Ideas

Communities of Commitment:
The Heart of Learning Organizations
Fred Kofman and Peter M. Senge

Managing the Dream
Charles Handy

Ahead of the Wave: Valuing Gender Perspectives
in Learning Cultures
Marilynne Anderson

Mastering Change
Rosabeth Moss Kanter

The Renaissance of Learning in Business
John W. Thompson

The Transformational Leader:
The Wellspring of the Learning Organization
Jayme Rolls

Why Smart Organizations Don't Learn
Lisa J. Marshall, Sandy Mobley, and Gene Calvert

Ten authors collaborate to start off this collection with their perspectives on values, purposefulness, and vision behind learning organizations. Grouped together in this opening section, the guiding ideas offered in these seven essays serve as a beacon for the reader throughout the remainder of this anthology.

MIT colleagues Fred Kofman and Peter M. Senge open with their comprehensive essay which examines the heart of learning communities. London author and professor emeritus Charles Handy addresses the personal challenges that accompany the dream of a learning organization, and Marilynne Anderson addresses the value of gender diversity in such an organizational transformation.

Harvard's Rosabeth Moss Kanter focuses on principles for mastering change as our business enterprises evolve into continuous learning communities. John W. Thompson examines the "renaissance of learning" in the business community.

Jayme Rolls offers perspective on the prerequisite leadership for achieving this transformation, while Lisa J. Marshall, Sandra Mobley, and Gene Calvert team up to help us understand why organizations can be so slow to learn, despite having so many intelligent leaders within them.

...it is clearly necessary to invent organizational structures appropriate to the multicultural age. But such efforts are doomed to failure if they do not grow out of something deeper, out of generally held values.

—Vaclav Havel

Fred Kofman (left) is the director of Leading Learning Communities, the educational program of MIT's Organizational Learning Center. He holds a PhD in economics from the University of California at Berkeley. His research focuses on the design and implementation of organizational learning systems. He integrates his interest in systems thinking, operations management, strategy and organizational behavior with philosophy, poetry and myth. His work with corporate partners includes studies on activity-based costing systems, strategic planning and organizational design, and he collaborates with them in seeking to develop a culture of wonder, respect, dignity, and compassion.

Peter M. Senge (right) is Director of the Center for Organizational Learning at MIT's Sloan School of Management. He is the author of the widely acclaimed book, *The Fifth Discipline: The Art and Practice of the Learning Organization*, published by Doubleday/Currency in 1990. With his colleagues Charlotte Roberts, Rick Ross, Bryan Smith and Art Kleiner, he is the co-author of the new book, *The Fifth Discipline Fieldbook: Strategies and Tools for Building a Learning Organization*. He is also a founding partner of the management consulting and training firm, Innovation Associates.

Senge received a BS in engineering from Stanford University, an MS in social systems modeling, and a PhD in management from MIT.

Communities of Commitment: The Heart of Learning Organizations

Fred Kofman and Peter M. Senge

Why do we confront learning opportunities with fear rather than wonder? Why do we derive our self-esteem from knowing as opposed to learning? Why do we criticize before we even understand? Why do we create controlling bureaucracies when we attempt to form visionary enterprises? And why do we persist in fragmentation and piecemeal analysis as the world becomes more and more interconnected?

Such questions have been at the heart of our work for many years. They led to the theories and methods presented in *The Fifth Discipline.* They are the driving force behind a new vision of organizations, capable of thriving in a world of interdependence and change—what we have come to call "learning organizations."

The Fifth Discipline generated significant interest, but a book is only one step toward bringing a new set of ideas and practices into the mainstream of management. Shortly after the book appeared, a group of us at MIT established the Center for Organizational Learning. The center now involves many organizations—including Ford, Harley Davidson, Electronic Data Systems, Federal Express, AT&T, Philips North America, Herman Miller, Armco Steel, and Intel—seeking major breakthroughs via partnership between researchers and practitioners.

Two years of intense practice and reflection have gone by.

Some pilot projects are beginning to produce striking results. But, we also have learned that it is crucial to address the opening questions. We have not found any definitive answers—nor were we looking for them—but, dwelling *in* the questions, we have found guiding principles for action.

Building learning organizations, we are discovering, requires basic shifts in how we think and interact. The changes go beyond individual corporate cultures, or even the culture of Western management; they penetrate to the bedrock assumptions and habits of our culture as a whole. We are also discovering that moving forward is an exercise in personal commitment and community building. As the late Dr. W. Edwards Deming said, nothing happens without "personal transformation." And the only safe space to allow for this transformation is a learning community.

So, we are coming to see our efforts as building "communities of commitment." Without commitment, the hard work required will never be done. People will just keep asking for "examples of learning organizations" rather than seeking what they can do to build such organizations. They will keep believing that the purpose of learning is the survival of an organization rather than its generativeness. And the larger meaning of this work will elude them. Without communities of people genuinely committed, there is no real chance of going forward.

But Commitment to What?

In this paper we will explore basic shifts in the guiding ideas of contemporary management. We argue that the main dysfunctions in our institutions—fragmentation, competition, and reactiveness—are actually by-products of our success over thousands of years in conquering the physical world and in developing our scientific, industrial culture. So, it should come as no surprise that these dysfunctions are deeply rooted. Nor should it surprise us that our first response, "to overcome these problems," is part of the very mindset that generated them. Fragmentation, competition, and reactiveness are not problems to be solved—they are frozen patterns of thought to be dissolved.

The solvent we propose is a new way of thinking, feeling, and being: a culture of systems. Fragmentary thinking becomes systemic when we recover "the memory of the whole," the awareness that wholes actually precede parts. Competition becomes cooperation when we discover the "community nature of the self" and realize our role as challengers to help each other excel. Reactiveness becomes creating when we see the "generative power of language," how language brings forth distinctions from the undivided flow of life.

Together these changes represent a new "Galilean Shift." Galileo's heliocentric revolution moved us from looking at the earth as the center around which all else revolved to seeing our place in a broader pattern. In the new systems worldview, we move from the primacy of pieces to the primacy of the whole, from absolute truths to coherent interpretations, from self to community, from problem solving to creating.

Thus, the nature of the commitment required to build learning organizations goes beyond people's typical "commitment to their organizations." It encompasses commitment to changes needed in the larger world and to seeing our organizations as vehicles for bringing about such changes.

This is a theoretical paper for practitioners. Contradictory as it may sound, there is nothing more practical than a good theory. The problem with "seven step methods to success," "keys to successful organizations," and similar "how-tos" is that, ultimately, they aren't very practical. Life is too complex and effective action too contextual. Real learning—the development of new capabilities—occurs over time, in a continuous cycle of theoretical action and practical conceptualization. The impatient quest for improvements all too often results in superficial changes that leave deeper problems untouched. Herein lies a core leadership paradox: Action is critical, but the action we need can spring only from a reflective territory that includes not only cognition but body, emotions, and spirit as well.

Areas of Cultural Dysfunction

Organizations are microcosms of the larger society. Thus, at the heart of any serious effort to alter how organizations operate lies a concern with addressing the basic dysfunctions of our larger culture. We believe that there are three fundamental problems with our current paradigm: fragmentation, competition, and reactiveness.

Fragmentation

We continually fragment problems into pieces; yet the major challenges we face in our organizations and beyond are increasingly systemic.

The analytic way to address a complex situation is to break it into components, study each component in isolation, and then synthesize the components back into a whole. For a wide range of issues, there is little loss in assuming a mechanical structure and ignoring systemic interactions. But for our most important problems, linear thinking is ineffective. Problems like runaway costs in our health care system or the decline of a corporation's vitality and innovativeness resist piecemeal, analytic approaches. We live in a world that is more like Humpty Dumpty than a jigsaw puzzle: All the king's horses and all the king's men can't put the system together again.

Our enchantment with fragmentation starts in early child-hood. Since our first school days, we learn to break the world apart and disconnect ourselves from it. We memorize isolated facts, read static accounts of history, study abstract theories, and acquire ideas unrelated to our life experience and personal aspirations. Economics is separate from psychology, which is separate from biology, which has little connection with art. We eventually become convinced that knowledge is accumulated bits of information and that learning has little to do with our capacity for effective action, our sense of self, and how we exist in our world.

Today, fragmentation is the cornerstone of what it means to be a professional, so much so that we call ourselves "specialists." Accountants worry about the books, operations managers worry about production and inventory, marketing managers worry about customer base, and nobody worries about the business as a whole.

The word *health* has the same roots as "whole" (the old English *hal*, as in "hale and hearty"). Like people, organizations can get sick and die. They also need to be cured and healed. Yet, like physicians who focus only on their specialty, most consult-ants operate from the analytic tradition. They fragment complex situations into symptoms, treat the symptoms, and rarely in-quire into the deeper causes of problems: how we learn and act together with a sense of shared aspiration. Consequently, man-agement experts have very little ability to influence organiza-tional health. All too often, their solutions contribute to a vicious pattern of "programs of the month" that fail and get replaced by the next program of the month.

In business, fragmentation results in "walls" or "chimneys"

that separate different functions into independent and often warring fiefdoms. Product designers, for instance, disregard marketing surveys and "throw the product over the wall" to manufacturing, which finds the design impossible to produce. After making the "appropriate" changes (appropriate in their minds, since they never bother to check back with design) and producing the product, manufacturing "throws it over" to sales. Salesmen find themselves stuck with a low-quality product that does not meet customer requirements. The product gets sent back and departments start blaming each other. This process constantly repeats itself.

In public affairs, fragmentation is making our society increasingly ungovernable. We know the problem as the dominance of "special interest groups" and political lobbies.

Pointing fingers at each other is now a favorite national sport, but recently a new variant has appeared: pointing fingers at the walls. Academics, consultants, and managers unite in blaming the barbed wire fences separating organizational functions for poor-quality, high-cost products. In response, many companies are trying to "re-engineer" themselves away from stovepipe structures and toward horizontal business processes that cut across traditional functions and power hierarchies. While potentially significant, such changes often prove difficult to implement and those that are implemented only "reap the low-hanging fruit."

The reason is that the walls that exist in the physical world are reflections of our mental walls. The separation between the different functions is not just geographic, it lives in the way we think. Redesigns that "throw down the walls" between different functions may have little enduring effect unless they also change the fragmentary mental models that created the walls in the first place.

Competition

We have become overdependent on competition, to the extent that it is our only model for change and learning. There is nothing intrinsically wrong with competition. It can be great fun. It can promote invention and daring. The problem is that we have lost the balance between competition and cooperation precisely at a time when we most need to work together.

In the United States, we tend to see competition among individuals as the ultimate mechanism for change and improvement in human affairs. We continually think in terms of war and sports analogies when we interpret management challenges. We need to "beat the competition," "overcome resistance to our new program," "squeeze concessions from the labor union," or "take over this new market." We have a metaphorical tunnel vision. We rarely think about how the process of developing leaders may be more like parenting than competing, or about how developing a new culture may be more like gardening than a military campaign.

Fascinated with competition, we often find ourselves competing with the very people with whom we need to collaborate. Members of a management team compete with one another to show who is right, who knows more, or who is more articulate or persuasive. Divisions compete with one another when they ought to cooperate to share knowledge. Team project leaders compete to show who is the best manager, even if it means covering up problems for which, ultimately, everyone will pay. Dr. Deming told a story of a man who discovered he was continually competing with his wife. The man was dumbfounded at the discovery. "Who would want to be married to a loser?" he asked.

Our overemphasis on competition makes *looking* good more important than *being* good. The resulting fear of not looking good is one of the greatest enemies of learning. To learn, we need to acknowledge that there is something we don't know and to perform activities that we're not good at. But in most corporations, ignorance is a sign of weakness; temporary incompetence is a character flaw.

How impossible it would be for a child to learn to walk if she were afraid of falling and looking foolish. Yet, that is exactly what happened in schools that made us feel foolish when we made mistakes, and continues in organizations that rank our performance on the basis of management-by-objectives.

In response, many of us have developed defenses that have become second nature—like working out our problems in isolation, always displaying our best face in public, and never saying "I don't know." The price we pay is enormous. In fact, we become masters of what Chris Argyris calls "skilled incompetence," skillful at protecting ourselves from the threat and pain that come with learning, but also remaining incompetent and blinded to our incompetence.

Overemphasis on competition also reinforces our fixation on short-term measurable results. Consequently, we lack the discipline needed for steady practice and deeper learning, which often produces few manifest consequences for long periods of time.

The quick-fix mentality also makes us "system blind." Many of today's problems come from yesterday's solutions, and many of today's solutions will be tomorrow's problems. What is most perplexing is that many quick fixes, from cost cutting to marketing promotions, are implemented even though no one believes they address underlying problems. But we still feel compelled to implement these "solutions." We need to show results, and fast, regardless of the long-term, system-wide consequences.

Reactiveness

We have grown accustomed to changing only in reaction to outside forces, yet the wellspring of real learning is aspiration, imagination, and experimentation.

As children, we accomplish some of our most astounding learning without any external motivation. We learn to walk, we learn to talk, we learn to be human not because we have to but because we want to. Eventually, however, we become conditioned to reacting to others' directions, to depending on others' approval. There is nothing intrinsically wrong with external authority; it would be inefficient to learn about the dangers of fingers-in-plugs experientially. The problem is that our current institutions exercise authority in a way that undermines our intrinsic drive to learn.

For most of us, reactiveness was reinforced on a daily basis in school. We solved problems identified by others, read what was assigned, wrote what was required. Gradually, reactiveness became a way of life. Fitting in, being accepted, became more important than being ourselves. We learned that the way to succeed was to focus on the teachers' questions as opposed to our own.

Reactiveness is a double bane of continuous learning. First, the attitude, "if it ain't broke don't fix it," prevents the steady improvement of products and processes. Moreover, when something is broken, the immediate reaction is to call an expert—a specialist—to fix it. Regardless of the specialist's success, his intervention will create a black-box mentality that prevents the organization from developing its own capacities for continual learning.

The pervasiveness of a reactive stance in management is

evident in the fixation on problem solving. Many managers think that management *is* problem solving. But problem solving is fundamentally different from creating. The problem solver tries to make something go away. A creator tries to bring something new into being. The impetus for change in problem solving lies outside ourselves—in some undesired external condition we seek to eliminate. The impetus for change in the creating mode comes from within. Only the creating mode leads to a genuine sense of individual and collective power, because only in the creating mode do people orient themselves to their intrinsic desires. It is a testament to how reactive we are that many leaders see the absence of vision as a "problem" to be solved in their company and set about writing and disseminating vision and mission statements as the solution.

It is a small step from the problem-solving orientation to a system of management that is dominated by fear, the ultimate external motivator. This is evident today in the simple fact that most leaders believe that people are willing to change only in times of crisis. This leads to the most pervasive leadership strategy in America—create a crisis, or at least a perception of crisis. Crises can produce episodes of change. But they produce little learning. Moreover, management by fear and crisis becomes a self-fulfilling prophecy. Because it *does* produce short-term results, managers see their crisis orientation as vindicated, people in the organization grow accustomed to "waiting for the next crisis," managers' belief in the apathy of the troops is reinforced, and they become more predisposed to generate the next crisis.

Roots of Our Cultural Crisis

These problems are deeply rooted. They are not just mistakes we keep repeating—they spring directly from our past successes. The triumph of reductionism and mechanical thinking has given rise to a set of conditions for which they are no longer suited.

Humankind has achieved unimaginable successes in controlling its physical and social environment. We have come a long way since the days in which our ancestors had to defend themselves from other animals, work continually to secure food, and survive in extreme weather conditions. We have learned to create safe dwellings, increase our food supply, harness powerful sources of energy, and provide for a level of material well-being beyond that previously available only to monarchs. In doing so, we have continually adapted and changed our environment to our benefit, to the point that today we appear on the verge of modifying the very genetic code that programs our species' development.

But this progress has not been without consequence. The very same skills of separation, analysis, and control that gave us the power to shape our environment are producing ecological and social crises in our outer world, and psychological and spiritual crises in our inner world. Both these crises grow out of our success in separating ourselves from the larger fabric of life. When we begin to understand the origins of our problems, we begin to see that the "existential crisis" of early 20th century philosophy and the "environmental crisis" of late 20th century ecology are inseparable—caused by the co-evolution of fragmentary worldviews, social structures, lifestyles, and technology.

There are two aspects to the story: one evolutionary and one cultural. The first concerns deep patterns of behavior established in the human organism over millions of years. The second concerns deep cultural beliefs that probably started with the agricultural revolution.

Throughout our history as a species, the primary threats to our survival came as sudden dramatic events: saber-toothed tigers, floods, earthquakes, attacks by rival tribes. Today, the primary threats to our survival are slow, gradual processes—environmental destruction, the global arms race (which continues unabated by the breakup of the Soviet Union), and decay of our nation's educational system and its family and community structure.

We are poorly prepared for a world of slowly developing threats. We have a nervous system focused on external dramatic events. A loud noise or a sharp change in our visual field brings us immediately to alert. Our adrenaline system heightens our awareness and strength. In extreme cases, our nervous system produces a state of shock that filters signals of physical pain, allowing continued reasoning and decision making. The irony is that all of these capabilities become potentially counterproductive in a world of slow, gradually emerging systemic crises. All our instincts are to wait until the gradual changes develop into crises—when it is often too late to take effective action.

Moreover, these threats were external; their causes were outside our control. Today's primary threats are all endogenous, the by-products of our own actions. There is no enemy out there to blame. As Pogo says, "We have met the enemy and they is us." Nor will blaming ourselves individually help. The causes lie in collective behaviors and unintended side effects of actions that make individual sense. There is no blame, there is no guilt, just a need to think differently.

This conflict between the nature of our most important problems and our instinctive ways of thinking and acting is no less catastrophic in organizations. Most of the primary threats to survival and vitality in organizations develop slowly, and they are not caused externally. The problems of General Motors and IBM, for instance, did not arise overnight. Arrogance, insulation, and rigidification developed over decades of success. At IBM, even as the symptoms of decline became more and more apparent, the sustained profitability of the core mainframe products allowed managers and investors to ignore growing signals of trouble. Only when an overwhelming crisis (record losses) occurred was there sufficient alarm to take bold action.

Thus, our evolutionary programming predisposes us to seeing external threats and to reactiveness. Layered onto it is a culture of fragmentation and competition, and together they hold us captive. But the capacity can be loosened if we begin to understand that our cultural history is but one historical path, a path that could have drifted toward a different present. The first step in exposing this illusory "naturalness" of our present way of thinking is to reflect on its genealogy. As David Bohm, a preeminent quantum physicist put it: "Starting with the agricultural revolution, and continuing through the industrial revolution, increasing fragmentation in the social order has produced a progressive fragmentation in our thought."

There is growing evidence that many pre-agricultural societies were not dominated by fragmentation and competition. The evidence is controversial because it contradicts the established orthodoxy to view ancient societies as having always been like us, but "less civilized."

Thomas Merton wrote of the magnificent Monte Alban culture that flourished in southwestern Mexico from about 500 BC to about 500 AD with "no evidence of militarism or war....Self-realization in such a context implied not so much ego-consciousness of the isolated subject in the face of a multitude of objects as the awareness of a network of relationships in which one had a place to mesh. One's identity was the intersection of cords where one "belonged."

Joseph Campbell spoke of the ancient Indo-European myth of the Goddess who "teaches compassion for all living beings. There also you come to appreciate the real sanctity of the earth itself, because it is the body of the Goddess." Recent advances in archeological research are suggesting that the myth of the Goddess may have predominated throughout central Europe in the late Paleolithic and early Neolithic cultures. These cultures may have been neither warlike nor male dominated, as long assumed. Riane Eisler claims that the period from approximately 5000 BC to 1500 BC was a "remarkably peaceful time," with little evidence of fortifications or implements of warfare. Men and women shared power, and that there was an overarching "quality of mind" based on "recognition of their oneness with nature." Such "partnership" cultures were eventually transcended by "dominator" cultures, according to Eisler—the cultures of the "thunderbolt hurlers, like Zeus or Yahweh," according to Campbell. Many now believe that the last broad flowering of partnership cultures in Europe occurred in the Minoan civilization on Crete.

The classic Greek culture and the emerging Christian era mark crucial crossroads that lead directly to the contemporary Western scientific and religious worldviews.

In ancient Greece, the world was a "cosmos," not an inert environment ruled by the abstract laws of physics. The earth was the space where gods and mortals shared their passion, wisdom, and folly. The Greeks walked with the gods. But classical Greek thought also established the foundation for the "scientific" view— the view that later set man as an observer apart from the world. Two thousand years later, building on Aristotle's classical category theory, Descartes propounded a rigorous split between subject and object, observer and observed, human and nature.

If classic Greece laid the foundation for justifying the split of man and nature, the Catholic Church institutionalized the split between man and God. According to Elaine Pagels, professor of religion at Princeton, the split lay at the very heart of the foundation of the church—in fact, it was the strategy used to differentiate the sect that eventually became the church from other early Christian sects that had very different interpretations of Jesus' teachings. "What we call Christianity (today) actually represents only a small selection of specific sources, chosen from among dozens," according to Pagels.

In particular, recently discovered "Gnostic gospels," banned as heresy by the early church, are based on belief in the human capacity for direct knowing or *gnosis*. "To know oneself," says Pagels, "at the deepest level, is simultaneously to know God; this is the secret of *gnosis*." "Abandon the search for God," wrote the Gnostic teacher Monoimus...."Look for him by taking yourself as the starting point. If you carefully investigate these matters, you will find him in *yourself*." By contrast, by the second century, the architects of the early church had established a very different view, the church as intermediary between man and God. According to Pagels, "God became accessible to humanity [only] through the church."

Thus were sown the seeds of the fragmentation evident today. Their fruit has grown steadily. "The belief that man was separate from nature," writes J. Krishnamurti, "evolved into the idea that nature was a resource for man's benefit. Nature became a "resource," a "standing in reserve." We became the masters of the world with a license to exploit it. We stopped living amidst objects and began living with disposable things that were just waiting to be used. "Because we do not love the earth and the things of the earth but merely utilize them," said Krishnamurti, "we have lost touch with life."

A Galilean Shift

The analytic model assigns a primary status to the parts and assumes that they exist independent from a whole. This view generates deep inconsistencies that lie behind many of our most pressing social and organizational problems. Its flaws are not surface but structural: David Bohm argues that the quest "to put the pieces together" is fundamentally futile when operating from a belief in the primacy of parts, "like trying to assemble the fragments of a shattered mirror." Worse yet, the analytic model doesn't accept its contingent status. It adopts the face of necessity and claims universal validity. As Bohm says, "Thought creates the world and then says, 'I didn't do it'."

Our work at the center began by putting separation and fragmentation into their historical context. This prepared us for the next step: exposing the limits of analysis and developing an alternative paradigm—one that can help to recover the memory of the whole.

As we move forward, we can use three fundamental theses to shift our understanding of ourselves and the world in which we live. Just as Galileo proposed that the earth was not the center of the universe, we are proposing here that parts, ego, and reality are not the center of a more meaningful way of life. Each reflects the fragmented worldview we have come to accept. Each needs to be reexamined.

1. The Primacy of the Whole

The analytic perspective involves a three-part process: (1) break the system into its component parts, (2) study each part in isolation, and (3) assemble an understanding of the whole from an understanding of the parts. The implicit assumption is that systems are aggregates of parts that interact relatively weakly and in a linear fashion. In this notion of systems, one can restrict attention to the parts and trust that optimizing each one amounts to optimizing the whole.

Decomposition is a time-honored way of dealing with complex problems, but it has big limitations in a world of tight couplings and nonlinear feedbacks. The defining characteristic of a system is that it *cannot* be understood as a function of its isolated components. First, the behavior of the system doesn't depend on what each part is doing but on how each part is interacting with the rest. A car's engine may be working just fine, but if the transmission column is detached from it, the car won't move.

Second, to understand a system we need to understand how it fits into the larger system of which it is a part. To use an example of Russel Ackoff's, we will never understand why standard cars have seats for four or five if we look at the physical properties of its elements. Human beings create teleological systems, systems with purpose. To understand the car design, we need to see how it fits into a society of families who travel together.

Third, and most important, what we call the parts need not be taken as primary. In fact, how we define the parts is fundamentally a matter of perspective and purpose, not intrinsic in the nature of the "real thing" we are looking at.

For example, consider an airplane. We might say that it is made of the fuselage, the wings, the tail, and a cockpit. But we might also say it is made of metal parts and plastic parts. We might also say it is made of a right half and a left half, and so on. What makes an airplane cannot be found in the parts—after all, a submarine also has a fuselage and a tail—but in how the parts emerge as distinctions from a coherent whole.

Rather than being objective, what we call the parts is highly subjective. No set of categories is natural or inherent to a system. There is no intrinsic right or wrong. It is a matter of purpose and awareness of choices, and of remembering the genealogy of categories invoked—the distinctions that we now see "out there" arose within a certain tradition and are contingent on it.

Rather than thinking of a world of "parts" that form "wholes," we start by recognizing that we live in a world of wholes within wholes. Rather than trying to "put the pieces together" to make the whole, we recognize that the world is already whole.

At the same time, the systems view recognizes that distinctions enable the observer to draw forth operational worlds. The whole may be more fundamental, but it is unmanageable. For example, the division of labor enabled societies to achieve levels of material well-being that would have otherwise been impossible. Henry Ford would have never been able to build as many cars as fast and as economically as he did had he not divided operations according to Frederick Taylor's principles.

But, once the workers become "workers" and the supervisors become "supervisors," rigidity sets in. To re-establish fluidity, the capacity for learning and change, we must remember the contingent nature of the distinctions within which we are trapped. We must once again confront the whole. Reflecting on what this means with one another, Martin Buber said:

> Even as a melody is not composed of tones,
> nor a verse of words, nor a statue of lines—one
> must pull and tear to turn a unity into a multi-
> plicity—so it is with the human being to whom
> I say Thou. I can abstract from him the color of
> his hair or the sound of his speech or the style
> of his graciousness; I can do this again and
> again; but immediately he is no longer my
> Thou.

2. The Community Nature of the Self

Newtonian physicists were startled to discover that at the core of the atom, at the center of matter there is...nothing, no thing, pure energy. When they reached into the most fundamental building block of nature, they found a pregnant void—stable patterns of probability striving to connect with other patterns of probability. This discovery revolutionized the physical sciences, initiating the quantum era.

By the same token, we are startled to discover that at the core of the person, at the center of selfhood there is...nothing, pure energy. When we reach into the most fundamental basis of our being we find a pregnant void, a web of relationships. When somebody asks us to talk about ourselves, we talk about family, work, academic background, sports affiliations, etc. In all this talk, where is our "self?" The answer is nowhere, because the self is not a thing, but, as Jarome Brunner says, "a point of view that unifies the flow of experience into a coherent narrative"—a narrative striving to connect with other narratives and become richer.

We normally think that the individual has a primordial origin and that selfhood is given to each one independent of the cultural or group practices in which that person happens to grow up. But, as Clifford Geertz says, "There is no such thing as human nature independent of culture."

When we forget about the social milieu in which we exist as people, we attain a spurious security and stability. We identify our egos with our selves. We take the contingent features of our current character and reify them into a substantive personality. Thus, we assign a primordial value to our ego (part) and see the community (whole) as secondary. We see the community as nothing but a network of contractual commitments in symbolic and economic exchanges. We think that encounters with others are transactions that can add or subtract to the array of possessions of the ego.

But the constitution of the self happens only in a community. The community supports certain ways of being and constrains the expressions of individuality to certain patterns of behavior—whatever we regard as acting "crazy" or inappropriate expresses our community of origin and upbringing much more than our intrinsic predispositions.

As with all deep cultural assumptions, the assumed primacy of the ego-self hides its contingent status, until we discover a different culture. For example, in many indigenous cultures of southern Africa the common greeting is "I see you." What it means to be a person in such a culture is to be in relationship. When we confront such a culture, where speaking a person's name acknowledges that person's existence, it seems "crazy" to us. After all, for us, the "self" is myself, isolated from other selves.

But a systems view of life suggests that the self is never "given" and is always in the process of transformation. Whenever we do not take the other as an object for use, whenever we see the other as a legitimate fellow human being with which we can learn and change—a "Thou"—we engage in a passionate interaction that can open new possibilities for our being.

3. Language as Generative Practice

In our everyday sense of the world, we see reality as "out there" and ourselves as observers "in here." Our Western tradition compels us to "figure out" how nature works so that we can achieve what we want. But what if what shows up for us as "reality" is inseparable from our language and actions? What if we are part of, not apart from, the world? What if our crisis is, at least in part, a crisis of perception and meaning, springing from a "naive realist" perspective of the observer as one who describes an external reality? What if observation itself is the beginning of the fragmentation?

The puzzle of the "ultimate ground" for knowing has confronted philosophers for a long time. There is a story of the humble novice who asks the great sage what it is that keeps the world from falling through space. The sage responds that the earth stays aloft because it rests on a great turtle. But, the student asks, "What is it that holds the turtle up?" "Why," responds the teacher, "it is because the turtle rests upon another great turtle." "But," cries out the student, "that turtle, too, must be supported." "Yes, indeed," responds the master, "it is turtles all the way down."

The alternative to naive "realism" is not solipsism, a view that there is "nothing out there," and therefore nothing to be learned, nothing to be valued. The alternative, we propose, is recognizing the generative role of the traditions of observation and meaning shared by a community. We invent structures and distinctions to organize the otherwise unmanageable flow of life. That organization allows us to operate effectively, but it can become a tranquilizing barrier to exploration and creativity. The more efficient a model of the world turns out to be, the more it recedes into the background and becomes transparent. The more successful the model's strategies, the more the map of reality becomes "reality" itself. The danger of success is that the thinking behind it can become entrenched and disregard the necessary context of its effectiveness. When a model loses its "situation" and generalizes its validity to universal categories, it sooner or later stalls our capacity to deal freshly with the world and each other.

The map is not the territory, but we can only guide ourselves with maps. As cartographers, however, we are far from neutral. Our perceptual apparatus, with its biological, personal, and cultural filters, is actively involved in the construction of these maps. So, where is the territory underlying the maps?

As philosopher Hubert Dreyfus says, "It is interpretation all the way down." The issue is deeper than recognizing that the map is not the territory. We have to face the possibility that we have no access beyond our culture to such a thing as a territory. We only have provisional maps permanently open to revision and recreation.

This may sound nihilistic. If there is no ultimate ground for values, why choose one system over another? Why is democracy better than totalitarianism? Why is anything better than anything else? Why even bother to care? The solution to the nihilistic dilemma comes from a self-reflective principle: Those contexts that display their precarious nature, those contexts that invite revision and recreation are inherently better than those which hide their precarious nature and fight revisionist attempts. The best constructs for explaining and organizing the world will imitate life itself. They will be in a continual state of becoming.

When we fail to recognize this principle, we lose the capacity to understand others. We become rigid. We lose the ability to learn. We lose the child within us who lives in awe and who understands what Einstein meant when he said that the most beautiful experience in the world is "the experience of the mysterious."

Operating Principles

As we endeavor to embody these theses in our work at the MIT Learning Center, several operating principles are emerging. These "principles" are neither rigid nor all encompassing. In effect, each grows out of a question, and in many ways the questions themselves may be the keys to moving forward— questions such as, "What do we mean when we speak of a *learning organization*?

There is No Such Thing as a "Learning Organization"

Along with "total quality management" and "process re-engineering," "organizational learning" has become the latest buzzword. Just as there is no such thing as a "smart kid," however, there is no such thing as a "learning organization."

"Learning organization" is a category that we create in language. Like every linguistic creation, this category is a double-edged sword that can be empowering or tranquilizing. The difference lies in whether we see language as a set of labels that describe a preexisting reality, or as a medium in which we can articulate new models for living together.

When we speak of a "learning organization," we are not describing an external phenomenon or labeling an independent reality. We are articulating a view that involves us—the observers—as much as the observed in a common system. We are taking a stand for a vision, for creating a type of organization we would truly like to work within and which can thrive in a world of increasing interdependency and change.

It is not what the vision is, but what the vision does that matters. In the early 1970s, Alan Kay led the researchers at Xerox PARC who developed the first true precursors to the personal computer. In fact, Kay and his colleagues were pursuing a different vision—they wanted to create the "dynabook," a fully interactive learning tool which would be as portable as a book. Unfortunately, they failed. The prototype they built was too large and was never produced in volume. It embodied, however, numerous component technologies, such as the "mouse" and an "iconic" interface that we all now know as the "Macintosh" interface—which eventually gave birth to the personal computer industry. That the Xerox researchers failed to produce the "dynabook" is now an obscure footnote in history, for the "dynabook" vision became, as Kay would say, "a forcing function for change."

What, then, are the types of changes we are seeking to encourage through pursuing the "learning organization" vision?

The Learning Organization Embodies New Capabilities Beyond Traditional Organizations

We believe a learning organization must be grounded in three foundations: (1) a culture based on transcendent human values of love, wonder, humility, and compassion; (2) a set of practices for generative conversation and coordinated action; and (3) a capacity to see and work with the flow of life as a system.

In learning organizations, cultural norms defy our business tradition. Acceptance of the other as a legitimate being—a Thou—(our meaning of love), replaces the traditional will to homogeneity. The ever-surprising manifestations of the world show up as opportunities to grow, as opposed to frustrating breakdowns for which somebody must take the blame (wonder). People understand that life is not condensable, that any model is an operational simplification always ready for improvement (humility). And when they encounter behaviors that they neither understand nor condone, people are able to appreciate that such actions arise from viewpoints and forces that are, in some sense, as valid as the viewpoints and forces that influence their own behaviors (compassion).

Learning organizations are a space for generative conversations and concerted action. In them, language functions as a device for connection, invention, and coordination. People can talk from their hearts and connect with one another in the spirit of dialogue (from the Greek *dia+logos*—moving through). Their dialogue weaves a common ongoing fabric and connects them at a deep level of being. When people talk and listen to each other this way, they create a field of alignment that produces tremendous power to invent new realities in conversation, and to bring about these new realities in action.

In learning organizations, people are always inquiring into the systemic consequences of their actions, rather than just focusing on local consequences. They can understand the interdependencies underlying complex issues and act with perceptiveness and leverage. They are patient in seeking deeper understanding rather than striking out to "fix" problem symptoms—because they know that most fixes are temporary at best, and often result in more severe problems in the future.

As a result of these capabilities, learning organizations are both more generative and more adaptive than traditional organizations. Because of their commitment, openness, and ability to deal with complexity, people find security not in stability but in the dynamic equilibrium between holding on and letting go— holding on and letting go of beliefs, assumptions, and certainties. What they know takes a second place to what they can learn, and simplistic answers are always less important than penetrating questions.

Developing such organizational capabilities will obviously require vision, patience, and courage. What is the nature of the leadership that will be required to move forward?

Learning Organizations Are Built by Communities of Servant Leaders

Leadership takes on important new meanings in learning organizations. In essence, the leaders are those building the new organization and its capabilities. They are the ones "walking ahead," regardless of their management position or hierarchical authority. Such leadership is inevitably collective.

Our conventional notions of leadership are embedded in myths of heroes—great individuals severed from their community who make their way through individual will, determination, and cleverness. While there may be much to admire in such persons, we believe that our attachment to individualistic notions of leadership may actually block the emergence of the leadership of teams, and ultimately, organizations and societies that can lead themselves. While we wait for the great leader who will save the day, we surrender the confidence and power needed to make progress toward learning organizations.

As the myth of the hero leader fades, a new myth of teams and communities that can lead themselves emerges. In 1983, successful grassroots community organizers from around the world gathered for a unique meeting in the United States. This group of "Ghandis of the world" produced a beautiful articulation of this new leadership myth:

> Our times are increasingly characterized by
> the awakening of the human force all over the
> planet, expressing itself in popular movements,
> grassroots communities, and local organiza-
> tions. This world force is a new kind of leader-
> ship capable of synthesizing the expressions
> of groups and organizing for action. Leader-
> ship from and of the group—and from the least
> among us—is the hope for change in our time.

The emergence of collective leadership does not mean that there are no "leadership positions" like CEO or general or president in learning organizations. Management hierarchies are often functional. But the clash of collective leadership and hierarchical leadership nonetheless poses a core dilemma for learning organizations. This dilemma cannot be reconciled given traditional notions of hierarchical leaders as the people "in control" or "in charge." For this, then, implies that those "below" are not in control. A hierarchical value system then arises that, as Analog Devices CEO Ray Stata puts it, "holds the person higher

One of the reasons the myth of the great leader is so appealing is that it absolves us of responsibility for developing leadership capabilities more broadly. Viewed systemically, there is a "shifting the burden" structure: a perceived "need for leadership" (a symptom) can be met through developing leadership capacities throughout the group or organization (the "fundamental solution") or through relying on the hero leader (the symptomatic solution). Success in finding a hero leader reinforces a belief in the group's own powerlessness (the shifting the burden "side effect"), thus making the fundamental solution more difficult.

Figure 1
Shifting the Burden

up the hierarchy as somehow a more important being."

Alternatively, the dilemma can become a source of energy and imagination through the idea of "servant leadership," people who lead because they chose to serve, both to serve one another and to serve a higher purpose.

Servant leadership offers a unique mix of idealism and pragmatism. At one level, the concept is an ideal, appealing to deeply held beliefs in the dignity and self-worth of all people and the democratic principle that a leader's power flows from those led. But it is also highly practical. It has been proven again and again in military campaigns that the only leader whom soldiers will reliably follow when their lives are on the line is the leader who is both competent and who soldiers believe is committed to their well-being.

As such leadership communities begin to grow, how will learning begin to be integrated into work?

Learning Arises Through Performance *and* Practice

It was common in native American cultures to set aside sacred spaces for learning. So, too, in our organizations today, learning is too important to leave to chance. It will not be adequate to offer training and hope that people will be able to apply new insights and methods. Nor will help from consultants be sufficient to bring about the fundamental shifts in thinking and interacting and the new capabilities needed to sustain those shifts. It will be necessary to redesign work if the types of ideas developed above are to find their way into the mainstream of management practice.

We believe that a guiding idea for redesigning work will be virtual learning spaces, or what have come to be known at the Learning Center as "managerial practice fields." The learning that occurs in sports teams and the performing arts is embedded in continuous movement between a practice field and a performance field. It is impossible to imagine a chamber music ensemble or a theater troop learning without rehearsal, just as it is impossible to imagine a championship basketball team that never practices. Yet, that is exactly what happens in most organizations. People only perform. They rarely get to practice, especially together.

Several design principles come together in creating effective managerial practice fields: (1) The learner learns what the learner wants to learn, so focus on key managerial issues. (2) The people who need to learn are the people who have the power to take action, so focus on key operational managers as opposed to staff. (3) Learning often occurs best through "play," through interactions in a transitional medium where it is safe to experiment and reflect. (4) Learning often requires altering the flow of time: slow down the action to enable reflection on tacit assumptions and counterproductive ways of interacting; or, at other times, speed up time to reveal how current decisions can create unanticipated problems in the long term. (5) Learning often requires "compressing space," as well as time, so that the learner can see the effects of his or her actions in other parts of a larger system. (Computer simulation and related tools may be needed for principles 4 and 5.) (6) This transitional medium must look like the action domain of the learners. (7) The learning space must be shamelessly integrated into the work space for an ongoing cycle of reflection, experimentation, and action.

If learning becomes more integrated into how we work, where does "work" end and "learning" begin?

Process and Content Are Inseparable

Because our culture is so caught up in separation, we have been led, according to David Bohm, "to seek some fantasy of action...that would end the fragmentation in the content (of our thought) while leaving the fragmentation in the actual process of thinking untouched." So, for example, executives seek to improve fragmented policies and strategies without addressing the fragmented and competitive relationships among the managers who formulated the strategies and policies. Consultants propose new process-oriented organizational designs without addressing the modes of thinking and interacting that cause us to focus on things rather than processes in the first place. Management educators treat either "technical" issues like operations, marketing, or finance, or behavioral issues like organization culture, decision making, or change.

In our normal ways of looking at things, the content or issues we are interested in are separate from the processes we might use to learn about them. Yet, this very separation may be the primary obstacle to potential breakthroughs in situations where content and process are inseparable. For example, early in one of our Learning Center field projects, the team began to address the company culture of punishment for bad news. But, rather than blaming the "culture" or "management," the members of the group explored their own reactions to hearing about problems, especially from subordinates. They began to surface their fears about mistakes and their automatic reactions and defensive responses, like heightened competitiveness or a tendency to cover up the problems. Gradually, they reached some deep insight into their "culture of punishment" and their own role in sustaining it.

If indeed it is possible to progress toward learning organizations, what are some of the reasons we might resist such changes?

Learning is Dangerous

Learning occurs between a fear and a need. On the one hand, we feel the need to change if we are to accomplish our goals. On the other hand, we feel the anxiety of facing the unknown and unfamiliar. To learn significant things, we must suspend some basic notions about our worlds and our selves. That is one of the most frightening propositions for the ego.

The conventional notion of learning is transactional. There is a learner who has a certain way of operating and a certain knowledge. If this knowledge proves to be incomplete or ineffective, the learner has the ability to drop part of it, change some of it, or add some new ideas to it. This may be an accurate description of how we learn to find better bargains or make better investments, but it fails to get to the heart of the type of learning involved when we are questioning deep beliefs and mental models.

The problem with this view is that the self is not separate from the ideas and assumptions that form it. Our mental models are not like pieces of clothing that we can put on or take off. They are basic constitutive structures of our personality. For all intents and purposes, most of the time, we are our mental models.

The learning required in becoming a learning organization is "transformational learning." Static notions of who we are must be checked at the door. In transformational learning, there are no problems "out there" to be solved independent of how we think and act in articulating these problems. Such learning is not ultimately about tools and techniques. It is about who we are. We often prefer to fail again and again rather than let go of some core belief or master assessment.

This explains the paradox of learning. Even when we claim we want to learn, we normally mean that we want to *acquire* some new tool or understanding. When we see that *to learn*, we must be willing to look foolish, to let another teach us, learning doesn't always look so good anymore.

It is little coincidence that virtually all spiritual disciplines, regardless of culture or religious setting, are practiced in communities. Only with the support, insight, and fellowship of a community can we face the dangers of learning meaningful things.

Theory in Practice: The Work of The Organizational Learning Center

The "liaison officers" of the MIT Learning Center are individuals from each participating company who work together to reflect on what we are learning and to translate these reflections into improved management practices for the center. It was in this group that we first began to realize that building learning organizations was grounded in developing leadership communities. A core question has occupied us throughout this year: "How do such communities form, grow, and become influential in moving large organizations forward?"

Ford's Vic Leo has suggested a three-stage "architecture of engagement": (1) finding those predisposed to this work, (2) core community-building activities, and (3) practical experimentation and testing.

Predisposition

It is easy to waste time attempting to bring about changes with people who do not want, or are not ready for, such changes. When the liaison officers reflected on how they became involved in systemic thinking and organizational learning, we discovered that there were aspects of each person's background that made that person predisposed. In some cases, it was academic training. In others, particular work or life experiences. In all cases, they were deeply drawn to the "systems perspective." They needed no convincing that much problem solving in organizations leaves deeper sources of problems untouched, and that the roots of these difficulties lie in how we think and how we interact. They were skeptical of conventional strategies for organizational improvement—reorganizations, training, management programs, speeches from "on high." Predisposition is important, especially in the early stages of building momentum when there are few practical results to point to.

Those not predisposed to systems thinking should not be excluded, but they may play less important roles at the outset. Over time, many people who are initially confused, threatened, or non-responsive to systems thinking and learning often become the most enthusiastic supporters. If they are not included, because they raise difficult questions or disagree with certain ideas, what starts as a learning community can degenerate into a cult.

Community-Building Activities

How those predisposed begin to know each other and to work together involves an ongoing cycle of community-building activities and practical experimentation. The former must be intense enough and open-ended enough to foster trusting personal relationships and to lay a foundation of knowledge and skills. The latter must offer realistic starting steps in applying new knowledge and skills to important issues.

For example, at the Learning Center, a five-day introductory course explores the tools, methods, and personal dimensions of the "Galilean Shift." There is practice with systems thinking tools and dialogue, and with reflecting on and articulating personal visions. Just as important, the cause often results in what the liaison officers called a "piercing experience," where the systems perspective begins to take on a deeper meaning and the nature of the journey ahead becomes clearer.

Moreover, it is a journey that we are all taking together. There are no "teachers" with correct answers, only guides with different areas of expertise and experience that may help along the way. Each of us gives up our own certainty and recognizes our interdependency within the larger community of practitioners. The honest, humble, and purposeful "I don't know" grounds our vision for learning organizations. In this sense, the five-day introductory course begins to forge the vessel within which the learning center staff and the company managers begin to operate as a community.

This vessel is reinforced and expanded through a variety of other meetings and communications media, including electronic mail, bulletin boards, and research documents. Especially important are semiannual "systems applications conferences," originally organized for reporting on projects under way in participating organizations. These large gatherings, which typically involve 100 to 150 people, have become an ongoing dialogue rather than a one-way reporting on various projects. Remarkably, we are finding that the more we organize around dialogue, and the less we plan out elaborate agendas, the more we accomplish.

Practical Experimentation and Testing

Ultimately, what nurtures the unfolding community most is serious, active experimentation where people wrestle with crucial strategic and operational issues. In our work at the center, we undertake learning projects in conjunction with groups of managers who have taken the five-day introductory course. Most projects focus on key issues, because of the resulting motivation for learning and because of the potential for significant improvement in business results.

Currently, two types of "practice field" projects are under way: dialogue projects and learning laboratory projects. Dialogue projects focus directly on the deeper patterns of communication that underlie whatever issues are being confronted by a management team.

Learning laboratory projects focus on specific areas such as new product development, management accounting and control systems, and services management. Here are some examples.

A team at Ford, responsible for creating the next generation Lincoln Continental, is also creating a New Car Development Learning Laboratory. The project has two interrelated objectives: to improve the effectiveness of the team in its current project and to develop better theory and tools that will lead to broader systemic thinking in product development at Ford.

One of the most daunting tasks in car product development is to balance autonomy of component engineering teams with optimal design for the car as a whole. For example, many component teams, such as electronic fuel handling and climate control, place demands on the car's electrical system. If every component team optimizes its own efforts, the total load can exceed the capacity of the alternator. Trying to convince each team separately that it should sacrifice accomplishes little; it may only raise fears that other component teams will then be able to command more of the alternator capacity.

This is actually an example of a general systems phenomenon called "tragedy of the commons." The term refers to situations in which there are common resources upon which all depend, like a commons for grazing sheep. Individual incentives, such as one family's efforts to increase the size of its flock, will eventually destroy the commons for all. Using system archetypes, Ford's team has been able to conceptualize the particular interdependencies involved in achieving an optimal total vehicle electronic system. They also have identified other basic "commons" that recur in all car development efforts. They are developing a general approach that can lead to early identification of commons and to establishment of specific management mechanisms to assure that commons are not "overgrazed."

At the same time, the team is developing a new car. Early returns show unprecedented levels of internal coordination. For example, at a recent checkpoint, the team had a level of "parts on time" twice the average.

Another example of a learning project is Chrysler's use of system dynamics computer simulation to introduce "activity-based costing" throughout the organization. The project's goal is to create an experiential laboratory where the users of the new system can reflect on the shortcomings of current accounting methods and the improvements of activity-based information. So far, Chrysler has used the laboratory in five new implementations, with all operations managers ranking an introductory session above 90 (ranking goes from 1 for terrible to 100 for best seminar ever attended).

The one-year program, the learning laboratories, and dialogue projects all spring from the "Galilean Shift"; all follow the operating principles articulated earlier in this paper. In all cases, what started as a "practice field" has led to penetrating insights into critical business issues. The practice fields are gradually becoming integrated into everyday company activities. When we started the pilot projects, we had a vision of transforming organizations through learning processes focused on significant business problems. We saw practice fields as a place where teams could meet to reflect on structures, identify counterproductive behaviors, experiment with alternative strategies, and design solutions for actual work settings. The core of the projects, in our minds, were "management flight simulators," computer simulations based on systems thinking. The simulators would enable managers to "compress time and space" so as to better understand the long-term consequences of their decisions and to reflect on their assumptions.

The management flight simulators are powerful tools that have shown their worth repeatedly, but the projects are yielding something more. We are finding that the notion of practice fields was far more radical than we originally believed. When people have a transitional medium where they can relate to each other safely and playfully, where they can openly explore the most difficult and "undiscussable" systemic issues, they begin to see their learning community as something precious. "People will misunderstand what we are doing as problem solving," said one senior manager recently, "when in fact we are creating a new way of managing."

Conclusion

Building learning organizations is not an individual task. It demands a shift that goes all the way to the core of our culture. We have drifted into a culture that fragments our thoughts, that detaches the world from the self and the self from its community. We have gained control of our environment but have lost our artistic edge. We are so focused on our security that we don't see the price we pay: living in bureaucratic organizations where the wonder and joy of learning have no place. Thus, we are losing the spaces to dance with the ever-changing patterns of life. We are losing ourselves as fields of dreams.

We believe that to regain our balance we must create alternative ways of working and living together. We need to invent a new, more learningful model for business, education, health care, government, and family. This invention will come from the patient, concerted efforts of communities of people invoking aspiration and wonder. As these communities manage to produce fundamental changes, we will regain our memory—the memory of the community nature of the self and of the poetic nature of language and the world—the memory of the whole.

This essay is reprinted, by permission of the publisher, from *Organizational Dynamics*, Autumn/1993. © 1993, American Management Association, New York. All rights reserved.

Charles Handy is a writer, teacher, broadcaster, and visiting professor at the London Business School. He has been an oil executive, an economist, a professor of management development, and the Warden of St. George's House in Windsor Castle.

He studied classics and philosophy at Oriel College, Oxford, and management at the Sloan School of the Massachusetts Institute of Technology. His published works include *Understanding Organizations; Gods of Management; The Age of Unreason; and Waiting for the Mountain to Move*, a collection of his "Thoughts for the Day" from the *BBC's Today Programme*.

Handy's most recent book is *The Age of Paradox*, which was previously published in the U.K. as the best-seller, *The Empty Raincoat*. He is a former chairman of the RSA (Royal Society for the Encouragement of Arts, Manufactures, and Commerce).

2

Managing the Dream

Charles Handy

In an uncertain world, where all we know for sure is that nothing is sure, we are going to need organizations that are continually renewing themselves, reinventing themselves, reinvigorating themselves. These are the learning organizations, the ones with the learning habit. Without that habit of learning, they will not dream the dream, let alone have any hope of managing it.

Just as the world has changed, so too has the process of learning. When the future was an extension of the present, it was reasonable to assume that what worked today would also work next year. That assumption must now be tossed out. The world is not a stable state, and particularly not the world of business. We are seeing change that not only accelerates ever faster but also is discontinuous. Such change lacks continuity and follows no logical sequence. During times of discontinuous change, it can almost be guaranteed that what used to work well in the past will not work at all next time around. The old approaches to change are simply too incremental. More than that, they are too slow.

Businesses today are especially exposed to discontinuous change. Gone are the cosy cartels, lasting technological superiority and market-niche security. When twenty or more countries around the world can produce Chardonnay wine to rival the French, nothing seems sacred anymore. No wonder that the average shelf life of corporations is only forty years, before they either are swallowed, die or merge. Those that do not change and keep on changing will eventually disappear.

Today we are hearing so much about change that the word is becoming a cliché. Rather than chant change, it is more accurate to say that we all—individuals and organizations—must acquire the learning habit, the new learning habit. It is a habit that changes many of the old assumptions about management. The learning organization is a different sort of place. But it is an exciting one.

What are these organizations like? How do they differ from traditional organizations? In this monograph, we will look at the qualities that characterise learning organizations and enable them to grow. We will then look at the actual process of learning. This process is like a wheel. It is designed to move. The challenge for organizations is to keep the wheel of learning in motion, to keep it turning. There are five key concepts which can help: subsidiarity, clubs and congresses, horizontal fast-tracks, self-enlightenment, and incidental learning. It is also important to have a leader who can provide vision, encouragement, and personal example.

Characteristics of the Learning Organization

The learning organization is built upon an *assumption of competence* that is supported by four other qualities or characteristics: *curiosity, forgiveness, trust* and *togetherness*. The assumption of competence means that each individual can be expected to perform to the limit of his or her competence, with the minimum of supervision. This idea is at the core of the concept of the professional. The assumption of competence in professional organizations is also what makes them so interesting to the talented young—a critical factor for those seeking to attract the best people.

For too long organizations have operated on an assumption of incompetence. The characteristics of this assumption are controls and directives, rules and procedures, layers of management and pyramids of power—all very costly. By contrast, the *assumption of competence* promotes flat organizations, with fewer checkers checking checkers. Flat organizations are far more responsive, efficient and cost effective. They put a high premium on early training, on acculturation in their ways and values and on some form of vetting or qualification before an individual is allowed to operate. In these organizations the learning habit starts early. Competence alone, despite all the prior learning it implies, is not enough to foster the learning habit. It must be accompanied by *curiosity*. Watch a small child learning. The questions are endless, the curiosity insatiable. But curiosity does not end with the questions. Questions beg answers, and the truly curious goes in search of the right answers. This often requires experimentation. This process is encouraged in the learning organization, provided there is an assumption of competence and a license to experiment within the boundaries of a person's authority.

Because experiments can fail, *forgiveness* is essential. Instead of failures, unsuccessful experiments must be viewed as part of the learning process, as lessons learned. One can also learn from successful experiments. That form of learning needs not to be forgiven but to be celebrated. One company known for encouraging constant experimentation at all levels and handsomely rewarding success is 3M. This company believes in praise, but it also believes in saying thank you to those who tried yet found a particular experiment did not work. Both are important in the learning organization.

None of these things—competence, curiosity, forgiveness or celebration—can foster a learning organization if there is no *trust*. While a person may be highly competent, you will not allow him to be competent unless you trust him. Of course, it is difficult to trust someone you don't know or have never seen in action. A person you know only by name from a memo is not a person to take a risk with. For the learning organization, the implications of this simple human fact are enormous. How many people can one person know well enough to trust? On the answer to that question hangs the whole design and structure of the corporation.

One solution is *togetherness*. Few, if any, of the problems businesses face nowadays can be handled by one person acting alone. That is fortunate, in a way, because curiosity, experimentation and forgiveness need to be shared. Lonely learners are often slow and poor learners, whereas people who collaborate learn from each other and create synergy.

Today we are seeing an increasing number of organizations made up of shifting "clusters" or teams that share a common purpose. The need for togetherness, both to get things done and to encourage the kind of exploration that is essential to any growing organization, creates the conditions for trust. Trust, in turn, improves togetherness.

Groups that are too big to feel any togetherness, or that lack a common purpose to hold them together, will not succeed in developing trust. When that happens, there are those who are quick to re-impose control and direction from the top, to assume incompetence in those below, to discourage experimentation and to withhold forgiveness. These conditions stifle creativity, making learning very difficult if not impossible.

Despite the presence of trust and togetherness, the learning organization is not a comfortable place for its leaders. It is an upside-down sort of place, with much of the power residing at the organization's edge. In this culture, imposed authority no longer works. Instead, authority must be earned from those over whom it is exercised. This organization is held together by shared beliefs and values, by people who are committed to each other and to common goals—a rather tenuous method of control.

Such an upside-down way of running an organization requires a powerful theory to justify it; in this case, a theory of learning. Real learning is not what many of us grew up thinking it was. It is not simply memorizing facts, learning drills or soaking up traditional wisdom. While these activities may be required in learning, they constitute only part of a larger process.

The Wheel of Learning

This process can best be described as a wheel—a wheel of learning. The wheel has four quadrants that, ideally, rotate in sequence as the wheel moves. The first quadrant consists of the *questions*, which may be triggered by problems or needs that require solutions. The questions prompt a search for possible answers or *ideas*, which must pass rigorous *tests* to see if they work. The results are then subjected to *reflec-* 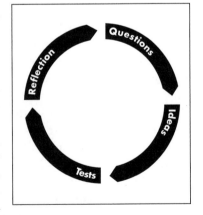 tions, until we are certain we have identified the best solution. Only when the entire process is complete can we truly say that we have learned something. There are no short cuts. This process lies at the heart of individual growth and of corporate success. Too simple, some would say. They should try putting it into practice.

Keeping the wheel in motion in a corporation requires great leadership, immense energy and a belief in the potential for excellence. There is little wonder at the fact that we have no examples of organizations that have got it all right. One reason is that it is so easy for a group or an individual to get stuck in one quadrant of the wheel, forever collecting more information without putting any of it to the test, or experimenting without pausing to reflect. Another pitfall is stopping after one set of tests proves successful, thinking that all the questions have now been answered. Like the wheel, the process is designed to move. To keep the wheel turning, we must continue to be curious, to ask the question again, to expect to find new answers.

The truth is that most of us work with an implicit model of learning that is out-of-date and wrong. We believe that learning is something we pass on from one person to another, by word of mouth or through books. These methods represent only one section of the wheel—the ideas. To believe that ideas form the whole of learning leads us to ignore, quite unconsciously, the other three sections. By so doing, we stop the wheel, inhibiting growth, change and development—both in ourselves and in those around us.

The historian Arthur Schlesinger once wrote, "Ignorance of the present, ignorance of the future, these are pardonable. But ignorance of how ignorant we are is unpardonable." Great leaders combine self-confidence with reasonable doubt, a skepticism that starts the questioning that turns the wheel. Organizations that have acquired the learning habit are endlessly questioning the status quo, are forever seeking new methods or new products, forever testing and then reflecting, consciously or unconsciously pushing round that wheel.

Keeping the Wheel Moving

Maintaining constant movement of the wheel is not as easy as it sounds. There are five key concepts which can help to keep it turning: *subsidiarity, clubs and congresses, horizontal fast-tracks, self-enlightenment and incidental learning.*

Subsidiarity. The word itself is rather ugly, but the concept is important. Subsidiarity means giving away power. While no one does that willingly in most organizations, the idea is at the heart of the learning organization. Subsidiarity is written in capital letters at the head of its statement of values and beliefs.

In these organizations power is given to those who are closest to the action. The centre then confines itself to such areas as strategic investments, R&D and the information infrastructure—the things which only it can do, or can do best, on behalf of all.

Television and journalism represent two arenas in which subsidiarity is practised. Both provide an opportunity to take responsibility publicly at an early age. It has to work this way because no one in the centre of a television or a newspaper company can specify in any detail what has to go into every programme or on every page. Those in power have to rely on control after the event, which can at times be embarrassing and even expensive. These mistakes are an inevitable part of trust. In good organizations, the mistakes are rare because the people are good; and they are good because they know that they will be entrusted with big responsibilities, including the chance to make mistakes.

Subsidiarity is managed, organizationally, by defining the boundaries of the job. There are two boundaries. The inner boundary defines the essential core of the job, be it an individual's job, a team's or a function's. This part of the job is defined, the roles and responsibilities clear. If these things are not done, then one is seen to have failed. The outer boundary defines the limits of discretion. In between lies the scope for initiative and for personal responsibility.

W. L. Gore, whose company does its best to foster the learning habit, makes a nice distinction between the two boundaries. There are experiments above the water-line, which do little harm if they go wrong, and there are experiments below the water-line, which might sink the ship. The former are encouraged; the latter are outlawed.

In traditional organizations, the space for initiative is limited. Many jobs are all core and no space. The water-line is set very high. Control is tight. There is no initiative without prior permission. In the flexible, responsive organizations that are needed today, the space has to be larger because the centre cannot define in advance the details of every job. Control then has to be after the event—with forgiveness if necessary. This means that each individual or team must understand very clearly which types of initiatives are acceptable and which are not.

Everyone has to agree on the definition of success. Control depends more on a common understanding than on budgets and procedures. Shared values reinforce constant and effective communications, all of which are essential if subsidiarity is going to work. The organization that talks together works together.

Clubs and congresses. The learning organization must provide opportunities for talking, for meeting, and for greeting. Unfortunately, the opportunities for such communication are rapidly decreasing as more and more executives work out of their briefcases. Unlike their predecessors, who did most of their work behind their desks, today's successful executives are away from the office much of the time, meeting with clients, customers, suppliers, or advisers. They communicate electronically when they have to and use their offices only as a base.

Costed per hour of occupancy, these offices are horrendously expensive. Rather than maintain private, under-utilised space, some say we should turn our offices into clubs—places for "members only" to meet, eat, and greet. These facilities include meeting rooms, dining rooms, libraries, and rooms equipped with telephones and computers. Members gather here for meetings, to gain access to particular resources and to generally keep in touch. Like much of the new learning, this is upside-down thinking. It builds on the strengths of the club and coffeehouse cultures as a way of encouraging personal and informal communications. Both are vital to a company guided by shared values.

Similarly, large organizations need their congresses. Values cannot be shared electronically via bits of paper. We need to meet one-on-one with the people who share those values to determine whether we also want to adopt them.

The boom in conference centres has provided organizations with facilities worldwide for such congresses. Assemblies of executives can now meet in centres near airports or attached to a golf course. They convene at these places to debate and discuss, to catch up on the latest news or to hear about new theories. But more important, they come together to reach a consensus on the meaning of success and to meet the people whom they will have to trust as they go about working for that success. While these congresses, small and large, can get expensive, they are now one of the "hygiene" functions of the networked organization. Like central heating, they are an essential precondition of effective working.

Horizontal fast-tracks. Competent professional people and flat organizations are both desirable goals, but in combination they can present several challenges. One is that people can become more and more competent about less and less, thereby inhibiting the shared understanding so essential to effectiveness. Another is that as organizations become flatter, ladders to promotion get shorter, creating fewer "conventional" opportunities to reward success.

In Japan such vertical fast-tracks for high performers are almost nonexistent. Instead, they rotate their best people through a variety of jobs in different parts of the organization. The Japanese believe that this practice more than compensates for any loss in specialised knowledge by increasing each individual's breadth of experience, contacts and overall understanding of the business. Their professionals build their reputations on the variety and quality of the assignments they complete; rewards are based on results more than on a particular grade for the job. Except in very specialised areas, where detailed expertise is required, horizontal fast-tracks are the preferred career paths for the successful, provided always that rewards follow achievement.

Self-enlightenment. The Japanese have no business schools, yet their young executives appear well versed in all the concepts of modern management and business. How did they acquire these skills and this knowledge? The answer they give is "self-enlightenment," a polite word for correspondence courses. Young Japanese recruits are expected to take one of the many correspondence courses available to learn what might be called the "language of management." He, and it is still universally "he" in Japan, completes such studies on his own time, although the company will pay for any costs. A good tradition, self-enlightenment continues on throughout the life and career of every Japanese businessman.

Making each individual responsible for his own learning does make sense. If you do not own the question, then there will be no motivation to turn the wheel. Some American corporations capture the same idea in the phrase, "individual initiative and corporate support." In Britain, one advertising agency put this idea into practice. It divided up its training budget and gave its executives a share to spend on professional development, the company's investment in their future. There was one proviso— the personnel director had to sign all cheques for course materials and fees. That proved to be no impediment for these executives. They quickly filled the queues to request the funds, confounding all the cynics.

Incidental learning. The quest for knowledge or skills is only the beginning. Self-enlightenment needs to move on to incidental learning. Incidental learning is not the same as accidental learning. Coined by Alan Mumford, professor of management development at International Management Centres, Buckingham, incidental learning means treating every incident as a case study from which we can learn.

Such incidents do not occur automatically; opportunities must be created for them to develop. For example, regular meetings of one's group or cluster can be arranged to review recent critical events. It is, in fact, the time-honoured way in which doctors, social workers and other professionals help each other to learn from their experiences. It requires honesty with oneself and with others, a sense of togetherness and trust. Incidental learning is the organization's way to build in time for reflection, the final segment of the wheel. A mentor from outside the organization or group can enhance the process by encouraging a free and frank exchange without acrimony.

Incidental learning is most appropriate when one is dealing with divergent problems. It was E.F. Schumacher, author of *Small Is Beautiful*, who first distinguished between convergent and divergent problems. Convergent problems have right answers: "This is the shortest route to Boston." Divergent problems, such as "Why do you want to go to Boston?" have answers only right for a particular person, time and place.

Once we have moved beyond the basics, all the problems of organizations are divergent, to be solved only by the process of the wheel. This is what makes organizations so endlessly fascinating, and also so difficult.

Some 2,500 years ago Heraclitus said that one could not step twice into the same river. The reason for this, according to this ancient philosopher, is that everything is always in motion; nothing stays in the same place. Some truths do not change.

Driving the Wheel

Theories and concepts are important, but the job of keeping the wheel turning remains the primary task of the true leader. While each will find his or her own way of doing it, *vision*, *encouragement* and *example* will be central to all.

At the beginning of the 1990s, companies began to talk increasingly about the need for corporate *vision*. Although unkindly mocked as "the vision thing," the truth is that no one is going to go through the ardours of organizational learning unless there is some point to it. Most people want to share in a task that is bigger than themselves. They want a purpose in life beyond themselves, one which is real versus a thing of rhetoric.

British Petroleum, as a first step to becoming a fast, flexible, focussed, friendly and fun place (to use Rosabeth Moss Kanter's mnemonic), spent a lot of time and money to gain a true acceptance of its vision and values from its top people. BP knew that without that acceptance, it could not create the energy to unlearn the past and to think upside-down and inside-out when this was required.

Visions, however, must be earthed in reality. Standards are the currency of vision. But standards need comparisons, which is one of the benefits of competition. Competition sets standards for us whether we like it or not. Benchmarking, a popular new tool, is really only a faddish name for an old habit: learning by voyeurism—spying on your neighbor and then doing it better. In business it means looking for best practices both in and outside of your industry. We would do well to cast our eyes as widely as possible, because good practices can be found in the most unexpected places. Professional partnerships, hospitals and universities, for example, are not obvious places to look for examples of good management, yet they have been running learning organizations for centuries. They have experience to offer and standards of their own, which businesses could learn from.

Learning needs constant *encouragement*. The best encouragement is the satisfaction of having learned something. Learning feeds on itself. Measuring results can help, because progress is then made visible. Recognition helps even more. Colleges and schools have ritual ceremonies to honour those who have learned. Organizations need to find their own ways to celebrate their learners, and they need not be expensive.

Ultimately, it is personal *example* which matters most in keeping the wheel moving. The leader who is perceived to be saying "learning is good for you, but I don't need it" will have few followers. Leaders once believed that they had to give out an aura of certainty, of invincibility and conviction. Today there are too many examples of misplaced certainty in both business and world affairs for that stance to inspire confidence. We would rather have a leader who is seen to be open-minded, questions himself and others, searches for ideas, is obsessed with truth and betterment, is ready to take risks, listens to criticism and advice and has a purpose beyond himself combined with an awareness that he cannot do it on his own. Give that leader self-confidence and a sense of humour, and most would be happy to follow his or her example.

There Is No Alternative

People once believed that there was a science and a theory of organizations which, like the laws of motion, would allow us to predict and determine the future. We now know that this is impossible. We have learned that chance happenings, like chaos theory, will trigger chain reactions, that the past will be a poor guide to the future and that we shall forever be dealing with unanticipated events.

Given that scenario, organizations have no choice but to reinvent themselves almost every year. To succeed, they will need individuals who delight in the unknown. The wise organization will devote considerable time to identifying and recruiting such people and to ensuring job satisfaction. Being a "preferred" organization will become increasingly important. One of the things that will set these organizations apart from the rest will be their emphasis on subsidiarity. Preferred organizations will be learning organizations. They will provide opportunities to exercise responsibility, to learn from experience, to take risks and to gain satisfaction from results achieved and lessons learned.

Such organizations will continue to defy conventional wisdom. They will be organizations of consent, not of control. They will be able to maintain a feeling of togetherness despite their size and far-flung locations. They will make many mistakes, but will have learned from them before others realise they occurred. They will invest hugely in their people and trust them hugely and save the salaries of ranks of inspectors. Above all, they will see learning not as a confession of ignorance but as the only way to live. It has been said that people who stop learning stop living. This is also true of organizations.

Marilynne Anderson is a Senior Vice President of Consulting Services for Right Associates, an international human resources consulting firm specializing in career management services. She sold her previous company, the first executive outplacement consulting firm in Minnesota in 1978, to Right Associates in 1988.

Beyond consulting activities, Anderson has an avid and abiding interest in the politics and practices of gender perspectives. Growing up female in the 1950s influenced her personal and professional decisions in both predictable and not so predictable ways. Hers is a generation that has seen significant strides in career opportunities for women, as well as in the redefining of professional expectations of 1950s women in the 1990s. From this personal experience comes her present involvement in creating leadership learning vehicles for women, actively mentoring women, and coaching both women and men through career transitions. She is a co-founder of The Women's Leadership Forum.

These efforts, as important as they are, have a larger purpose, however. That purpose is to value and promote an integration of *all* perspectives for the healthy growth of organizations and people.

3

Ahead of the Wave: Valuing Gender Perspective in Learning Cultures

Marilynne Anderson

We've each been invited to this present moment by design. Our lives are joined like the tiles of a mosaic; none of us contributes the whole of the picture, but each of us is necessary for its completion....More important, the depth, the richness of the picture in its entirety is enhanced by our fulfilled dreams.

—Karen Casey & Martha Vanceburg
The Promise of A New Day

My windshield wipers threaten to stop in mid-motion as gusty sheets of rain blur my vision. "Why didn't I have that damned wiper motor fixed?" I exclaim as I grip the wheel. My fear is palpable as the wind insists that I and my car move farther toward the right shoulder of the road. "This is how it will be—learning to bring more of my self, my voice, my authenticity to the workplace—difficult."

I note my reactive response. "Why must I work so hard to keep the car and me on the journey?" I continue. "After all, the road is a straight, easy shot north to the training center, and I want to get there. I'm looking forward to the good, hard work of becoming more aware of how I listen, how I deepen a dialogue, how I influence and am influenced by others in the learning community we've been creating the past four days. I want to continue to engage in a multiplicity of opportunities to learn from a host of individuals through a great variety of interactions. From each, I am learning about learning, either from participating or from observing others learn from one another."

The torrents of wind and rain haven't diminished in intensity. Nor have my desires. As I think beyond the difficulty of the moment, I renew my choice to take this journey, and I'm eager to share the meaning of this moment with my new community.

My experience in the storm was a moment of grace and a segue into what I intend to focus on in this essay: the gift of diversity of perspective, the impact of an integration of the feminine perspective in the workplace, and the simplicity and importance of learning from one another one at a time.

As we rise to the waves of crisis, change, and choice in our personal and professional lives, perhaps we need a periscope—that instrument whose mirrors and prisms permit observation from a position displaced from a direct line of sight—to guide us through uncharted territory. Let's raise our periscopes and look at what we cannot yet fully see—the changes that a full engagement of gender perspective will precipitate in the organizations of the future in which we all will learn.

Voices Of Diversity—The Gift

Recognizing, including and valuing perspectives of gender in the building of learning cultures honor the voices of diversity. The melting pot theory has proved to be a woefully inadequate construct for creating workplace equity and community. Personally, I feel illumined and energized by the vision of a grand mosaic or tapestry. I anticipate that its design and creation will emerge from each of our unique contributions, that each contribution will further a continuous effort, and that the outcome will be valued by all. My fear is that all of us won't be able to contribute if we fail to commit to creating endless opportunities in organizations for exchanging differing perspectives.

When I do not listen to your voice, your difference, with my heart as well as my head, I miss something beyond your uniqueness—an opportunity to learn about my *self*. In the learning culture we created at the conference I mentioned, one of my learning partners told me that her first goal was to learn to listen differently. I observed her in dialogue in her skills group and shared my perception of her impact on others. As she observed me in dialogue, she reflected on how I listened. When we closed our "learning partner loop" at the end of the week, she thanked me for reflecting what she needed, for providing a mirror from which she could learn. From our work, I, too, learned about my self.

My values are strengthened by, and often derive from, a deeper self-knowledge. You give me the gift of my self by being in continuous dialogue with me. I become more aware of boundaries, the point where I leave off and you begin. Through identifying our boundaries, I become more powerful. I am freer to be creative, to seek responsibility, to speak more truthfully. With truthfulness, I invite your truthfulness. Together, we delve deeper to clarify assumptions about each another.

In delving deeper, I believe we are understanding that as few as two establish a system, a reality based on individual perception and agreement as to when and how and what the two of us will say and do and be together. This reality exists only between the two of us and, while affected by external events, is continuously co-created. As a result, we have an ongoing opportunity to change this reality, a continuous learning opportunity.

Today, continuous learning is expected and affords us endless opportunities to be proactive rather than reactive. Historically we have not valued mutuality—that condition of holding mutual interests in common. Duality, however, whether it be looking through the lenses of male or female, white or of color, young or old, has perniciously and persistently pervaded our thinking. Going forward, I believe we must create opportunities to discover, respect and integrate the perspectives of feminine and masculine within each of us. For if we fail to assimilate the feminine perspective into the leadership of tomorrow, we will continue to suffer a preponderance of transactional leaders in the face of a critical need for transformational interactive leaders, leaders who are authentic—self-disclosing, self-regulating and collaborative.

Gender Perspective—The Impact

What is masculine? What is feminine? We need to repeatedly ask these questions of each other because the answers are in flux. What descriptors come to your mind? What kind of energy do you think about? Does the feminine perspective reside only in females? Does the masculine perspective reside solely in males? Are the skills formerly thought of as feminine—communication, relationship and social sensitivity skills—presently *leading* dialogue in workplace dialogues? Rarely. Some male voices are beginning to speak, however, about the underutilization of human assets and the resulting losses of innovation, productivity, and competitiveness in organizations by not engaging the feminine perspective. On a personal level, more and more males are responding to their nurturing capability within and demonstrating it within their families in nontraditional ways.

What is the feminine perspective? I think it is important to create a picture that may be illuminating. In my work as a career transitions consultant, I use the nine dots puzzle to illustrate the concept that a client must be open to possibilities to co-create an employment situation. During fifteen years of such counseling, I have seen many individuals earnestly try to follow instructions, to do what they have been told, to draw the box. Those who "come out of the box," create a drawing comprised of the *diagonal* line, the line of energy. This is good; however, at some level, this exercise reinforces linear thinking in the face of the need for holistic thinking using the right *and* the left brain. What is needed is the *curvilinear* line, the line that defines the circle, one of the most common shapes in nature and one of the most useful motifs for learning from one another...a motif familiar to women.

Curvilinear thinking encompasses the possibilities of both the diagonal line which connotes direction, energy and purpose, and the gentler curved line which suggests inclusion and flexibility. Flexibility aligns with opportunity—opportunity for reflection, for turning round for feedback, for redesign, for moving forward, with involvement, direction, optimism, and new thoughtful connections. Moreover, the curved line suggests collaboration—a blending of perspectives. It suggests integration of the characteristics commonly ascribed to the masculine perspective—bold, firm and decisive—with characteristics of the feminine perspective—nurturing, communal, and flexible. Separate, and, presently, not equally valued perspectives.

Will the feminine perspective have an impact on learning cultures within organizations of the future? According to some experts, the single most significant force for social change in the western world since the industrial revolution is the influx of women into the labor force. Recent data from the U.S. Bureau of Labor Statistics, and other sources, are illuminating:

- By 1992, the number of women in the labor force had reached 57.8 million, an all-time high.
- By 1992, women held 47%, or 14.7 million, of all managerial and professional specialty jobs—up from 40%, or 9.7 million, in 1983.
- In 1992, women-owned businesses employed as many individuals as all of the *Fortune* 500 companies combined.

Add to these startling statistics the estimate that white men, who now dominate as business leaders, will constitute only 10% of the U.S. work force by the year 2000. Clearly, women will be one significant voice in the chorus of individuals aspiring to leadership in organizations of the future.

How will the feminine perspective manifest itself? Today, more and more women are elected and promoted to positions of authority and influence. Women's gains are real. Glad to express their voice, women are excited by the prospect of leading change, of serving as role models and mentors for our partners, sons, daughters, sisters, mothers, brothers, friends and workmates.

Do the women currently in leadership positions lead organizations and institutions differently than men? Will they in the future? What will be the outcome of a greater concentration of women leaders? Because we don't have definitive answers to these questions today, the questions seem all-important, especially to women, reflecting the stage of change we are currently experiencing.

As we move from a known state to an unknown state we are often in "the neutral zone," as William Bridges calls it in his 1980 book, *Transitions*. Being in the neutral zone is extremely frustrating. We are plagued by doubt and energized by opportunity. Change is "in our face." Many women are in the neutral zone today. We are asking the wrong question if we focus on: Will women lead *differently* than men? This is a *divisive* question. A better question is: What will be the *meaning, emphasis*, and *extent* of women's influence?

Prisms and Mirrors—The Simplicity and Importance of Learning from One Another

Cultural change happens in two transformational ways— from the *inside-out* of each individual, as well as from one individual in dialogue with another. Both occur well before public voices are synthesizing and mirroring change for us. Inside-out individual change is critical, for it forms the vortex around which larger systemic change will continue to occur. We only have dominion over ourselves. *One at a time* we can shift a cultural perspective which discounts differences to one, which embraces and values the uniqueness of each of us.

We each must commit to self-development, personally and professionally, manifesting the understanding that "locus of control" rests within, that change happens from the inside-out. Today more and more women are showing the way to other women and to men by being intentional about self-development. A guiding self-development principle is our socialized (or inherent) tendency toward forming "learning from one another" circles. In the circle, we feel free to tell our personal stories, to speak about our vulnerabilities and our strengths. We *listen* to one another to nurture and learn from one another. In these simple ways which celebrate our uniqueness, we invite one another:

- To be authentic—the *meaning* of our influence
- To create community and celebrate mutuality—the *emphasis* of our influence
- To seek balance by celebrating the integration of the feminine and masculine aspects of our natures—the *extent* of our influence.

> *AUTHENTICITY—"the state or quality of being genuine, authoritative"*

On a Minnesota bone-chilling-cold January day, a woman, unknown to me, called me and another woman to arrange a meeting to discuss whether our three organizations might co-sponsor a marketing event. The event would highlight a nationally known author-lecturer who would discuss women's leadership potential for the Nineties. This serendipitous meeting resulted in the creation of a significant opportunity for women to share their voices—The Women's Leadership Forum.

The central design principle of The Women's Leadership Forum is to circle and learn from one another in some depth... *to raise our individual periscopes*. We meet in circles to share our opinions, to be genuine with one another, to experience our authority. We listen to and respond to our individual and collective voices.

The Forum has generated circle discussions on such topics as women as leaders in the Nineties, women as change agents; women's leadership lessons from abroad; women and humor; women and economic issues and trends of the Nineties, and women and the meaning of work. These and other forums have elicited "outstanding" evaluations from participants, who are women in business and academia in the Twin Cities of Minneapolis and St. Paul.

Why have they been so successful? Because learning from one another is as *contemporary* as it is an ancient form of *cultural wisdom-sharing* and a vehicle for receiving the feedback so critical to achieving authenticity. Some indigenous cultures sew small pieces of reflective glass into ceremonial costumes or glue them onto masks to remind themselves that a mirror is a metaphor for reflection. Upon "reflection," we give ourselves and one another the opportunity to be authentic.

In Women's Leadership Forums we provide an environment for cultural wisdom sharing of the feminine perspective, and we model authenticity by:

- the *willingness* with which we disclose our personal stories—a powerful tool for building community and shared vision in organizations
- the *naturalness* with which we invite disclosure
- the *inclination* to listen carefully, from a nurturing heart, to the story of another's journey
- the *trust* that we extend to signify that we believe in one another's ability to succeed

We leave each forum with several gifts: a sense of shared meaning and community gained through the power of honest dialogue and a shared understanding of the work that remains to be done. Empowering gifts. What is the potential take-away here for all of us? It is this: it is but a small step to formalize the use of learning circles within our organizations so that we can benefit from both the feminine and the masculine perspective. Learning circles of diverse perspectives of gender, race, age, functional levels, etc. will contribute to an individual's understanding that one person always makes a difference when listened to with the head and heart of another.

> MUTUALITY—"possessing or holding in common mutual interests"

About the same time as The Women's Leadership Forum began to sponsor learning forums, another idea, with a unique focus on women's leadership potential, was conceived in Minnesota. Two women meeting at a business dinner discovered a similar passion and commitment for the advancement of women within organizations and co-created Minnesota 100, a mentor-mentee program of far-reaching consequence for the progress of women leaders and the organizations they serve.

Gayle Holmes and Mary Mahoney, veterans in the corporate training and education field, have since successfully developed a service based on the key concept of learning from one another. Corporate leaders responded to their message: "We know of the leadership potential inherent in the women in your organization. Enroll one, two, three, or as many women as you wish, and we will match their development needs with 100 male and female Minnesota executives who will serve as their mentors for one year. Since the mentors will not be from your company but from other Minnesota companies, your organization and your employees will accrue unique benefits from the differing perspectives of the mentors, framed by the organizational cultures within which they serve." I have had the privilege of being a Minnesota 100 mentor in 1992, 1994, and again in 1995. My experience and that of others has shown that this relationship pushes the learning edges of both mentor and mentee.

What is so powerful about this creative effort is that leaders are being developed one at a time, or, as the Minnesota 100 co-founders would say, mano á mano. Mutual interests in building strong, cooperative, and spirited organizations are being served by the men and women who are learning from one another through disclosure of their gender's perspective in relation to experiences of failure and success in organizations. How does this happen?

- Mentors *actively listen* so that they can give appropriate feedback to further the self-development of mentees
- Mentors *self-disclose*, share their experiences, to inform through the power of the personal story
- Mentor and mentee *clarify* the meaning of words together and take the time to find shared meaning, learning from one another how each thinks and feels and values. Words don't have meaning, people do. Shared meaning engenders commitment.

Male and female mentors have enthusiastically embraced this program. One male senior executive of a large firm declared: "A greater presence of women in all kinds of leadership is welcome, necessary and overdue. I believe the development of women requires equal parts of ambition, performance, opportunity and advocacy—it's just plain smart business. I have two young daughters, and I don't want any real or perceived barriers to stand in the way of their future."

Female mentees completing a Minnesota 100 program have also enthusiastically embraced this program. One mentee commented: "I've strengthened my leadership skills and outlined steps and a plan to continue my growth in this area. As a result, I've gained a lot of confidence and visibility within my company." Another expresses: "I have worked on 'letting go' of total job absorption and used that time to concentrate on setting a balance with my personal goals. I now know that a well-balanced person translates into a more productive employee."

This last comment leads to another significant outcome of an emphasis on integration of the feminine perspective when creating learning forums within organizations—balance.

> BALANCE—"A state of equilibrium or equal relationship; Harmonious proportion, as in the design or arrangement of parts of the whole."

At the heart of career management consulting is the concept of an internal locus of control, of effecting change by first looking inward at one's strengths and weaknesses and then acting from a clear understanding of the unique interrelationship of interests, abilities, and values. In my work, I repeatedly see that it is our values which drive our decisions.

What does this imply?

We are seeing signs of the influence of the feminine perspective through a transformation in values which drive our work/life decisions. A recruiter recently told me about a change that she has seen over the last two years in the questions being asked by men in their late twenties and early thirties when introduced to an employment opportunity by her firm. Two years ago, the first questions asked were "how much does the position pay?" and "what are the responsibilities of the position?" etc.

Today, individuals in the same firm are asking, "how much travel is there?" and "how much time away from my family?" Most have working wives. Most are in pursuit of balance in their lives, of having "time" to attend to the feminine characteristics within themselves, those qualities of giving nurturance and support, of listening, of being present in their families. Balance and integration issues. Values issues.

It isn't just that we need more "time" in our lives, however. "...More important, the depth, the richness of the picture in its entirety is enhanced by our fulfilled dreams." (K. Casey & M. Vanceburg). How often is it that we are asked or given the opportunity to express our dreams in organizations? Generally we exist in workplaces driven by linear thinking and task oriented behavior. Dreams belong to another realm, the realm of spirit, of personal values, of integration of the feminine and masculine perspectives within us. From our dreams, we create those personal visions which pull us towards self-development, self-fulfillment, and self-regulation which increase our contributions in the workplace.

Women, in particular, who have left larger organizations speak about the sense of freedom, balance, and self-development they are able to fashion for themselves in their worklives. A thirty-six-year-old national accounts manager put it this way: "I graduated from college summa cum laude and entered the world of business. Fourteen years later I felt I had gained a fair amount of success as measured by salary and responsibility within two corporations. When I was laid off, there was a part of me that breathed a sigh of relief. I felt released from the 'super woman' syndrome. I determined to take the time to explore how I could fashion a worklife which would incorporate my values of attending to my family, to my self-fulfillment, and to my self-development."

There is a strong need, if we but notice it, to create spirit-filled environments within organizations in order to attract and keep valued, talented individuals who are increasingly committed to attaining "harmonious proportion" in their personal and professional lives. Values issues.

In the fifteen plus years since outplacement began in my state, I have seen but a small shift on the part of forward thinking companies and individuals, from a perspective of individual employment entitlement, to the "employability" concept. Employability means that the company no longer implicitly guarantees employment but that it commits to providing individuals with development and directional counseling based on an understanding of abilities, interests, and values that derives from this type of counseling. By promoting self-development, a company is changing the cultural climate of the organization to one which charges the individual with ownership of his or her career, and therefore of employability internal or external to the company. Ownership and authenticity are but two sides of the same coin. Both lead to self-regulating individuals. Self-regulating individuals seek balance and integration in their lives. Values issues.

Passage

Twenty years ago, Elizabeth Janeway wrote *Between Myth and Morning: Women Awakening*. In the introduction, she quoted Victor Turner in adapting Martin Buber's use of the word community to the form communitas. "At certain life crises," he wrote, "such as adolescence, the attainment of elderhood, and death, varying in significance from culture to culture, the passage from one structural status to another may be accomplished by a strong settlement of 'human-kindness' a sense of the generic social bond between all members of society."

We have the opportunity today to be intentional about valuing the "generic social bond" between all members of society and of being intentional about integrating the masculine and feminine perspectives within each of us. We will all benefit from:
- the boldness of being nurturing,
- the decisiveness of committing to community, and
- the firmness with which one can be flexible.

Our emphasis must first be on doing the difficult work of dialoguing with each other at the one-to-one level, sharing the meaning of individual values. Systems will follow. Organizations will become organic, evolving cultures, representing authentic, self-regulating individuals.

Perspective

As I close this essay, I am reminded of gazing up at the ceiling of St. Paul's Cathedral in London last year, where I saw the majesty of millions of golden mosaic pieces depicting the stories of the Judeo-Christian heritage. Each tile was a glittering jewel. The power and magnificence of the whole was awesome.

I believe that if we each visibly embrace the concept that we are called in this life to be learners and teachers to one another—in mutuality—we will have a simple yet elegant guiding principle for co-creating "learning cultures," golden mosaics, in our respective organizations.

The message is so simple we may not "get it." The message is one person always makes a difference. One person learns in dialogue with one other person. Together, we create a system. Together, we learn in that system. Together, we change that system. It's never easy. In fact, it's very difficult, and...it's well worth it.

Rosabeth Moss Kanter is an internationally known business leader, best-selling author, and advocate for change in business, government, and health care management. She holds the Class of 1960 Chair as Professor of Business Administration at the Harvard Business School. From 1989-1992 Kanter was also editor of the *Harvard Business Review*, a finalist for a National Magazine Award for General Excellence in 1991.

Her book *When Giants Learn to Dance: Mastering the Challenges of Strategy, Management and Careers in the 1990s* received the Johnson, Smith & Knisely Award for New Perspectives on Executive Leadership and was translated into 10 languages. Other books include *The Change Masters: Innovation and Entrepreneurship in the American Corporation* and *Men and Women of the Corporation*, winner of the C. Wright Mills Award for the year's best book on social issues. She has published 11 books in total and over 150 articles.

4

Mastering Change

Rosabeth Moss Kanter

We are living in a time when mastering change is probably the most important thing that leaders can help their organizations do, because the conditions under which businesses and governments are functioning today are more turbulent, more chaotic, more challenging than ever. I like to think about the changes which are affecting the world of management in terms of "the new game." In America, we are very fond of using sports images to talk about the work of management: "The ball's in your court!", "Keep your eye on the ball!" I realize that this is a culturally-bound image, because as I travel to other countries, I hear different kinds of images. In France, for example, I hear a great deal of food images used to describe management: "That deal stunk like a cabbage," a "chou"; and in Britain, I keep hearing gardening metaphors: "You tend your patch and I tend mine." But in the United States, we talk about sports.

In recent years, as I have been trying to convey to managers the magnitude of the challenge of change they face, I have begun to describe the work of management in terms of my favorite game: the croquet game in *Alice in Wonderland*. This is a game in which nothing remains stable for very long. Everything is in constant motion around the players. Alice tries to hit the ball, but the mallet she is using is a flamingo, and just as she is about to hit the ball, the flamingo lifts his head and looks in another direction, which I think is a perfect image for technology—for the tools we use. Technology, particularly information technology, is changing today at a more rapid pace than ever before in human history. In fact, the pace of change in technology in recent years has been greater than in any other period for fifty years beforehand. This puts pressure on organizations and on the people in them in order to constantly master new challenges, as the tools, systems and the technology that they use keep changing.

The second part of this croquet game, which I think so accurately describes the challenges managers face, is that the ball that Alice is trying to hit is a hedgehog. It is a living creature with a mind of its own. Rather than just lying there waiting for Alice to hit it with whatever she has got, the hedgehog, when it feels like it, unrolls, gets up, moves to another part of the court and sits down again. This is a perfect image for employees and customers—the human factor in business. They, too, are in motion; they, too, are putting pressure on organizations to change. Study after study around the world shows that employees today are less loyal, less committed and more mobile than ever before.

To some extent, in some occupations and professions, there is already a world labor market. There is a world labor market for talented engineers, and a world labor market for professionals, such as nurses, who may be in short supply in one country. In the Boston area where I live, for example, many of our hospitals staff their nursing departments with nurses from Ireland or the Philippines. The labor market increasingly crosses borders, but, in addition, employees themselves no longer have the same expectations of long-term relationships with particular organizations. This finding holds true in Japan and those countries that once had lifetime employment—at least for the section of the labor force which was fortunate enough to work for a large and stable organization. The promise of long-term or lifetime employment is harder and harder to keep, as organizations want a flexibility to restructure, to move in and out of businesses, as circumstances change. In response, employees express less loyalty and less commitment than they did ten years ago.

This puts pressure on organizations to be more responsive to the needs and desires of the people who work in business to get more rewards, more satisfaction, today rather than waiting to get them in the future.

There used to be an implicit contract between employees

and their employer that somehow, over the long term, people would get all of their needs met—but perhaps not directly related to the contributions they made today. For example, people would go to work for a large employer, sometimes a government bureaucracy, sometimes a large manufacturing organization. They might start out young and energetic, and they would over-perform and be under-compensated for it, they thought; but over the next thirty or thirty-five years they would gradually rise through the ranks in the organization until they would finally reach a position in which they could under-perform and be over-compensated!

Jokes aside, the attack on the compensation of people at the top is a very political issue in the United States today. The idea was that somehow, over the life cycle, things would be fair, things would work out. But today's employee will no longer wait in the corner like the hedgehog for the employer to deliver the appropriate rewards for the efforts people have put in. They want more opportunities now to share in the results of what they contribute to the company. This is the phenomenon that we see growing all over the world.

But the most important hedgehog in this new game of business—*Alice in Wonderland*-croquet game—is the customer. Because the customer, too, like the hedgehog, is no longer lying there just waiting for us to hit it with whatever we have got. Customers, like employees, are mobile and have choices. In industry after industry, customers—whether they are institutional or individual customers—are less loyal, more fickle, more willing and able to shop for choices. They have access to more choices; they are more sophisticated and informed. They are increasingly aware of what the whole world has to offer, even if it is not offered in their own local area.

In industry after industry power is systematically shifting away from those who produce goods and services towards those who buy or consume goods and services. In retailing, for example, when most retail outlets were small, sometimes family-owned, it used to be the manufacturers who had the information about which products were selling. The manufacturers established the brand identity of their products and manufacturers could set the terms. The retailers had to buy on these terms.

As retail organizations have been consolidating all over North America and Europe, becoming bigger and more powerful, tapping the power of information technology through scanning systems which now allow the retailer to have more information than the manufacturer about which products are selling, power has systematically shifted from the manufacturer to the retailer. Just-in-time delivery is a wonderful system for a retailer because it allows the retailer to shift costs—the costs of carrying inventory—back to the manufacturer, so power is systematically shifting to customers in the retailing industry.

The United States pharmaceutical industry has been very powerful until recently. Now the pharmaceutical industry is facing a new and different kind of customer: not the individual physician anymore, but the large consolidated managed health plan. And if this customer has consolidated and become more knowledgeable and more powerful, he, too, can demand of the manufacturer better terms that favor him. Revolutions are taking place because of the growth of customer power, because of the access to choices to shop for goods and services everywhere in the world.

Sometimes, even political upheavals occur because of the increase in access to global choices. I do not want to attribute the entire fall of communism in the Eastern Bloc to the consumer revolution, but let me tell you one revealing story. Recently, I attended a small dinner with a Hungarian minister of economy and his wife. He got up and spoke to our group about the reasons for the changes in Eastern Europe. He talked about currency rates, oil prices, trade relations and a variety of macroeconomic factors. And when he sat down, his wife got up and said: "I am not sure that I understand everything that my husband just told you. But I want to tell you that my friends and I, we want to go shopping."

Knowledge of the best that the world has to offer—the knowledge that the choice exists somewhere in the world—is often enough to make customers more demanding even in local areas, even of suppliers who only supply local needs. The customer, like the employee, is less loyal, more fickle and, therefore, demands a different kind of response from organizations: more flexibility, greater innovation, more attention to where the customers' needs are heading in the future, rather than just expecting them to take today's goods and services.

Finally, the last part of the *Alice in Wonderland*-croquet game image is that the hooks through which Alice is trying to hit her ball are card soldiers. They are a deck of playing cards being ordered around by the Queen of Hearts. Just as Alice finally feels that she understands the flamingo, can make the technology work, and that she is more responsive to the hedgehog, more flexible and innovative, all of a sudden the Red Queen barks out an order, and all the hooks reposition themselves on the court. The final challenge of change that organizations face today is not only that tools and technology keep moving and changing, or that customers are more demanding and employees want more rewards and power now, but it is also that the very structure of the game itself is changing, the boundaries between industries are blurring and the boundaries between countries are blurring.

I am always amused, from a North American perspective, to look at the questions that are being raised in Europe about whether or not there will be political unity, because political change is following economic change. Trade exchange and cross-border relationships that blur the boundaries between the interest of one nation and the interest of the other are already happening, and politicians are merely rushing to catch up with it.

The chairman of a leading Anglo-Dutch company said to me recently: "Why did we work so hard to make sure we got rid of state bureaucracies in Eastern Europe only to try to recreate them in Brussels." This was his opinion; I will not push it on you. But the very structure of the world in which businesses are merely trying to do their job is now subject to rapid and unpredictable change. Unlikely combinations are occurring between industries and unlikely alliances are occurring between companies that cross borders to create joint ventures and strategic alliances. Then, of course, changes in the capital market which have permitted takeovers, mergers, and acquisitions, also change the very structure of the world in which we are operating. It is not that only the technology is changing, that customers are more demanding, that employees have to be listened to in a different way today, we also need organizations that can operate in a world where everything is subject to constant change.

How do you win a game like this? How do you master this kind of change? You certainly do not win this game the old-fashioned way, with top-down chains of command, with all decisions having to flow to the center, to headquarters, before anybody in the field can act. You would not be responsive enough—be able to act quickly enough—in a world of change. Nor can we win the game with organizations that are oriented toward rules, traditions, procedures in which people are told: "Follow the rules and do not depart from exactly what you are told." You would lose "the new game." Instead, the new game is being won by organizations that are putting into effect four principles which I would like to think about in terms of four "Fs."

Organizations which are winning the new game are more *focused, fast, flexible* and *friendly.* In fact, think of Alice's croquet game for a moment and try to identify with Alice, as the executive. Alice can win her game, even the fast-moving game, if she is extremely focused on depth of skill, depth of know-how, and never loses sight of her major priorities. She can win the game if she is very fast, if everything is lined up to hit the ball, and she just goes ahead and hits it. She can win it if she is flexible, if she can change tactics, if she can put resources together in new ways to respond to an emerging situation. And she can win the new game if she learns to be friendly, to collaborate. What if, for example, Alice forms a joint venture with the flamingo to design a new technology to her specifications, so that she understands it at the same time she is learning to use it? What if she forms an alliance or a partnership with the hedgehog customer so that she is innovating at the direction of the customer? And what if she forms alliances and partnerships with all the sources of turbulence in the environment, so that she is not the victim of change, but rather helping direct change? This, in fact, is what is happening.

The companies that are succeeding today are succeeding via the four "Fs." First, companies are much more *focused* today, and focus is considered an important element of business strategy. It is important in a world of change to pick only those areas in which you can be excellent on all dimensions, or you lose the new game. It is no longer good enough in the global economy to be the best in your neighborhood, or the best in your community, or the best in your local market. National champions, including many of the European national champions—I can think of some computer and electronics companies in France, for example—are beginning to fade in prominence, because, while they are maybe the best in their protected local market, they cannot compete effectively with the best that the world has to offer. Increasingly, as the terms of the competition broaden and as the game becomes one of constant change, it is important to master change by picking areas in which the company can meet the highest standards of the world, and perhaps not engage in activities where it cannot meet that highest standard. This is beginning to change the terms of competition as businesses become more focused.

Fifteen or sixteen years ago, when I was beginning to engage in an active career as a consultant as well as an academic, my colleagues and I started a consulting firm. We wanted to take out an advertisement identifying our first clients, because we were very proud of the companies for which we were working. Our ad was going to say "We work for the Generals": General Electric, General Motors, General Foods, General Dynamics, General Tyres. Today, I cannot imagine wanting to advertise that we work for some of those companies—General Electric, maybe. General Foods does not exist, General Motors has been having problems, but the more important point is that I cannot imagine a company beginning today which would call itself "General" anything.

Companies are focusing, instead, on the specific value they are providing for specific customers. In fact, the troubles that many of the world's giant companies are having today, in part, are troubles because they have spread their resources and their attention too thinly over too many activities, some of which were not clearly related. They never got the power of synergies which came from having an integrated and focused organization.

IBM, for example, a company that still has wonderful technology, was attempting to be all things to all people—often at high costs—because a customer who just wanted one thing was often paying the costs of a corporate staff for a much larger organization. The troubles which IBM has had, in part, did not come because it has faced one single formidable competitor. It is because it has faced many, many focused competitors, each of which only wants one part of IBM's business. If IBM has a whole range of businesses, along comes a Sun Microsystems in work stations which says: "We do not want most of the business, we just want the work station business over here." And then a personal computer manufacturer says: "We just want this end of the business." The problem that the giant, all-purpose organization has is being nibbled to death—bite by bite by bite—by specialized and focused competitors.

The solution for those giants is to break themselves up into smaller, more focused units which can meet the standards of the best of the world in that focused area rather than simply riding on the advantages of being part of a large umbrella organization which adds costs. Businesses are rethinking their portfolios of activities to pick related areas where they can focus and have depth of strength. They are rethinking their portfolios of internal services to include only those services internally in which they also provide the best.

Out-sourcing or unbundling of the corporation is a major movement—an important movement. Companies have begun to realize that they do not necessarily have to provide services and functions internally by employees in order to have control over them, but that they often get higher quality if they use specialist service organizations which can provide this service as their business focus, allowing the attention of executives to remain on the core business. In fact, we recently completed a Harvard Business School case on a Swiss holding company which has grown dramatically in recent years, and which began as the out-sourcing of the logistics and support functions of a German retailer. By out-sourcing these functions, the German retailer cut costs and improved the quality of service. A new company was formed, an entrepreneurial company, to provide those services to the retailer parent and also to sell those services on the open market. It is now a focused company, focused on cleaning services and environmental recycling, and logistics and transportation. In the name of focus, corporations are being reshaped and rethought in dramatic new ways.

But focus is not just a matter of the business strategy and those activities done under the roof of the corporation—under its umbrella. It is also a matter of what the leaders of the company convey to the people who have to take action in the company. Increasingly, in this "Alice in Wonderland"-croquet game we are playing, companies must count on the actions and decisions made by hundreds or thousands of people in millions of daily interactions to make the focus real. It is one thing to state the strategy or the policy or the values at the top of the organization, and it is another thing to make sure that every single person who must take independent action is taking it in line with the organization's own focus. It is an old lesson that real strategy is not set at the top of the organization, at least real strategy as the customer sees it. Real strategy is set at the front line by all those people who interact with customers or who make decisions about goods and services, about how much quality is acceptable, how many defects are acceptable, what does quality mean, should we let this product go in this form or not. In the name of focus, there is also more explicit attention today paid to the kind of focus that leaders provide by transmitting their values and priorities to all of the ordinary people in the organization, so that these values and priorities are embedded in their hearts and minds and direct their daily action toward the organization's goals.

In a world of change, it is impossible to rewrite the rules fast enough to take account of every new situation that employees are going to face. So the new control systems which organizations are putting into effect in a world of change are controlled through shared values, through shared understanding of the focus of the organization. Whether it is, for example, Max Link, the head of Sandoz Pharma, who has his top 400 or 450 people thinking about the same sets of priorities and the same explicit statement of values everywhere in the world, or whether it is Mochtar Riady, the current chairman of the Asian Bankers' Association and head of Lippo Group, deciding that synergy is the most important goal to unite the financial conglomerate he has built. Riady invests his own time and energy in transmitting to his top people the value of synergy and then expects them to transmit the importance of this value to the people below. These leaders understand that the new organization which masters change can only do so because of an agreement by everybody in the organization to be focused on the same sets of priorities. Focus is the first important tool in mastering change.

The second tool is to be *fast*—to increase speed. There are three kinds of speed that companies need today in order to be effective. The first is innovation speed, to be in the marketplace first with the goods and services that customers want, to be constantly innovating and experimenting with new features that give the customer what the customer desires, before you run the risk of losing the customer. In this world of intensified competition, organizations can no longer afford to be followers, to wait for somebody else to innovate. They must get the advantage of the first-mover. If they are not there first with something new, something improved, something that the customer desires, it may be too late, because the competitor will already have taken that customer. Innovation speed is the first kind of speed which is very important

Organizations that are successful at mastering change sometimes seem as though they have a crystal ball: they know where markets are heading, which products are going to be desirable, which geographic territories are the best. In reality, they do not have a crystal ball at all: they are no better at predicting the future than anybody else. But what they are good at is constant experimentation, constant testing of new ideas and new concepts that have them ready for in whatever direction markets may shift. In fact, because of their innovation they are not simply trying to predict the future, they are creating the future by developing new products and services that transform how everybody else in this industry must operate. Speedy innovation is, in part, a matter not of rocket-science, of waiting for the next big breakthrough. In some industries a big breakthrough means a company can crest for a long time: in pharmaceuticals, the next big drug; in energy businesses, the next oil field that you find. But for most organizations it is not the huge breakthrough, it is the constant experimentation that gets this first kind of speed.

In the United States, General Motors, as part of its drive to revitalize, defined its eight-year, car-of-the-future project, the Saturn project. It actually turned out to be a twelve-year, car-of-the-future project. They now have a wonderful new car—they are not making money on it yet—but during those twelve years, how many new models did Honda and Toyota put on the market? With how many new features? They are already just as good as the Saturn, if not better, through constant incremental experimentation. In fact, in comparing the difference between innovation speed, cycle-time for new products in the US, Europe and Japan in the automotive industry, it turned out that the Japanese companies were often four to six times faster than the American and European companies. Part of the key to this speed was that rather than define only the gigantic project over the long term, the Japanese companies tended to define many, many more short-term projects and continued to move on to the next level of innovation and to the next project, as soon as they had completed the short-term goal. By the way, this is a wonderful lesson for mastering any kind of change: take a big goal and divide it into short-term achievable product projects that give those demanding employees the gratification of success today, reward them for this short-term project success, and then quickly move on to the next project, to the next experiments.

The second kind of speed you need is speed at processing everything through the organization, and the third is recovery speed—the time it takes to respond to and fix problems. Reduction in cycle time has become the goal of major world organizations. For Asea Brown Boveri, for example, it is the T50 project that cuts the time in half that it takes to do everything. What is the secret of being faster at processing things and achieving problem-solving speed when there is a mistake? The secret is my third "F," *flexibility*.

Organizations which are faster-moving are also more flexible in how they use people. They are much more likely to have broader rather than narrower definitions of jobs, to treat every employee as a professional who knows and understands some disciplines and, therefore, to give them professional tools which can be used to solve problems and get results, and to build project teams that bridge functions and departments. Organizations which move faster, which can innovate more quickly, which can move things through the organization more quickly and which can solve problems more quickly, are much more likely to be organized around cross-functional project teams than they are to be organized in old-fashioned hierarchical departments. They are more likely to emphasize the horizontal dimension of the organization—how we bring people together across departments to tackle something new or to solve a problem—than they are to emphasize the vertical dimension up and down the hierarchy.

The reason this kind of flexibility helps organizations master change is because, first of all, it overcomes the major source of resistance to change which exists in most bureaucratic organizations. This source is employees who say: "That is not my job, my job is.... I am the receptionist. The building is burning down around me, but I do not do anything about it, because the procedures manual says that the maintenance department takes care of the building and, besides, the last time I tried, I got in trouble with the union for doing work that was not in my classification." This was the old-fashioned bureaucratic method of organizing work.

Whenever employees have only a narrow territory and a narrow scope of action, they are more likely to resist change, because both they do not know what to do and change threatens the control they have over their own territory. I have spoken to many blue-collar workers, who say: "I know what innovation means. Innovation means I am going to lose my job." Organizations that master change are ready for new challenges and have eliminated the resistance people feel when their territory is being threatened by giving them broader territories, by putting them on teams and by building those important cross-functional links. In the organization of the future, people will be oriented toward short-term projects and, in fact, I hope that the most valuable title in the organization of the future will be project-leader or team-leader.

Finally, the kind of cross-department, cross-functional collaboration that is required inside needs to be matched by collaboration outside. This is my *friendly* "F." Organizations cannot be focused if they do not understand how to be friendly. In order to be focused, you must also be friendly. If an organization is going to narrow the range of things in which it engages, it will need more partners. If organizations are going to master constant change they need to be linked more closely to their suppliers and their customers. And if organizations are going to tackle new business opportunities emerging across borders and across industries, they will have to do it through partnerships.

There is not sufficient time to learn everything internally that we need to know to tackle something new. For example, in one of the major emerging industries of the world, multimedia, the linkage between computers, telephones, video and other forms of data transmission, there is not sufficient time for any one of the companies in these separate industries to gain mastery of all the skills they need. There is not sufficient money for them to buy all the other competencies they would need. They can only operate through partnerships. And my assumption is that in the organization of the future in this world of constant change, collaboration across companies will become a more and more important part of the companies' own strategy.

Look at how the computer industry has changed. Sun Microsystems, for example, currently has about 10,000 employees and about 2 billion US dollars in sales. The head of Sun Microsystems says that they are going to grow, they hope, to 10 billion US dollars a year in sales in the next five years and they will still have only 10,000 employees. They are going to remain focused on the core skills which are important, and they are going to do the rest of their growth through the choice, the careful choice, of partners with whom they will work very closely. Among those partners will be the customers who are going to play a bigger role in designing products directly, and the suppliers that are going to add their capabilities to Sun's in order to create a powerful combination.

We have spent too long assuming that the boundaries of the corporations were important and needed to be maintained. Today, we are breaking down those boundaries on every front. We are breaking down the boundaries between nations, between industries, but we are also breaking down the boundaries between companies and their customers, companies and their suppliers, between levels of the hierarchy, between departments and functions internally. And this provides the ultimate flexibility which helps people master change.

I began by saying that there were four "Fs" for success in the world ahead, but let me end by adding one more "F"—and this is *fun*. Because if it is not fun, we are not going to get anybody to do it. And I do not mean fun in the sense of play or humor or that it is a joke. I mean satisfaction. I know that we Americans are often accused of being very fun-loving—of treating everything like it is a party—but we are very serious, too. What we do understand, and I see leaders all over the world beginning to understand, is that if we do not pay attention to the kind of satisfaction people gain from their work, that they find it pleasurable and enjoyable, we are not going to find people to staff the new organization, because the challenges of change are too overwhelming.

We live in a world in which we need constant learning. This means that nobody can go to sleep on the job anymore. We used to talk in big bureaucracies about the people who had "retired on the job." This would no longer be possible. We are talking about a world where we want constant innovation, a world where we want people to move faster, to work more collaboratively, to spend more time in teams. This means more meetings. It is a world which is inherently overloading. It is true, change is more work, and it is harder work. But it can ultimately be more satisfying work if we make it fun. And the clue to making it fun is putting people in charge of the change rather than imposing the change from the top.

I was amused a number of years ago when I was approached by one of the world's leading computer manufacturers who asked us about developing a program for them on mastering change. And I said, "This is wonderful. You mean you want to encourage more innovation, more initiative on the part of your people so that they can create new things and anticipation of market shifts?" They said, "No, no, no. We want a program that will help people be more receptive to the changes we impose upon them!" So I said, "We cannot do that kind of program." Change is always a threat when it is done to people, but it is an opportunity when it is done by people. The ultimate key to creating pleasure in the hard work of change in this challenging and demanding environment is to give people the tools and the autonomy to make their own contributions to change.

I hope that I have given you a great deal to think about. I think that these principles are the right principles for the times ahead, and if they are the right principles then you not only must do them, but you must do all of them. Piecemeal programs are not good enough. Only total transformation will help companies— and people—master change. Thank you.

John W. Thompson, PhD, is founder, president, and CEO of Human Factors, Inc., an international management consulting company that works primarily with key executives and senior management of Fortune 500 companies. Thompson is also the founder and chairman of the board of Acumen International, Inc., an educational software company focused on the application of expert-based computer technology to management and leadership assessment and development. He has been in the educational field for the last two decades and has delivered educational programs to well over 100,000 professionals.

Thompson has held numerous management positions and taught in the College of Business at Utah State University and the University of Oregon. He has published numerous articles including "Leadership In The 21st Century," in *New Traditions in Business*, and the book, *The Human Factor: An Inquiry into Communication and Consciousness*.

5

The Renaissance of Learning in Business

John W. Thompson

Intense and global competition, an explosion in information technology and the emergence of a knowledge-based economy are continually reshaping the world's business environment. As never before, success, indeed survival, requires American corporations to become learning organizations. They must create the organizational conditions that lead to the continual acquisition of what Dr. W. Edwards Deming termed "profound knowledge." The purpose of organizational learning and the acquisition of organizational knowledge is to provide the foundation for rapid, dramatic organizational change; increasingly the fundamental requirement for organizational success.

A company's ability to learn and innovate is a direct driver of the company's capability to increase revenues, profits, and economic value. To launch new and superior products, to continually improve operating efficiencies, and to create more value for customers requires the ability to learn. The penetration of new markets and the achievement of sustained market leadership demand applied learning. U.S. corporations' weaknesses here have invited, over the last thirty years, a succession of successful assaults on the U.S. marketplace by foreign competition. Two-thirds of the firms that made the 1960 *Fortune* 500 list no longer exist today! Clearly market dominance and large size, without the ability to learn and adapt rapidly, are not sufficient even for survival.

Organizational learning is increasingly being recognized as a critical factor in an organization's ability to create ongoing economic value for its shareholders. However, scientifically sound processes for successfully developing the organizational capabilities and competencies required to become a learning organization are not widely understood.

The term organizational learning is actually a misnomer. In fact an organization itself doesn't learn—people learn. Any given condition in an organization is affected by the applied knowledge of its membership. In order to understand how organizations learn, we must understand how people learn and share knowledge, the processes that support attitudes and behaviors essential to learning, and the psychological issues that underlie resistance to learning.

A Relationship for Learning

One attribute of true learning is a sense of curiosity and wonder. A second is an experience of openness to new possibilities. A third is that the process of searching for an answer is more important than having an answer. Finally, it is necessary to have an approach to one's environment characterized by experimentation: accessing information, analyzing that information, and looking for new connections and relationships.

Very young children are extraordinarily good at learning. The relationship a very young child has with his or her environment is one of openness, curiosity and a sense of wonder. The child engages in a rich process of experimentation, acquiring new understandings that flow from an openness to feedback when interacting with its environment.

The way a child experiences feedback is a model for the way living systems, other than adult humans, actually function. They pay very careful attention to the environmental response to their behaviors. They learn very rapidly to build cause and effect relationships. The very young child maintains a playful, light-hearted relationship to the environment, and is not discouraged when an experiment does not work. Rather, they try again.

Contrast these behaviors with your own experience of how people in organizations generally behave in relationship to new possibilities, other points of view, and feedback. As adults we are poor learners. One could make a strong argument that we're demonstrably much poorer at learning than many adult animals. To understand why, we must examine the influences that shaped our relationship to learning as adults.

Family Influences

A fundamental deterioration in our relationship to learning begins at an early point in our lives—in the family. There is general agreement in the field of cognitive psychology that by the onset of puberty, children have built up a set of causal relationships in their minds and have developed a general theory of who they are, what their relationships are to their environment, and cause and effect relationships. This is termed a personal framework of reality, or a "personal paradigm," that they then begin to think and behave from. Once this cognitive map is in place, the basic relationship children have with their environment shifts to become virtually the opposite of a learning relationship. The child begins to exhibit automatic rather than exploratory behavior, becomes defensive rather than open, and is less curious, less creative. It is my belief that the family is largely responsible for this sudden reversal in attitude.

The two dominant figures in the family—the mother and father—based on their own experiences of being parented, function in what they believe to be a proper role for teaching the child. This role is based on extending rewards and punishments for behaviors that the parent believes the child should or should not exhibit.

Parents either consciously or unconsciously extend love and affection for behavior they approve of, or withhold love to impose punishment for behavior that does not meet with their approval. The child's reality of the relationship between cause and effect becomes very narrowly prescribed within the parent's view of the world, which includes how they believe the child should or should not behave. Thus, parents shape the child's paradigm, teaching them that it is necessary to act in certain ways in order to receive love. In this way children learn, unconsciously, that disagreement with authority figures or experimentation with behavior outside the parents belief system is an unwise practice. This system of parenting which has been in place in the western world for the last 150 years is the initial cause for the deterioration in our ability to learn.

Educational Influences

The child's relationship to learning is further eroded upon entry into the educational system. The child is taught, sometimes in very harsh ways, not to share information or collaborate in the acquisition of knowledge. Our educational system is organized primarily around the memorization of information and the ability to produce that information upon demand. The focus is not on creativity and the exploration of new possibilities.

The way children are evaluated is based upon their individual acquisition of information and their ability to demonstrate that they have memorized the information, or have the "correct" or "socially accepted" answer to a particular question in a given area of inquiry. Children are publicly evaluated, relative to their peers, on their individual ability to demonstrate the acquisition of prescribed information. In many cases they are actively discouraged or even punished for any attempt to collaborate with others in the discovery of new knowledge. The paradigm that the child lives within becomes even more deeply encoded with behaviors and ways of thinking that directly inhibit the ability to learn or the ability for any group of people to share knowledge. It is well documented that the child's creativity quotient starts to decrease upon entering the public school system and never recovers.

Our educational system generally does not encourage creative, original work (the educational equivalent of organizational innovation) until graduate school, either in the Masters thesis or, in most schools, in the Ph.D. dissertation. By this time the ability to be creative and actually advance understandings in the field of study has been largely lost. This is supported by the fact that over 70% of all Ph.D. candidates in this country do not complete their dissertation and fail to receive the degree.

Thus, the focus of the American school system is not true learning. The creative processes of experimentation and the sharing of knowledge, which are the fundamental driving forces for innovation, are discouraged. Young people are not taught how to learn, but how to memorize and recall. These are profoundly and fundamentally different processes. As we explore organizational learning we must understand that the public school system did not contribute to our learning capability, but eroded it.

The Double Bind of Organizational Learning

If we were to describe the mental condition of young people entering the business community, we would conclude that they believe they are supposed to have the right answers. It is not okay to reveal that they do not have the answers for fear of retribution, of ridicule, or of being evaluated as being less intelligent or effective than other people. They believe they are supposed to meet explicit or implicit expectations of authority figures. It is not okay to ask questions or share information. It is not okay to experiment or to make mistakes. It is not okay to challenge the status quo. Finally, they believe that it is not okay to test or go outside of currently prescribed means and methodologies of performing any given task or process.

These beliefs represent the opposite of the mental conditions required to learn in a new environment. Because of these attitudes and beliefs, corporations do not have the fundamental practices in place to truly become learning organizations.

As organizations grapple with this challenge of organizational learning they face a double bind. People have been molded into a relationship to learning that is the antithesis of what is truly required to learn. In addition, organizations have not had good models for managing people other than their experience of the family and the educational system. Our general management population of today has not been exposed to, or trained in, any healthy model for maximizing the performance of a business system in a rapidly changing environment.

Managers treat their direct reports and co-workers in ways similar to how their mothers and fathers treated them. It is a family system. The same principles of punishment and reward are used to exact desired behaviors. Performance management, if practiced at all, is a system of control rather than a developmental process aimed at organizational learning and the development of human capability. Therefore, workers entering the organizational system find themselves face-to-face with the same influences that created their dysfunctional relationship to learning in the first place.

Thus, people in our corporations today typically have a dysfunctional relationship with learning. The corporate systems, processes and culture are those of a dysfunctional family—they actively discourage those behaviors most related to individual and collective learning. There are no proactive forces in the corporation championing experimentation and real learning. So we have a double bind: the person in the organization has a dysfunctional relationship to learning and has entered a system which keeps that dysfunctional relationship to learning in place.

Unwittingly, those who stand to gain the most economically from corporate learning are also part of the problem. Peter Drucker recently pointed out that our corporations have increasingly become owned by institutional investors focused on short-term return. The CEO is constantly pressured to maximize the results of the next quarter. This demands that the CEO focus on the wrong thing: the maximization of short-term economic value. This precludes systematic investment in the human assets of the corporation. As Drucker puts it, the job of the CEO is not to produce economic value but to grow the capacity of the corporation to produce economic value. This is a subtle but fundamental and crucial distinction. Focusing on short-term profit forces the CEO to compete with available human assets rather than systematically investing in development of human assets as a long-term competitive strategy.

With these strong forces arrayed against organizational learning, a major, system-wide intervention is required for a company to actually become a learning organization.

A Renaissance in Learning

The rapid rate of change, combined with what is happening to our global economy, has brought corporations worldwide to a crisis of unprecedented proportions. Organizations no longer have the luxury of conducting business as usual. They must learn in order to adapt and change and they must change in order to survive. Yet they do not possess the fundamental attitudes, culture, and processes that will be required to make the necessary changes.

It is a well documented fact in social psychology that when a social group of any kind feels threatened, they are much more open to change or to doing things in a different way. The rate of change and global economic forces are demanding that our corporations re-invent themselves in order to survive. As a result there is an unprecedented openness to finding effective responses to the competitive challenges that we face. This set of conditions will become the driving force for a "Renaissance in Learning." This renaissance represents an unprecedented opportunity to engage corporations and facilitate their understanding of the conditions that support learning within the organizational setting. We must establish the essential relationship to learning as well as the organizational systems that will be necessary for members of the corporation to learn and for knowledge to be shared system-wide.

The challenge is to fundamentally reshape our understanding of what learning is. Then we must acquire the attitudes and behaviors that are prerequisite to being able to truly learn. Finally, we need to apply that learning to organizational innovation. We have sadly "learnt" a lot of the wrong things. Achieving a proper relationship to learning is really a process of un-learning and re-framing what learning is.

Such interventions are a very challenging undertaking. We are dealing with human conditioning that has been passed on for generations. There is much debate about whether people who have patterns of thinking and habits of work that have been deeply ingrained for many years are able to learn and change their approach to work. The debate would not continue if not for a lack of understanding of the required conditions for learning in adults. This is the real issue. As adults, we have an amazing capacity to learn when immersed in a proper learning environment.

Blocks to Executive Learning

The challenge for executives is to continually learn about themselves, their organizations, and their environments in a way that will lead to enhanced individual, team, and organizational performance. The problem is that adults who find themselves occupying senior positions in corporations tend to have a firmly anchored worldview of how they should operate in the organization, evidenced by past successes. And they tend to have a great deal of authority, which creates compliance rather than questioning from others. These are not strong motivational factors for learning.

The question is how to effectively engage an individual—who has a dysfunctional relationship to learning but a great deal of authority and power—in a process that will lead to a renewal of their capacity to learn. Concerning learning, such individuals live in a state of unconscious incompetence. This means that they are incompetent in certain areas crucial to organizational innovation and are unaware of their own incompetence.

When there is no awareness of incompetence, motivation to learn in that area is missing. Areas of conscious incompetence—where the individual is aware that they have a learning challenge—receive all the person's attention. Symptoms of unconscious incompetence include certainty, righteousness, being closed to others' views, denial and delusional thinking.

Delusional thinking means to hold beliefs about one's own performance or the performance of the organization that are inconsistent with well established facts. An example of delusional thinking is the policy of planned obsolescence practiced by General Motors and other American automobile manufacturers for many years. They believed that the American public would continue to tolerate it even when a better product became available to them. Another case of delusional thinking was the belief at IBM that, in spite of evidence that the world was moving to microcomputers and networking capability, the market for mainframe computers would continue to grow.

Awakening Learning Capacity

The starting point for learning in the natural world is curiosity. Therefore the process of learning for executives must begin with the reawakening of curiosity. People who are exhibiting symptoms of righteousness, denial, or delusional thinking are not curious about the things they are in denial about. The crux of the problem of engaging business leaders in a learning process is the challenge of converting their relationship to the subject of learning from one of denial and defensiveness to one of curiosity.

The strategy we employ at Human Factors, Inc. to engage corporate leaders and senior managers in the learning process is to move individuals from a condition of unconscious incompetence to conscious incompetence by exposing and exploring limitations in their current ways of thinking about issues and behaving. This is done by structuring learning situations. The person or group is asked to perform a task where they bring their business skills and capabilities to bear, only to discover that their skills and capabilities are insufficient to the task. We then begin to explore with them what contributed to their deficiency in performance in that situation.

Since their immediate experience in the learning exercise is fundamentally inconsistent with their assertion of their own competence in this area, they have to question their own assumptions about themselves and their capabilities or competence. Once that question is opened, they will begin to move from a sense of confusion to an attitude of curiosity. This is the natural state of mind of human beings when there is something that is not understood. Once people begin to be curious—if they are in a well structured learning environment—they will then begin genuinely and honestly to experiment with new possibilities.

Science and Learning

Many experiments conducted in science aim at proving something to be true. The pure scientific method is composed of five steps: first, establishing premises or hypotheses about possibilities; second, designing and conducting effective experiments to test those hypotheses; third, making observations and gathering data from one's own experience and the experience of others; fourth, analyzing that data and reaching relevant conclusions; and finally, applying those conclusions to real time or real world issues. The most important underpinning of the scientific method is that a proper attitude is taken in approaching both the experiments and the analysis of the data. What is required is an attitude of objectivity or non-attachment to the outcome of the experiment—that is, to hold the discovery of truth as more important than any particular truth which might emerge from the experiment. This is the learning strategy we use with our clients.

Once people begin to experiment from this attitude of intellectual neutrality, they begin to make discoveries or have insights about things they were unaware of when they were in denial or delusional thinking. When people begin to make discoveries that lead to new insights, they have begun to learn. While part of the learning process, discovery or insight on the part of an individual is insufficient to actually apply those insights to their daily work life, achieving what we term real competence.

What must be provided to an individual or group of individuals in an organization for them to achieve competence in the subject of inquiry is a program of practice and feedback. Practice and feedback are fundamental ingredients for acquiring real competence (see Figure 1).

Once individuals understand that it is okay for them not to be as competent as they would like to think of themselves, and that the organizational incentive is going to be for learning rather

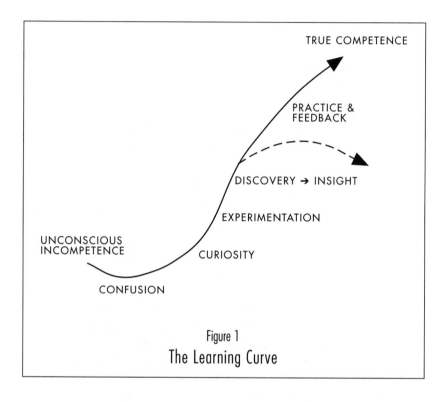

Figure 1
The Learning Curve

than on knowing or being right, their natural instincts take over. People begin to follow their natural orientation to learning, to achieve greater understandings, and to acquire improved capabilities. This allows them to make a larger contribution to whatever they feel part of, whether it is an organization, family or community.

From Individual to Organizational Learning

In the future, it will become increasingly difficult to differentiate oneself based on information alone. All competitors in a given marketplace are going to have access to the same information. The critical strategic advantage for the 21st Century will be the relative capability of the members of an organization to learn from that information and to apply those learnings to create a strategic advantage.

A corporation that intends to become a learning organization must create the conditions within the organization that lead to what Deming termed "profound knowledge." As he described it, profound knowledge involves the acquisition of new knowledge and competence, as well as the ability to transfer that understanding to others so that they come to have the same level of knowledge together with the ability to pass it on to others. This is the essential ingredient in moving from individual learning to organizational learning, the process of transferring knowledge across the organization in an on-going stream.

As described above, organizational learning involves the acquisition of new information and the ability to analyze that information creatively, learn from it, and apply that learning in useful ways. This leads to strategic advantage as well as improved human capabilities and conditions within the organization (greater vitality, motivation and sense of spirit). All of these factors combine to drive toward the ongoing creation of economic value.

In the attempt to build a learning organization, we direct executives to the natural world and the principles involved in the learning of living organisms. For example, all living creatures have elaborate systems of corrective feedback. The human body has countless such systems that are constantly sending information to the brain to make adjustments in the chemistry, temperature, water content, etc. of the system to keep it alive and thriving in constantly changing environmental conditions.

Yet when we look into organizations, we find that most have elaborate systems that actually *preclude* feedback. This stems from an unwillingness to confront areas of threat, incompetence or lack of understanding.

Human Factors' role in affecting such a transformation is to become a catalyst for change in the organization. Our job is to support the executive group and senior management in understanding the problem of learning. We assist them in defining and coming to an understanding of the requirements for change that are described here. We support them in securing the understanding and commitment necessary to fundamentally re-engineer the company to emulate the learning mechanisms of living systems and to build the support systems, processes, attitudes, and behaviors that are prerequisite to becoming a learning organization.

As one client CEO put it, "the purpose of this initiative is to organize this company around one thing—the ability to change and continually reinvent ourselves."

Organizational Conditions for Building a Learning Organization

There are a number of conditions we consider critical success factors which must be created within the organization to provide an environment where people will feel supported and encouraged to enter a new relationship to learning. These critical success factors include:

- Senior management committed to making learning capability a key part of its ongoing competitive advantage
- A compelling vision of the desired learning organization that people feel part of and excited by
- A clear blueprint for change
- Milestones—identified, achieved, and celebrated
- Committed leadership willing to model desired changes and drive fear out of the organization
- Immediate corrective action with leaders who resist change
- Senior management committed to significant investment of time and resources
- A performance management system that links compensation to achievement of the desired vision
- Encouragement and acknowledgment of experimentation, collaboration, innovation, and new paradigm thinking
- Urgency—but no quick fixes
- Multiple feedback structures
- Multiple learning channels

In the press of day-to-day business, these conditions are very difficult to create. As one client CEO put it, "The challenge that lies in front of us is the equivalent of changing a bicycle tire in the Tour de France while in a full-out downhill sprint."

The single most powerful mechanism for creating a learning environment is that the leadership of the organization be willing to model the approach to learning that they want others to embrace. Members of an organization must have a clear model for the kind of change that will be required of them as they reorient themselves to learning. The Chief Executive Officer and the other senior managers of the organization will make the critical difference by their example.

If the learning problem is truly a double bind, and both individuals and the conditions of the organization have to change, then organizational conditions will not change until individuals change. Albert Einstein stated it very eloquently in 1946 when he said, "The problems we have created in the world today will not be solved by the level of thinking that created them." Management, and most particularly the executive group, must understand the fundamental problem of achieving a proper relationship to learning. When they have committed themselves to the quest for that relationship to learning and offered themselves as a model, they will be able to discover, through their own learning processes, what the organizational inhibitors to learning are, what organizational changes will be required, and be able to mount the commitment to make them happen.

Perhaps the greatest difficulty in becoming a true learning organization is that we live in an age of instant gratification. To change the fundamental paradigm an individual or group operates from is to fundamentally reorient an individual or a group to learning. Given the attitudes and behavior that have been molded into them, and the conditions that surround them in an organization, this is no overnight task. It takes years. If one speaks with those corporations today that are most recognized for having accomplished fundamental change and have succeeded in becoming learning organizations, they talk in multi-year time frames. As a culture, we are not used to thinking in these terms; rather, we think in terms of this month, next quarter, or the current year.

Our firm has fourteen years of experience working with *Fortune* 500 companies that have engaged in the process we have outlined here. They all committed significant resources and time, in most cases a number of years, to the development of those organizational conditions, systems and processes, and those individual attitudes and behaviors that truly create a learning corporation.

One CEO's Story

One CEO's (George) story records this journey into learning. In a first meeting, George, CEO of a Fortune 500 company, revealed that the company was in a "technology discontinuity." The company's products, once hi-tech, were now low-tech and the market was moving away from them. Eroding market share threatened the company's survival. George expressed his frustration that for the past three years he had attempted to create a new strategic direction for the company and mount an organizational change process, only to watch management slide back into "business as usual."

Soon after, George and the executive team, followed by other key managers, began the learning process described earlier. Utilizing assessment data that we generated, George and the other executives were able to confront and work through their own denial regarding the root causes of this inability to mobilize real change in the organization.

By learning to apply newfound skills to listen, inquire, and apply creative thinking, they were able to forge strong relationships with the senior management group in the company. Collectively, in a spirit of partnership, the 100 senior managers, led by George and the executive team and supported by our consulting team, attacked the problem of producing ongoing economic value on three fronts: Agreeing on a new strategic positioning for the business; identifying, through Gap Analysis, the organizational capabilities and competencies required to execute the strategy; and finally, identifying and bringing to life a set of cultural conditions that employees were yearning for.

CREATING SUSTAINABLE ECONOMIC VALUE

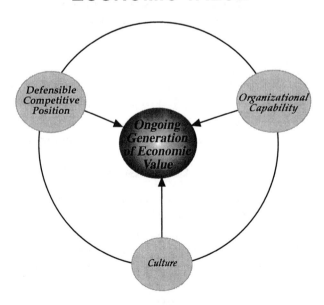

Defensible Competitive Position

Organizational Capability

Ongoing Generation of Economic Value

Culture

In the following three years this company has been able to migrate their core competencies into new cutting edge products and services, re-engineer core systems and processes, and bring over 1,000 managers into the new way of functioning. Today the culture is described as one where people are respected and cared for, new ideas are honored, innovation is rewarded and learning is the norm. Their success is evidenced by continuous improvement in products and processes. The company is not only maximizing the application of collective intelligence to future success but people in the business are moving forward together in a heartfelt commitment to the contribution they are making to their customers.

In the time Human Factors, Inc. has supported such organizational change efforts, we have confirmed that, when executives and senior management actually step forward and take responsibility for creating the conditions for organizational learning, the results can be extraordinary. An organization that has the heart, intention and courage to see it through can achieve sustainable economic growth coupled with organizational conditions where employees say, "This is a great place to work."

Jayme Rolls, PhD, is president of Rolls & Company, Inc., a Santa Monica, California-based organizational transformation consultancy. Rolls & Company, Inc. is working with organizations like Ernst & Young, John Hancock Mutual Life Insurance, The New York Times, Digital Equipment Corporation, Bank of Boston, Lotus Development and Southern California Edison.

She is a psychologist and holds a Ph.D. in organizational transformation. Formerly, she was founder and president of a multi-million dollar communications corporation, a Fortune 500 communications manager, and professor of mass communications. She serves on the Board of Directors, World Business Academy; Board of Directors, American Society for Training & Development; is a member of the Society for Human Resource Management; Organization Development Network; Human Resource Planning Society; and the Board of Directors, Family & Children's Aid.

6

The Transformational Leader: The Wellspring of the Learning Organization

Jayme Rolls

Business is changing. It's changing from the inside out and from the outside in. From the sociocultural forces driving demands for a meaning-rich worklife and from the economic pressures leaving American industry with marginal profits.

American business is working hard to become competitive. According to *Business Week*, the "economic recovery" began in March 1991, but since then the economy has been weighed down by defense cuts, heavy debt, and sluggishness overseas and has only been able to grow a couple of percent. That is slower than any recovery in the past 30 years. Companies have been able to raise productivity but they are squeezing payrolls and overall output is lagging.

Employment costs are rising faster than capital costs. Companies are resorting to buying labor-saving technology rather than hiring. The combination of global competition, increased cost of health care benefits, and inexpensive computers has slowed job growth. Since 1987, benefit costs have risen far faster than inflation.

There are countless examples of corporate "resizing." One example is an Owens-Corning plant which once operated with 500 employees and was closed in 1987. It will reopen in 1994 with only 80 employees. The insurance industry eliminated

33,000 jobs. The wholesale trade industry lost 53,000 jobs. IBM, United Technologies—the list is long.

Sociocultural Change

At the same time, there are sweeping sociocultural changes as employees are seeking a deeper sense of meaning from their worklives.

In Swedish the word for business is *Narings Liv,* which means *nourishment for life.* This is far different from our experience over the past generation here in the U.S. There are far-reaching problems affecting employees today that are interfering with their search for meaning from their work—their "nourishment for life."

This search by employees, coupled with the intense economic pressures on American business, have resulted in a new relationship between people and organizations in the workplace as people address the pressing issues and try to find answers to staying solvent in a whitewater environment. They are joining in partnership to learn together, to rethink the ways in which their company does business in order to survive—psychologically and financially—and to thrive.

People want to define their lives and their work in their own terms. Employees want to enjoy work, to feel they can make a contribution, to feel respected as people, and to learn and grow. The workplace has not been the worker-friendly, flexible structure that would accommodate sociological changes. So the corporate inhabitants have been forced to re-invent the organization, living with their natural resistances and their feelings of upheaval and insecurity that change brings.

Organizational transformation deals with the deep issues of personal growth, vision, trust, creativity, purpose, leadership, mastery, and cultivating organizational and individual spirit. Today, the leader responsible for helping to transform corporations is charged with fostering growth, with leading cultural change.

Leadership and the Learning Organization

Change is the constant. The only way to survive is as a learning organization—to continually adapt, learn, be change-responsive, to reinvent the reality and the future, to transform. Organizations that excel in the future will be those that understand how to gain the commitment of people at all levels and continually expand their capacity to learn.

A learning organization is a place where, through learning, people are continually re-perceiving their world and their relationship to it, discovering how they create their reality and their future. A learning organization adapts a willingness to identify and challenge its existing paradigms, valuing output and the skills necessary to yield that output, rewarding the thinking, not just the doing, eliciting input and commitment to the vision, values, and performance expectations from employees at all levels within the organization, providing opportunities for growth, accepting and encouraging mistakes. It makes use of the learning of its individual members, encourages and rewards widespread and spontaneous learning. It engenders open debate and questioning to remain flexible in the long term.

The cornerstone of the successful learning organization is its ability to repeatedly become. The leader of a learning organization has to create the conditions in which employees have the supporting psychodynamics and infrastructure that allows them to move from "change fragile" to "change agile." He/she helps encourage a shift of mind that is the learning organization's constant task, where managers see their primary job as facilitating members' experimentation and learning from experience.

Highly attuned to his/her employees, the new leader is relationship-driven and creates a work intimacy that unleashes the human spirit. The assumptions in a learning organization are that everyone can be a source of useful ideas, learning flows up as well as down in the organization, new ideas are valuable, and a mistake is simply an opportunity to learn.

These transformational leaders provide the critical set of conditions under which employees can unfold, transform, grow, and flourish in uncertainty. They model and teach the skills needed to build a learning organization. They don't delegate responsibility but they invite subordinates to interpret the ideal future in terms of their roles and to determine how to close the gaps between current and future states.

The transformational leader embodies the characteristics of leaders who have a mastery of the "five disciplines" as identified by Peter Senge in his book, *The Fifth Discipline* (see Figure 1, on the next page). He/she is responsive to the unspoken needs of employees. Here is a model of some of the competencies leaders need in order to manage a learning organization juxtaposed to what employees want for themselves in their work environment.

The Five Disciplines	Leadership Competencies	Followership Expectations
Systems Thinking	expansionist thinking understanding of connectivity intuition perspective integration	understanding the whole
Personal Mastery	compassion self and other acceptance shared power authenticity nurturance of spirit moral leadership sensitivity humility mastery growth oriented risk taking self directed tolerance value ambiguity learning commitment trust spirituality ego subordination	encouragement acceptance empowerment trust self discovery someone worth working for dignity autonomy fulfilled potential growth supported choice independence space to make mistakes support in transition learning responsibility self/other connection ownership of results
Mental Models	insight introspection challenge assumptions innovation	innovation meaning challenge assumptions
Shared Vision	principles personal/co. values alignment inspiration goals vision vitality mobilize commitment	sense of purpose personal/co. values alignment motivation clarity co-develop vision engagement commitment
Team Learning	cooperation dialogue listening creativity promote harmony encourage relationship	co-design self expression contribution creativity social unity relationship

Figure 1

The Work of the Transformational Leader: A Model of Leadership Competencies and Followership Expectations

While both managers and employees need to practice the Five Disciplines to create and sustain a learning organization, what employees need requires that the leaders pay particular attention to their desire for the fulfillment-rich qualities inherent in Personal Mastery, Team Learning and Shared Vision.

Transformational Leaders

For both the leader and employee, Personal Mastery may be the most impacting, difficult, and demanding challenge because this is where the greatest self-evaluation and personal transformation is required. It also offers the greatest reward because it is those who have transformed who can help others through their transformation.

Coming to terms with oneself through deep personal reflection and change is the preparation for transformational leadership. Only by deeply examining core values and beliefs can a shift occur and inner growth be achieved. An internal change is often characterized by a value shift, a new frame of reference for understanding context and mission, a broadened perspective, and a heightened respect for meaning.

People who have successfully negotiated transformation appreciate that it is both necessary and difficult to live for an extended period of time in the "not-knowing"—in the resolution-pending stage—to examine and challenge "truths." Once they have traveled this highly intense and personal path, they can help others find their paths, their courage, and help them inhabit the inevitable limbo and share their challenges and triumphs.

The leadership qualities most in demand, and the rarest, are those that result from the inner journey: integrity, vulnerability, awareness of the human spirit, courage in relationships, curiosity, predictability, breadth, comfort with ambiguity and presence. Leaders who have successfully navigated deep personal change are transformational and can create and manage learning organizations.

Corporations need leaders who have been through their own transformation to facilitate the transformation of others. They need leaders who value people, growth and learning, and who can help employees tap into inner reserves, re-invent themselves, become more attuned to interrelationship, connect to and value their own wisdom, work with colleagues in co-creation. Without these leaders, it will be difficult to build a high performance learning organization.

Through self-reflection and change, leaders find a new place of truth within them that propagates service and connection. They develop a stronger platform from which to conduct their lives, a capacity for outreach, a commitment to right action, and a reverence for truth.

The Organizational Perspective

The new organizational model further underscores the need for a transformed leader. It hears people's needs—the internal and external customers—as they themselves define them. As we move culturally from authoritarian to libertarian values, people want a broader range of choice. The movement is customer- and employee-led, owned, and believed.

People don't want experts internally or externally to decree, they want co-design, co-creation, to arrive at solutions jointly, to own what is developed. People want to express their individuality and have it acknowledged. Greater creativity and innovation are prized by organizations as well who need the best possible ideas to compete successfully.

The learning organization must be market-driven and customer-focused. Customers ask that service providers know their business, get closer to their issues, and relationship is an increasingly important part of the equation. It requires that employees be more flexible than ever before, that they learn and adapt quickly. In this framework, employees have increased accountability and authority, they have the task of self empowerment. Managers are asked to move from a "command and control" function to become counselors, mentors, coaches, and facilitators. They are expected to exhibit a new level of honesty, sensitivity, trust, communication, and innovation.

There is more inclusivity, resulting in a blurring of boundaries as we have known them. Now customers and service providers are part of the same team created to solve production problems. There is a new role for peers, in assessment, mentoring, and recognition.

A new emphasis on partnering requires flexibility as leaders and followers alternate roles, experience shared leadership, and function as teams. Social unity and organizational cohesiveness are prized. Whether it is cross-functional teams or virtual corporations, short-lived, outcome-based alliances are being formed and dissolved continuously. This further blurs boundaries as one-time competitors cooperate when temporarily partnering in a virtual corporation; then, when the alliance is disbanded, they become competitors again.

With increased information and speed of change, and the lack of grounding that constant change brings, there is a greatly heightened need for more authentic and frequent communication.

We are moving to a "market of one," where needs are customized, where we manage one-by-one, where one size no longer fits all in working with the internal and external customer. There is an emphasis on relationship-based client interaction, where products and services are custom configured, and delivered to the precise needs of the customer. Clients want targeted, meaningful, "just for me" service and attention.

The New Leader

The new leader understands this organizational model and breaks dramatically from the old management paradigm. He/she becomes a facilitator, moral architect, coach, steward, relationship builder, teacher and models the values required of all stakeholders: trust, authenticity, courage, commitment and partnership.

We're moving toward whole-self integration with no separate selves for work and personal lives. The new leader supports an intimacy that believes in disclosing true selves in an environment of nurturance and acceptance. He/she encourages employees to free up energy from protecting themselves, to show that sharing feelings is encouraged and that the company supports people who want to learn.

As people seek heightened authenticity, compassion, wholeness, and meaning outside of work, their newfound growth and expectations will come to work with them. They will choose to work for those firms that deliver on the promise of empowerment. We need to provide workplaces that nourish and foster personal and organizational change. We need to discover how deeper meaning can be accessed in our worklives.

Organizations must transform to survive. Their inhabitants must transform for the organization to transform. This happens with the help of change agent leaders who possess unique characteristics; corporations need to create understanding, resolve, and commitment to identify and develop these leaders who are essential to organizational health and the survival of American business.

Transformational leadership occurs when managers broaden and elevate the interests of their workers, when they generate awareness and acceptance of the purposes and mission of the group, and when they motivate their people to look beyond their own self-interest for the good of the whole group. The new leaders have an extraordinary effect on their subordinates because they create meaning for them.

The transformational leader can create conditions in which employees can experience *Narings Liv*—nourishment for life—self esteem, connection, dignity and security, where they can create and feel alive, be listened to and cared for, become, live their values, self discover, risk in an environment of safety—where they can live with meaning and meaningfully contribute to the art and practice of the learning organization.

Lisa J. Marshall (left) is vice-president of Syntax Communication Corp. and principal at The Learning Advantage. Her clients have included Ford's Electronics Division, EDS, Compaq, MCI, Legent Software, and the United States Departments of Agriculture and Treasury. She holds a BA from Bennington College.

Sandra Mobley (center) is a founder and Senior Partner in The Learning Advantage, created to help organizations full of smart people learn more effectively. Her clients have included DuPont, M/A-COM, EDS, Rust Engineering, National Education Corporation, Albemarle Corporation, LCC, Inc., and the U.S. Department of Agriculture. She was Manager of Executive Development at Hewlett-Packard and was head of Training and Development for The Information Consulting Group. She earned an MBA from Harvard Business School.

Gene Calvert (right) is the author of *Highwire Management, Risk-Taking Tactics for Leaders, Innovators and Trailblazers*, and President of Carpe Diem, a risk strategy consulting firm, and founder and Senior Partner in The Learning Advantage. He is an adjunct Professor of HRD/OD at Johns Hopkins University. He has a Masters Degree from Harvard, and a PhD from Case Western Reserve.

7

Why Smart Organizations Don't Learn

Lisa J. Marshall, Sandra Mobley, and Gene Calvert

It is not news that change is the order of the day. How we're handling it is, however, cause for some concern. Consider this:

- A small manufacturing company in the Southwest pursues and wins the Malcolm Baldrige Award for Quality in 1990. In the midst of the rush of recognition that follows, management fails to notice that the business is going down the tubes. It enters Chapter Eleven.

- A hugely successful public television station abruptly loses most of its corporate funding. Unable to believe that the money won't be replaced, station executives continue to pay themselves very high salaries for three years, by which time the station is nearly bankrupt.

- A very smart consultant leaves a firm after working there for over a decade. He is determined to create a "healthy company" full of strong, capable, motivated and empowered employees. Within a year, it is clear he has simply recreated the hated image of the parent company, complete with controlling owner who fails to listen to other people's ideas, weak employees who can't be trusted to be "empowered," and customer service running a weak second to profits.

Dozens more examples of this sort can be cited. The question is: What causes an organization to succeed at one moment in time and fail at another? While each example has its own circumstances and constraints, we believe they all share one thing in common. They were built and staffed by brilliant people who became convinced that they had figured out "THE WAY" to run their organizations. They were right, given their initial circumstances. Yet when the circumstances changed, these brilliant people failed to see, accept or adapt to these changes. In other words, they failed to learn.

Organizations have always been challenged by the question of how to develop their workforce. Traditionally, the greatest effort has been invested in developing "the best and the brightest"—those with high potential, the fast-trackers. These were people identified early on, and then groomed for organizational success. In the (relatively) orderly business world of the 1950s, 1960s, and 1970s, common sense indicated that this would be an easy group to develop, since most of them had excelled scholastically.

In today's turbulent environment, however, Eric Hoffer's pungent comment that "In times of change, learners inherit the world, while the learned remain beautifully equipped to deal with a world that no longer exists" is all too true. It isn't enough to *be* smart: you have to be able to continuously learn. Smart is no longer a destination: it's a journey.

Yet we have a system in place that nourishes certain kinds of smarts at the expense of others—and at the expense of learning how to learn about those others. And what are they? They're areas that aren't addressed in most university programs;

- an ability to see current reality unfettered by biases and beliefs;
- the capacity to notice and modify your own behavior, depending on the results you are seeking;
- and the ability to work with others to effectively set goals, make plans, and carry through in a systematic fashion.

Chris Argyris, of Harvard University, has done provocative work on this subject. His 1991 *Harvard Business Review* article, "Teaching Smart People How to Learn," was the genesis of the thinking that resulted in this essay. He labeled the ability to assess the environment and make changes as "single-loop learning." The ability to look at the mental models you hold about the environment and your resulting behavior, he called "double-loop learning." He documented numerous examples of consultants from major firms who were extremely bright, yet lacked the ability to do double-loop learning. As a result, they failed to notice the impact of their own behavior and discover ways to change it.

This is a critical question we believe organizations need to struggle with today: *If greater smarts don't lead to better learning, what's the cause of this paradox? And what can be done about it? How do we build better learning strategies into individuals and organizations?*

Defining Intelligence: What Is Smart?

> *My own, highly personal definition of what it means to be smart has changed over the years. When I was in the second grade, "smart" meant being able to read a word like Mississippi and then correctly announce how many syllables it had (four, right?) . During my college days, smart people were the ones who wrote the most complex and amazing computer programs. Today, at college plus twenty years or so, my definition of smart means being able to deal honestly with people, yet somehow avoid the twin perils of either pissing them off or of committing myself to a lifetime of indentured servitude by trying too hard to be nice. In all three cases, being smart means accomplishing something beyond my current level of ability...*
>
> —Robert X. Cringely
> *Accidental Empires*

"Smart" as used in the business world is a very narrow definition of human capability. An entire generation of business school graduates, with their high verbal skills and enormous capacity to analyze and manipulate reams of data, reflects this common definition. Much commentary has already been generated about their inability to actually manage businesses in an effective way.

Over the last decade, a considerable amount of work has been done in developing new "theories of intelligence." One of the most thought-provoking of these is Howard Gardner's concept of "the seven intelligences," as defined in his 1993 book, *Frames of Mind:*

- **Linguistic, or verbal intelligence** is the ability to convey ideas. Thus, this kind of intelligence can be shared by salespeople, rappers, executives, a Winston Churchill and a Stephen Hawking.

- **Musical intelligence** is the ability to appreciate and create pleasing combinations of pitch, rhythm, and timbre.

- **Logical-mathematical intelligence,** also described as sequential-linear, is the capacity to abstract reality and manipulate it through long chains of reasoning to some conclusion that can then be tested. Chess players, engineers, computer programmers, financiers, and research scientists all have this intelligence.

- **Spatial, or visual-spatial intelligence** is the ability to perceive, recognize patterns, transform and modify those patterns. Examples might again include engineers, as well as architects, sculptors, painters, and specialists in geometry.

- **Bodily-kinesthetic intelligence** is defined as "two capacities—control of one's bodily motions and capacity to handle objects skillfully." Typing skills and Nintendo may be the most common forms of kinesthetic intelligence practiced in our country. Examples range from athletes, actors and dancers to artisans, the surgeon, and the karate teacher.

- **Intrapersonal intelligence,** says Gardner, is "access to one's own feeling life—one's range of affects or emotions...[and] to draw upon them as a means of understanding and guiding one's behavior." It's the ability of the poet and the diarist.

- **Interpersonal intelligence,** he notes, "is the ability to notice and make distinctions among other individuals, and, in particular, among their moods, temperaments, motivations and intentions." This is the capability of the skilled diplomat, mediator or process facilitator, as well as political and religious leaders.

All of us have one or more of these intelligences, in a vast variety of combinations. Almost no one has all of them. They influence what and how we learn. Each of us must find our own balance—both in our internal appreciation of them and our external use of them in teams, communities and nations.

Robert Sternberg is another important scholar currently reassessing our definitions of intelligence. In his 1988 book, *The Triarchic Mind*, the bulk of his attention is directed toward practical intelligence, or "mental self-management," the area least studied to date. He defines intelligence as "purposeful adaptation to, selection of, and shaping of real-world environments relevant to one's life and abilities."

His work further divides intelligence into three arenas: analytic, creative, and adaptive. Analytic he also labels "academic or white collar," creative is "generative," and adaptive, "practical or blue collar." (Again, we have all three and are usually dominant in one.)

Both Gardner and Sternberg offer useful ways of looking at "smart people." Whichever lens one chooses, what is clear is that the kinds of smarts traditionally rewarded in the academic world—from elementary school on—are not necessarily what will stand us in best stead in the age of "permanent white water." Yet for most professionals today, one's standing is based on immersion in a highly technical field that continues to promote and reward linguistic, analytical/mathematical and visual spatial intelligences and barely recognizes any others.

Individuals who have exceptionally well developed verbal and linear-mathematical learning skills, (academic/analytic) while lacking intra- and interpersonal abilities (adaptive/practical) seem especially prone to single loop learning. We've focused on this combination because :

- Logic tells us that without those intra- and interpersonal abilities, the ability to do double loop learning is greatly impaired;
- This represents what we see as a typical pattern in organizations;
- It is such a disabling paradox, at both the personal and the organizational level; and
- It is one most organizations have not figured out how to resolve.

The Power of Paradigms

The mental models of the world from which we operate—our assumptions about how the world is and ought to be—are frequently invisible to us. The result is that often smart people don't know that they don't know. Indeed, in the Information Age, how could one not know? We educate smart people for content, without regard for context. Yet in times of rapid change, context is everything: no fact, by itself, is as important as it is when applied and economic, social, environmental and political realities are factored in.

Context, however, can be invisible if one's filters preclude its existence. (This dynamic is most often described these days as "paradigm paralysis"—the inability to see how and where the world has changed.) "I'll see it when I believe it" is exactly accurate. Eileen Shapiro, author of *How Corporate Truths Become Competitive Traps*, comments that:

> *Filters have become our expectations and our preferences, and those expectations and preferences encourage us to see and hear what it is we expect and want to see and hear....Acting on the real facts is a painful process."*
>
> —*Industry Week*, February 3, 1992

Utilizing Context

Two key elements are needed to fully assimilate and use context. One is curiosity—that driving sense of wonderment that always assumes there's more to learn. Curiosity allows us to be fascinated by how each of us arrives at our different views or opinions without assigning blame or deprecating that path. The second element is courage, which we'll explore more fully in the discussion of risk.

If our filters, our biases, and our assumptions are transparent to us, how do we uncover them? The answer is the same for individuals and organizations—by taking in feedback. By accepting that perception is not the same as reality, we begin the journey to discovering our mental models. Peter Senge observes that "the discipline of personal growth and learning" is the first step towards learning organizations.

Learning begins when people know their goals and know their current situation. We believe that knowing your goals includes being sure that your values are incorporated into those goals. Like individuals, organizations also need to know their goals and values, key elements in our mental models of the world. When organizations align around a shared purpose or vision, one can often see resistance to learning melt away in favor of the common goal.

Organizations which face hard truths and learn through that process often emerge stronger. Johnson & Johnson's strong corporate credo enabled it to handle the Tylenol crisis in a way that inspired public trust and confidence. Contrast that with Salomon Brothers' insider trading scandal, Union Carbide's Bhopal disaster, or Exxon's Valdez oil spill.

The Missing People Skills

Reading the literature on successful change efforts—places and times when smart people *did* learn—we were struck by the important role that improving intra- and interpersonal skills played. For example, organizations which underwent major transformations, such as Ford, did so in part by making skilled facilitators available every time a meeting took place. This enabled those with the weaker people skills to benefit from more effective group processes without having the skills themselves. It created the kind of atmosphere in which greater truth telling could successfully take place. Learning naturally followed.

Over and over, the story is the same: people skills are the subtle difference that makes a difference. In this difficult economy, Nordstrom is thriving while many other retail chains are facing bankruptcy. For anyone who has ever shopped at Nordstrom the high level of interpersonal skills and empowerment of their salespeople is noticeable.

Another example: Apple Computer, which began with the premise of making a personal computer that would be easy for people to use, is still generating strong sales. When customer feedback told them that high price was a problem, they quickly responded with several lower cost models, unlike a competitor which was unable to respond to complaints about price without undergoing a significant management shakeup. People skills such as listening don't guarantee learning, but they do increase the chances.

Similarly, research on successful and derailed executives supports the need for solid, consistent people skills. This was documented by Morgan McCall and Michael Lombardo in 1983. Technical skills and business know-how may get you to the top, but interpersonal effectiveness is more and more what is required to keep you there. That includes being able to create compelling visions, to build mutual understanding and bridge between differences, to recognize current reality and to continuously learn. As GE puts it, today's managers "must inspire, not force, performance."

Risking to Learn

Learning involves risk: looking dumb, feeling frustrated, losing time, wasting money, appearing stupid, and so on. The universal risk-reward ratio applies to learning: the higher the risk, the greater the reward, and vice versa. Without risk taking, any learning is probably of minimal value.

Learning risks have the same four core components that all risks involve: uncertainties, gains, losses, and significance. Your risk assessment involves considering what you don't know (uncertainty), potential gains and losses, and how significant the risk is to you and your organization.

For example, in deciding whether or not to write a book on learning organizations, you would attempt to find out what you don't know—are there books on learning organizations, how well are they selling, is every niche covered and covered well? Gains include reputation as an author (if the book is good), and higher income streams. Loss assessment would include what you would otherwise be doing with your time that earns income, as well as potential loss of stature if the book bombs. Significance may include recognition for a body of work you created and are proud of (which may carry greater weight than the possible financial gains).

Given the fear that most well-educated people have of looking, sounding and feeling foolish, it isn't surprising that so little real questioning of basic assumptions—the "context" discussed earlier—takes place, even in supposedly safe organizations. If the entire reward system is based on "do more of what we think we already do well," it takes considerable gutsiness to say something isn't going to work any more. Those who try it and get "slam-dunked" for their efforts are especially reluctant to try again. The concept of the CLM—Career Limiting Move—is real in many places. After a decade of down-sizing, right-sizing, mergers and acquisitions, a job is a terrible thing to waste.

Organizational Learning Risks

Organizational learning entails taking risks at three levels: financial, opportunity, and political. The *financial risks* obviously involve money—specifically the two to six percent of revenues that must be invested annually to maximize employee learning.

For many retail and manufacturing organizations, these percentages make the difference between red and black ink. And many industries, such as high technology manufacturers, find profit margins shrinking every year. Yet not making these investments may prove even more costly.

The *opportunity risks* include everything given up in exchange for everything obtained from the risk. That rough calculation often leads to risk avoidance unless the competitors who take the risk gain market share, and then it is often too late. What businesses often fail to calculate is the double opportunity loss that comes from failure to chose either the risk or its best alternative.

The *political risks* center on career consequences:
- of not staying at the peak of your skills technically and interpersonally,
- not knowing what's happening organizationally, and/or
- not building strong networks.

As a manager, you may be told that your learning mistakes become more visible and costly professionally and more humbling and embarrassing personally. Often, the only learning you have time for is on-the-run, brain-picking, making-it-up-as-you-go learning. It becomes more and more difficult to admit "I don't know." Sadly, this failure to admit to not knowing may be one of the greatest learning risks any manager can take. The opportunity to transform individual "not knowing" into organization-wide learning can be the catalyst for true transformation.

Learning Risk Reduction

There are ways to improve the probability of your learning risk succeeding:
- risk sooner, rather than later;
- risk big;
- and risk for a worthy cause.

By risking sooner in your career, you have an earlier and longer payoff time, plus more time to recover. The very process of getting support for big risks helps to surface problems, raise issues you may not have thought of, and generates ideas for selling your plan. Worthy risks are ones that solve important problems or support noble causes, are usually more visible and offer more recognition when they succeed.

Other ideas to improve your success with learning risks include:

- question your assumptions,
- play Devil's Advocate,
- get a critical view from others,
- increase learning risks incrementally,
- gradually increase the scale of the risk.

In any case, you must walk a tightrope between gathering enough data to be sure you've thought through the risk thoroughly versus waiting until all the data is known and probably losing the opportunity to others. In today's resourceful marketplace, there are worms only for the earliest bird.

Creating Learning Environments

We believe organizations can do a lot to create an environment where people are willing to learn—and are rewarded for learning. As a first step, define accurately the costs of NOT learning. The examples we cited at the beginning are a useful starting point. Rest assured, your own organization can provide you with several just as compelling. Then, tie learning's value to critical business needs. Smart people are so pressured these days that you've got to get their attention with something that's compelling from their point of view.

The quality movement has been a powerful force for helping "smart people" and "smart companies" learn. By increasing involvement to include multiple functions and levels, assumptions can be questioned and mental models explored. For example, one organization brought marketing, engineering, and support together to figure out how to make a breakthrough improvement in customer support. The support managers believed support could only be done with engineers in every city because that was the conclusion reached after extensive study of the issue earlier. The marketing people questioned that assumption because two competitors were providing great support from a centralized office.

When the discussion was over, support managers realized that their old analysis no longer applied, because of technical breakthroughs available through on-line diagnostics. However, without marketing questioning their assumptions, they might not have revised their old mental model.

This questioning of assumptions is also increased as quality efforts lead people to work more in teams. Effective teamwork requires greater sharing of information, exploring other perspectives and options, and greater diversity in approaches. This allows a group to come together quickly and work more effectively. Once there's mutual understanding of goals and specific tools for communicating and problem solving, teams can move quickly into high levels of performance. In addition, with proper training, teams learn how to involve *all* members, using techniques such as brainstorming for maximizing group creativity, to create an atmosphere in which people can be more open with each other.

Similarly, the quality practice of benchmarking to explore "best practices" and leverage the learning process, and, the concepts of process analysis and re-engineering have provided platforms for companies to review their work, question their mental models about how that work gets done and make improvements.

Another benefit of *quality* is the concept of continuous improvement, which sanctions questioning the status quo in order to always do better. This concept allows people to get the feedback that is so necessary for learning. And, by exposing "mistakes" at an early stage, companies do not have to repeat them: they utilize the learning that occurred instead.

Other Tools and Strategies

Modeling: Another powerful tool for increasing individual and organizational learning is *modeling*, identifying an ideal and then copying it. First, discover those individuals who function well in your fluid, dynamic business environment to discern exactly what they are doing and how they are doing it. Second, be open and willing to incorporate those behaviors into your own, on an ongoing basis. This means articulating and demonstrating them for others. In short, through modeling one both learns the skills of effectiveness and makes them learnable for others.

Dialogue: The process of *dialogue* explores issues from the base of their assumptions and allows underlying beliefs to be surfaced, prior to decision-making. The old process of advocating our own ideas prevents listening, understanding and recognizing whether our current mental models apply. Moving from an advocacy stance to simple curiosity models an openness to learning, makes it easier to get feedback from others, and presents additional opportunities to learn.

Double Column Technique: Argyris' *double column technique* is a valuable technique for surfacing confining mental models. He documents the actual dialogue—"undeniable data"—in meetings, and then allows people to comment in writing on what they were actually thinking as the conversation unfolded. By sharing that feedback in written form with each other, assumptions and beliefs can be illuminated and addressed.

Action-Reflection Learning: This is a process that says that learning doesn't stop when action is taken. Rather, that's when learning begins. When we reflect on the action, we come to better understanding about what happened, what worked or didn't and how we should act in the future. By building in pauses to reflect and digest, participants draw on their real-world experiences as the primary source of their learning.

Whatever the means, (be it the ones we've just described or creating champions or skunk works or any dozens of other tools and strategies), the issue of getting outside information into the organization and addressing its meaning has to be managed if learning is to take place. Both organizations and individuals need to create "permeable boundaries," ones strong enough to maintain identity and flexible enough to allow input from the outside world that continuously reshapes understanding.

Conclusion

Three key elements shape the organizational learning process: our narrow mental models about the nature of intelligence (what we encourage and reward in our organizations), our lack of emphasis on the importance of people skills both as the lubricant of effective organizational functioning (and as a source of learning), and our fear of the risks involved in learning. Addressing these three issues will enable organizations to take a far firmer grip on their learning processes.

Double-loop organizational and individual learning comes from interactions with the world. All types of intelligence are needed for this to happen. "Smart" as it is currently understood tends to support rationalizing information from the environment into our current mental models by deleting, distorting or generalizing the data to make them fit. Curiosity, plain and simple, supports learning. In the next decade, learning, truth telling, teamwork, changeability and sensitivity to our customers are likely to be the final discriminators of personal and organizational success.

PART TWO

Theories/Methods/Tools

Stories:

Stories for Learning
Diane Cory and Paula Underwood

**The Seventh Story: Extending Learning Organizations
Far Beyond the Business**
Barbara Shipka

Dialogues:

Dialogue: Capacities and Stories
Judy Brown

**Mindshift: Strategic Dialogue for
Breakthrough Thinking**
Sherrin Bennett and Juanita Brown

**Language as Action: Linking Metaphors
with Organization Transformation**
Susan J. Bethanis

Coaching:

**Generative Coaching:
A Surprising Learning Odyssey**
Kendall Murphy

Systems:

Building Learning Laboratories to Create More Effective Distributed Decision Making
W. Brian Kreutzer

FASTBreak™: A Facilitation Approach to Systems Thinking Breakthroughs
David P. Kreutzer

Tools:

The DNA of the Learning Organization
Robert Dilworth

Wisdom at Work: An Inquiry into the Dimensions of Higher Order Learning
Joel Levey and Michelle Levey

In this segment, we look at ways of making a transition from "know-it-all organizations" to learning organizations. Thirteen authors attempt to answer a variety of "how" questions, offering useful methods of bringing about constructive change. The benefits of story-telling, dialogue, coaching, systems thinking, and other specific strategies are offered in these ten essays.

Diane Cory and Paula Underwood lead off this section, with their own unique approach to stories-for-learning in community. Barbara Shipka starts her essay with a dream she experienced, tying it into her vision for learning. Judy Brown looks at capacities and their relationship to stories and storytelling.

Sherrin Bennett and Juanita Brown focus on strategic dialogue as a way of contributing to paradigmatic shifts. Susan Bethanis explores the roles of metaphor, language, culture and structure in organizational transformation. Kendall Murphy elaborates on the value of generative coaching and includes some inspiring personal anecdotes.

W. Brian Kreutzer describes learning laboratories as methods for systemic team learning and David P. Kreutzer shares a story of the development of one model of a systems thinking facilitator. Robert Dilworth looks at the road to learning in comparison to the building blocks of DNA.

Joel and Michelle Levey inquire into consciousness and higher order learning, examining both the apparent and not-so-apparent mental skills.

Diane Cory (left) is author of the *AT&T Teaching Tales* and *AT&T Teaching Verses*. She has led programs with numerous organizations, including Arthur Andersen, Coca-Cola Company, Motorola, Bank of Hawaii, Texas Utilities, Internal Revenue Service, as well as AT&T.

She is a member of the board of trustees for the Robert K. Greenleaf Center in Indianapolis, Indiana and is a member of the Executive Committee for The Past Is Prologue Educational Program.

Paula Underwood, MA, (right) is the developer and director of The Past Is Prologue Educational Program, a nationwide program awarded Exemplary Educational Program status by the U.S. Department of Education in 1986. This program is used from kindergarten through corporations and is listed in the catalogue of "Educational Programs That Work."

Her first book, *Who Speaks for Wolf*, won the Thomas Jefferson Cup for quality writing and has since been declared an Environmental Classic. She is featured on "Working Together," a regular broadcast produced for Radio for Peace International, Costa Rica.

8

Stories for Learning

Diane Cory and Paula Underwood

Diane Cory has extensive experience in working with story-for-learning in organizations such as corporations. Paula Underwood has developed an educational program based on her Native American learning tradition, in which story is often used to enable learning. This essay represents a dialogue between Diane and Paula, whose two traditions are reaching toward each other.

DIANE: Who can know why I awake in the night so regularly? Sometimes my dreams call me to consciousness. Sometimes my spectacular gift for worrying arouses me to begin gnawing again. Then again, it might be that in a household blessed and bursting with the presence and energy of children and animals, I am simply fond of the intense privacy and stillness of the middle of the night.

This particular night I opened my eyes quickly and was awake in the push out of the bed. From the deep darkness of the bedroom my eyes aimed immediately at the lighter landscapes just outside our bathroom window.

The back of our house faces a large cleared backyard that ends in an expanse of Maryland forest. Tangled and tattered are these forest lands. Neither beautiful nor spectacular, they are mostly scraggly. Thin tall pines and hardwood, abundant brambles and unattractive low-lying vegetation, they are best appreciated from a distance where their details become a more attractive whole.

I stood gazing out the six-foot bay window. On the shelf of the window, fifteen sentinel orchids watched silently with me as new snow fell fat and fluffy.

The orchids are keepers of the crossing place—the between place. They remind me of the thin membrane that separates our inner and outer worlds. Even though they have no eyes as we understand eyes, their job is to *see* everything. Watchers. Observers. Witnesses. They practice the many, varied kinds of perception. They practice the subtlety and nuance of perception.

Visitors from another world, they have traveled here to my home. Called by my soul's need for beauty. They have answered with their secret ways. Soothing my mind's incessant searching inside of mystery, they perform healing with paradox—an incredible hardiness of plant with an exquisite delicacy of bloom.

I am watching with these spirits from the soul of nature as another teacher from nature swirls around our house. I am thinking of this essay on stories and I slowly realize that this isn't just snow dancing and whirling like Sufi saints caught in the arms of ecstasy—this is stories a-birthing.

For tomorrow the stories of this winter siege of weather will continue as we meet and greet each other. News reports on radio and television will chronicle the many facets of this series of storms. I know my mother will call and check on us because she has watched weather reports and she will want to know we are okay.

I will tell her the stories of the wild songbirds who gathered on our deck to eat their breakfast of sunflower seeds in six-inch snow. She will laugh when I tell her how our two dogs and five cats lined up at our wall of windows to stare in unison at the peck-peck, hop-hop, flutter-flutter of the winged ones.

I can already feel the stories begin their rising and cooking in the bakery of my imagination. I know I will begin telling stories to my family and friends and then to the participants of my workshops—about how my three daughters and seven animals followed me around the house like a caravan of shadows as I foolishly attempted to work.

My children are like Zen master teachers for me. These teachers of mine, however, are clad in habits and robes of sweaters and soccer shoes. They display an intense devotion to mangling me into my learning.

Exhibiting many of the awesome characteristics of our Jack Russell terrier, Rusty, they can catch even the faintest whiff of learning and will pursue it down any rat hole of inquiry, just in case something is there they can sink their mental teeth into.

They are not afraid of the darkness of unknowing. They are not afraid of the fierce and sly creatures of mystery, paradox, and quandary with their blood-red eyes and gleaming, piercing teeth. They are not afraid of the quick incisor bites from the animals of learning. Mongoose children have no fear of the cobra. They can stare into the hypnotic eye of unknowing, quivering with anticipation of the dance.

These children/teachers of mine already know about how stories teach us. Their favorite form of learning is stories. They intuitively recognize that stories engage us more wholly and completely than a linear presentation of facts. Stories breathe life into our learning; they require us to bring our spirits, our souls, our emotions, our imagination, our reasoning, our analysis, our creative juices.

How do stories help us learn? They engage our mind/bodies completely rather than just our intellect. The cells of our skin, lungs, and liver are just as curious as those of our brain. And they process learnings differently, in ways we need just as much as those of the brain.

Stories are capsules of time-released learning. They release possibilities slowly and with impeccable choice when we need the learnings, regardless of whether or not we think we are ready, willing, and able. The same story can and will release new learnings every time we hear it—matching the learnings to our emotional and mental states with the precision of cell replication.

Stories are alchemy. They are medicine, healing, mystery, paradox, power, and many other things, allowing us to feel, taste, touch, hear, and see the stories around us. They are chaos, order, complexity. Stories are fractals. They are necessary, basic, and dangerous in that they can't be controlled by our striving intellects. They are the container, the elements, the process, and the trigger of transformation.

As a spiritual tradition, alchemy was about the transformation of lead into gold. Stories as a spiritual tradition are about the transformation of power into love.

When we have been blinded by our intellect and reason, by our need to control and not to fear, stories serve us not so much as guide dogs (they are rarely, if ever, so tame) as they do guide wolves, tigers, and hawks. They teach us to learn by teaching us to hunt.

So what do stories have to do with organizational learning? How can we use them? What roles can they play in our work? In our lives?

Let's start by defining stories. What are they? Where do we find them? What can be a story? As we move into considering these things I am going to move from the more esoteric to the more practical. Circling and weaving in and around, back and forth between these two poles as a way to understand story.

What is a story? A beginning, a middle, and an end. Characters. Mood and movement. Conflict, climax, resolution. Meaning. Perspective. All of this can happen in one sentence.

Stories exist all around us. We might be more used to thinking of them as novels, anecdotes, fairy tales, folk tales, opera, drama, movies, history, biography, science, articles, and so forth. But they are also found in the form of paintings, photographs, dance, song, sculpture, meals, clothes, buildings, and gardens. Stories are both tangible and intangible.

As we are considering how we might use stories as a way to deepen organizational learning, we can begin by thinking about what we believe stories are and where we can find them.

When I am working with stories I use every form that I can find that is appropriate to the moment and the individual or group that I am working with. I use video, music, songs, cartoons, poetry, children's books, quotes, personal anecdotes, fairy tales, folk tales, and short stories.

Stories are everywhere—so they are always at hand when you might want or need them. If we just had the right kind of eyes to see them.

* * * * *

Note on terminology from Paula: *"I write from my Native American tradition, rather than from the more general Western tradition. It is important to convey accurate meaning. Terms frequently used in English may not do that for my tradition. For instance, I use Mind Image here advisedly. It is not the same as the*

*more usual term in English, 'mental image.' In my
tradition, Mind is understood as the way Body and
Spirit talk to one another. A Mind Image, then, is much
more like a religious symbol which can convey transcendent meaning [more] than the term 'mental image'
can convey.*

*In my tradition there are also considered to be
two-drumbeat (. .) thoughts and three-drumbeat (. . .)
thoughts. In Oral presentation, this awareness requires
a pause . . a silence . . In order to portray this on the
printed page, I use . . or . . ."*

PAULA: We are weaving Diane's thoughts with mine in this
writing. Now I invite you to consider what Diane has accomplished—through story—in just a few pages. Through the Mind
Images of her thoughts, she invites us toward sensitivity, toward
awareness . . . by inviting us with her words into her edge-of-
woods space, she creates visual images, cleared of any other
thought, in which we can consider the nature of her sharing with
us . . and learn from that sharing . . she beckons us toward story
as an opportunity to learn and grow . .

Look at the conceptualizations she has spun from the stuff
of her experience! Maryland forests "best appreciated from a
distance." Orchids as "keepers of the crossing place." "Hardiness
of plant," "exquisite delicacy of bloom." Will we ever look at
orchids the same way again? Will they ever again be "just pretty
flowers" to us?

If the purpose is to learn, to grow past our present limitations, to expand our vision to include more and more of the whole,
story makes an excellent tool to move us in that direction. And yet,
we have grown out of the habit of using story in our daily lives. Or of
recognizing it when we do use it. Story to describe individuality.
Story to describe unity.

Coherent cultures share their general stories. These can be
the fairy tales we heard in childhood or seeing *The Wizard of Oz*
on television when we were young. These can be the *story*
contained in the Bhagavad-Gita, the Torah, the Bible, or the
Koran. Such stories lead to a common, shared understanding of
the collective history of our people, an understanding of who we
are . . together.

It is like this in the coherent culture of corporations and
other organizations as well. Every organization has a story, the

story of its beginning and its growth, the story of how it came to be what and where it is. This story may or may not be shared. If it is shared, then the people in that organization probably understand what is expected of them a little better. If the corporate story also talks about where everyone is going together—a vision statement— then they probably work toward that goal more effectively.

There is more to story than this. Stories create a "safe place for danger," as Lana Leonard says. They create a kind of mental sandbox in which to play with options before the cost is too great. But most of all, they can create a learning opportunity, a space in which learning can occur.

Diane tells me that experience shows that the most effective way to work with story in organizations and corporations is to proceed in a logical, sequential way . . then tell a story . . then back to the logic . . then another story. Thus, alternate thought-ways are woven and braided together. My Native American tradition explains how this structure works well because it has two benefits.

First, it gives us some mental breathing room to absorb what has already occurred and to experiment with these ideas at the many levels of our thinking. Not taking enough time at this stage is the principal reason people *thought* they understood, then don't! There isn't enough time or enough space allowed for that internal dialogue that *must* take place for thinking to be coordinated and integrated. In corporations as in other organizations, merely reaching a decision will not be enough if the organizational community has not really assimilated that decision. Uncoordinated response may destroy original purpose.

For instance, a cousin of mine decided to use one of the Learning Stories handed down in my tradition, *Who Speaks for Wolf,* at his next design and planning meeting at one major manufacturing company. When the meeting was ending and everyone had aired all their concerns about potential design flaws they were willing to share, he asked the ancient question, "Who Speaks for Wolf?"

Of course, no one had any idea what he was talking about. So he told them the story. *Wolf,* you see, asks us to stop and think about what we have forgotten to consider.

After he finished, *six different people* said that they had a concern about design, but they had hesitated to take the group's time. Now they spoke.

My cousin decided to track the results. He found that raising these six concerns had saved his corporation $40,000. From then on, he ended every planning and design meeting with the ancient question, "Who Speaks for Wolf?" The story communicated his request that everyone speak up better than any language he had been able to devise in decades of corporate experience. This is only one of story's many uses . . .

Second, effective story has a capacity to link our logical left brain with our holistic right. In fact, this is one of the principal benefits of effective story—the right brain *is* that mental sandbox in which we can experiment with ideas before they get too costly. When we access this whole-thinking, experimenting, creative part of our intellectual equipment, we increase our capacity for processing thought—geometrically. We begin to integrate thought with purpose, mind with heart. Organizations and the individuals that comprise them need this unity of purpose.

Experience tells us that there are several things that need to be true for story to have such an effect.

Completeness

A story needs to be complete in itself. Rather than having only a beginning, a middle, and an end, a story can be seen as a circle, a design that begins and ends but, like a circle, a design which *implies* future possibilities and future decisions. Each story circle then, effectively done, expands our awareness, as Diane's Snow Orchid story did. Each completed circle is an expansion of that circle, an expansion in awareness, in understanding and, as the circle expands, it becomes a spiral—a spiral of growth and greater creativity.

Wonder

You see how this is different from our usual way of thinking of story? We think of stories as having a beginning (laying the groundwork), a middle (fleshing out the story), and an end (the resolution of the theme of the story). That might make a good movie, but it isn't enough for a story that works for thinking, for organizing, for experimenting. Such a story can create a small world in which to wonder, perhaps in which to wander! This is the gift of a real learning story. Space to think in and ideas about which to think.

Touching

To be effective for any learning purpose, story needs to touch us, to awaken our broader senses, to find its way to more aspects of our being, to speak to our inner senses as well as to our five physical senses.

Space . . and Sensitivity . . . here is one of Diane's poems that describes space . . . and encourages sensitivity . . .

Fear

I want
fear
to have
a face

I want
fear
to be a
place
I can
pass
in and
out of.

I want
fear
to be

something
I can
hold
in my

hand
and crush.

But
what I
find
is that
fear

is my
shadow

always

behind
below
beside
in front

of me

depending
on the

light.

— Diane Cory

With these few words, she brushes away cobwebs that limit our thinking and expands our awareness.

Notes on terminology from Paula: *"In my tradition, Learning is considered so important that it is considered Sacred. Therefore, words which relate to any process of profound Learning—such as a Learning*

Story—will be capitalized to denote greater emphasis and to support the inherent spirit of the theme and presentation of this section of this essay.

Thought and Thinking are two different events. Thought is Whole. It is much like the light bulb that flashes on in the cartoon balloon. Thinking is a spinning out of that Thought into something one can ponder in a different way and possibly communicate."

In my tradition, after any Story, any Poem, any Song meant for Learning, we ask that ancient question, "What . . may we learn from this?"

Silence

Now we can value, now we can judge, whether or not we have a true learning, a true Learning Story! Now it is time for the storyteller to maintain absolute silence . . and wait . . and wait . . to learn . . . whether any learning at all occurred. If that learning is particularly deep, if it truly touches the soul, if it awakens deep understanding, perhaps no one will be able to reply.

So *let* silence invite. Let silence give permission to think and to absorb. Let it help each listener to be conscious of the choice they are making . . to speak . . to ask . . to consider. Wait a while before going on. Ask them . . perhaps tomorrow . . what they learned.

In her poem, Diane creates space in which to consider the fears that beset us all.

The Bullfight

A story I tell for this purpose is about Portuguese bullfighting. It is my favorite example of how we can address our fears, our traumas—both as individuals and as organizations—in ways that enable growth and learning. It carries with it a clear Mind Image of what is necessary.

It is like this . . .

We all hold in our minds a clear image of a Spanish bullfight with its swords and *banderillas.* Blood seeping into the sand. Severed ears to the winner.

A Portuguese bullfight is not like that. It grows more directly from the Minoan roots of this ritual. There are no spears, no swords. There is no matador, no killer of bulls. Rather, the torero creates a dance of bull and cape and man . . again . . and again . . until at last the bull is tired and confused . . until at last the torero understands the bull's nature . . and faces his own fears.

Now the torero walks up to the nearly immobile bull, places his hand on the bull's forehead, turns, and walks away! He shows that he has, at least for now, mastered the bull. He shows that he and the bull have reached a balance point, a place of temporary safety in the midst of the inherently dangerous.

Most of all, the torero shows that he has mastered himself in relation to great danger. He has taught himself a difficult lesson . . to face this great danger with equanimity, to learn to understand its nature, to turn, to walk away with impunity.

A Portuguese bullfight has a happier ending. The bull goes out to stud—and the torero, having killed no one at all, goes on to a better life, aware of his own ability to face and overcome a most fearful possibility.

With the cape of story, we can work with our own terrors and, learning to know them through this work, walk up to them, touch that reality, turn and walk away—we have become a more whole person, a more whole organization. We have become more effective.

Your Corporate Community

Story helps us expand the mental space in which we operate. We can never do this all at once. It takes time and opportunity to explore learning space. It takes some patient experience to become effective users of story, practitioners of the art.

Let's say that you can see the economy changing around you, that your organization doesn't presently produce anything you see as marketable in five to fifty years. Everyone in the organization is likely to be so busy trying to think their way out of the situation that they can't even see it's only a paper bag . . the paper bag of your assumptions about who you are and what you are doing . . your story . . so far!

It is as if . . the way you presently operate, the way everyone in your corporate community already understands, is a circle of light in which you know how to function, a light that allows you to see. Your group is like a circle, a circle that is generating this light. You see everything inside that circle because *you know how to*. Your vision, your light is more than adequate to accomplish that goal. You have clear vision . . within those limits.

But times change. Now your vision needs to extend *past*

your own limits.

Now it is as if . . someone in your group uses story to shine a spotlight here . . and there . . just outside your circle, the circle of your understanding, the circle of your clarity of vision.

If all of those participating in this exploration of possibilities begin to see, through story, this part . . and that . . of the landscape *outside* your corporate conceptualization . . you may begin to discover new territory, new possibilities that you thought irrelevant before. You may discover new depths of understanding in yourself and in others.

Story creates a safe place for danger, somewhere to experiment before the cost gets too high.

Remember, we said spotlights . . plural. This is not a transition that's easily made with one thunderclap. It takes time, slow efforts to think through possibilities in new territories. Stories can begin to illuminate the darkness, show you what you hadn't considered before, and, over time, the unknown becomes the slightly known—a place that has less danger, one you can begin to explore with that effective logical left half of your thinking apparatus.

Really effective story is the process of creating a world where people can go in and out and experiment with possibilities before those possibilities arrive at your door, before it's too late to steer a different course.

As to that mental sandbox, we discover possibilities much better through play, because when we aren't playing we are simply weaving the things we already know into new patterns. When you have time to play, just fool around, generally frolic, new possibilities come up. That useful left brain is much too predictive. It will always try to build houses out of wood instead of out of something new. People in New Mexico are beginning to build houses out of straw bales now. Nothing at all they learned from an instruction manual.

Circles

Diane also talks about ways in which to begin creating an environment where learning is fostered and supported. Circles create one such environment. This is one reason why quality circles work well in the manufacturing process. The equality of input that is implied in a circle encourages everyone there to contribute their best. It discourages them from limiting themselves to echoing back what they believe is expected. Answers come. Solutions crystallize.

Story probably works best for group learning—for learning to be a learning organization—if all are seated in a circle, preferably with no table, no barrier between them.

At other times, tables are not barriers. They facilitate certain kinds of work and establish organizational structure. But when you seek creativity or creative learning, they can interrupt the threads of connection between us. It may work best to remove visual barriers, to arrange it so that everyone is equidistant from the center of the circle. A circle which grows lopsided into some corner prevents too many eyes from meeting, puts too many people out of focus.

Perhaps you want your group to truly focus. Then no distraction, please. No posters with extraneous messages, no windows overlooking a park.

But if your purpose is to open, to expand—then put posters on the wall, flowers here and there, indications that there's more to life than this circle, more to Thought than we presently understand.

Most meetings have need for both circumstances.

Now ease the circumstance—say something that makes it easier for your listeners to participate. Say something that makes it clear that you are both, you are all human beings. Diane's Snow Orchid story is an excellent example. We *feel* her as a human being. She sets an example of creative thought that encourages us to try, to experiment with possibilities. By being herself, she gives us permission to be whoever we are, to make the best contribution we can, being that person. She gives our natural creativity permission to express itself.

And yet, her thoughts are so beautiful that they may discourage some from speaking up. They may doubt they can match her brilliance. Say something that makes it clear that we are all on an even footing. My father used to say that we are *all* stumblers along the path, catching one another from time to time.

Say something that implies a future, that makes it clear that there's time to learn, time to grow. Encourage comments, but don't ask for evaluations. The job . . right now . . is to go with the flow, to allow story to happen. Later, sort and analyze.

The circle of story will be more complete if they have the feeling that you, the storyteller, are and will be accessible to everyone. Remember, traditional storytellers *lived* in the community they served. The ultimate accessibility. This gave them a wonderful opportunity to monitor the effects of their storytelling and it made them subject to those effects. More to gain. More to lose.

In my tradition, we say that a Learning Story needs to create visual space, space within the mind. There is a natural geometry to any Learning Story—circles of wholeness, triangles of acuity—that enable us to create mental space in which new learning can occur. You can see this space forming in the beginning of *Who Speaks for Wolf*:

> *Almost at the edge of the circle of light cast*
> *by Central Fire—Wolf was standing. His eyes*
> *reflected the Fire's warmth with a colder light.*
> *Wolf stood there . . looking at the Fire.*

Do you see the circle? Can you discern the triangle?

As you can see in Snow Orchid, *noticing life* is the most effective way of gathering stories, stories that work, stories that are real, stories that provide a new space in which to learn.

The Storyteller

Professional storytellers find it works to center yourself within the story before you begin. This means simple things like—don't begin the joke until you remember the punch line!! That can be a very critical learning. It means more complex things like—allowing the story to be, creating a space within yourself in which it can occur, then letting the story tell itself.

My own way of reminding myself of the wholeness of the story before I begin is this:

Say or imply that you are about to tell a story.

Stop.

Be silent.

Feel yourself in that story. Center yourself in the images the story creates for you.

When I am comfortable in that place, I bring my hands together to remind me of focus, of the need to stay where I am; then I outstretch my hands to include everyone there as witness to the story, as the "Listening Ears" without which story cannot take place.

In my mind I have opened a circle, a circle that invites everyone to its edge without insisting. This circle is so large that it extends *up to* the center of each person there. It *never* extends farther. I make no effort to *insist* on including people by making the circle so large they are forced, willy nilly, to be within it. Some people need to move in and out. Sometimes you can see them leaning back in their chairs, moving *away* from what's happening. *If they have that right,* if you don't try to hold them against their will, if they are comfortable moving in and out, they may become some of your most effective workers-with-story. If they feel trapped . . that won't happen.

I have found that these Mind Images encourage me to include without insisting, to remain focused within the story, whether or not there are interruptions. I have found that they work.

When we learn to focus in this way, story is a wondrous adventure. And the story does, indeed, tell itself.

The first task here is to become a person ready to tell heartfelt stories, to tell stories from the heart. You cannot do this if you shy away from the content.

The second task is to prepare your group to hear this story with an open heart. As Diane describes, music may work here, or poetry, or everyone taking a turn at telling a personal story; something that paints Mind Images without troubling your logical sequencing too much.

Any such story can probably not be about the issues your organization means to address. They need to be stories that build visual space, that heighten a capacity and a willingness to feel. If you are unwilling to feel the pain of failure, there's a good possibility you won't recognize it as it approaches.

Story can help build awareness.

As we have seen, story is the process by which any organization explains itself to the people within the organizational family (employees, stockholders, directors) and those related people outside the immediate family (the customers, the public, the funding agencies).

If your organizational story is good, it will evoke the ethos of your organization. If this is done well, details won't matter.

If your story is "true," further details will just flesh it out without arguing with the basic story itself.

If your story is clear, it doesn't need to be long.

As we have seen, story can create the space in which new and necessary thinking can occur. It can be the process through which we build increasing awareness of Life and its many options, through which we show ourselves—in time—the many paths that lie open to us.

A Final Story

Ode to Quantum

Silence is
a beating
heart

And
if you
walk
into it

you will
eventually
come to

a room
that
has been
calling
your name

since before
you were
born.

There
you will
find the

mirror
of darkness

reflecting
back to
you

everything
you cannot
see.

The invisible
and intangible
will be
revealed
as real

and your heart
will find
its peace

and your mind
will find
its terror.

The
heart of
silence

is a
beating

mirror

that lets
us see
all of the
opposites
as one.

Reality
is a
tiger
whose stripes
are the
waves
of possibility.

—*Diane Cory*

Let us learn to see that it is so.

Barbara Shipka consults to corporations primarily in the arenas of creating a global orientation, anticipating increasing interdependence, leveraging growth and transitions, working with differences and diversity, and developing resilient work roles. Among her clients are Cray Research, Honeywell, IDS Financial Services, Levi Strauss, Medtronic, The Pillsbury Company, and Wilson Learning.

Shipka serves on the Board of Directors of The World Business Academy and initiated the Minnesota Chapter. In addition to the corporate sector, she has worked with the United Nations, government agencies, the non-profit sector, and the education sector. She has lived and worked in Lebanon, The Dominican Republic, Somalia, Ethiopia, The Sudan, Czecho-slovakia, and Switzerland.

Shipka is a contributing author to several anthologies including *When the Canary Stops Singing, Leadership in a New Era, Community Building,* and *Rediscovering the Soul in Business.* She is profiled in *Merchants of Vision* by Jim Leibig and *Who We Could Be At Work* by Margaret Lulic.

9

The Seventh Story: Extending Learning Organizations Far Beyond the Business

Barbara Shipka

We dream to wake to life!
—Stephron Kaplan-Williams

Anyone who recognizes what is going on in the world and is not insecure is just not awake.
—in a speech by a Fortune 500 CEO

In 1987, I had a powerful nighttime dream—filled with metaphors representing aspects of our lives today. It went like this: *A handsome, highly intelligent, impeccably dressed American corporate businessman is driving the car as we wend our way toward our destination. It is slow going and he is using extreme caution to avoid the throngs of people moving in the opposite direction. They seem frightened as they coax children along and clutch meager belongings.*

"What's going on?" I ask.

"It's because of the fire," he explains.

"Oh, I see," though I didn't see at all. I had absolutely no idea what he was talking about. But, not wanting to appear any more ignorant than I already had, I didn't ask, "What fire?"

As we approach the only tall building for miles around I recognize the familiar six-foot concrete wall topped with jagged-edged glass from broken bottles—a common form of security in many parts of the world. A mass of humanity envelopes the outer perimeter of the wall. Though these people exude intense urgency, for the most part they appear settled, living on the streets and in makeshift homes constructed of what others have discarded.

The building is beautiful! Once we pass through the gate, a sense of spaciousness, quiet, and ease embraces us. As we ascend to the top of the building, the seventh story, I mention that I am struck by the urgent, frenetic mood outside the gate.

"Yes," my colleague responds. "But, lucky for us, it's not something we have to worry about."

The seventh story is one large room—an elegant yet conservative reception space. There are several people in the room when we arrive. Most are men between thirty-five and fifty-five who also appear to be highly successful executives like my colleague. There are only a few other women and no children or old people. The mood is upbeat—jovial, in fact. As I walk across the room, passing and greeting people along the way, I glance out the windows to the south. Across the entire horizon I see fire. In front of the fire there are no trees or animals, only dry savannah grass and people on the move. A pit forms in my stomach—I feel shock and terror.

I turn and run from the room and down the stairs two at a time. I want to help. I want to offer my energy, my money, my intelligence—whatever. To save lives! But, what can I do? I find myself running haphazardly through the streets. I become just one more person among the teeming masses. I notice I am dissipating my resources without having the slightest positive impact.

With a heavy heart, I return to the building. On my way I glimpse many creative attempts to survive the fire. One especially stands out. Two boys have rigged up a teeter-totter/pulley system over a sewer. Thus, one boy comes up to breathe as the other is lowered into the vat of sewage to cool off.

After passing through the gate into the building's interior garden, I climb the first flight of stairs. I notice a small darkskinned young woman descending. Her eyes are downcast and she holds a newborn baby in her arms. They are both soaked through so I know she somehow got permission to use the shower. I think to myself that this may be the last time either of them will be cool. For an instant I consider taking them upstairs with me. That, at least, would be something I could do.

As we meet, she looks directly and unabashedly into my eyes. I am stunned by the calm, the compassion, and the comprehension I see. I witness generations of ancient, timeless wisdom in her teenage face. Without a word she communicates that she knows I cannot take her and her child upstairs; that not only would they be refused entrance, but so would I. Tears fill my eyes as I receive her forgiveness and, at the same time, feel my own despair and helplessness.

When I enter the room on the seventh story again, I notice that cases of beer and snacks have been set out. People are conversing, laughing, and dancing to the music of Bruce Springsteen. I see the fire moving closer. The smoke finds its way to the windows.

"Look!" I shout. "Please look! The fire is rapidly approaching. What are we going to do?"

My colleague smiles consolingly saying, "Don't worry. It's okay. You'll be okay. We'll all be okay as long as we stay up here." He asks someone to pull the curtains to block out the unpleasant sight of the fire. "It might get hot in here for awhile. And it might become difficult to breathe. But we will survive. We are survivors, after all. When the fire has passed we will go back downstairs and begin to rebuild."

"But," I think to myself, "How can I ever again leave this room?"

Transforming the Fire

Many images of my dream are daunting even when considered individually—the fire, the cavalier attitude of people of the seventh story, the absent children and old people, the lamentable circumstances of the boys with the teeter-totter and the teenager with the baby. Combine them and they become so overwhelming that it is possible to feel consumed by feelings of helplessness, hopelessness, and despair.

Even more breathtaking is that the dream, while symbolic, is not unreal. It fairly represents one view of the world in which we live today.

Whether we can feel it or not, we are affected by what happens on the rest of our planet. And, most certainly, business is not exempt. Most people *know* this to be true. But the question is, "What can we *do* about it?"

The first response, often, is feeling afraid and helpless. This can lead to running down the stairs two at a time as I did in the dream. Many of us feel a true sense of urgency and a desire to positively affect the outcome. Responding out of urgency tends to lead us to finding a "cause" where we can make a contribution. The paradox is that most of the causes treat symptoms, rather than establishing, understanding, and impacting the roots of systemic problems . Thus, it is critical to distinguish between the urgency of our plight—which leads to panic—and the necessity for taking responsibility for it—which leads to learning more about its nature.

Where there is deep and radical learning, transformation occurs. It occurs simultaneously at the most personal and the most global levels. Thus, to the extent that each individual and the system as a whole can learn, there is probability of transforming the fire.

A Daytime Dream

The nighttime dream has given me the opportunity to be more awake to what's going on in our world at this time. It has allowed me to safely be with and face very difficult emotions. Most of all—because the dream is so vivid, so compelling, and so real for me—it has prompted me, stirred me, to balance it by developing an equally vivid and compelling counterpoint daytime dream— a vision.

My vision is that we devote ourselves to making the world of business, the seventh story, a living, learning, and profitably thriving organism—a milieu that supports human evolution for eternity while accomplishing the goals of today. Given the power of business on one hand, and the powerlessness of much of the rest of our world on the other, it's likely none of us will survive if the global business infrastructure doesn't succeed.

If we truly want a world in which we can do business, those of us on the seventh story will passionately assume more responsibility for the well-being, integrity, and survival of our larger living system.

What does that mean—assume more responsibility? It means that "sound" business decisions are those which ensure the viability of a discrete business, to be sure. In addition, however, sound business decisions are those which take into account the implications of the course of business beyond itself— in both geographic space and linear time. Thus, the true learning organization is larger than the boundaries of any one business. True learning organizations creatively incorporate—in balance— both present and future, both local and global, both within and beyond themselves.

Around the time I had the dream, I was at a decision point about whether to resume my corporate consulting practice or accept a three-year contract with the World Bank in Papua New Guinea. The dream made it crystal clear that, given the types of work I had been doing in Africa for the better part of the three preceding years, continuing my international relief and development work was akin for me to running through the streets dissipating my resources.

Thus, I made my choice. I would return full tilt to the seventh story and sometimes shout, sometimes whisper, "Look! Please look! The fire is approaching rapidly. What are we going to do?"

Since then, the tone of my voice, the way I shout or whisper my warning has changed. My mission has become a very sacred task and I am less scared. Continuously awakening anew to the current predicament of our world and pushing through the hopelessness and despair, I experience hope and creativity.

And companionship. Over time, thank goodness, I have discovered others who share this awareness, these values, and a similar vision. And I have found them on the seventh story.

But, even though we may have a clear sense of purpose, even though we may have hope and a vision, does not mean we know what to do. It doesn't mean we have answers. It does mean, however, that as much as we are able, we are willing to live in the questions and engage in learning. It means we are willing to explore the edges of our consciousness—our minds, our hearts, our spirits.

Together We Will Be Learning

In Chinese, the character that represents crisis includes both danger and opportunity. We currently live in crisis, in a state of emergency. It is essential that we navigate the emergency routes to new landscapes for it is often in times of emergency or crisis that we have major breakthroughs. That is where the hope and opportunity lie. But to get there we will have to work in new ways. We stretch ourselves beyond where we've ever been before—and we do this together.

Together we will:
- delve into deep inquiry of the unanswerable questions and dilemmas of our times—and live with the discom-

fort of not having ready-made answers.

- develop unified, resolute, ardent vision—and engage in creation.
- literally change and, thus, grow our minds.
- draw from the deeper, less physical senses—and then trust more and more what we learn from them.
- discover ways to transcend time.

Let's look at each of these directions for our learning together.

Together we will delve into deep inquiry of the unanswerable questions and dilemmas of our times—and live with the discomfort of not having ready-made answers.

How can the seventh story more fully reflect the nature of the human family—whether literally or symbolically? How do we weave more of the generations of ancient, timeless wisdom into our lives? How can we more fully bring into the workplace the innocent child's freedom for learning, creating, and making mistakes along with the experienced elder's wisdom, long view, and reflection?

How do we face the challenges of disparity of resources and differences in cultures represented by the two sides of the concrete wall? How sturdy is the wall? How can we create safe harbors where we can rest, relax, restore, and restock ourselves without having the harbors be elite or exclusive?

How can we more fully learn from the creative resourcefulness of the boys with the teeter-totter? How can we develop and express more of the calm, the compassion, the comprehension of the teenage mother?

How can the destructive fires be transformed into heat, energy, and passion that can serve all life?

Together we will develop unified, resolute, ardent vision and engage in creation.

Early in *The Fifth Discipline*, Peter Senge distinguishes between "adaptive" and "generative" learning. Adaptive learning is learning that maintains survival. Generative learning is learning that leads to creating the future.

In our learning we will deeply scrutinize commonly held assumptions that set limitations on our ability to engage in generative learning. One assumption that limits is the recently popularized word meant to describe efforts toward creating a workable world. The word is "sustainability." "Sustain" is not a word of hope or creation. It means "maintain," "shore up," "buttress." An alternative, for example, is "viability." "Viable" means "alive," "vital," "prospering." "Sustainability" cannot truly engender deep images of thriving. It stops at notions of surviving because it implicitly calls for adaptive or survival learning rather than generative or creative learning!

In our quest to generate common vision, we will become clearer about our assumptions and values. From the vision, we must risk creating new forces, new forms, new systems, and new rituals.

While it is an essential tool, conventional rational problem-solving is insufficient. We will push ourselves much further. As far as we know, our creativity is a truly limitless resource.

Together we will literally change and, thus, grow our minds.

We will recognize that the mind has capacity for infinitely more than thinking—though thinking, of course, is part of the equation. We will also open ourselves to believing in possibilities until they are disproven, rather than waiting until they are proven.

We will recognize that individually and collectively, no matter what, we choose and create our future. Daily, we will entertain the possibility that the folk saying, "Be careful what you wish for because you just might get it," just might be true! We get what we put our attention on—whether loving or fearful. For example, it seems that the more resources we devote to the "wars" on crime, drugs, and poverty, the more murder, drug trade and use, and homelessness we seem to have!

On the other hand, ignoring the issues altogether does not make them go away. Denial is a choice that directly determines the future by *not* consciously creating it.

Together we will draw from the deeper, less physical senses—and then trust more and more what we learn from them.

Our five senses, while they keep us alive and well in the physical world, are inadequate to handle the tasks that face us. As with all of life, we are "in process." We are evolving as a species. One locus of our evolution is the arena of our "sixth sense." But it is much more than a sixth sense—it's an entire cadre of senses. Call them what you will—inner knowing, intuition, psychic power, the small quiet voice—we are coming to comprehend that there's more going on and more available to us than what we can see, hear, taste, touch, and smell. We are also recognizing that this cadre of senses is available to all of us—not just to the religious, the specially endowed, or the weird few on the fringe.

Author Gary Zukav calls this "the emergence of multisensory humanity." In an essay entitled *Evolution and Business,* he writes, "The human species is now leaving behind the exploration of physical reality as its mode of evolution and, simultaneously, the limitations of the five senses. Five-sensory humans are becoming multisensory humans—humans that are not limited to the perception of the five senses."

Together we will discover ways to transcend time.

We don't have much time. But acting out of urgency alone doesn't produce the creative results we need. Nor does giving up.

Here, again, we have assumptions to challenge—like, "Things take time." Some processes do take time. On the other hand, some processes can change direction in an instant or perform an unexpected quantum leap—especially in our minds when we're learning and creating.

Given the force and momentum of the flailing and failing life support system on our planet today, we will push ourselves to create by moving beyond linear time. At a minimum, we will bend time. Even better, we will learn more about how to "tesseract." Do you remember reading *A Wrinkle in Time* as a child or to your own children? For those who don't know it, I'll let Mrs. Whatsit explain it as she did for the children in the story:

> *"Explanations are not easy when they are about things for which your civilization still has no words. ......traveling at the speed of light......of course is the impractical, long way around. We have learned to take short cuts wherever possible." ......Mrs. Whatsit looked over at Mrs. Who. "Take your skirt and show them." ......Mrs. Who took a portion of her white robe in her hands and held it tight.*
>
> *"You see," Mrs. Whatsit said, "if a very small insect were to move from the section of skirt in Mrs. Who's right hand to that in her left,*

it would be quite a long walk for him if he had to walk straight across."

Swiftly Mrs. Who brought her hands, still holding the skirt, together. "Now, you see," Mrs. Whatsit said, "he would <u>be</u> there, without taking that long trip. That's how we travel. ......In other words, a straight line is <u>not</u> the shortest distance between two points.

Esoteric experiences like telepathy, clairvoyance, and pre-cognition are examples of learning that transcend time. But breakthrough ideas, spiritual conversions, choosing anew, and comprehending something for the first time are also examples. They are examples of common, everyday experiences that are not linear and that transcend time. They happen in an instant and can change everything about how "reality" appears as a result.

Conclusion

My nighttime dream ended but it did not have a conclusion. There is room to realize the daytime dream, the vision. The fires of destruction can be redirected—in my heart and soul, I'm sure of it—to become alchemical fires of transformation.

By living in the unanswerable questions of our lives and times, by exposing them to constant, continuous, and rigorous inquiry, we can influence our individual and collective futures toward as yet unimagined creative solutions. We can direct our journey away from the systemic global problems and toward our own evolution as a species and the evolution of all life on earth.

Judy Brown is an educator in private practice in the Washington, DC area. Her work revolves around the themes of change, quality, diversity, and renewal. A writer, speaker, and facilitator of retreats and workshops, she is writing a book on organizational and personal renewal, and produces a series of working papers on topics of interest to leaders.

She has served as a White House Fellow, and holds a PhD from Michigan State University. She has been associated with major universities, The Aspen Institute, and organizations across all sectors. Brown's work reflects the values of the learning organization, and she is best known for the manner in which she draws the wisdom from groups, and weaves the insights of participants together with the ideas of influential thinkers in ways that allow for important and productive individual and organizational change.

10

Dialogue:
Capacities and Stories

Judy Brown

I have come to view dialogue as a process central to the development of learning organizations. I have also come to view dialogue as a capacity we each possess. We may have forgotten our capacity for dialogue as individuals and as organizations. Thus learning about dialogue is really a matter of rediscovery, of recalling what we have forgotten to remember. This paper is about dialogue understood in that light.

I know no way to convey this understanding of dialogue but to tell a story.

Not long ago, I was working with a group of *Fortune* 500 executives in a retreat. Two days into a session on teamwork, this group was struggling with the perverse effects on teamwork of an element of its financial incentives package. As only one of the firm's operating units, the group had no power to unilaterally change corporate policy. They saw no leverage for getting the corporation to change. It was clear that the incentive structure made real team effectiveness nearly impossible. This had been frustrating them for a long time. It had become an insurmountable impediment to much that they wanted to accomplish.

I suggested that a struggle like this could be seen as a kind of hologram, containing all the patterns and problems that were interesting and important to the corporation and to their work. I asked if they would be willing to take a couple of hours and work on this issue in a slightly different way. They were delighted to try something that might "loosen the knot." A change of pace seemed welcome so they quickly agreed.

I asked if they would follow some simple guidelines for a different kind of conversation: Only one person could speak at a time and, as they spoke, they were to hold a small rock (I carry a small polished heart-shaped rock and I fished it out for the occasion). They were to relinquish the rock only when they had completed their thought. They should then pass the rock to someone else who had signaled they wished to speak, or place it in the center for someone else to pick up. They were to begin by talking about where they were with this issue in the moment. They were to speak from the "I" and from the moment, and "listen from the perspective of the group."

One man took the rock. He spoke with deep passion about how rotten the current policy made him feel and how painful it was for him to explain it to his subordinates. He deeply wanted to change it. The rock passed from person to person. Sometimes the energy of an idea would cause someone to "piggyback" quickly on the idea or to finish someone's sentence, and people would laugh and say "remember the rock" or "you have to have the rock." The conversation sped up. It slowed down. There were periods of silence.

One person took the rock and said "I am not where I was when we started this conversation. Something really has changed my way of thinking." Bit by bit there emerged an entirely new way of conceiving the problem and shaping possible solutions, until finally, after a long silence, one person said "I see how we might work to change this...." He proposed a very participative and involving process for incubating a new approach, with a clear goal of greater fairness and equity. He volunteered to contribute his own financial gain to the pot to make it work. People began to weave together an approach that would have seemed impossible when they began the conversation. They ended in silence.

I asked if they felt finished and settled with this issue that they had been gnawing at for months and years. They said "yes," perhaps sensing that each of them had a clear idea of the collective goal, and would immediately do whatever could be done to move forward on this work, realizing that after this conversation there was no way not to do what they had given voice to.

What is dialogue then, as it emerges in this experience?

In a sense, dialogue is not complicated. It is good conversation, over the "back fences" of our lives. It is continued, thoughtful exchange about the things that most matter. It is time to sit under the apple tree together and talk, as the ideas and thoughts come to us, without agenda, without time pressures. It is the kind of conversation that we have forgotten in the pace of western, modern life. Or, in the language of both Maya Angelou and Paula Underwood, who speak to us from the African-American and Native American traditions respectively, from cultures that practiced dialogue, it is reminding us of "that which we have forgotten to remember."

The concept of dialogue comes to us from many historical and contemporary sources. One form of it comes out of the Greek tradition of Socratic dialogue in which the student is led by the master to a greater level of wisdom. Some form of dialogue is found in most traditional pre-industrial and pre-agricultural societies. It is particularly visible in the Native American culture, where the process acknowledges that it is necessary to "talk and talk until the talk starts."

In contemporary management literature, dialogue figures most prominently in the work of Peter Senge's *The Fifth Discipline*, where it serves as one of the processes central to systems thinking. It finds its intellectual roots in the work of British physicist David Bohm. Various forms of dialogue are reflected in the work of Bill Isaacs and his colleagues with the MIT Dialogue Project, in the work on "organization as community" and the concept of work as "nourishment for life" of the Naerings Liv project of Juanita Brown and David Isaacs, in the exploration of corporate strategy employed by Diana Smith, and in the work about the nature of learning and inquiry of Parker Palmer. All of us are part of a contemporary, virtual community exploring the power of dialogue, in a variety of different ways.

The pattern of dialogue requires new ways of thinking about and evaluating communication. If the goal of communication is to decide something or do something, we are unable to discern the way in which dialogue enables individuals to focus their personal energies so that they can go forth and act in a remarkable level of concert. We may believe that, without action plans or coordination or checking, focused action seems impossible. However, such patterns have been noted in the modes of communicating of Asian and Native American cultures.

Dialogue taps ways of communicating not often represented in the dominant Western culture—ways that may be more reflective of minority cultures, of marginal cultures, or the cultures less visible in our organizational world. These ways are not going to feel comfortable or familiar for leadership elites which have achieved great success by communicating in modes decidedly un-dialogue-like.

Dialogue is a different and often unfamiliar way of being together in communication. We should acknowledge that and be prepared for it. If we overlook the unfamiliarity of this mode of communicating, we will also make it unlikely that others can accurately evaluate its benefit in our organizational lives. Instead, we will mistakenly evaluate it in traditional modes (of decisions taken by meeting's end and measures of closure) and judge it within the time bounds of the meeting, rather than in the longer and more important time frames of future action and alignment.

In negotiating with Asians, many North Americans consider the process of talking and silence without any seeming progress to be pointless and unproductive. The same North Americans have found the level of accord and speed of implementation quite astonishing. Seldom do they realize the relationship between the slowness of speaking and the ease of implementation.

In very powerful dialogues, I have found participants unwilling to evaluate the experience during the session. In one case, after I had asked the group to evaluate a pilot experience with dialogue, one usually driven and outcome-oriented executive said to me after a long period of collective silence, "I cannot do this. I can't evaluate this. For three days we have engaged in a level of communication and exploration, the likes of which I have not experienced before. I, for one, am not willing to stop the dialogue in order to evaluate it. For three days we have suspended judging and instead we have listened to each other. I'm not going to stop now."

Yet the practice of dialogue is not without its dark side, its seeming dangers for people. We know from heatedly negative reports of "dialogue sessions" that for some people the process is powerful, for others it is "full of sound and fury, signifying nothing." For still others it may open their understanding in ways that are emotionally overwhelming and that the process is not prepared to help them handle. There may be instances in which dialogue leaders are using the intensity of the mode for their own purposes, subtly and invisibly manipulating the process to meet their own needs.

Because it makes space for people to explore very difficult things, this methodology must be handled with great care—very gently and very ethically. This means that we must, as those designing and leading dialogues, be aware of our own power and of the seductive power of the process and ensure that it is not coercive. We must build real safety within the experience.

What purpose does dialogue serve?

I think of dialogue as seeking to build deeper understanding, new perceptions, new models, new openings, new paths to effective action, and deeper and more enduring, even sustainable, truths. Dialogue's purpose is to honor development of individuals and ideas and organizations, at a very deep level. It opens paths to change and clears space for organizational transformation by changing the inner landscape. We change the world by changing the way we perceive the world, the way we think about cause and effect, the way we conceptualize the relationships among things, and the meaning we ascribe to events in that external world. Organizational change means changing our internal landscapes as leaders. Such change is undertaken by us only when we reach a place in our lives where we want to change those landscapes. Such changes are encouraged by the openness and the reflective and collective process of dialogue. Dialogue opens pathways for change—within us and among us. From that opening comes space for organizational and social change.

Most of the traditional thinking about change is more mechanistic, and shows change as structured and planned, change as engineered and driven into organizations. We believe that resistance is a necessary component of managing change. We say that managing change means managing resistance. Perhaps we should note instead that resistance is a natural part of managing change the way we have managed it so far. It is "natural" no doubt, when change is managed in instrumental, mechanistic ways. But dialogue builds capacities that dissolve resistance.

What capacity does dialogue build within us?

Dialogue builds capacities in the same way that exercise builds capacities in the human body, slowly and over time giving us new strength.

Those capacities may include:

- Listening as an ally, listening for understanding, for the piece of the mosaic that might be missing from our own and the collective understanding, the piece which is key to a decision or to successful implementation.

- Asking questions from a "place of genuine not knowing." Dialogue increases our skills at inquiry.

- Allowing for the time and space to finish a thought. Bringing forth thoughts in real time that are not finished, that are fresh and passionate and alive.

- Finding value in silence, in time to think, in reflection.

- Granting others the respect of being an authority about their own thoughts and feelings.

- Noticing our own internal responses and learning to coexist with those responses. We notice what is happening in our response to an idea, without needing to actually respond.

- Building a hospitable, bounded and open place for the consideration of perspectives so that we can build a powerful mosaic of common understanding.

- Learning to be provoked and not close down, to step into the center of the provocation, to consider equally the ideas which provoke us and those that resonate with us.

- Learning to listen deeply without the urge to fix, nor counter, nor argue.

- Noticing the nature of our thinking. We learn to give up blaming and judging others, and to become more compassionate with ourselves.

- Dialogue helps us to develop the capacity to move into and toward difficult issues in a welcoming fashion because we can notice the difficulty without being "hooked."

We come then to understand dialogue as a way to build mental, spiritual and interpersonal muscle with power in our lives and in our organizations. It builds it, not overnight, but over time and that muscle develops differently in different people.

I recall a dialogue with a CEO and part of his leadership team on "freeing the human spirit." Originally I had designed this strategic dialogue as being about "quality, diversity and change."

But the CEO had said that while he realized that such specific topics were more understandable to engineers like himself, the real challenge to the corporation was "freeing the human spirit" and we might as well say it straight out. He was convinced that we had to learn to make it possible for people to come to work with all the talents, energies, and power that were potentially theirs. Now we were in the midst of a three day exploration of how to free the human spirit, and were using excerpts of readings from a broad range of literature (Martin Luther King, Peter Senge, Charles Handy, Paula Underwood, Carol Gilligan, and others) to spark our conversation. We were talking about learning, and knowing, and mental models.

The morning's readings began with Plato's "Allegory of a Cave" in which the ancient Greek philosopher describes human beings chained to a wall, looking at shadows cast by figures behind them, figures which, because of the chains, they don't know exist. They see the shadows as the only possible reality. This is the conversation about mental models and how we know what we know, from over 2000 years ago. Tough and serious questions emerged.

"Once we've been out of the chains and realize the nature of reality, what are we required to do?" someone asks. "We're required to return to the cave...," someone answers. "And?" Long silence. "And tell the others what we've learned." "Or to take their hand and lead them out." "But they are still chained." One executive, a senior woman says, "I don't want your hand. I just want you to listen to me." Stunned silence. What does it mean to listen to those we believe are chained? Who are wrong? Who are not yet enlightened? The question is still on my mind eighteen months later. And on theirs.

In a later dialogue, a group of engineers is wrestling with the same reading. I have given them a task: "Draw the cave that Plato describes. Do the specs of the cave." A group of men are circled around the flip-chart calling out to the man with the magic marker "No, no, it says right here that there is a wall in the back of the cave, and so it would have to be this way, so the light comes in at an angle...." Detail by detail they sketch the cave, more and more clearly. As they finish, one engineer says "Well, you could draw it the way we have, or...," he says, flipping to a clean sheet of newsprint, and doing a quick sketch "you could draw it like this." His sketch is of the human brain. There is silence.

After a small group dialogue about what Martin Luther King

had to say to us in his "Letter from the Birmingham Jail," and
after reflecting about what great gap King would now point to
between our vision and the current reality, about what he would
require of us, and about what action we should take, one of the
plant leaders says, "My life is changed by this letter. How could
we ever have seen King as just a trouble-maker? The issues he
raises are for all of us, not just for Blacks. I, for one, am going to
take this letter back and read it with my guys in the plant. We all
have to read this and talk about what it means for us."

How do we start dialogue and how do we sustain it?

There are many possible prompts or beginning points to
dialogue: meditation, quiet, writing, reflective exercises, readings, music, the practice of certain communications techniques.
Bohm suggested that there be no explicit prompts, no formal
process, yet many of us may find it less daunting to enter a space
of dialogue by following some recognizable road signs, or paths.

For me, perhaps because my early training was in literature, I find the written word, particularly carefully excerpted
pieces of literature from diverse genres and diverse cultures, an
effective prompt to dialogue. People have said to me that because
of such readings received and read in advance, they find themselves in a different frame of mind when they arrive at a dialogue,
as if they have begun an internal dialogue already, which then
becomes collective and involves the voices of others, when they
come together with others around the table. The readings create
a reflective space in advance of our coming together. Readings
that are classic, or from other cultures, remind us of the serious-
ness and importance of those issues with which we are struggling, and they remind us that the thoughts of others can be a
resource to us in the struggle.

I would suggest, moreover, that whatever the opening to
dialogue, it should encourage our examining of our own assumptions, and ways of thinking, and it should also move us to
consider different ways of thinking that allow for healthy change.

We might characterize dialogue as a profound openness to
the vitality of real diversity. It is a process which, even with a
facilitator, produces a collective examination of ideas, a collective
sense of participation, and a collective wisdom. It is a collective
process in which wisdom emerges not from our finding the
appropriate path of thinking like the wise one at the head of
the table, but rather from coming to a deeper understanding

than any one of us had to begin with.

Dialogue is perhaps born out of a sense of incompleteness, of needing something more, and of being hungry for something that is currently beyond us. It seems to reflect a collective sense of needing to move beyond where we are at the moment, without necessarily having a destination in mind nor a particular problem or crisis that pushes us. It is an inquiry, a questioning, a wanting to move to a more satisfying place, together.

What contributes to dialogue?

Here is my list of what contributes to dialogue. I encourage your additions, from your own experience:

a. Readings, sent out in advance, which put people in a different frame of mind; they model the image of multiple voices and perspectives, over time and space, and make considering the diverse wisdom within the room less of a leap since we are already considering the wisdom from outside the room. Individual reflective writing, completed quietly as a prelude to dialogue, is also very effective.

b. A program design which focuses on "emptying" a space for people to fill with reflections, rather than filling an already-crowded space with more concepts.

c. The choice of a setting which is reflective, calm, away from the fray.

d. A round table or circle to give people a sense of shared leadership and to allow all individuals to see each other more completely, listen more completely, and be heard more completely.

e. Communication about the process that puts people in a frame of mind to slow down, back off, listen, and reflect. Here we must attend to the introduction of the process in a way that meets people where they are and enables them to settle into the process. It is important not to suggest that dialogue is something that only the initiated can do. Dialogue taps a capacity in each of us that can easily come to the surface, given the space in our lives to do so.

It is important to set the stage in quiet ways, ways that value who people are and where they are, and in ways that open pathways to dialogue. Beginning with some thoughts about the process itself and having individuals do some quiet work on personal perspective-setting is helpful. I often begin with Ira Progoff's stepping stones exercise, asking people to list for their own reflection the steppingstones that have brought them to where they are in their lives as a way to put this present time of their lives in perspective. Sometimes I provide simple written or verbal guidance on dialogue, for each of us to use to reflect on our own contributions to the process. The guidance includes:

- Speak from the heart and the moment, and from your own experience; listen from the community, from the collective;
- Listen without thinking about responding;
- Listen for information, not confirmation;
- Begin thinking in terms of "I wonder..." or "Where I am on this issue now is...;"
- Allow for silence; it may mean people are thinking, considering;
- Suspend assumptions and consider alternative ones that might be just as useful;
- Assume that the ideas and observations of others come from a desire to contribute;
- Expect that ideas build upon each other even if they don't link logically one to the other;
- Remember that difference of opinion can be helpful, because it sharpens our understanding;
- Move away from conclusions and toward observations; notice what you are noticing, and what meaning you are making of it;
- Sometimes in communication, less is better, and slowly is fine.

With this guidance, I believe we help people rediscover the power of dialogue, the capacity for its emergence everywhere in their lives and in their organizations.

Conclusion

Let me end with two stories on the capacity in each of us for dialogue, and the potential for dialogue to emerge anywhere, everywhere, even in the most unexpected places, when we give it space to do so.

I was working with a global organization examining the potential for becoming a learning organization in order to increase its effectiveness with its clients. Forty of its young stars— peppery, hard-charging, talented people from all over the world— had been together for a week. As part of our work on shared vision, I had asked them to draw pictures of their individual visions of us as a learning community. Remarkable pictures emerged on the sheets of newsprint, which were posted on the walls. One man said, as he was drawing a pattern of different colored X's to represent the group, "Wow, it's in the shape of a heart." The man beside him said "You stole my idea...," as he, too, found that his pattern was heart-shaped. We sat in a circle on the floor with our art work taped to the walls as a backdrop and dropped into a deep, quiet space of dialogue, talking quietly and slowly about what we saw in the drawings as we worked on them. Our dialogue ended and we were back in our seminar room, out of the circle, in the rows of chairs. One of the men said, "That was a remarkable conversation, but I don't see how it could happen with clients, or with our partners. I don't see how we could do it. It's easy for you," he said of me, "to lead us to such a deep place because that's your work, but I can't imagine," he said, searching for words, "that we could get the average...teamster, for instance...to participate in such a dialogue." It was as if he had punched me in the stomach with his words. Before I could censor my words, I blurted out: "I started my work life as a teamster." There was stunned silence. For a minute. Two minutes. Longer. Then a quiet voice from the back of the room said, "I think I just adjusted my mental model."

Months later, I was flying home after a long stretch on the road. The big jet was full. I'd been upgraded to First Class where the only empty seat was next to me. The wind was so strong that it was rocking the big plane while we were still at the departure gate. The last passenger strode on board and slid past me into the window seat on my left. He was a big scruffy man, tattooed, with an unruly beard. The flight attendant asked if he'd like anything to drink "A double whiskey," he said. "I hate to fly." I thought it was going to be a long ride home.

As we lifted off in the great shaking gusts of wind, he regaled me loudly with stories of how the rich were soaking life out of the working poor and why the unions (of which he was a representative) were being decimated by the efforts of the rich to get the little guys. It was getting very cool in First Class. Then he was quiet and so was I. After some time he said, "Look down there. Isn't it beautiful? Sometimes I think how it must have looked thousands of years ago to those who lived here. When I go on vacations with my family, I drive them nuts, because I like to go to cemeteries where great people have been buried and sit next to their tombstones and think what they have done for us, for all of us." Another long silence followed. As we approached Washington he said, "It really is beautiful down there. You know, we're funny, we human beings. We buy all those lottery tickets in hopes that some day we will win the big prize and what we don't realize is that we won the prize the day we were born."

Sherrin Bennett (left) is president of Interactive Learning Systems, an international consulting firm and publisher of multimedia "tools for change." Her clients include corporations, national governments, educational and health systems in the United States, South Asia, and Scandinavia, including Cathay Pacific Airlines, the United Nations Development Program, Kraft General Foods, Procter & Gamble, Aspen Institute and National Semiconductor.

Juanita Brown (right) is president of Whole Systems Associates, an international consulting consortium dedicated to strategic change management. She has worked with corporate clients throughout the United States, Europe and Latin America. Brown has served as program faculty at the John F. Kennedy University School of Management, the California Institute of Integral Studies, and the University of Monterrey, Mexico. She is a Fellow of the World Business Academy and has served as a member of the core team with the Dialogue Project at MIT.

11

Mindshift:
Strategic Dialogue for
Breakthrough Thinking

Sherrin Bennett and Juanita Brown

> *Strategic planning is not strategic thinking. One is analysis and the other is synthesis....Through the discoveries based on serendipitous events and the recognition of unexpected patterns, learning inevitably plays a, if not the, crucial role in the development of novel strategies.*
>
> —Mintzberg

How can we as a team improve the way we think about the work we do? What strategic challenges do we face? What dilemmas have we encountered that need to be resolved? Questions such as these lie at the heart of strategic dialogue, a special type of collaborative inquiry which supports the discovery of breakthrough insights that can substantially improve business results.

Strategic dialogue is built on the operating principle that the stakeholders in any system already have within them the wisdom and creativity to confront even the most difficult challenges. Given the appropriate context and support, it is possible for members of an organizational community to access this deeper knowledge about underlying causes and leverage points for change. The role of outside content "experts" is minimized in favor of the kind of support that allows members to draw deeply on their own "memory of the whole" in order to think in systemic ways about key challenges and opportunities.

Strategic innovation is more likely to occur in an organization when its members are able to articulate the mental models which shape key decisions as well as the deeper beliefs and core assumptions underlying both thinking and action. Strategic dialogue enhances this capacity for interactive learning, transforming new knowledge into coordinated action. The reflective skills developed in strategic dialogue can help strengthen the organization's resiliency and sustainable advantage in a rapidly changing environment.

In this essay we explore the strategic imperative, the spirit of inquiry, the dynamics of dialogue, and the way that learning happens among a collaborative team. The "scenario" which begins each section of this essay and the conceptual reflection which follows invite you to join the inquiry regarding the practical ways strategic dialogue can serve businesses and communities, as well as public and private institutions, as they struggle with the deeper questions at the heart of creating a positive future.

Scenario 1: The Strategic Imperative

Our leadership team was uneasy. Our responsibility was to chart the organization's strategic course. In recent strategic planning sessions we had studied trend data, statistical reports, financial results, and forecasting models. Our company's mission, vision, and values had been distributed widely throughout the company.

Still, something was missing. Even though we were not in crisis, it was clear the game was changing. The next stage in the life of our company would require a quality of thinking and strategic insight that our traditional planning process somehow never seemed to produce. We knew that our choices and the thinking behind them were more important than ever. They would impact not only our business results but our key relationships with employees, customers, suppliers, the community, and other groups with a stake in our future.

I had been exploring new approaches to organizational learning and coordinated action involving companies like ours. Strategic dialogue had appeared as one approach which seemed to show real promise for the kinds of issues we were facing. When

I shared this with my team, they perked up. I had heard that strategic dialogue enables people to look beneath the surface to the core assumptions and operating principles which underlie thinking about current strategies in order to discover innovative possibilities and see the whole picture.

Even though some team members were skeptical, they agreed to experiment with strategic dialogue. One member commented, "Well, it can't hurt. This strategic dialogue stuff seems kind of like an investment in R & D. We spend millions of dollars and huge amounts of time. Sometimes we get a hit and sometimes we don't. We still make the investment though, because, if we get a breakthrough in our thinking, it can make a big difference to our future. Let's go for it and see what happens." Another added, "Well, if we learn something interesting we can begin to test it with other folks and begin to link it into the regular planning process."

We agreed to go off-site to experiment with strategic dialogue in an effort to understand our strategic issues more clearly. We realized that, like all development work, strategic dialogue was not a one-shot deal. It would involve a number of follow-up conversations. I knew that team members held very different views on the company's challenges. I wondered if there would be conflict once we really began to look under the surface.

Making Decisions of Strategic Importance

We are all faced with the challenge of making decisions of strategic importance in the face of critical uncertainties. These are decisions in our personal lives as well as those taken by a management team on behalf of the organization. Decisions are strategic in nature, according to Peter Vaill, when the choice:

- involves commitment of significant resources,
- may move the organization into a new domain not in the organization's prior experience, "a whole new ball game,"
- involves long cycle feedback—it won't be known for some time if the decision was a wise one and if the intended benefits are occurring,
- will have lasting impact.

The strategic imperative is to reflect on these choices using the highest quality of collective thinking. We are all too familiar with "group think" which has been described as the tendency to confirm our existing assumptions without question in order to avoid conflict or responsibility and to save face among peers.

Even the fact that the current assumptions guiding business strategy have been rewarded with past success doesn't guarantee that they are appropriate in today's rapidly changing environment. High stakes in the midst of uncertainty creates the genuine imperative for strategic thinking.

Strategy-Making Requires both Analysis and Synthesis

In his 1994 article in the *Harvard Business Review*, "The Rise and Fall of Strategic Planning," Henry Mintzberg makes an important distinction. Strategic thinking must integrate what executives learn from all sources—from their own and other's experience, from analysis of financial data, and from trends in the larger environment—into a coherent sense of direction for the business. *Strategic planning isn't strategic thinking. One is analysis and the other is synthesis.* They inform one another. Strategic planning, with its usual focus on analysis of trend data and performance figures, has not proved adequate to produce breakthrough thinking among management teams. It does not assure that core assumptions will be explored and improved. Planning often relies on outside expertise in a way that doesn't create and refine shared mental models to guide decision-making throughout the organization. Strategic dialogue creates a continuing conversation in parallel with the regular cycle of strategic planning. It supports a team in doing what Ikujiro Nonaka has called articulating the company's "conceptual umbrella"—identifying the core concepts that link seemingly disparate activities into a coherent whole.

Strategic Thinking is Generative Learning

Strategic thinking identifies and resolves dilemmas at the heart of strategic issues by shifting the context in which they are understood. Exploring questions of strategic importance together allows team members to examine their mental models or sets of working assumptions about what drives the business, the intentions of their competitors, the customers' needs, and the dynamics in the larger environment. Shifts in the core assumptions that guide business strategy are a major source of innovation that can create the organization's most significant growth opportunities. Done well, strategic thinking assures resiliency and informs coherent decision-making in a rapidly changing environment. It is a practice that helps the enterprise to become a learning organization, which Peter Senge has described as an organization that is continually expanding its ability to create its future.

Metaphor and Analogy Provide a Language of the Whole

In his landmark 1986 book, *Images of Organization,* Gareth Morgan explores how strategic objectives are embedded in dominant metaphors that guide the organization.

> *Organizations enact metaphors. To manage an organization as if you were operating a mechanism, steering a ship or wielding a weapon is to embody that metaphor in action. Managers may unwittingly construct a reality they dread through an incapacity to reflect upon the metaphor in use.*

Senior managers give voice to a company's future by articulating metaphors, symbols, and concepts that orient the knowledge creating activities of employees. These images shape the organization's possible future. Shift in strategy often requires a shift in guiding image.

Strategic dialogue becomes a forum for exploring these guiding images and the deeper assumptions which give rise to them. In strategic dialogue, the language of metaphor and analogy helps us move from tacit or implicit knowing to the explicit realm where, together, we can see relationships and strategic opportunities that were not evident before. As Susan Bethanis points out on page 189, "Metaphors make language come alive: language becomes action...."

Figure 1
Engaging the Dialogue

Scenario 2: The Spirit of Inquiry

Our leadership team gathered for the dialogue in the large library of a nearby inn. The comfortable chairs and warm tones created an atmosphere of relaxation and informality as we sat in a circle to begin. I opened the conversation. "Strategic dialogue may help us chart new territory and make new maps. We have all our trip equipment and supplies—ourselves and our previous experiences with the dilemmas we are facing as well as all the information and data we could ever want. Let's go for it."

Then I introduced Carlos, a skilled facilitator, and Janis, a specialist in visual language and systems thinking. Janis would use the large wall panels that surrounded us on several sides to record in words and images the linkages and patterns of our key ideas as they emerged. To begin, Carlos asked us each to "check-in" around the circle by first reflecting on the following and then sharing our thoughts.

If there were one core question that underlies all the strategic challenges you face, what would it be? Why is that question important to you?

Carlos asked us to listen carefully to each person and notice when our own question (or a better one that arose as we listened) could link to or build upon what we were hearing. He asked us to notice when we felt uncomfortable or disagreed since that could be a sign we were bumping up against our own assumptions. He emphasized that strategic dialogue is not about agreement or consensus. Rather, it's about listening for deeper understanding and insight. And that's not easy. I was surprised at how uncomfortable I felt with the ideas of several other members. I realized how hard it was to listen fully without jumping in with my own reactions.

As we were checking in, Janis was recording our questions with colorful graphics on the large wall panels. After the check-in we were invited to go on a "gallery tour" to begin to get a "feel" for the questions which had been contributed. People seemed intrigued and started to comment on common threads.

As we adjourned for the evening we knew that whatever happened, this was going to be an important conversation. I could tell that people weren't yet saying all that was on their minds but this opening session had been different and engaging. People left curious to see what would happen when they gathered the next morning. Many went to the lounge to continue talking.

Creating a Spirit of Inquiry

One of the fundamental goals of the early phases of strategic dialogue is to create a climate of discovery, questioning, and exploration—even mystery and adventure. Without this *spirit of inquiry*, it is more difficult to move through the tension that often accompanies the process of strategic dialogue. Developing a spirit of inquiry is also important in order to reach the deeper understanding of underlying assumptions, organizing images, and core beliefs that are crucial to strategic thinking. In the early stages of a gathering there are several key elements that can help "create the context" and evoke the spirit of inquiry:

- Choose a setting where the normal distractions can be minimized.
- Encourage informality, relaxation, and personal relationships.
- Assure that all voices are heard and "in the circle" from the very beginning. Create opportunities early for members to discover what they have *in common.* For example, it is useful to hear the ways in which people, despite their differences, care about the challenges they face together.
- Honor the knowledge that is alive in the people present. Evoke initial questions that will enable members to look toward the "heart of the matter" from their own experience of the situation.
- Focus on questions which create curiosity, "wondering" and anticipation rather than abstract lists of issues or topics.
- Acknowledge that it is normal for people to experience uncomfortable as well as comfortable reactions to others' perspectives.
- Demonstrate innovative and interesting tools, like visual language and graphic recording which enable people to begin to "see" the connections between ideas.

The Art of Strategic Questioning

The properly shaped question always emanates from an essential curiosity about what stands behind. Questions are the keys that cause the secret doors...to swing open. What is behind the visible?
—Clarissa Pinkola Estes

Strategic questioning plays an important role establishing that the deeper insight we seek is "findable" through the dialogue. Fran Peavey, a pioneer in the architecture of powerful questions, shows how they serve to energize a "resonant field into which our own thinking is magnified, clarified and new motion can be created."

Continuing to focus on questions rather than answers in a strategic inquiry has a paradoxical impact on the evolution of both individual insight and collaborative discovery. Clear, bold, and penetrating questions which elicit a full range of dynamic responses and energy tend to open the social context for learning. They enable individual members to discover that we need not be limited by our individual isolated positions or static political alliances.

Questioning together begins to demonstrate that as individuals we have the capacity to become part of something larger than ourselves. Those in the dialogue begin to *share* a concern for deeper levels of shared meaning. People begin to realize "If we continue to think like we've always thought, we'll continue to get what we've already got." It rapidly becomes clear that, in these dynamic and turbulent times, "what we've already got" will not create the kind of future we desire.

Paying Attention to the Words and the Music

Inquiring into our most critical challenges and simultaneously *noticing* the way we think about them has the potential to yield insights which neither can do alone. As members experiment with strategic dialogue, they realize that the way we *think* about things is in large measure the source of fragmentation, reactiveness, and competition in modern organizational life. Most interestingly, the organizational community begins to discover that they, together, have the power to change these modes of thinking into more coherent, integrated, satisfying, and effective ways both of being and of doing.

Scenario 3: The Dynamics of Dialogue

The next morning we began to delve more deeply into the core strategic questions which we generated the previous evening and added others as they arose. We established a rhythm of work in which we periodically "stopped action" to reflect on our own working process and to notice the principles and practices of the dialogue itself as it unfolded. Carlos encouraged us to notice both

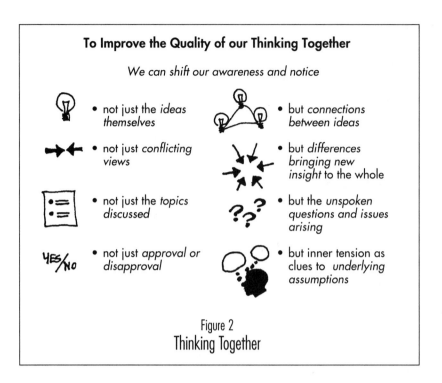

To Improve the Quality of our Thinking Together

We can shift our awareness and notice

- not just the *ideas* themselves
- but *connections between ideas*

- not just *conflicting views*
- but *differences bringing new insight* to the whole

- not just the *topics discussed*
- but the *unspoken questions and issues arising*

- not just *approval or disapproval*
- but inner tension as clues to *underlying assumptions*

Figure 2
Thinking Together

what was happening within ourselves as well as among the team as a whole.

We did not dampen or "cool down" passionate stances as too dangerous to handle. We learned to see each other's passion and advocacy not as an indicator of one person being closed to others but as a sign of deep caring about a question. Rather than "cooling it down" we were encouraged to "slow it down" so that we could "listen into" the varied perspectives that were being expressed.

We were asked to listen underneath the tone and style and even the words to search for the special contribution that might be present in each person's offering to the conversation. At one point, a member of the group who had been silent through most of the morning commented, "I'm just realizing as I try to listen to what we're saying here that even though we're all from the same company we speak different languages. We don't mean the same thing even when we use the same words. No wonder we have trouble thinking together."

That started us on a path of exploring more deeply what people were saying—the distinctions and interpretations embedded in the language we used—the meaning beyond the positions.

All the while, the graphic recorder was capturing key ideas and images and the group began to help the recorder, making sure that what she was capturing reflected the essence of what we thought was being shared. "It's really amazing how Janis seems to be building a kind of web out of our different viewpoints," the Director of Operations commented.

But, it wasn't easy. People felt frustrated as they got stuck in their long-held certainties. At times, things got polarized. Slowly we learned to see polarization as a resource—an opportunity to see how we identify positions with people and then "take sides." At one point Carlos asked, "Is there some common pattern underneath the apparent irreconcilable differences here?"

That did it. We began to see that what we had in common was our rigidly held assumptions and beliefs. No matter how apparently "right" they seemed to one or more of us, our "noble certainties" were inhibiting our capacity to see new possibilities for strategic leverage and coordinated action. Like peeling an onion, we began to "unpack" the assumptions underlying the different positions and the perspectives being explored.

By this time, the conflicts which flared up earlier and the differences that seemed to divide people began to take on a new tone. People began to metaphorically place their different points of view into the center of the circle or graphically onto the wall panels to be "held by all." Our frustration and fragmentation was yielding to a new level of coherence and collaboration as we began to "think together."

Weaving a Web of Connections

Dialogue is a process of collaborative conversation. Bill Isaacs, Director of the MIT Dialogue Project which has conducted pioneering research in this area, emphasizes that it differs markedly from the casual discourse of daily life, persuasive discussion, negotiation, or formal debate. Dialogue is most useful for learning about complexity where no one has "the answer." Rather than trying to understand an issue by breaking it into its parts, the practice of dialogue draws attention to the whole. As each person offers a unique contribution to the conversation, the intent is not to persuade but to explore from another perspective. Together, people in dialogue weave a web of connections between their own thoughts and what has been said before. Gareth Morgan points out that the process of strategic insight that emerges "is always dependent upon reciprocal connectivity that can never be predicted and controlled."

Embracing Diverse Perspectives

Like a photographer exploring various perspectives of a subject, each comment offers a picture from a different vantage point in an effort to tell the whole story. The whole picture in soft focus brings better understanding than detailed pictures of fragmented parts. Each person adds to the common pool of ideas rather than trying to prove or persuade from their own point of view. Part-

Figure 3
Creating the Field of Shared Meaning

ners in dialogue are challenged to find a *coherent interpretation of their multiple perspectives.* Each comment is seen as true in its own right and as a valuable clue essential to revealing the mystery of the whole. This expectant attitude can ignite the sparks of insight that bring about innovation.

Noticing the Dialogue Within Us and Between Us

In the practice of dialogue, participants focus both on the dialogue within and the dialogue among themselves. When we hear another speak from their unique perspective, we typically notice a process of comparison that goes on within the listener sensing whether or not the other's meaning matches our own. Agree or disagree? Disagreement is often felt as tension within the body and is expressed as defensive reaction or restatement of our own preferred view. Agreement usually leads to head nodding and statements in support of the other. This judgment generates the usual argument or debate.

Strategic dialogue goes deeper. We move from advocacy to inquiry and from evaluation to exploration in service of the whole. When feeling disagreement, we search for differences in the assumptions or core beliefs underlying our views. This practice deepens the conversation into dialogue. As each of us reflects on and shares our underlying assumptions it becomes clear that others have constructed their own knowledge and meaning in another way.

Allowing Listening to Transform Us

Listening deeply and taking in the other's meaning, we risk being changed by what we hear. In this sense, listening is a radical act. The willingness to allow this process to unfold gives dialogue its transformative power. We cannot enter into the mutuality of dialogue while maintaining defensive and reactive postures. It requires humility, softening our certainties, and allowing ourselves to learn and change in the company of one another. Through mutual reflection, dialogue begins to clarify the places where our assumptions are tangled or seem to contradict themselves. David Bohm suggested that dialogue can function like the immune system in the body. It clears up material that cannot be assimilated into the existing pattern of dis-ease. At a social level, dialogue recognizes and clears up the incoherence of our thought. This happens both within us and between us. Dialogue is a core process for improving our own "pictures of the world" as well as refining and extending the shared mental models that guide decision-making for the business. As a community of colleagues, we make shared meaning of our diverse perspectives and experiences by surfacing, testing, and improving our collective thinking in the context of a changing environment. This is the dynamic that makes concerted action possible. Nonaka points to the importance of this process for team learning in today's organizations:

> *Teams play a central role in the knowledge-creating company because they provide a shared context where individuals can interact with each other and engage in the constant dialogue on which effective reflection depends. Team members create new points of view through dialogue and discussion. They pool their information and examine it from various angles. Eventually, they integrate their diverse individual perspectives into a new collective perspective.*

Using Visual Thinking

The integration of the verbal with the visual is very important to the emerging practice of strategic dialogue. Our minds make meaning through analogy, symbol, and metaphor. Graphic recording and the use of visual as well as verbal language during strategic dialogues assists in clarifying the underlying metaphors, symbols, and core images that are at play in a strategic inquiry. Visual recording helps illuminate the group's perspective on the whole because they are literally surrounded by the larger picture as it emerges around them in the room. It enables relational thinking to emerge organically from the conversation.

Visual recording and the interdependencies it highlights often become the platform for more formal learning regarding systemic patterns and underlying structures influencing desired outcomes. Computer microworlds and other systems dynamics tools then serve as powerful and exciting vehicles for deepening the organization's strategic capability. The combined verbal and visual approach also allows incoherence, fragmentation, and polarities to be noticed and experienced more immediately and acutely. "This just doesn't make sense." "What's the pattern here?" "How come the pieces don't fit together?" "There's a 'hole in our thinking' and the missing piece is over there in the upper right hand corner."

Scenario 4: Shift Happens

By this time the room was alive. The tone was spontaneous, playful, irreverent. The team was beginning to have "serious fun." Several of the walls and the large panels surrounding the circle were covered with drawings, diagrams, and key phrases reflecting areas of connection or need for further exploration. There was a special wall panel which contained subjects on which people felt they had reached a common perspective or a greater sense of clarity. These were not agreements or decisions but rather key leverage areas where we had come to share a new frame of reference within which to see our challenges and core strategic questions. It was not the shift of "content" but rather the shift of "context" that seemed to make all the difference and opened new possibilities.

It had become clear that no one had all the answers. One of the guys said, "Whew! I thought I had it all figured out before I even came in here the other night, but I think we've got to deepen our understanding and explore the larger picture. I don't think we've ever really gotten this close to the heart of it before." One of the women in the group said, "You know, we've all been really humming together. It's great but we've been at it now for several hours non-stop. It's amazing how time has seemed to dissolve. Maybe we should take a little walk and get out in the fresh air. Let's just take some alone time to see what new ways of thinking might come up.

When we reconvened, people were very thoughtful. There had been pauses in the conversation before, but this time the silence seemed to have a different quality. The tension of earlier times in the conversation was gone and people simply sat together, enjoying the quiet.

One of the members spoke up, "Something different is happening here. It feels like we are all a part of something important that is larger than just ourselves in this room." The Finance Director added, "I really believe that the questions we have been exploring are going to make a difference not only for the company's bottom line but also for us personally. The head of Sales added, "This kind of thinking together can also make a difference for our employees, our customers and suppliers, and the larger community. Somehow, we've come to another level together." The marketing guy commented, "I have confidence in the direction we are sensing here but it's important to now explore these questions and insights with others. We need to continue these meetings ourselves and also begin these kinds of conversations with larger circles of people who have a stake with us in the future of the company."

The Pot Thickens

We feel a shift of mind when learning happens—Aha! Learning in community means getting to "aha" together. As Senge has said, "Through learning we re-perceive the world and our relationship to it....A learning organization is a place where people are continually discovering how they create their reality and how they can change it."

What are the conditions that make this shift possible? Strategic dialogue is like making a good stew. At first the broth seems watery and thin. We add ingredients with different textures and flavors while spices bring their special aroma to the mix. We continue to stir. As we keep the heat on, there is often a moment when we notice that "the pot thickens" and what, only a few moments ago, appeared to be a thin mixture has now become rich and fulfilling without losing the unique qualities of its original ingredients.

It's that way with strategic dialogue. We place our core

questions and strategic issues into the "stew," looking at them from different angles and perspectives. Simultaneously we become aware of the "heat" as we examine our own reactions and discomfort with others' perspectives and try to suspend the certainties and rigid assumptions that tend to hold us in their grip. No one loses their individuality or unique contribution to the stew. As the pot thickens, we discover we are a community sharing deeper understandings which feel rich and fulfilling.

In his research on psychological satisfaction, Mihaly Csikszentmihalyi has described the sense of total involvement in a satisfying activity as the experience of *flow* through which each of us integrates conscious experience into a meaningful whole. The "ahas" come as we recognize that a new integration is occurring. Like a kaleidoscope, where pieces of colored glass hold a pattern until a slow turn of the barrel causes them to suddenly cascade into a new configuration, generative learning creates coherence at a new level of complexity. The strategic insight that emerges out of complexity and chaos enjoys a simple elegance. It satisfies and creates the energy required for committed action.

Getting to the Heart of the Matter

In Spanish, there is the word *el meollo*. El meollo means the *essential nature or substance of that which is being seen or explored.* In strategic dialogue the search is for the essence, the source, the heart of things. It is symbolized by the center of a conch shell that has been cut to reveal the spiral pattern of growth. In the dialogue we sense a spiraling downward as we follow underlying assumptions and discover how they are linked. The

Figure 4
Getting to the Heart of the Matter

conversation deepens. Silence seems full rather than empty. And from this depth of reflection we return as the energy shifts releasing upward new insights and creative opportunities.

In dialogue, the process of change feels like giving birth to new meaning, out of which we realize creative possibilities for action. Then we know what Rainer Maria Rilke recognized: "That which we call the future goes forth from within...the future enters into us in order to transform itself long before it happens."

This is the unfolding of the implicate order Bohm described. With it comes the profound realization that the way we have linked concepts in our minds gives rise to patterns of thought and feeling as well as perception of the world and thus our actions in daily life. If we have difficulties, they are *our* difficulties, and the resolution of them often lies in re-conceiving with one another our pattern of thought itself. These cognitive structures frame the issues we perceive and our sense of what is worth doing.

The Opportunity and the Challenge

Strategic dialogue can provide a vehicle for focusing and deepening the ongoing conversations that Alan Webber has identified as critical for organizational success in the growing knowledge economy. The *opportunity* is for strategic dialogue to serve as one key approach for initiating and linking generative conversations and creative action throughout the organization. The *challenge* is to recognize innovations in thinking as they occur and to integrate them into an increasingly effective set of core assumptions and guiding images which enable the development of coherent strategy.

Strategic dialogue can help uncover patterns in apparent chaos, resolve strategic dilemmas, and open new possibilities. This type of learning expresses itself as *knowing in action* which does not require the level of formal planning and control that characterizes traditional hierarchies. Strategic dialogue encourages the kind of self-management required by the more flexible and responsive organizations that are now emerging.

In their research on the future of collaborative work and "communities of practice," John Seeley Brown and his Xerox PARC colleagues help us see that as learning conversations expand, larger numbers of stakeholders are encouraged to join the growing circles of informed participation and empowered action that form the foundation for a democratic society. New discoveries lead to new questions. New questions lead to new discoveries. A community of inquiry and commitment begins to form. Excitement and forward movement in the service of a shared vision for a positive future begins to happen.

Strategic dialogue can extend beyond the organization to include unions, customers, suppliers, and other stakeholders. It holds promise for conversations during the formation of strategic alliances and mergers. Strategic inquiry may be able to support more creative negotiated resolutions of intense regional conflicts. It may provide forums for engaging broader perspectives in the renewal of health, education, and government institutions.

With patience and discipline, the practice of strategic dialogue can become part of a dynamic and reinforcing process which helps create and strengthen the "communities of commitment," which Fred Kofman and Peter Senge emphasize lie at the heart of learning organizations capable of leading the way toward a sustainable future.

Susan J. Bethanis is an organization consultant and educator in the San Francisco Bay Area. Her primary work is in organization transformation; she emphasizes the critical relationship of language, communication, and change for leaders. She works with a variety of people in transnational and national companies, non-profit organizations, and county agencies in supporting their transformation efforts.

Bethanis holds a master's degree from Stanford University and a doctorate from the University of San Francisco, and she is an adjunct professor at USF. She is a member of the editorial board of *Vision/Action*, the journal of the Bay Area Organization Development Network.

The diversity of her experiences includes traveling in Asia and Europe. She has conducted participatory research in Thailand and China, and in 1993, she spoke at an international conference at Chiang Mai University. Her paper was entitled "The Language and Interactiveness of Leadership: An Interpretive Approach to Transformation."

12

Language as Action: Linking Metaphors with Organization Transformation

Susan J. Bethanis

A Meaningful Conversation

My life's work involves conversing with people in the business and non-profit sectors. Attending to words and interpreting the meaning of clients' and colleagues' stories is at the core of my organization transformation consulting practice. In my conversations, I consistently try to become aware of peoples' assumptions, reach mutual understanding, and offer ideas to create new meanings and new possibilities. These actions are at the center of interpersonal and organization change.

One afternoon a couple of years ago, I had a particularly illuminating conversation over lunch with Mark, a real estate broker in the Los Angeles area. At that time, not surprisingly, Mark had been deliberating as to whether or not he should get out of the business. He seemed to be having a conflict about his purpose. I clued into this because he mentioned, almost as an aside, that he always had to gear up to make *presentations* to potential sellers in order to drum up business. As he spoke, he was lamenting the discomfort of making presentations. I sat and listened a bit more. Then, I offered a suggestion: "Instead of going in and doing a *presentation* with these clients, why don't you sit down with them and just have a *conversation;* just sit and talk with them, like you are talking with me right now."

About a year later Mark came to San Francisco for a state-wide real estate convention. One night, he and I were having a conversation with his boss. At the time I was in the throes of writing my doctoral dissertation. Fittingly, Mark's boss asked me what I was writing about. This is always difficult to explain in a succinct manner. "It's about language and change in organizations, specifically how leaders understand what metaphors do in everyday situations," I said.

I started to offer some examples; however, Mark stepped in and said, "I know what you're talking about, Sue—it's what you told me that day a while back about having a *conversation* with my clients, that there is a distinction between *presentation* and *conversation*. That has made such a difference in my work! I use that language all the time now, in what I say, in my letters and memos. And I *think* so differently now about why I am doing real estate work." I smiled with contentment.

This revelatory moment—this shift in Mark's assumptions about how he "sells" his real estate services—was especially gratifying for me because Mark is my brother.

Now another year has passed; Mark had great results in 1993—tops in his company—and his community's peers nominated him for president of the Burbank Board of Realtors. He started his tenure in 1994 as the youngest president ever.

Language and Organization Transformation

In Mark's case, making distinctions between metaphors (e.g., *conversation* versus *presentation* as metaphors for sales strategy) led to shifts in his thought and action. It is important for both organization consultants and organization members to understand the link between language and organization transformation.

Think for a moment about two very different organizations with which you are associated. Perhaps one is the company where you work and the other is a community-based organization where you volunteer. If you are an organization consultant, envision two different client companies. Think of one metaphor that most aptly describes each of the organizations; here are some examples—organization as machine, culture, political arena, game, living organism, psychic prison, or family.

How we envision an organization in *language* is likely how

we move in it! How people act in a *machine*—a mechanistic entity made up of many components—is vastly different from how people act in an organization thought of as a *culture*. A *culture* emphasizes the interconnectedness of people. Organization cultural norms come from a blending of peoples' deeply held assumptions, thoughts, language, and actions. In a *machine*, people are isolated entities that input and disseminate information. In a *culture*, people interpret and create in a broad context; people are the organization, not a mere part of it.

Many theorists and practitioners whose thinking reflects past management "science" approaches suggest that, in order for transformation to take place, an organization must strategically change the structures—different parts—of that organization. This prevalent viewpoint flies in the face of the more *relationship-based* approach I described above. In her book *Leadership and the New Science*, Meg Wheatley points to the problems inherent in the *machine-like*, externally-focused approach to organization transformation:

> In organizations, we focused our attention on structure and organizational design, on gathering extensive numerical data, and on making decisions using sophisticated mathematical ratios. We've spent years moving pieces around, building elaborate models, contemplating more variables, creating more advanced forms of analysis. Until recently, we really believed that we could study the parts, no matter how many of them there were, to arrive at knowledge of the whole. We have reduced and described and separated things into cause and effect, and drawn the world in lines and boxes. A world based on machine images is a world filled with boundaries.

Rethinking the way we s*tructure* organizations will not transform organizations; rethinking the way we *think* may begin this process. This is not an easy task, nor is it a short-term answer to the presently perceived "ills" of organizations. Most of the time we want to "fix" things immediately. We solve problems based on what we already know. We want to get better at what we already do. A *culture*, as opposed to a *machine*, does not have fixed boundaries because people in conversation have the power to shift things by virtue of their relationships. People and their organizations will survive and prosper only if they discover new meaning in these conversations: they disclose different assumptions that provide the context for even more discoveries and new applications.

Structure vs. Culture

This distinction between *structure*—which is associated with an external, model-building motif—and *culture* is critical. The title of this book offers a good example. Originally, the title was "Learning Organizations: Developing *Structures* for Tomorrow's Workplace"; a week before the final manuscripts were due, the title was altered to include the word *Cultures* instead of *Structures.* The supportive and *generative* community that surrounded the editing of this book gave the opportunity for an author to suggest the change. This parallels a significant shift beginning to take place in organizations—going from *adaptive* learning organizations to *generative* ones. Generative cultures have no boundaries. People in *generative* cultures value the constant flow of ideas.

Valuing the purely observable, and constantly reacting and adapting based on these measurable observations, is giving way to a study and application of what's behind these behaviors—values, attitudes, deeply held assumptions, and everyday thoughts. There are also key connections being made between the individual and the organization (i.e., how shifting our assumptions or "mental models" and actions will shift an organization).

The role of language in this continuous process of organization transformation is not getting the same attention in the academic or practitioner's literature.

Language is a medium of change. There is an inextricable link between language, thought, and action. Language can also be a perpetuating medium because metaphors are embedded in the relationships that make up an organization. These metaphors are reinforced in the organization culture over and over—in discussions, internal written memos, marketing materials. These metaphors become tacit, or taken-for-granted. These assumptions, or root metaphors, eventually are not questioned, and we stop learning.

Sometimes metaphors perpetuate domination and control over people. For instance, military metaphors are often used for amplification. I have heard, and felt, numerous examples in my consulting experiences: "We'll need to *gather the troops* for that marketing meeting." "We have to *bite the bullet* on that account." "It's a *minefield* out there. It's important to *divide and conquer* when you are heading this project." Of course, these type of metaphors infiltrate—and create—culture on many layers. One use of language that I found created a disturbing view of a culture was, surprisingly, on National Public Radio. The reporter described China's rural agriculture as the "*detonation* of China's current economic *explosion.*"

The age of technology is not without it's troubling metaphors. Look at the hostile language connected with computers: abort, execute, crashed, killed, megabyte, boot, virus. Fiona Wilson writes about gender-biased reality created by such technological language in *Human Relations,* in her article "Language, Technology, Gender and Power." Also, the technological mega-advancement that is implied in the trendy term "information superhighway" is being embraced without much concern and critical reflection. What does the *information superhighway* mean for human contact and conversation?

Certainly, metaphors can have an *empowering,* rather than *overpowering,* energy if we do not take them for granted. It is this illuminating and creative quality that will be the focus of the rest of this article.

Metaphor as Light: Illuminating the Way for Interpersonal and Organization Transformation

The concept of metaphor will be explored here as the energy source of language. Metaphors make language come alive: language becomes action because metaphors can spark people to different actions. Metaphors are more than the clever, figurative nouns that we first learned about in elementary school (e.g., that *person* is a *rock;* this *relationship* is a *peak and valley*). Metaphors are not merely figures of *speech*—they are figures of *thought.* G.B. Madison suggests that a "metaphor is more than just an odd way of saying things with words, it is a superbly effective way of doing things with words, of altering our way of being-in-the-world." When we "do things with words," human beings pay closer attention to the interplay of their own and others' expressions. If we listen carefully, for example, we can better discern what people mean by what they are saying. We can clarify by asking questions. When we speak, we can be more conscious about how words reflect our deeply held assumptions and thoughts. We can be aware that what we say is in line with what we do. Figure 1 demonstrates how metaphor is central to these processes.

The triangle reveals the fundamental ways metaphors come forth in conversations. Metaphors emerge as: 1) thoughts and assumptions (root metaphors); 2) communication for mutual understanding (bridging metaphors); and 3) creativity for new meanings (generative metaphors).

First, *root metaphors* are assumptions that are deep in our memory or on the surface. In either case, our assumptions about anything—our existence in the world, our relationships, our organizations—come forth when we speak. The many words in the previous section (e.g., *structure, machine, minefield, troops,* and *detonation*) have roots in the mechanics of science and the hierarchy of the military. On the other hand, *conversation* (in contrast to *presentation*) and *culture* (in contrast to *machine*) have roots in a participative and systemic approach, rather than a hierarchical and mechanistic one.

Second, when we are in *conversation,* the intentions are different from when we engage in a discussion or debate. Both Peter Senge and David Bohm make distinctions between debate, discussion, and dialogue. *Conversants* are dedicated to reaching mutual understanding. In order to do this, a conversant must clarify (or bridge) meaning by using metaphor. Especially in a small group meeting or an interactive workshop, one conversant may help other conversants understand one another by using a

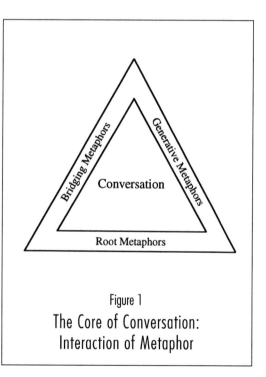

Figure 1

The Core of Conversation:
Interaction of Metaphor

bridging metaphor. Naturally, a person will suggest a different word or give an example in order for a conversation partner to understand something better. I am proposing here that consultants, workshop leaders, and organization members should become far more conscious in their listening and *bridge* more often.

With clarifying, a conversants' root assumptions will come across. *Bridging* is especially appropriate in the early stages of a consultant–client relationship to understand the client's needs and determine mutual expectations. I will customarily ask these kinds of questions: "Do you mean *educating* or *training;* and what is your understanding of *'interactive training'*?" "Do you think the workshop will *change* people or have them question and *shift* their assumptions?" "What do you mean by leadership—*empowering* others or *motivating* others, or something else?" "Do you want your managers to *manage* or *lead,* or both?"

Bridging is "active listening" and more. One of the important notions of active listening is repeating words to acknowledge the speaker. *Also* inherent in *bridging* is that humans are interpretive beings. We have different understandings of the same words and/or similar understanding of different words. Thus, a conversant dedicated to reaching understanding will clarify by asking questions and/or offering different interpretations. Such was the case when I was talking with a colleague, Bob Myers, about his company's core business issues and senior staff strategies. Bob said, "As a group, you want to get out of managing *low fruit,* you even want to get out of managing *high fruit;* you want to get into the business of finding out where you should be planting the next seed that's going to grow the next tree." Here is another example: In workshops and project meetings, I co-create *bridging* lists on flip charts with the participants. These short lists of metaphors live throughout the workshop or meeting. They are designed to include or cover different understandings of certain concepts or ideas so the group as a whole has a mutual understanding.

Third, *generative* metaphors provide the impetus for conversants to disclose *new* understandings. Metaphors are a spark for new meanings to emerge. The opportunity exists for root assumptions to shift. By offering a so-called "sales strategy" that was *conversational* rather than *presentational,* I sparked my brother—and myself—to new understandings. He shifted his thinking and actions regarding how he runs his business. I shifted my assumptions about my brother.

Generative metaphors, especially, have a critical link with organization transformation. Creativity expressed in language allows for new possibilities and new actions. Whereas *bridging* metaphors are comforting—the intention of the conversants is to reach trust and mutual understanding—inherent in a *generative* conversation is discomfort, intrigue, and paradox. Why is this the case? Generating a new interpretation (new metaphor) of an established idea makes something that is *familiar, strange.* This creates tension. Thus, *time* becomes a critical factor: After reflective time, we begin to understand the tension and shift our assumptions.

I noticed this creative tension over a six-month period consulting with a small company. A small group started with the conventional mission of *strategic* planning. Much of the process generated new ways of looking at things; there were often questions about the company's founding assumptions. Certain metaphors (e.g., *shift* instead of *change, consultation* instead of *training, interrelationships* instead of *strategic* relationships) sparked new understandings. People began to shift their assumptions: *Strategic* action gave way to *communicative* action. At the end of the six months, there was a strategic sales role; however, strategic planning was not the root assumption driving actions. Rather, the emphasis was on client relationships and internal company communication.

Figure 2 links metaphor with transformation. Conversation, with metaphor at the core, supports the on-going process of organization transformation. In developing this design, I have synthesized ideas from a number of theorists, practitioners, and interpersonal experiences. The primary grounding of the design is philosophical and cultural rather than psychological.

The action of language is the basis for transformational shifts in interpersonal relationships. Since these relationships make up organizations, conversations have tremendous implications for organization transformation. The arrows in Figure 2 suggest that meaning is spread, or shared, and leads to organization transformation (i.e., a *collective* paradigm shift and overall culture change). Notice that all the facets of the design float in a sea of conversation. Over time, new paradigms eventually become old paradigms; however in a *generative* learning organization, metaphors continuously *spark* new meanings. These bits of *energy* give conversants opportunities to question old assumptions, which lead to new assumptions (root metaphors), new

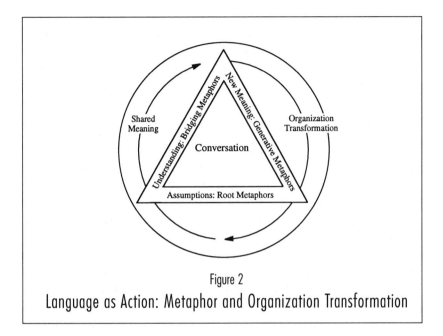

Figure 2
Language as Action: Metaphor and Organization Transformation

shared meaning, and a different paradigm.

Conversation is also a *sun:* It continues to shine through thick and thin. With all the downsizing, technological advancements, endless competition, and restructuring, some people are overwhelmed and under a constant *cloud cover.* Thus, when *sunlight* does shine brightly enough to make us blink—when metaphors spark something new—instead of donning our sunglasses mindlessly, we must stop and take notice.

More Implications for Consultants and Organization Leaders

In my work as a consultant and educator, people either praise me for my wordsmithing abilities or denounce me as being the word police. I am either lauded for being able to articulate a vision with creativity and clarity, or accused of being too sensitive about the importance of words. People either seek my advice and relish its cleverness, or avoid talking with me because they are afraid I will tell them they are not "walking their talk." Such is the life of an interpreter.

Fortunately, most of my clients see my services in the positive light of the former attributes mentioned above, rather than the latter ones. I suppose my life and work would be smooth sailing if everyone thought of themselves as interpreters or managers of meaning; however, that's exactly why I am in the organization transformation consulting business. I serve others in their journeys to understand the centrality of language in organization transformation: the shifting of the deepest fabric of the organization—the culture.

Shifting culture—people's assumptions, language, and actions—is certainly not a short-term affair. Thus, so-called "change" consultants should offer organization members *ideas,* not *remedies.* In using his or her own experiences to spark clients' discoveries, the consultant is *anecdotal,* not *antidotal.* The client and consultant, together in conversation, discover and disclose inner wisdom in order to make decisions about what to shift. For example, when it is appropriate—usually after I have developed trust with a client or colleague—I offer *generative* metaphors and *stir the waters.* In a true partnership, a consultant is seen as a *coach stirring things up,* rather than an *expert pouring knowledge* into a client or participant. This *"to and fro"* acts as an exemplar for how conversations take place among members of organizations.

Summary

What are the key learnings to share with your colleagues or clients? First, acknowledge the link between metaphor and transformation; in concert with this, take *time* to shift your practices. Here is a summary:

LISTENING—take *time* to listen and read; verify with people what their words mean and what assumptions (root metaphors) these words reflect.

EXPRESSING—take *time* to attend to the words you are saying and writing; what do you mean, how do the words reflect your assumptions (root metaphors)?

CLARIFYING—take *time* to ask questions; offer different metaphors (*bridging*) for clarification and for mutual understanding.

GENERATING—take *time* to offer different metaphors (*generative*) in order for new meanings to emerge, for new understandings, and new actions.

REFLECTING—take *time* to reflect on conversations for learning purposes.

I hope that some of the metaphors in this essay have *stirred the waters* for you. Refer back to the italicized distinctions. Take time to reflect; perhaps my offerings will spark a new meaning for you. I welcome your interpretations and the opportunity to generate new understandings and interpersonal transformation. *Language as Action* certainly holds the energy for far-reaching, long-term shifts.

> *The metaphors, symbols, or narratives produced by imagination all provide us with "imaginative variations" of the world, thereby offering us the freedom to conceive of the world in new ways and to undertake forms of action which might lead to its transformation. Semantic innovation can thus point towards social transformation.*

—Richard Kearney
The Narrative Path

Kendall Murphy is a principal of MetaLens Consulting, Inc., which specializes in coaching individuals and organizations in the art of creating sustainable excellence and creating human systems that are required to succeed with organizational transformations, including Total Quality. Murphy has thirty-five years' experience in technical and management positions in the communications industry, including positions as controller for Pacific Telesis and vice-president of quality for Pacific Bell, before his retirement in 1991.

He has lectured and taught both technical and leadership subjects in a number of corporate and educational institutions and has co-led public seminars on generative coaching and dialogue. He is a member of the World Business Academy, the Bay Area O.D. Network, the Institute of Noetic Sciences, the American Society for Quality Control, and the Total Quality Corporate Advisory Committee for the San Francisco Unified School District.

13

Generative Coaching: A Surprising Learning Odyssey

Kendall Murphy

HAWK

Through outstretched arms of the oak
I feel the hawk.
I wonder what it feels as it circles endlessly on invisible seas.
The resistance of the air does not impede the hawk
   but supports it.
How many past resistances have I struggled against
   when all they offered was a helping hand?
The hawk knows what I still seek to learn.
It offers its secret openly, but in a language that is unfamiliar.
It, too, has choices—but sees the currents as friends.
A Mozart on the wing, it makes its contribution
   not as a creator, but as a vehicle through which creation flows.
Man, easily fooled, sees only the final product
   and relates it to the last, the closest step.
Having thus learned wrongly, he fights the currents
   and tries to persuade others to his new found wisdom.
Others, doing likewise, push back.
The hawk smiles, achieving sustenance and beauty without effort
   providing its song
   to a world that does not hear.

—Ken Murphy (1991)

It seems odd that my thinking has arrived at its current point of evolution. After all, I was brought up in the "scientific era" with its Baconian ethic of domination of nature. Moreover, I was trained as a mathematician and was highly successful in applying such analytic techniques to business problems—including those involving people. My job was organizing, controlling, solving problems, and overcoming resistances, and I did it well! As a result, I moved rapidly into middle management. I had become a manager par excellence! Why would I change?

Looking back, it amazes me how foolish this now looks. "Managing" people is a guarantee that one will never create a learning organization! Even now, most managers don't yet understand how manipulative most human resource approaches are and how such approaches invisibly undermine their very purpose: excellent performance. Such systems must be replaced if what is wanted is to create non-manipulative, high performance, high quality learning organizations. Among the changes needed is to move from *managing* people to *coaching* them. I don't mean "coaching" as organizations usually use the word, but a form of coaching that I will call "Generative Coaching," based on the work of James Flaherty of New Ventures West. It is a fundamentally different way of working with people that creates more satisfying results for both the organization and the individuals within it.

Even in the early part of my management career, I began to notice things that disturbed my belief in the power of analysis and control. I remember going into my first district manager job at Pacific Telephone where I was responsible for about 600 people. Having no experience in this position, I had little idea of what I should do, let alone how to do it. So I talked with people and sat in on group meetings that my subordinate managers had convened. Since I was unable to provide any direction, I just listened, asking questions when I didn't understand something. My great skill in planning, organizing and controlling—the "holy trinity" of good management—was temporarily disabled.

Amazingly, results began to improve anyway!

It turned out that, in spite of my ignorance, my questions caused my subordinate managers to reflect on how they were doing the job in the areas that I questioned. In doing so, they discovered and invented new ways to do it, causing district results to steadily improve. So much for planning, organizing, and controlling!

Nevertheless, my habits ran deep. When I finally learned the ins and outs of the district's operations, I again began to plan, organize, and control—although now tempered by the experience of my first several months. In one particularly difficult area, I devised a plan to improve the district's performance. When I shared the plan with my subordinates, it turned out they had already developed one of their own. Once they described it to me, it was clear to me their approach had several serious flaws. Mine was much better.

I was convinced their plan would not work, but they were so enthused about it I didn't interfere.

I assumed that after they discovered for themselves that their approach wouldn't work, they would be more receptive to my wise advice. Sure enough, they encountered the flaws I had seen. But they were so sure they could make their plan work, they kept at it, adjusting it as needed until it did work. My perfect planning was no match for their excitement, creativity, and persistence.

I began to observe a pattern: Given a little elbow room and support, people can surprise you!

Having begun to observe a pattern in my work environment, it was only a small step to start noticing things at home that had previously been invisible. I noticed that my wife, Katie, who I felt greatly undervalued logical thought and overvalued intuition, often made decisions that turned out far better than mine. This was true in business decisions as well as those of child rearing (Thank God, she was there to save our kids from my well-intentioned theories!!) Could it be there was something to intuition? Was there some other, more subtle, way of knowing something than straight-ahead logic?

These observations were the beginning of a personal odyssey that was to completely unravel all my prior thinking about the science and art of management.

A World Turned Upside Down

Sometimes awakenings are gradual. But sometimes the ground is ripped out from under us in a flash! In 1987, my entire universe collapsed.

Katie had been experiencing abdominal discomfort and scheduled a medical appointment to see what was the matter. Some tests were performed and she was given an appointment to come in and review the results. Since it seemed routine, I stayed at work, coming home a little early to inquire about the findings and treatment. Since she wasn't yet home, I became concerned and called the doctor's office to see if she was still there. I was informed that she had left some time ago and had been sent to the hospital to see one of the specialists there. I called the hospital and was told she had left an hour before. Now beginning to panic, I rushed to the hospital to track down where she was.

When I reached the hospital, I found her sitting on the curb crying. My heart stopped! I jumped out of the car and wrapped my arms around her as she sobbed uncontrollably. When she was finally able to talk, I discovered she had been diagnosed as having advanced ovarian cancer. The whole world had changed! All those hopes and dreams we had been working on for over 28 years had gone up in smoke! Within twenty-four hours, beliefs and habits I had held for decades suddenly and radically shifted. Things I once held as of paramount importance, were no longer important at all. Many of my models were immediately and thoroughly shattered! All the prior resistances I had held to changing these beliefs and habits evaporated. This all happened, not through any analysis, but through some strange and immediate knowing that is not possible for me to articulate adequately.

My wife's diagnosis and eventual death led to a reflection on how many times I had been sure of something that later turned out to be completely or partially wrong. I began to understand the importance of never being certain.

Beliefs, principles, and visions are important. They provide a guiding light for one's actions in life. But once one feels that they are "truths," they also become traps, fences, barriers to growth. They also become screens that prevent us from really hearing and fully considering the views of others. This is the shadow side of beliefs and principles.

A Learning Journey

The most important aspect of this learning journey might be described as becoming more spiritual, if one thinks of spirituality as more sensitivity to and placing more importance on the whole.

Over time, the cumulative force of these gradual "noticings" and sudden "shocks" led me to reflect on their patterns and originating structures and to investigate alternate ways of seeing things. This, in turn, led to further changes in both my approach to management and to my personal way of being.

I became much more experimental in my approach to life and work, relying less on carefully constructed plans. With issues involving people, detailed plans usually don't turn out as planned anyway. Nor can time-consuming planning anticipate all the secondary effects of implementation. Experimenting, combined with a sensitive feedback system and rapid adjustment to what came up, seemed to work much better. This shift had a surprising side-effect: When people saw my willingness to change the plan on the fly, they started offering a lot more suggestions. With my previous mode of tight planning and control, most felt that offering suggestions was a waste of time.

Having observed what people do when supported and given a little elbow room, one of my new roles became providing "air cover"—i.e., providing a heat shield from the pressures, changes, and general static that often came from higher management levels. As a general manager, and later as a corporate officer, I even began to speak openly about the importance of love in the business environment. While this had developed as an unspoken ingredient in my approach to management, I am indebted to Roger Harrison for his article, "Strategies for a New Age," for focusing and adding to my thoughts and for providing the impetus for helping me articulate them in the business environment.

These changes in me often happened without much conscious effort. They seemed to be happening as a by-product of my seeing things differently.

Results and Implications

I was impressed by how successful my changed approaches were in actual application inside a multinational company that, by and large, didn't believe in or support this stuff.

Results improved. Costs went down—not because of budget cuts, but because individuals stopped doing things that didn't make sense and large numbers of people became very creative. Staff groups that traditionally had no responsibility for revenue generation found ways to market their internal "products" outside the company. People began finding more joy in their work! In effect, I got away with this radical behavior because it worked!

As this learning journey continued, I noticed that increasingly I was operating in a very different way from the company norm. Since my peers seemed intent on staying with their own ways of managing, I started observing those differences more consciously.

One major difference was the way of dealing with folks, caused by different assumptions about people in general. Somewhere along the way, with strong pushes from Frederick Taylor and B. F. Skinner, business accepted and institutionalized the premise that people can be treated like things and that their behavior can be successfully manipulated to produce results desired by management. Even the term "Human Resources" implies that people, like other "resources," are disposable inputs to production. Such assumptions worked to a degree and were consistent with management thinking in the early part of the twentieth century. However, they are not consistent with more current approaches to revitalizing organizations, such as Total Quality, which require individuals and teams that are self-generating and self-correcting. As quality guru W. Edwards Deming tried to point out for years, these more effective approaches require a complete re-thinking of organizational assumptions about people. This is especially true for those attempting to create a "learning organization."

The whole idea of managing may need to be tossed out in favor of an approach that recognizes the irreducible wholeness of the human being. It is neither possible nor desirable for people to bring just part of themselves to work and leave the rest outside. Shared meaning and commitment to a common goal, for example, will not come about by applying new techniques to the "human resources." It will come when our thinking changes about what it means to be human and part of a human community.

An important part of these changes is to move away from managing people and toward coaching them.

Generative Coaching

The type of coaching that I referred to earlier as Generative Coaching has potential leverage in implementing the ideas of learning organizations. It is based on Flaherty's research and on his work with both organizations and individuals.

Generative Coaching is, above all, a way of understanding people in their wholeness, followed by conversations (language) and actions (practices) consistent with that understanding.

Beware of the simplicity of this statement! It deserves close

---

Long-term (sustainable) Excellent Performance
that is

- **Self-Correcting,** and

- **Self-Generating**

Figure 1
Goals of Generative Coaching

---

study because it represents a radical shift from current organizational practice.

The goals of Generative Coaching call for long term, sustainable excellent performance that is both self-correcting and self-generating. These goals apply to *commitment* as well as to *competence*. While these goals appear to be simple and sensible, they are very different from both the goals and the outcomes of almost all "human resource" efforts in U.S. organizations today. Traditional human resource approaches produce none of these results. Rather, they set up barriers to them.

Principles of Generative Coaching

Principle 1: Relationship

Generative Coaching is possible only by establishing and maintaining a mutually satisfying relationship with the "client" of the coaching. This mutuality must exist in four areas:

- **Mutual Commitment**—Both coach and client must be committed to the same thing. Generative Coaching can only happen in that region where the coach's commitments and the client's commitments overlap.

- **Mutual Trust**—This means that both coach and client are sincere in making their commitments and both have the competence to meet those commitments.

- **Mutual Respect**—Both coach and client must believe that the other is being authentic—their intentions are sincere and they put forth themselves and their positions without guise or hidden agendas. They also must have a positive view of the other's position. This doesn't

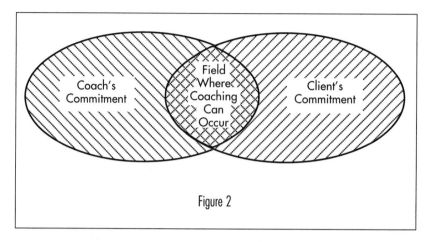

Figure 2

mean agreement—only that such a view is reasonable and acceptable.

- **Mutual Freedom of Expression**—"Expression" refers to *both* sending and receiving. Each party must feel they can speak openly, even on sensitive subjects. Also, each must be open to being influenced by the other. In other words, their listening must be highly receptive and they must be willing to reflect on what is said, even if it challenges closely-held beliefs and habits.

Mutual respect and freedom of expression need only exist in the dimension that is being coached. If the subject of coaching is customer service, it does not require that mutual respect and freedom of expression exist in the dimension of one's personal life.

In addition to these four areas of mutuality, it is also vital for a coach to approach the client as a whole human being and not simply as a functional "part" as defined by the client's role in the organization.

Without such a relationship in place, Generative Coaching cannot occur.

Principle 2: Pragmatism

The worth of any coaching effort is assessed by its outcome. It is rigorous in its pursuit of what works and its relentless correction of coaching efforts based on outcome. In other words, it is based on a "feedback loop" that assesses progress against standards and uses that information not to judge people but to ensure a self-correcting process that will lead to the desired outcome.

My observation of conversations in business, political, and social settings is that people spend an inordinate amount of energy asserting and debating which position is right or wrong. Such thinking is not only destructive but flawed, because we always see the world through a particular filter or lens, or what Peter Senge calls "mental models." The world is so complex that people *must* simplify it in order to deal with it. There is no other choice. But all models are "wrong" by definition. They can only be simplifications of reality, not reality itself. There is nothing wrong with this. Where we go astray is when we confuse our models with reality and become sure that they are "right." The important question, however, is not whether something is right or wrong, but is it *helpful* for the purpose at hand. Such a small shift in thinking could greatly ease the way to creating a much more productive and much more human world. It would certainly go a long way towards removing some of the more serious barriers to learning and to creating learning organizations.

I am not proposing that one should not have beliefs and principles. The danger lies in confusing one's beliefs, one's models, with "truths." Being 95% sure may provide a helpful "guiding light" as long as one is continually looking for that 5% that might be off!

I remember how strongly I had believed in the "holy trinity" of planning, organizing, and controlling. I also remember how sure I was that there would always be time "later" to spend quality time with my wife Katie. It is humbling to look back at all the times I was so sure of something that turned out to be wrong in some respect! I learned that even one's deepest beliefs can only be approximations and interpretations and are therefore best kept open to constant examination and adjustment, or even outright change. This one profound learning, perhaps more than any other, freed me to become more open to possibilities that were invisible to me or were out of reach in earlier years.

Principle 3: Two Tracks

Unlike the traditional model where a teacher attempts to impart his/her knowledge to the student, Generative Coaching assumes that both the coach and the client are in a learning process. The client is on a track to learn a new competency or quality; the coach is on a track to learn how to coach this particular human being as well as being open to modifying some of his/her own cherished beliefs and assumptions. Both are on a joint, interconnected and mutually dependent learning path. This is quite different from the usual way of viewing a teacher, trainer or consultant as the "expert" who comes already equipped with "the answers." In Generative Coaching there are always two tracks of learning, both of which require observation, reflection, and action.

Principle 4: Always—Already

Before moving to the next paragraph, you might consider putting this book down for a moment to make a list of the four or five most important things going on in your life. Some may be positive; some negative. Don't worry about it or judge it. You might even want to make a list of your most immediate concerns and hopes as well as a list of your longer-term dreams, ambitions, and fears. Be as honest as possible. You can burn the list later!

You might even hold this list in your mind for a few days and notice how these things affect your mood, your reactions to others, and the thoughts that constantly flow in and out of your mind. Then, ask yourself what you might have learned from this.

One important lesson is that, like you, people are "always already" in the middle of their lives. What they are up to always affects anything new that tries to come their way. But the traditional behavior of teacher to student (or manager to subordinate) implies an assumption that the student comes "empty"— just waiting to be taught and led. As one educator said, "What we have assumed to be a failure to learn is more often a failure to teach effectively." In other words, it is a failure to understand the individual and to coach that person in a way that is effective for that individual person. Each person already has a way of doing things, understanding things, reacting to circumstances, justifying his/her actions, explaining the actions of others, and, in every other way, is always in the middle of life!

No matter how illogical it may seem to others, what people do always makes sense to *them*!

What people are in the middle of is heavily influenced by the culture they grew up in, their experiences, what has already worked for them and what hasn't, what their values and goals are, and their orientation towards life, not to mention genetic characteristics they were born with. All of these make each individual a distinctive human being, different from all others, even though certain characteristics may be shared.

Successful coaching requires that such differences are

recognized and taken into account. It also requires the coach to:

(1) Find out how the person sees the world: How do they interpret it?

(2) Shed new light on what the client is currently in the middle of.

(3) Help the client let go of that long enough to see new possibilities and to make new choices.

In 1990, a team of eight people in a large multinational company was assembled to redesign a process that was not working effectively. Each person was expert in his/her own area. Pete had worked on similar projects before and was very skeptical about the value of this one, feeling that management never implements the recommendations of such task forces anyway. Due to his resistance, the project team was ineffective in performing its task. Carmen, on the other hand, felt that this was a unique chance to correct a process that was hurting some customers and wanted to try to make it work. However, she didn't have the training required to carry out her part of the project.

In Carmen's case, the coaching was straightforward: Provide the support needed to help her acquire a new skill without delaying the project, paying attention to what learning modes worked best for her. This was worked out by attaching an instructor to the project and by using the project itself as a case study for the training.

However, it was useless to take this approach for Pete until his mood of skepticism was addressed. In his case, the coaching required discussions to find out what could be provided to Pete that would allow him to temporarily suspend his skepticism long enough to see another possibility. Not only was the project successfully implemented, but both Pete and Carmen became advocates for following the team's approach on other projects.

People in organizations are often treated as if they all have the same motivations, the same understandings, the same ways of seeing the world and coping with it. This is never the situation. As in the case of Pete and Carmen, by assessing each individual's way of dealing with the world and taking it into account, coaching can help a team achieve continuous improvement that is self-correcting and self-generating—i.e., it opens a space where continuous learning can occur.

Principle 5: Techniques Don't Work With People

Have you ever experienced a situation where someone, maybe your boss, learned a "technique" for dealing with people—then tried it on you? How did it feel? I have observed that people often like to use techniques, perhaps because it simplifies things for them, but they don't like being "techniqued." William Barrett provides much of the foundation for this principle in his book, The *Illusion of Technique.*

When it comes to working with people, techniques are fundamentally manipulative. Sooner or later, people figure out what is being done to them and begin to resist and resent it. The unspoken premise of techniques, fostered by the behaviorist school of psychology, is that people are things that can be readily understood and easily manipulated. Neither premise is true and both undermine the dignity of people.

People subjected to techniques don't become competent or committed. Rather, they become skillful at making it appear that they are cooperating so as to avoid any negative consequences. This drives their resistance and resentment underground where it does the most damage, because underground attitudes tend to fester and become fairly permanent. Such feelings impact the organization in subtle but destructive ways as they come out in "safe" ways of expression, such as sabotage and withholding of commitment. Anyone who has worked for long in almost any large organization can testify to the existence of such symptoms.

The Premise of Generative Coaching

Most attempts to improve "human resource" practices fall into the category that Harvard's Chris Argyris calls "single loop learning" in his book *Overcoming Organizational Defenses.* That is, it takes place without challenging the basic premises of the accepted paradigm. Generative Coaching, on the other hand, is the result of what Argyris calls "double loop learning" in that it challenges the fundamental assumptions of existing theory and practice. This reexamination of the fundamental premise produces some major changes.

Both the behaviorist and the generative coach are looking for results (although the behaviorist is usually looking for results that benefit someone other than the client, whereas the coach focuses on the client). Both agree that behavior is a major determinant of results. A key difference, however, is that the behaviorist focuses directly on influencing behavior, usually with some form of rewards and punishments (however disguised). Applied to humans, this has some problems associated with it. For example, remove the incentive or control and the behavior usually reverts to its original form. In addition, controls, rewards, and punishments often have a number of undesirable side effects. Not only is the overhead for such supports very expensive, but people have been known to spend a great deal of energy to "beat the system." These and numerous other negative side effects are well documented.

In contrast, the premise of Generative Coaching is that behavior is only a symptom, not a primary cause or leverage point for change. Working on symptoms may sometimes be necessary to cope with short-term emergencies, but such action will not produce sustainable, excellent performance that is self-generating and self-correcting.

A higher leverage point for change is how a person sees and interprets the world (as discussed under "Always-Already")—what Flaherty calls their "Structure of Interpretation."

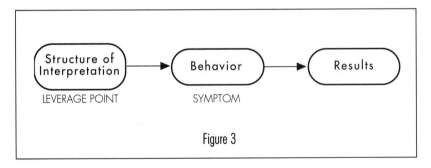

Figure 3

If one wishes change to be self-correcting and self-generating, the focus must be on intervening in the Structure of Interpretation, not directly on behavior. For example, in the earlier example, focusing directly on Pete's behavior may induce temporary compliance, but self-correcting behavior isn't likely to be forthcoming. For that to happen, the root cause, his skepticism, must be addressed in a way that Pete can begin to see things differently.

There are two fundamental ways to influence Structure of Interpretation:
- through Language and
- through Practices.

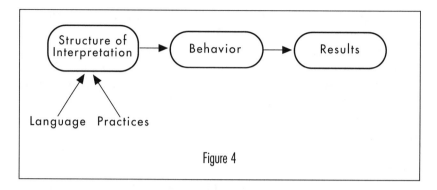

Figure 4

The task of Language is to provide a new way of perceiving and observing—to help the client see the world through a different set of lenses and filters; to put light on areas that may not be currently visible to the client. Working with a coach is different from getting expert advice. The coach does not tell clients what they should do. It is the coach's job to help the client see new possibilities and to invite the client to consider making new decisions based on a broader set of possibilities.

The task of Practices is to both help the client see new possibilities and to move the client's mental shifts into the body. Moving mental shifts into the body means replacing old habits with new ones. Learning is never complete until it moves into the person's automatic response system, into the nervous system—the body. Think about how you learned to drive a car or ride a bicycle and you will understand the importance of practices. Recall when you wanted to change an old habit (eating, exercise, some personal trait) and you will understand both the power of habit and the need for constant practice if one desires to change permanently.

The Process of Coaching

Establishing a Relationship. Many attempts to supervise, teach, "coach" or advise are thwarted because there is no relationship that permits it. Relationships based on role are not sufficient. A coaching relationship must be based on mutual:

1. Commitment
2. Trust
3. Respect
4. Freedom of expression.

Recognizing Openings for Coaching. Coaching cannot take place unless there is an opening for it in the mind of the client. Many openings go unrecognized because our culture has taught us to cover them up or to make them disappear. Chris Argyris has discussed this at length in his books and articles. As an example, when a person doesn't succeed in something, a common reaction is for the person to engage in psychological assessment (self-criticism and/or criticism of others). For those trying to help the person, the culture teaches us to try to treat it as a problem to be solved and to solve it by trying to "rescue" the person—smooth it over; make the pain go away. None of this is really helpful to the person. It robs them of any learning opportunity.

In contrast to this, Generative Coaching focuses on the learning opportunity presented by the breakdown: What is it and how can the coach help the client see the opportunity presented? Breakdown is treated as an opportunity to create something new, not as a problem to be solved. The most serious breakdowns, while painful, can be invitations to significant reassessment of one's long held beliefs and assumptions, thus opening up whole new worlds of possibilities that were previously blocked. My wife's cancer and subsequent death was such a breakdown for me. The kind of transformation that it triggered in me is an experience I share with many cancer patients and their loved ones.

Observing and Assessing. Since the coaching must fit the individual client, assessment must precede the actual coaching. This especially applies to addressing a person's Structure of Interpretation, since it is that structure that determines how a person sees the world and therefore guides every action that is taken. That being the case, observation is done within a framework that provides useful distinctions for the client. This may be both within the framework of the discipline being coached (baseball, Total Quality, brain surgery, etc.) as well as within the framework of understanding the client as a whole human being (e.g. the framework of Generative Coaching)

Enrolling the Client. Enrollment is about getting the client's permission to coach him/her. This step is often skipped, leaving the would-be coach to wonder what went wrong and, often, to blame the client for not being cooperative. Enrollment is a stage in coaching where expected outcomes are made explicit, possible barriers and breakdowns are anticipated and addressed ahead of time, and mutual commitments are made as to what will happen when such obstacles are actually confronted. This mutuality is important because either the client or the coach can become discouraged when difficulties are encountered. Because of this, trying to coach without enrollment is often just wishful thinking.

Coaching Conversations. This deals with interventions designed to impact the client's performance in a way that is sustainable, self-correcting, and self-generating. To understand coaching conversations in depth it is necessary to first have a grasp of the nature of language itself. Language is more than just a tool for communicating. It is a representation of the culture in which we live and, as such, frames the possibilities and meanings that are available to us. It is also important to understand the structure of language so that it is used effectively. Often when communication goes astray, it is because some important structural aspect of the necessary language is missing. Effective coaching requires effective language.

An essential part of coaching is to use language to provide the client with a way to see something that he or she could not see before. That is, to shine a light on something that was previously

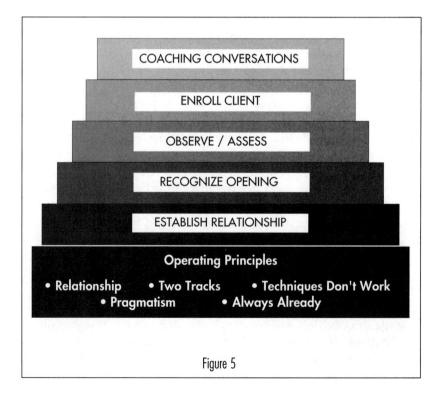

Figure 5

dark to the client. When this happens, immediate change can happen. What is sometimes taken as a resistance to change is often just blindness to certain perceptions. When a light is shined on such an area, a person can change immediately, voluntarily and effortlessly—sometimes even with great joy at seeing something once hidden. In this way, a coach does not persuade or even "tell," but rather frees the client to take action by lighting the way. In doing so, the coach must also speak in a way that the client can hear.

The process of coaching stands firmly on the base of the five Operating Principles of Generative Coaching (See Figure 5 on page 212):

Skills and Qualities of a Coach

Because the assumptions, principles and processes of Generative Coaching are so different from current practice, the aspiring coach usually has some work to do in order to acquire new skills and qualities. These include:

- **Skills**

  Speaking (in a way that frees the client to act)

  Listening (in a way that meets the criteria discussed)

  Resolving breakdowns

  Assessing a person's Structure of Interpretation

  Designing coaching conversations and practices.

- **Qualities**

  Rigor (upholding the standards of the discipline being coached)

  Creativity (being inventive)

  Flexibility (being experimental while staying "tuned" to the client)

  Self-consistency (holding oneself to the same standards)

  Patience (persisting and waiting without complaint)

Facing the need to acquire these skills and qualities can be intimidating, especially for higher level managers. This is not so much because of any inherent difficulty in developing the skills, but more because one's habit system is so strongly set and because moving in this direction implies that one's current set of skills and qualities is no longer adequate. This can strike at self-esteem, which is to strike at something that is often highly protected. Coaching in such an area is a delicate task.

Parting Thoughts

Many well-meaning attempts to change organizations don't work because of a failure to question and rethink the traditionally accepted assumptions behind the "human resource" systems that permeate business and other organizations. Successful intervention requires moving away from a direct focus on behavior and toward the root cause of resistances to sustainable change. Those root causes are embedded in what Flaherty calls a person's Structure of Interpretation. The process of Generative Coaching can provide a very effective means for a practical intervention at this root cause level.

It is not so easy, however. What is easy is to stay on the path that one is already on. My own learning odyssey was one of staying in my comfortable "knowing," resisting all attempts to pry me out until breakdowns made it impossible or until the evidence piled up so high I could no longer ignore it. It was at those times that I realized how much energy it took to hold onto what I already "knew" or "had." It was such a waste of my time and my life.

Ultimately, one must question such fundamental assumptions as to what end do I want to make an organization more "effective"? For starters, moving away from the kind of manipulative approaches that are embodied in almost all "Human Resource" systems would be a very positive step. Generative Coaching provides a way to take such a step without sacrificing the organization in the process.

> *When the Master makes a mistake, she realizes it.*
> *Having realized it, she admits it.*
> *Having admitted it, she corrects it.*
> *She considers those who point out her faults*
> *as her most benevolent teachers.*
> *She thinks of her enemy*
> *as the shadow that she herself casts.*
> —Tao Te Ching (Chapter 61. Translation
> by Stephen Mitchell)

W. Brian Kreutzer is an associate at Gould-Kreutzer Associates, Inc. where he is responsible for directing the company's research and development efforts and for designing and building multimedia graphical user interfaces for system dynamics (mathematical) models that allow non-technical managers to use and understand them. He also teaches courses on systems thinking to their client base and has taught graduate level courses in systems thinking at Lesley College.

He writes user manuals for the firm's custom interfaces and designs and develops teaching materials for it's systems thinking courses. Among his publications are the second edition of *Managing A Nation: The Microcomputer Software Catalog* (co-edited with Drs. Gerald Barney and Martha Garrett), two articles in *The Fifth Discipline Fieldbook*, and hardware and software reviews for *NewMedia* magazine, *The Whole Earth Review*, and *The Systems Thinker* newsletter.

14

Building Learning Laboratories to Create More Effective Distributed Decision Making

W. Brian Kreutzer

When we first encounter an unfamiliar system with which we need to work, we attempt to learn as much about it as possible. We experiment with it, study it, and observe it until we develop a "good understanding" of how we think it works. We often call this understanding a mental or conceptual model. When we "simulate" these models in our minds, we are attempting to solve a multi-order non-linear differential equation, something that is almost impossible to do. Our intuition often gets us successfully through the problem but intuition cannot be easily transferred; when the person with the intuition leaves, so does the understanding and skill.

There is, however, a methodology for capturing these mental models, converting them to a mathematical format, and then using a computer to simulate them.

Once a mathematical model has been created, an interface can be attached to it, producing a "Management Flight Simulator" which will allow non-modelers to explore and experiment with them.

At the heart of these Management Flight Simulators (MFS) are mathematical representations of the systems that affect the problem the company is facing. Attached to that mathematical model is an interface which makes it easier to use and communicate additional information. Users can then vary the input for these models to see what outcomes they produce. In this way they can explore, in an experiential way, the underlying structure of the system. These MFS can then be used to share their mental models of strategic issues with other managers, practice and teach decision-making skills, facilitate strategic and scenario planning, and enhance corporate learning. They do this by: allowing the users to experiment with the simulation by trying different strategies and decisions, making the modeling insights accessible through a gaming interface, and allowing a non-technical audience to explore the assumptions and causal links behind the mathematical model.

The process of building a Management Flight Simulator-based learning laboratory can be divided into four steps:

1. Capturing the group's mental model
2. Converting that mental model to mathematical equations
3. Creating and connecting an interface to those mathematical equations
4. Designing and implementing the learning laboratory itself.

There are many different ways of building MFS. They can be divided into three main approaches: a) the black box approach, b) the create-and-share approach, and c) the participatory approach.

The black box approach is the process where a company hires an outside consultant to implement the four building steps listed above. At the end of the process, the company is given the "answer" to their problem and told what to do. They are also sometimes given a piece of software which they can then use in their internal learning laboratories. Since most of the learning is done during the process of actually creating the model, the consultant is the one who learns the most about the underlying system in this approach.

The create-and-share approach is the second process where a company hires an outside consultant to implement the four building steps. At the end of the process the company is also given a piece of software. In addition they are given all the notes and materials that document the learning process. The consultant then teaches the managers of the company about the system. In this approach the consultant still learns more about the system then the company managers but can transfer some of that learning to the managers.

The participatory approach is the process where the company hires an outside consultant who then trains company managers to be part of the modeling and MFS building team. Together they go through the model-building steps. At the end of this process, the company not only has a piece of software, but they also have experienced the learnings about the system first hand and have developed the internal expertise to continue the learning process in-house. In this approach the company managers often can learn as much about the system as the consultant.

The following case study is an example of how our firm, Gould-Kreutzer Associates, uses the participatory approach to building a Management Flight Simulator. It is a hypothetical case, combining many different experiences we have had and is for illustrative purposes only.

Overview

One of our Latin American clients asked us to help them build a learning laboratory to help train mid-level managers in strategic decision making. We didn't learn until after the project was completed that the following high level debate had occurred.

The Dyno Petroleum Company (not its real name) was facing a crisis. The only solution they saw was to get better thinking from their management teams. The main implementation hurdle they had to overcome was that for decades their industry had been characterized by traditional top-down hierarchical organizational structures where both the decision making power, the intuitive understanding, and the experience in dealing with big picture issues were limited to a few people at the top of the hierarchy.

The accelerating pace of change had overwhelmed this group's ability to keep up with and understand how these changes were affecting their company. They had even less of an idea what adjustments in their organization would be necessary to respond to those changes. They had heard reports about other companies solving this problem by moving towards a less hierarchical organizational structure and allowing "empowered" teams to make more decisions and take the responsibility for implementing them. They decided to have a meeting to discuss using this same approach at Dyno Petroleum. Some of the team members thought that this was the wave of the future and not only a solution to their problem but the only way Dyno Petroleum could keep up with their competitors. Others were skeptical. In fact one cynic, their director of marketing, asked:

> Why would we want to broadly empower our people to make these kind of vital decisions and be responsible for the future success of our company? These people don't have the training, experience, background, motivation, or sense of responsibility and accountability necessary to make high level strategic decisions in such a complex environment. We're only here because we are a highly select group who have filtered to the top of this organization because of our special talent for making these types of complex decisions. We have been given extraordinary training and career development opportunities to give us the right kind of experience so we would better understand the whole system.
>
> We also know that if we don't "do it right" we would not only lose our jobs but be exposed to massive public humiliation. However, if we do play it right we will achieve great business success, and perhaps even become enormously wealthy and have the glory of high level promotions. This meeting came about because we realize that we're in over our heads. What makes us believe that if we're in over our heads that managers with less training, experience, and motivation are going to do any better?

Carmen Manchez, the director of human resources replied:

> There are new ways to accelerate the kind of system wide understanding, judgment, and even wisdom of which we think we have so much. These are the learning laboratories that are built around "management flight simulators." Why would we think that the only way to learn is by facing the "slings and arrows" of experience? There are in fact new and better ways to accelerate learning. All that I am asking is that this group endorse a small experiment. We would like to create a learning laboratory to test this concept and to show how these learning laboratories can help improve team learning and transform mid-level managers into more effective high-

level decision makers." (See page 354 of Daniel Kim's essay for a description of why you should use Learning Laboratories).

Pre-work

The first thing Carmen did after she received the endorsement of the management committee was to contact us. She told us that she would like us to create a learning laboratory as well as teach some introductory systems thinking courses for Dyno Petroleum. We told her that we would be delighted to help them create a learning laboratory and teach the courses. We also explained that it would be necessary for a team of their managers to be an integral part of the process. Converting mental models to mathematical models involves a great deal of learning about the system. It forces one to think long and hard about the interconnections within the system. It is important that members of the client's management team share in this learning.

Carmen and her fellow high-level managers decided that the first step in empowering their managers was to teach them to think holistically about the company. Since company-wide decisions had historically been the province of only the highest level managers, most middle managers only thought about how their decisions affected their own departments. It didn't occur to them to consider the affects their decisions had on the rest of the company. In order for the high level managers to trust middle managers with more responsibility, they decided the first step was to teach the middle managers to begin seeing the company as an interrelated whole.

It was decided that one way of approaching this purpose was to create a simple model of Dyno Petroleum and allow the mid-level managers to play president for a day. They would get the opportunity to make high-level strategic decisions and then see the impact those decisions had on the entire company. It was hoped that at first they would make the decisions that would be optimized for their individual departments and experientially discover that while these decisions helped the individual departments, they hurt the company as a whole. Once we agreed on the overall purpose we began to discuss the specifics and wrote a couple of paragraphs in our project log documenting this step.

Now that we knew what we wanted our participants to learn, we began thinking more deeply about who those participants were going to be. We came up with a detailed description of what our audience would look like. We asked ourselves questions like; How much computer experience do they have? What is their level of managerial experience? What is their level of technical experience? Are they going to be enthusiastic about coming to the learning laboratory or are they going to have to be forced? How do they see themselves within the company? It is our belief that by taking the time to research who our target audience is, we can customize the interface to their needs and make sure that the interface itself doesn't undermine efforts to achieve the goals. We wrote up our findings and included it as the second entry in our project log.

Capturing the Mental Models

After our first course we identified two managers as having the vision, the enthusiasm, and the personal skills to be on the modeling team—Taisen Suzuki and Sita Shastanantra. Carmen decided she'd also like to be a part of this team. We also identified two members of our firm to be on the modeling team—a professional model builder and a professional interface designer. At our first modeling team meeting we reviewed the purpose of our learning laboratory and the audience description that we had written up. An in-depth discussion followed where both documents were revised slightly.

Next we discussed who at Dyno Petroleum had the information on the company that we would need to build the model upon which our learning laboratory would be based. We identified a number of "experts" within the company. This team consisted of a number of high-level managers from different areas of the company who were known for their "understanding" of the entire company. We called them the "mental model team." Carmen was given the task of getting them together for one meeting. It was not expected that all of them would be able or interested in attending so we identified more than we actually needed.

The first step in any modeling effort is to define a problem that will be modeled. This problem should not only support the purpose of the learning laboratory but also be relevant to the target audience. The entire modeling team met and discussed a number of different problems we could model that would engage our target audience as well as support our purpose. In the end it was decided that our modeling problem would be almost the same as our purpose; how to pilot an oil company through an era of perpetual change.

We were now ready to meet with the members of the mental model team. Carmen had been able to schedule a time when most of the managers identified could attend. There were about twenty members of the team. We started the meeting by reviewing the purpose of the learning laboratory and the problem we had identified. We used FASTBreak™ (see essay by David Kreutzer on page 229) to move from the event level, represented by the mental models of our team, to a map of the underlying system structure, called a causal loop diagram. This map describes the feedback structure that our simulation model would represent, and line charts (Reference Modes) showing the behavior over time of key variables.

Converting Causal Loops to Mathematical Models

Our model builder explained that what we would be doing was an iterative process and would take time. We would use the causal loop diagrams and reference modes as guides as we converted the causal loop diagrams to their mathematical equivalent. We would then compare the output with the behavior shown in the reference modes, continuously refining and adjusting the model until we had created one which produced the same behavior as the real system.

Next we needed to determine what software tools we would use to create the model and the MFS. We had to do this before we began the actual modeling process because not all modeling software is compatible with all interface generation software.

Since I held the role as the interface designer I gave the team an overview of the MFS building process. I told them that because we are interested in using this model as the simulation engine to a MFS, we needed to think a little more about what we wanted the interface to look like. This can be done easily and quickly using storyboards, a method movie and cartoon makers use to design the flow of action in their films. We can use the same concept to design MFS. The process is quite simple, you create a map that shows the events your user will experience when using your interface. While we are creating the storyboard we are actually designing the user experience, and hence the user interface. All the features you want your interface to contain are identified in this process (including sound effects, movies, and animation).

Once we determine the features our MFS needs in order to achieve our purpose, we can choose the interface development software that is capable of producing all of these features. It is then an easy task to identify the modeling software that attaches to that interface development software.

We were now ready to begin to convert the causal loop diagram to mathematical equations. This is an iterative process. The team may need to repeatedly return to the mental model team for clarification and additional information. We encouraged the team to keep a list of system insights and issues that arose during the model building process. This is crucial since it contains some of the main learnings of the process that may need to be incorporated into the interface at a later date. Once the model builders had completed the process and were sure that it reproduced the behavior shown in the reference modes, we invited the mental model team members to use the model. We asked them to review it with several things in mind: Did it accurately reflect their mental model? Did it behave the way their intuition said it should? If not, was it a faulty mathematical model or faulty mental model? The discussions that followed were exciting and informative. The modeling team recorded the mental model team reactions and suggestions and refined the model to reflect their insights.

Attaching an Interface

Based on the initial purpose and the insights from the modeler's insight log, we were now able to determine exactly what key lessons we wished the target audience to learn. We once again examined our target audience to determine the best way to communicate these lessons to that audience.

While it is true that most of the lessons should come through using the MFS itself, some may need to be communicated with on-line causal loop diagrams, stock and flow diagrams, help screens, and the method of displaying the output. Some of the key lessons may need to be elicited during the debriefing session. We created a storyboard for the learning laboratory itself to help us make sure that the users were given all the information that they needed in order to experience the key lessons we wished them to learn. We discovered that there were several new features and screens that had to be added to our interface storyboard due to the fact that we now had more lessons which we wanted to communicate. We updated the storyboard with these new lessons.

We took our interface storyboard around to all our mental model team members and elicited their comments, evaluated those comments, and made the appropriate changes to the storyboard. I told our modeling team that we needed to evaluate the usability of the interface. Sita asked how we could do a usability evaluation on software that doesn't yet exist. I explained that we actually do two usability evaluations when creating an interface—one at the design stage and one on the software itself. Solving problems at the design stage is much less costly and disruptive then attempting to solve them once the software has been written.

The point of the usability evaluation is to ensure that there is nothing in the software which sabotages or hinders the user from easily using and benefiting from the software. This evaluation has a number of prongs to its attack—a human factors review, a display review, and a compositional review.

In order to allow the other members of the modeling team to participate in the usability review, we had an afternoon session talking about the main issues in the three prongs of our attack. For the human factors review we kept it simple and introduced our team to the main points of Don Norman's book *The Design of Everyday Things*. We then led them through the process of applying them to our interface. Since the purpose of this project was not to teach a course on human factors, we kept their role in the usability review as simple as possible and did a more thorough and traditional usability review on our own.

The main thrust of the display review is to make sure that the screens themselves emphasize the correct points. In this step we examined our choices of color, output charts, input devices, instruction screens, and debriefing screens. The main purpose of the instruction and debriefing screens is to make it easier to use the software and to reinforce the learnings. The display review attempts to make sure that the displays are drawing attention to the correct thing. Growth share matrices (bubble charts) are great, and graphically spectacular, but if your main point is to communicate the value of a single variable it would be a mistake to randomly select two other variables just so you could use the matrix.

The last usability review we had to do was the compositional review. This review is done from an artistic point of view.

The main questions here is whether or not the composition of the interface distracts the user from the interface's purpose and does the composition draw the users attention to where you want it drawn.

While a full human factors review includes a lot more issues than the ones listed here, these were the ones that the modeling team were responsible for implementing.

The storyboard was changed to reflect the results of these evaluations. We now turned our attention to actually building the interface. We tested the interface by dividing our modeling team into two groups. We then ran the model and the interface simultaneously to make sure we got the same results using a number of different inputs.

The final step in this stage is to redo the usability review on the software version of the interface. This is done because problems often surface in the actual software implementation of the interface that are invisible in the storyboard version. The interface must be refined to correct the problems identified by the testing, validation, and human factors review.

Designing and Using the Learning Lab

There are three main parts to learning laboratories: the briefing, the use of the interface, and the debriefing. The preliminary learning laboratory storyboard we created told us what each of these sections needed to communicate.

Our briefing contained two elements: a brief introduction to systems thinking and its limits, and the underlying structure and assumptions of the model. In order to help the users shorten the learning curve, we also created slides to help walk them through a base run of the simulation in the briefing.

Before we created the user guide we took out our audience description and discussed it one last time. We needed to focus the user guide efforts for our intended audience. We have found that user guides tailored to a specific audience are much more helpful to that audience then ones tailored to the general public. A user guide that computer programmers would thrive on could be considered nonsensical techno-nonsense by a non-technical manager. Conversely, user guides written for non-technical managers could have programmers climbing the wall because of excessive "hand-holding."

The user guide had several sections. There were sections which documented the underlying model. Sections which provided a step-by-step guide, sections which listed a number of scenarios that should be run, and sections which gave instructions for how to run user defined scenarios.

Despite the fact that we planned our debriefing to be done in a conversational format we believe strongly that it should be organized and written out ahead of time. It's important that the users actually draw their conclusions from the debriefing themselves in their discussions. It is the job of the facilitator to ask the questions which lead the discussion to the lessons you wanted to teach.

It is just as important to test and review your training materials (briefing, user guide, and debriefing) as it was to test the model and interface. There are two different ways of testing this material. One is to formally review the materials using a set of criteria that are found in a number of books on training. Another is to test the material with representative members of your target audience and then run post laboratory tests and interviews to make sure the laboratory had its desired affect. Both should be done.

We used our mental model team as a test group and ran the completed learning laboratory with them as the participants. Members of the modeling team helped facilitate this learning laboratory.

Final Thoughts

This learning laboratory was considered extremely successful by Carmen, the modeling team, and the mental model team. At Carmen's suggestion we invited the director of marketing (the cynic in the debate) to participate and observe one of the learning laboratories in action. He was impressed and joined with Carmen in recommending to the executive committee that additional learning laboratories be created to further test their usefulness in training mid-level managers to begin thinking in a systemic way.

As you can see from the above case study, a great deal of learning about the system occurs during the process of building a learning laboratory. Involving members of the client's management team in the model building process may allow managers to share in this learning, giving them the ability to continue to use and evolve the model, interface, and learning laboratory once the consultants have gone home.

David P. Kreutzer is president and co-founder of Gould-Kreutzer Associates, Inc., a management consulting firm in Cambridge, Massachusetts. The firm specializes in systems thinking, a management perspective that focuses on how to change the structure of a company in order to enhance its performance with System Dynamics Models, Management Flight Simulators, and Executive Strategy Systems.

Prior to founding the company in 1989, Kreutzer had been on the Systems Dynamics research team at the Massachusetts Institute of Technology for eleven years and is the joint director of the MIT System Dynamics Summer Session. He has extensive experience in the fields of computer simulation and corporate strategy, as well as in applying a systems thinking approach to organizational learning within companies throughout the world.

15

FASTBreak™:
A Facilitation Approach to
Systems Thinking Breakthroughs

David P. Kreutzer

> *The significant problems we face cannot be solved at the same level of thinking we were at when we created them.*
>
> —Albert Einstein

How can we transform our "level of thinking" to arrive at a creative problem solving breakthrough of the sort Einstein refers to? Even more importantly, how can we facilitate this kind of transformation in management teams that are stuck in a rut or in a conflict? A number of systems thinking tools such as causal loop diagrams, system dynamics simulations, and management flight simulators have demonstrated great potential at assisting managers in making this transformation. However, these tools are often challenging to implement in real time consulting situations.

This paper describes a strategy for improving the implementation success of such systems thinking tools by embedding them in a specifically designed sequence of facilitation processes. The first process engages the management team "where it is at"—making visible the "level of thinking" of the team when it created the problem. In systems thinking we call this the "event" level and it is often symbolized by the man in the domino cartoon.

Arnie Levin, © 1992. Reprinted with permission from the artist.

The domino man cartoon (above) represents a typical manager who thinks he has solved a problem. He wants more room, so he does the first thing he can think of to create more space. It's obvious, isn't it? If you need more space, push down the wall. It's exactly what any decisive, action-oriented management hero would do. But, as you can see, because the dominoes are in a particular pattern, this manager will eventually get exactly the opposite of what he really wants. In short, he's going to get flattened.

Seeing the Big Picture

The question is: what would happen if this manager could suddenly stand up, turn around, and see the pattern? If he could see the relationships, the big picture, and he still wanted more space, what could he do instead?

The difference between getting what you really want and disaster often depends on your ability to see the big picture. If you're about to push over a domino, but instead you move your chair forward, or push the dominoes down from both sides, that's learning. That's improving the quality of thinking and decision making. This is also an example of how a transformation of viewpoint can get you the kind of outcome you want in a real tangible sense. In today's complex systems, the dominoes are connected in ways that we don't always understand—to our teammates, to our customers, to our suppliers, to our competitors, and to other nations. If you can't see the big picture, if you don't understand the connections, you're likely to do the wrong thing, or something that seems to reward your company in the short term, but destroys your organization over the long haul.

Systems Thinking Tools

One goal of systems thinking and system dynamics is to provide tools to transform the perspectives and mental models of managers so that their decisions and actions lead to real sustainable long-term improvements in their organizations. Not just a succession of quick "better before worse," short-term improvements.

My personal experience with systems thinking began in the late 1970s. It was an exciting time at MIT. As a research associate, I felt very fortunate to be studying under people like Jay Forrester, the founder of system dynamics, and Ed Schein, the innovator of process facilitation, and to work on a research team with the "up-and-coming" masters of systems thinking.

I remember how incredibly impressed I was with the power of the systems thinking tools, which give the ability to map whole systems, to test and to refine the quality of people's mental models and assumptions, and to design learning laboratories and management practice fields. Inspired by this potential, I worked hard to master the methodology and tool kit, and then naively set out to conquer the world.

Implementation Issues

However, when I started to practice systems thinking in my first major consulting engagements, I was in for a big surprise. Implementation was an uphill battle, and—as with Total Quality Management today—success came more slowly than one might have expected, especially given the power of the tools.

The systems thinking tools are powerful, but implementing them was difficult. The fundamental reason was that we were so fascinated by the power of the tools that we were not paying enough attention to the underlying learning processes. One of most important lessons I learned from the systems thinking "school of hard knocks" was that if you want to enhance your chances of implementation success, it helps to embed the systems thinking tools in a well designed and flexible facilitation process. You have to pay just as much attention to the process of facilitation itself as you do to the tools that you use in the process.

Another important question was: how could we help teams create a shared picture of their most important business assumptions, a group-shared mental model? A mental model is a map, a picture of the territory. We live in our own interior worlds, in the worlds of our own experience, in our individual versions of reality. Team members may use the same words, the same language, but much of the *meaning* is very personal. Not that everyone has to agree with each other, but it helps if you understand what each person is thinking, and what each team member is really trying to say. Instead, in my first attempts at implementing systems thinking models it often seemed as if the team members were speaking different languages. It was like the Tower of Babel. They all had different mental models. Team members were often drowning in a sea of different assumptions, different interpretations, and different meanings. Creating *rapport* and *shared meaning* in a group was not an easy matter, but essential to achieving implementation success with systems thinking tools.

So, we discovered that implementing systems thinking was not just about tools, or just about the facilitation process, or just about creating rapport in teams. The real question was: how do they all work together? How can you do them all at the same time? After trying to apply systems thinking training in organizations, I was convinced that the systems thinking tools were extremely powerful, but they certainly weren't always the right place to start a conversation with a management team. On the other hand, the basic process facilitation tools were great for starting a conversation, but managers usually got impatient and frustrated after awhile, and asked, "Okay—so where do we go from here?" I needed a springboard, some way to jump from assumptions about "what's going on here and how did we get in this mess" captured in the event map, to the "big picture" a systems map where effective change can actually occur. The facilitation and conceptual methodologies that empower a team to make this transition are the defining objectives of FASTBreak™. This is a systems thinking facilitation process enabling the team to combine the best features of both worlds.

The FASTBreak™ System

During that period, I was invited by Royal Dutch Shell to introduce the systems thinking tools to their Global Planning Group. It was on that visit that I met Tony Hodgson, a British creativity and organization development consultant. He had developed a way to use color-coded magnetic hexagons to do fast and flexible brainstorming and creativity exercises (Hodgson 1992). My first thought was, "Wow! What a clever way to improve the process of drawing causal loops with management teams!"

One of the bread-and-butter tools in systems thinking is the "causal loop diagram," a kind of visual map which allows you to see the big picture and the interrelationships among the key variables in a system. A causal-loop diagram is a picture of the underlying systems structure which, from the point of view of systems thinking, is both the cause of system behavior, as well as the level of most effective intervention. In a causal loop diagram you ask yourself, "What links to what?" and then you draw a connection between Variable A and Variable B. As you continue the process, you usually discover important feedback loops, situations where, if you do something to the system, it tends to circle back. The purpose of causal loop mapping is to identify these feedback loops, which helps you to intuitively deduce possible outcome behaviors which your system might exhibit over time. Causal loops are a powerful language for describing systems: a language which, metaphorically, makes the invisible dominoes of your situation—visible. Unfortunately, it's not a language in which most people are fluent.

Now, just imagine that you're a member of a management team and I'm here to facilitate your strategic planning process with causal loop diagrams. And I say, "Hello, thank you very much for inviting me here. Now tell me your most important thoughts and concerns. But wait! Make sure that each one of them is expressed as a proper variable, and use arrows to link them in terms of cause and effect. And, while you're at it, put either an 's' and 'o' next to each statement depending on whether the variables in a causal loop move in the same or opposite direction. And, by the way, it would be very helpful if you could identify all of the reinforcing and balancing loops by putting an 'R' or 'B' in the middle of all loops." That's just too much for most management teams that are still novices in the systems thinking languages. It's a real conversation stopper.

An additional process difficulty in applying causal loops in management teams in the past was that we would almost always need to redraw the diagrams about ten or eleven times before we got them right. And all that redrawing and rearranging of the variables on flip charts was distracting enough to sometimes lose the attention of the group.

So, I thought, "What a great solution! We'll put the variables on magnetic hexagons and then we can move them around." This was the first step towards creating what is now known as FASTBreak™, a systems thinking facilitation process specifically designed to manage the transition from ideas to causal loop diagrams and other advanced systems thinking tools. FASTBreak stands for a facilitation approach to systems thinking breakthroughs.

Most importantly, FASTBreak™ has been used, with great success, to allow managers to experience the transformation from the "events" to the "systems" perspective. It is often said that systems thinkers are able to move back and forth among three different ways of looking at reality: 1) seeing discrete events, 2) recognizing patterns of behavior over time (or trends), and 3) seeing the big picture, or the underlying structure itself.

Fixating on Events

The manager in the domino cartoon is stuck at the level of events. He just lost a big order, a delivery is late, staff morale is down, he's got to finish a report. Because this manager is so focused on events, he only sees what's right in front of his nose. He sees a domino, he wants more room, so he pushes it down. In organizations dominated by this mentality, people race from one crisis to another. Since they are trapped in event-level thinking, they are catapulted from one problem to the next. This fixation on short-term solutions keeps them from seeing the patterns of change behind the events.

Charting the Trends or Patterns of Behavior

When teams and managers operate solely at the event level, they get locked into a "fire-fighting" mode. So at this second level, you are encouraged to get up from the chair and look at the relationships among the individual events. When you look around, you begin to notice that there are trends or "patterns of behavior of events over time." Identifying these "variables", and charting how they behave over time, provides a window or a gateway to the systems level.

Seeing the patterns of behavior over time is like saying, "Hey, wait a minute—isn't this just another version of something I've done before?" Someone in the sandbox hits you, and pretty soon you're both fighting. This exchange takes place exclusively at the event level: "I hit him because he hit me." However, if you look around for a moment, you might see a *pattern* there. You begin to see the nature of the *trend* ("I hit him, then he hits me").

Unless one person breaks that pattern, the *events* will escalate into all-out warfare. Pattern-of-behavior explanations help you to break the grip of short-term thinking and to see, in this case, the *pattern* of escalation. This insight enables you to find the leverage in the situation. Rather than simply reacting, you could offer to share your toys, therefore breaking the escalating behavior caused by this feedback loop. Learning to see the underlying *patterns* that cause *events* is one of the goals of systems thinking.

Seeing the Big Picture

At the third level, you finally turn around and see the big picture—the systems structure. Once you see the *system,* you can answer the questions, "What causes the patterns of behavior? What is the underlying structure behind the trends?" You have found the points of power and high leverage for successful change. You may not be surrounded by hostile dominoes, but there are all sorts of cause-and-effect relationships—seemingly invisible—that can produce unexpected results. For example, let's say your company is in a cash flow crisis. What do you do? You lay people off, because layoffs reduce costs.

You think you've solved your problem—profits are up, cash flow is up—but wait! If you laid off your R&D department, and your competitors introduce a new product, your sales will go down, and your profits will drop even more. So the very thing you did to fix the problem eventually made things worse. That's an example of a "Fixes that Fail" archetype, one of a library of systemic patterns that occur over and over, again and again. (See Figure 1.)

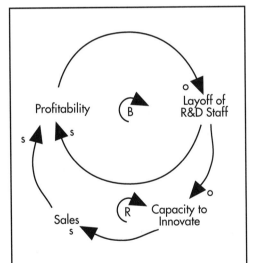

The *Fixes That Fail Archetype* is an example of a causal loop diagram that shows that while the system impact of R&D layoffs is to improve profitability the unintended long-term effect is to reduce it by reducing the capacity to innovate.

Figure 1

Systems interventions can be very powerful. Once you can draw a picture of the whole system, you can focus your actions on high-leverage interventions. When you focus only on events, your interventions will usually produce only low-leverage change. You may have "fixed" the symptoms, but your illness will get worse in the long run.

FASTBreak™ Stages

The tools and the facilitation steps in FASTBreak™ are designed to lead a team through these three stages from the "events" to the "patterns of behavior" to the "systems structure".

Step One: Focus on Core Issues

The first phase of FASTBreak™ uses color-coded magnetic hexagon shaped disks to surface each team member's concerns and mental models around some theme question. You ask each person, "What are the most important ideas and issues from your point of view?" "What are your strongest opinions?" "What do you feel is holding us back?" You summarize each response in three to four words and write it on a hexagon. You place the hexagons on the board in sequence. At first, you don't attempt to arrange the ideas. This step can also be done with Post-it Notes™, however, the hexagon shape is the most convenient geometric shape for making the maximum number of connections with no blank spaces.

Hexagon maps capture the event level—the world of who, what, when, where, and why. That's where you want to start, because you first have to connect with people's worlds in their own language. So they begin talking in their everyday language, and with symbols that people understand. But, since your goal is to build a shared understanding, you have to go beyond simple brainstorming. You want to explore the reasoning—and the emotions—behind their statements. So, if someone says, "We need to raise prices," you would probably ask, "Can you tell me more about that?" And then maybe they say, "If we don't raise prices, this company is going to go under, because we won't have enough revenues to support R&D!" The challenge is to capture the essence of each person's position in just a few words, so that the hexagon can serve as a vivid reminder for the entire group. You're really using the hexagons as a prop that allows people to clearly express their ideas, to really speak their minds.

Then you zero in on the core issues, the big-picture areas

that percolate to the top. You ask, "Which of the hexagons seem to go together?" and you start moving them around. You find the hexagons that seem to go with each other, and then you move them into the same general area on the board. Once you have reviewed the positioning, you draw a circle around each grouping and then give each cluster a title, a name. Maybe you put your first title up there, and someone says, "Let's change it, that's not quite right." That's the reason we do this with magnets, and on dry-erase surfaces. It's an organic process. You take each small victory as is it occurs. And you start to develop a common language with the team.

Every team has a continuously changing issues agenda of key assumptions they need to be challenging or discussing. However, at the outset or when their circumstances change, they don't know what this agenda is. As a consequence they should regularly surface and test their issues agenda together. Every individual says, "Here's what I think is important, here are the issues I want to see resolved, here are the things I think we should talk about." The titles of the most important clusters become what Hodgson calls the "emergent agenda"; these are the hot spots according to the group.

Step Two: Finding the Variables

If this is all we had up our sleeves, many of you would say, "So what? We already know how to do affinity diagrams, and we've done lots of brainstorming. But now we start to shift into higher gear. In FASTBreak™, this is where the action really begins.

At this next stage of the process, you use tools to identify the most important trends and patterns of behavior over time. Variables, and charts of the patterns of behavior they exhibit over time, are the springboards which allow you to jump from the event level to the systems map. A variable is something that can increase or decrease. So if you were concerned about the economy, you might say, "We could have a depression!" A *depression* , however, is not a variable. Once you define a depression as eight consecutive quarters of declining GNP, you've found your variable. GNP *is* something that can increase or decrease. You can also use "soft" or qualitative variables—"morale" or "quality" can increase or decrease; both morale and quality can change over time.

What we're looking for are the system's dynamics. When you look for key variables, you're really asking, "Can you tell me an interesting story of how something in this system might change over time?" At Gould-Kreutzer Associates, we surface the key variables by asking a set of transition questions about the most important groups of hexagons on the board: "What do you really want? How would you know if you got it?" "Who are the other key players? What might they want? How would they know if they got it?" "What are your key choices?" "What are the key uncertainties?" "What are the most important trends?" You're trying to make the shift to the systems point of view, and it takes some skill to navigate into that domain. But, once you've identified the trends, the variables, you'll be amazed at how quickly you can move to a systems map. Additionally, if the team has used this process to ask itself what are the most important issues, key players, goals, choices, and uncertainties, the resulting map is more likely to represent the most important "big picture" of their system.

Step Three: The Systems Thinking Tools.

The systems thinking tools—especially the causal loop diagrams that show the structure in a comprehensible way, and the systems archetypes—are a great way to foster high-quality thinking, communication, and decision making in teams. These visual maps offer a vivid and engaging way to tell your company's most compelling stories. If you can create a causal loop diagram which allows each team member to see the complete story on a map, it can bust through log jams and resolve disputes. But remember, for real breakthroughs, the maps must focus on the group's key problems and objectives. If they do not, they can easily degenerate into meaningless spaghetti diagrams.

Systems Thinking's Fairy Tales

In systems thinking, certain classic stories occur so frequently that they are called systems archetypes and given names like "Limits to Growth," "Shifting the Burden," "Tragedy of the Commons," and "Fixes that Fail." These archetypes are so prevalent in systems behavior that it is often wise to heed the advice of the police inspector in *Casablanca* to "Round up the usual suspects!" The Systems Archetypes provide a very accessible way for novice users to begin to recognize systems behavior.

However, it is also important to remember that systems thinking is not simply a multiple-choice test. If you go to your CEO and say, "Tell me about your problem? Is it a 'Shifting the Burden?' 'Limits to Growth?' 'Fixes that Fail?'"—that's probably not the best way to start. You can always come up with a correct and interesting archetype, but that may not be your best shot at an effective intervention. However, when used properly, the archetypes do allow you to practice a kind of "systems judo," where you don't fight against the system, but you use the system's forces to your advantage. This is because, once a systems archetype has been identified, it will always suggest areas for high- and low-leverage change.

Coming to Closure with the Team

In learning organizations, "it's the process of learning that's important, not the content outcome of any particular lesson." Despite this, however, at the end of that process, other people will still want the "hard facts." They'll ask, "Where's the output?" And if you don't have anything to show them—"Oh, we don't have any output, but we learned a lot along the way!"—you'll be in trouble. People will say, "Was it really worth the expense? How do you know?"

So you should make a real attempt to document your learning process. Take photographs of your hexagon maps and clusters; your behavior charts, and your causal loops. There's an old Chinese saying that "a picture is worth a thousand words." So, now we have people saying, "Instead of giving you a thousand-page report, we're going to send you our hexagon maps and our causal loop diagrams."

Remember where you started with the hexagons? You asked, "What are your most important issues?" And someone said, "Price is too high." Now go back and retell those stories from the systems thinking perspective. So, if someone said, "Look, we need layoffs to reduce costs and improve cash flow," and than someone else said, "Yes, but if we lay off the R&D department, we'll lose our capacity to innovate. And if we lose our capacity to innovate, our sales could go down, and our cash flow could actually get worse"—that's learning! What looked like a decisive action at the hexagon level now looks shortsighted from the perspective of the causal loops. That's the kind of thing you can document. The real value is the sudden insight: "I never thought of it that way before. I was about to do this, but now on Monday morning I'll do that instead."

Empowerment and Team Learning

I was talking about empowerment to a manager from a command-and-control culture, and he turned to me and said,

"Why would we want to empower incompetent people?" And to him, "incompetent" meant that those people couldn't see the big picture. As Peter Senge says in *The Fifth Discipline,* "There's no guarantee that energetic, committed local decision makers will be wise decision makers. Local decision makers can be myopic, and fail to appreciate the impacts of decisions on the larger systems in which they operate." Without a way to improve the quality of the team's mental models, group decision making tends to drift to the lowest common denominator.

A lot of companies are talking about "empowerment," "breaking down hierarchies" and "self- managing work teams." But in many cases you're not empowering your people with the tools and processes they need to create a shared team mental model. Without the ability to do that, team decision making just won't work. People will just get stuck in their individual mental models, identify with their "positions," and fixate on their personal assumptions about "how things really work around here."

What if one member of the team says, "I think prices ought to be high," and I say, "That's the stupidest idea I've ever heard!" Now it's a face-to-face battle. The argument's not really about pricing anymore. It's about who's going to win or lose the debate. So people start to become very cautious. They begin to withhold their insights, and to refrain from challenging each other's assumptions. That's because, if you challenge that person's assumptions, you'll be perceived as challenging that person. So you begin to hold back, and the quality of thinking in the organization begins to degenerate. By separating the ideas from the people this process encourages more aggressive and constructive challenging of assumptions which can lead to higher quality thinking in teams.

How can we create a shared mental model? How can we connect to the wisdom that resides in each person's mind? A lot of companies are struggling with these issues right now. Is there a way to take advantage of diversity as a source of strength, and, at the same time, not get bogged down in endless confusion, arguments, power plays, and fights? That's the focus of FASTBreak™. To the extent that we can learn to learn from people who are different from ourselves, we can actually do a better job. That's the real benefit of "diversity." A lot of people are starting to see diversity as a genuine business opportunity, not just as something we "ought to do."

Even more important, the understanding of structure fully

opens the door to extremely robust exploration of policies and modes of operation through simulation, modeling of the structure, and development of a management practice fields. User-friendly enough for executive teams, the potential for active use in real-world management is enormous.

Visibility Works

How do we improve the quality of thinking, communication and decision making in teams? To borrow a phrase from my friend Gary B. Chicoine-Piper, "visibility works." First, you have to make your assumptions visible. The next step is to ask, "Now that we can see our assumptions, is this the best we can do? Is there something missing? Can our models be improved?" You have to be willing to step back and look at the larger picture, and be courageous enough to say, "We're systematically, over and over again, doing this in reaction to that, and it's not working, let's change it." Surfacing individual mental models, testing them, building a shared group mental model, and learning are key notions.

Summary

The thing I like about FASTBreak™ is that it keeps everything visible. Not just the final output, but throughout the entire process. The process has a way of keeping people in the present moment. My guess is that if you could count the percentage of people and teams who are able to surface, challenge, test, and change their most crucial business assumptions and group shared mental models in present time and in common with everyone else on their team, in both the real system and in practice fields, that would be one interesting way to measure your progress towards becoming a learning organization.

At the outset, team members may see different parts of the problem. Then they start by generating key issues, then collecting the key variables, putting them on the board, and connecting the dots. Once they make the transition to the systems level, and started asking, "What are the structural forces that are creating change?" insights, understandings and opportunities break wide open. At this point the team can stand up, look around, and see the dominoes. Now they can see the problem at a different level from the one at which it was created. To me that's an improvement in the quality of thinking, decision-making, and action. Now they can get more space by moving the chair forward instead of being flattened by dominoes.

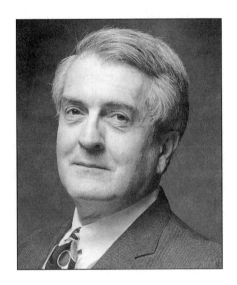

Robert Dilworth received his Doctorate from Columbia University following his retirement as an Army brigadier general in 1991. He then joined the faculty of Virginia Commonwealth University as an Assistant Professor of Adult Education and Human Resource Development. He has experimented with Learning Organization-related concepts in both government and industry and has extensive experience with quality management.

Dilworth serves as National Director of the International Society for Quality Government, as well as on the National Executive Committees of the Management Science and Policy Analysis Section of the American Society for Public Administration and the Learning Organization Network of the American Society for Training and Development. His research focus is transformation of organizations preparatory to introduction of quality management.

16

The DNA of the Learning Organization

Robert Dilworth

An organization's ability to survive and prosper in our turbulent age requires new ways of thinking and organizing the business enterprise. It demands the confluence of two streams of thought. They are continuous improvement (Kaizen) and continuous learning, characterized by what has come to be called the learning organization. This is as much art as science, where gentle subtleties and intricate ambiguities can be more important than concrete constructions.

The Nordstrom department store employee handbook covers only one page and lists but one rule: "Use your own good judgment in all situations." This is the mental model that drives the Nordstrom culture. You can deduce several concepts and values from this one-page handbook and its simple guidance: empowerment, trust, commitment, and shared vision—each of them important components of a true learning organization.

Corporate values represent a key ingredient of "organizational DNA." You can define organizational DNA as the internalized values and beliefs that govern individual and team behavior. They operate much like a genetic code. In high-performing organizations like Nordstrom's, employees operate fluidly within a broad vision. Learning becomes embedded in day-to-day work activity. One could also term such a phenomenon as holographic—in the words of V. Marsick, "just as the whole can be recreated from any of its parts in the laser-created photograph called a hologram." This connotes inclusiveness rather than fragmentation within an enterprise, with both hierarchical and horizontal boundaries of greatly reduced significance. The goal becomes an enterprise, without boundaries, fully integrated in terms of both quality and learning processes. Peter Senge speaks of a systems thinking learning process, where it is the "models we carry in our heads that determine what we actually perceive and how we make decisions."

Organizational integration demands a model that has not yet been fully defined. As K. Watkins and V. Marsick write:

Learning organizations grow organically and each company will create a different configuration. A learning organization requires thinking like a sculptor. The sculptor . . . has to see in her mind's eye, and shape structures toward, that which nurtures learning and then create, sustain or alter existing approaches to foster this capacity.

The purpose of this chapter is to call attention to the gaps in current thinking and to show how the DNA of a learning organization can be created. It involves the design of a strategic architecture that brings business and learning processes together as part of a single system.

> *Strategic architecture...is the invisible intellectual, philosophical and even normative 'DNA' which programs and lends coherence to virtually all important business decisions, whether they be strategic or operational.*
>
> —N. Kiernan
> *The New Strategic Architecture*

Principal Barriers

There are at least five principal barriers to organizational learning. The first is a tendency to treat learning as an individual phenomenon rather than as something that can involve a group of people. Senge talks about the importance of team learning as a group skill. The second is a fixation with formal training, with scant attention given to informal learning. (One telltale sign of this is the setting aside of a fixed percentage of payroll for training, as if it represents the sum extent of learning that will occur.) The third is to treat business and learning processes as entirely discrete worlds. A fourth gap relates to "nonlistening" work environments. Non–listening effectively blocks communication and the kinds of idea interchange necessary to promote organizational learning.

> *A company that becomes a learning organization may eventually evolve into a place where everyone is cross-trained and enjoys learning continually, but it's got to start with someone listening, really listening, to someone else.*
>
> —B. Filipczak
> *I am a Learning Organization*

Finally, the barriers generated by hierarchy, and the autocratic leadership styles, create an atmosphere of distrust, fear, blocked communications, fragmentation of work effort, and stultification of organizational learning. Until this aspect of organizational culture is dealt with, there is little likelihood that meaningful organizational learning activity will occur.

How do you know when such gaps are being closed? A metaphor perhaps says this best. It can be described as the difference between a combustion engine and a diesel engine. A combustion engine requires a continuous spark to operate, much as an organization reacts to an autocratic leadership environment. A diesel engine, once the starter motor has activated it, becomes self-firing. An organization that reflects creative freedom, prudent risk taking, employee self-initiatives, and wide–ranging communications flows is on the way to closing such gaps.

Bringing Business and Learning Processes Together

Firms that are on the cutting edge of the quality movement understand the need to reengineer, not simply refine processes. It is necessary to analyze processes in depth and ensure that they support the purpose of the enterprise and its vision for the future. Processes must also interrelate in seamless ways across the business. This is not an easy task and can demand years of attention to achieve in a comprehensive way. It rarely succeeds unless fundamental changes in organizational culture take place as well, including the empowerment of workforce and a shift to a matrix form of process management rather than holding to the archetypical functional relationships. Quality management initiatives fail to get off the ground when no pre-work is undertaken to prepare the corporate culture for a new way of doing business. It is as if a farmer accomplished seeding before tilling the soil. We would think the farmer strange, yet we regularly introduce new approaches in organizations with little, if any, preparation whatever, and then we puzzle over the absence of seedlings.

The better quality initiatives now address the creation of learning organizations but such development usually gets treated as a separate area of activity, instead of being interactively modeled with business processes. This is a major gap. Closing this gap is the single greatest challenge of the 1990s. To continue the DNA example borrowed from genetics, the business and learning processes must become strands in a common chromosome.

> *The two streams of business development*
> *and organizational development...are seen as*
> *parallel (and interconnected) rather than as*
> *sequential.*
> —R. Beckhard and W. Pritchard
> *Changing the Essence*

It is *not* a case of attending to design of learning processes after business processes have been re-engineered. It must be done concurrently. In some cases, the strategic needs related to learning processes may dictate that they take precedence over what might otherwise have been a pure business process decision. This can be true, for example, when positioning the human resources of a company for the next generation of technology and work complexity.

The separation of learning from work is not new. They have come to be treated as essentially discrete areas of activity.

> *Around the turn of the century, learning*
> *was separated from work. The notion then*
> *became one of classroom training taking place*
> *at one site and work being conducted at an-*
> *other. Learning wasn't continuous; it wasn't*
> *holistic; it wasn't integrated with work.*
> —Ernst & Young
> *Valuing the Learning Organization*

If one accepts the premise that interactive modeling needs to occur, what form should it take with respect to learning processes? It is *not* a case of rolling out traditional training which focuses on instrumental learning, namely task-oriented problem solving. While formal training programs are represented in the new paradigm they are increasingly supplanted by experiential forms of learning, with a heavy emphasis on action learning. Workplace becomes classroom, supervisors become coaches, and fellow employees serve as cross-peer tutors at the work site.

Specific Strategies

What follows is a survey of some specific strategies that can become an embedded part of the way the organization functions. They do not represent a single system or all-inclusive list of strategies. Strategies will vary widely depending on circumstances in a given organization. What they all hold in common are conscious efforts to better integrate the business enterprise. They also help create the kind of DNA necessary to perpetuate individual and group learning processes in direct juxtaposition with the business processes.

Cross-functional teams or task forces can continuously serve to globally integrate the business, even as individuals and the teams themselves learn. The art is in the composition of such teams. As Kiernan writes:

> ...the deliberate selection of directors, executives, and managers with a diversity of skills and backgrounds to promote divergent viewpoints and debate.

In an example directly known to me, each cross-functional team in a large organization contained membership from every traditional organizational subcomponent. This challenged team members to work on problems outside the bounds of their prior knowledge (one common feature of action learning). Members also then became agents in providing learning feedback to their departments.

Job rotation can be a potent way to promote a continuous process of learning. When accomplished across business processes in a systematic manner, it broadens employee knowledge in ways that open up new approaches to process refinement. It represents an effective way of "up-skilling" a workforce in preparation for future demands. The Japanese are very good at this and carry it to a point far beyond that customarily found in the US. The requirement for multiple competencies inherent in a

self-directed team focus also underlies the job rotation orientation in Japan. Employees are expected to have broad mastery of
process, and understand the relationship of their contribution,
and that of their team, to the overall enterprise.

Work-outs, an organizational development strategy that
lines up closely with action learning, were invented by GE in
1989. In this process, groups are brought together either as
natural teams or as an admixture of people who may never have
worked together before. They go through an intensive problem-
solving experience that lasts roughly three days. Most GE employees have now experienced a workout. As many as fifty
individuals undergo the experience. During the session, participants are further broken down into smaller groups to work on
specific issues.

This organizational development approach is so compelling
because it consciously sets out to empower attendees. It also
commonly focuses on improvement of business processes. A
work-out culminates with work-out team proposals to top management that must be dealt with on-the-spot.

The work-out pioneered by GE is perhaps the best example
in corporate America of how business and learning processes can
be consciously engineered to create a new DNA and transform
the company. According to Beckhard and Pritchard, GE's CEO,
Jack Welch, determined:

> ...that a change in 'genetic code' is required to
> produce a different kind of leader-manager in the
> future. The work-out serves as a tonic in achieving
> this end.

The work-out is now embedded in the GE culture. When the
design characteristics of work-outs are considered, the inter-
twining of business and learning processes within a strategic
plan becomes evident. First, it is common to have work group
members come from sources other than company employees. Up
to one-half of participants may be customers or suppliers, causing cross-pollination of ideas and sharing of widely varied perspectives. Employees see problems through the eyes of the
customer. They are forced to deal with uncertainty, and draw on
their own inner strengths, coupled with resources of the group,
in arriving at solutions. This is where you enter the territory of
team learning. Group synergy in such circumstances can elevate
the plateau of knowledge and produce opportunities for perfor-

mance breakthroughs. Such efforts to modify DNA in major ways is not something undertaken timidly.

> *Radically altering the genetic code of a large successful corporation requires revolutionary action. Since 1981 John F. Welch has been struggling to break the company's old genetic code.*
>
> —Noel Tichy, *Crotonville: A Staging Ground for Corporate Revolution*

Action learning is a basic ingredient of learning organizations. The principal pioneer of action learning, a term coined by Kurt Lewin in the late 1940s, is Reg Revans of England. Revans' work with corporations in Belgium underscores the importance of inducing new thinking by conscious consideration of group content, called an "action learning set." His model centers on the belief that *setting* (or environment) and *problems* to be considered have an important link to group composition decisions and the depth of the learning experience. Revans further characterizes settings and problems as either familiar or unfamiliar.

Revans contends that team learning gains fullest expression when both setting and problem are unfamiliar. In Belgium, action learning sets of five senior managers from different industries were formed. They then proceeded to visit and diagnose an industry other than their own, sharing observations among themselves in arriving at new understandings. Revans calls such an experience "partners in adversity." Pursuit of complex problems causes the group members to bond closely in sharing their ignorance and insights. Such an experience induces fresh questions by those not immersed in the biases and texture of the problem set being examined. In Belgium, major break-throughs occurred, including a discovery that procedures dating back more than 150 years were hamstringing the ability of a major steel producer to meet demands for new alloy steel.

There are a number of engineering options available, such as the staff of one hospital examining another hospital. General Electric Company of England tends to examine unfamiliar problems in familiar settings. Finally, when "questioning circles" are brought together (a term Revans developed), it can be a self-directed work team struggling to improve a process.

Succession planning is almost always confined to the more senior management ranks. An essential ingredient of the continuous process of learning is a succession design that covers *all* levels in the organization.

A fundamental feature of a broad-based succession plan is that when the person an individual is earmarked to succeed is absent, the next in line physically covers that role and has *equal* accountability for outcome. In the 1990s, the person in line of succession may link laterally because of the flat hierarchical structure and focus on management by process. To actually move the understudy to the incumbent's role is a powerful way to induce meaningful learning as part of work processes.

One might argue that the physical movement of the understudy to the role designated in the succession plan can play havoc with continuity in the organization and create unnecessary turbulence. This can be true at a tactical level. From a strategic perspective, it breeds an unusual depth of operating strength, sense of cohesion, and depth of capability, which more than compensates for what might be construed as the senseless interruption of a person's work life.

Career pathing is closely associated with job rotations, but from the standpoint of DNA engineering it takes on a more global character as well. It involves the artful marriage of the evolution of processes with the just-in-time readiness of workforce members to deal with those processes. It is a case of keeping the human resource base aligned with processes in terms of skill sets and overall level of knowledge. The only way such a balance can be properly struck is through parallel and interactive modeling of business and learning processes.

Mentoring programs tend to receive inadequate attention. The Japanese, in contrast, have turned it into an art form. Peter Drucker describes their "Godfather" system where senior level managers not earmarked for advancement are assigned a group of junior managers. They then nurture and monitor their development. The system is the product of many generations of development, with its roots traveling back more than four hundred years to the Samurai warrior ethic. Protégés have the opportunity to turn to a trusted advocate outside of their normal line of supervision.

As a different way of mental modeling, the Japanese speak of *Sempai-Kohai* in considering mentoring relationships. It holds that mentors learn from their protégés, even as the protégés learn from them. Such a philosophy is not normally a part of the way mentoring is approached in the United States. Those who foster such an approach and watch it play out in organizations see mentors learn a great deal from the act of mentoring and from those being mentored.

Employee exchange programs allow cross-peer coaching to occur as a natural and planned result of the experience. Ideally, this is engineered so that there is an overlap to begin the process. One exchangee begins by understudying the other at their work site. Each exchanges knowledge with the other. New perspectives result. It is also reminiscent of the Revans' model in terms of having to operate in an unfamiliar environment while dealing with unfamiliar problems. Exchange programs are perhaps most successful when sufficient time is involved, such as six months, to cause the exchangee to accept accountability for some of the decisions made. As in the case of succession planning, the DNA is designed to immediately adjust assigned roles to compensate for the absence of any given person. It creates a learning environment where absence of one individual, or even groups of individuals, has little impact because of the sense of team membership and unity.

Distributive learning uses a well-developed computer network. Employees can tap into instructional resources from a work station. Instant learning feedback is possible, including sharing of solutions by individuals in different organizations. Such delivery even can be accomplished internationally.

Because of the ability to reach across international frontiers, it becomes possible to address multicultural issues in ways not formerly possible. Managers engaged with a common business process internationally can, in effect, compare notes in working through a common instructional package.

For a variety of reasons, such distributive learning approaches represent an important part of the DNA of a true learning organization.

Formal training continues to play a role but it becomes much less of a factor in organizational learning. Perhaps one of its more important roles becomes the generation of a broad appreciation for the business, corporate values, and vision–driving corporate goals and planning. Classrooms can also serve an important role in bringing together cross-sections of employees for interactive experiences, to include team–building techniques, quality management approaches, and shared problem solving.

Town meetings provide an opportunity to broadly mix people who normally would not work together or know each other. In some cases, the meetings can take the form of an inspirational address that lends added emphasis and credence to corporate values.

Such gatherings can also take the form of leaders addressing corporate goals and building a sense of unity, with employees able to address questions to the leaders, much as might occur at a meeting of shareholders. In fact, it is not uncommon for companies today to speak of their employees as shareholders or stakeholders.

Theatrics can sometimes be included to reinforce a message through symbolism. A classic of such an approach occurred at Microsoft. Senior leaders arrived on stage on Harley-Davison motorcycles. The were quickly followed by CEO Bill Gates in a convertible with the word "Windows" (designating its new software product) etched across the windshield as the music "Leader of the Pack" played in the background. Such approaches may seem too carnival–like, but to the extent they put forward a message, build a sense of cohesion, and inform the general workforce about corporate goals, they can be a valuable learning experience at several levels of the corporate psyche. Collectively, they can represent a Gestalt of key importance to corporate success.

Celebrations of success can represent a key aspect of the learning process. They can also help to drive out fear as they teach employees to concentrate on actions and processes that can most assist in corporate success. Celebration is best done within the employees' work environment. Increasingly, it will not involve reward of an individual, but rather reward of a team.

The manner in which success is rewarded projects the organization's personality. In the 1990s, reward systems are shifting from extrinsic to intrinsic. Extrinsic rewards that do occur have less involvement with bonus payments. It becomes a case of feeling that the team goals have been advanced. A member of a special task force in a high-performing organization told me:

I am not after bonuses. My reward is in seeing the team succeed. It also relates to self-esteem, namely being viewed as a person of great worth. In the last few months I have had the opportunity to brief a senior vice president on several occasions. That is in and of itself a personal celebration of success. It is also a wonderful learning experience.

Self-directed teams are at the essence of the learning organization. Most companies are expected to be employing them by the year 2000. What isn't commonly appreciated is, that once the empowerment of self-directed teams takes hold in an organization, it becomes a prime way of both conducting business and advancing learning.

The City of Hampton, Virginia, makes great use of teams of employees, and leads many cities in customer (citizen) satisfaction levels and services-to-cost ratio. Hampton was, in fact, one of five cities in America selected in 1993 by the commission headed by Vice President Al Gore to "Re-invent government." What is particularly interesting about Hampton's city government is that some teams spring up on their own and then dissolve naturally. It is once again a different mental model than most organizations practice in America. Bob O'Neill, the city manager, does not know on any given day how many teams are operating. He told me: "Those who might wonder why I don't keep absolute track of what teams exist simply don't get it." Such broad use of teams unlocks myriad opportunities for learning to occur through shared responsibility and action.

E-mail interconnections tend to be structured around strata in the organization, with middle managers talking to middle managers, and top managers talking with top managers. Lower levels in the organization often have no involvement. In the learning organization such interconnections become much more generalized, with communications crossing hierarchical lines and lateral boundaries. The reach even extends to customers and suppliers. The information management architecture of the firm can even provide for common interest or trouble shooting networks, where employees at all levels can interact around common issues.

When dealing with this area, you must go well beyond considerations of having the necessary technology accessible to all. The principal blockage to interaction via a medium such as E-mail is the associated sense of empowerment. Lower–level employees do not usually capitalize on the opportunity to communicate with others at different hierarchical levels. To the extent that the opportunity for idea interchange is shaped (e.g., communications related to a specific topic) and encouraged, it occurs. Leaders must also model behavior by being broadly interactive.

As CEO of an organization, I had an E-mail network allowing *direct* communication with roughly 400 employees via what was called a "Suggest" network. Initially, few communications were received. But as it came to be understood that top management would often respond within thirty minutes, the network activity climbed to a high level. It opened up vast opportunities for organizational learning and a number of solutions to persistent problems were identified that otherwise would have gone undiscovered.

Cross-peer tutoring becomes a natural occurrence in a learning organization. It is not common in traditional organizations where it can seem demeaning to have a peer offer tutoring support. In a true team environment, this becomes as natural as one member of a football team showing another how to throw a block. Given the fact that basic skills competencies exhibited by employees vary widely in many companies, cross-peer tutoring carries with it the opportunity to gain assistance in sharpening their skills.

Summary

To be of true value, there must be interactive modeling of business and learning processes. While many of the strategies outlined will seem familiar, they are usually robbed of their force by narrow or nonexistent application. It is not a case of the cart before the horse. Both are horses, and both are carts. They must be considered together. Sometimes learning for long-term corporate advantage must take precedence over short-term business interests. For example, a process might be re-engineered to bring in a foreign subsidiary in order to begin forging a long-term collaborative learning process, even though short-term interests might suggest a process loop limited to US subsidiaries. While specific strategies must be fitted to the circumstances of the firm, the aforementioned interactive modeling of business and learning processes must occur if lasting gains are to be realized.

In the broadest sense, *all* organizations *learn*. The problem is that many organizations today are learning disabled or cause workforce members to learn business practices ill-suited to the times. Antiquated formal training practices are a prime contributor. The key is to produce organizations that learn naturally and effectively. Creative engineering of DNA to produce wide and varied connections between internal corporate players and those in the environment, such as customers, is the road to a true learning organization. Action learning principles are one means of keeping the pump primed and operating smoothly once DNA is in place. The goal is confluence of two streams of thought: the continuous process of learning and the continuous process of improvement.

Joel Levey and **Michelle Levey** are co-founders of Inner Work Technologies, Inc., a Seattle-based firm that works with leaders in business to build high performing, change resilient individuals, teams and organizations. Over the past twenty years their pioneering work has been field-tested in over 150 leading organizations. The effectiveness of their work was recognized by US Army West Point logisticians as, "The most exquisite orchestration of human technology we have ever seen!"

As core faculty for the International Center for Organization Design, the International Institute for Innovation, and The Performance Edge, the Leveys' work with leadership and change strategy teams from large organizations focuses on building synergy between personal, professional, and organizational learning, and development. They are co-authors of *Quality of Mind: Tools for Self-Mastery & Enhanced Performance*, and Nightingale Conant's best-selling business audio program, *The Focused Mindstate*.

17

Wisdom at Work: An Inquiry Into the Dimensions of Higher Order Learning

Joel Levey and Michelle Levey

> *The world we have made as a result of the level of the thinking we have done thus far creates problems that we cannot solve at the same level (of consciousness) at which we have created them....We shall require a substantially new manner of thinking (and learning) if humankind is to survive. [emphasis added]*
>
> —Albert Einstein

The current generation faces a learning challenge of an unprecedented magnitude unique to any time in history. For more than 99% of human history we lived with less than 7 million people on earth. Life was simpler, sparser, and shorter-lived. Survival depended upon learning.

Our ancestors' attunement to the multidimensionality of their inner and outer worlds awakened the insight and innovation necessary to meet the challenges of their world. Each bird's song, each change of the wind, every dream or vision revealed something of significance and worthy of attention. This deep listening taught us how to assimilate every experience into a rich tapestry of meaning that revealed a clear sense of purpose and direction for our daily life and work.

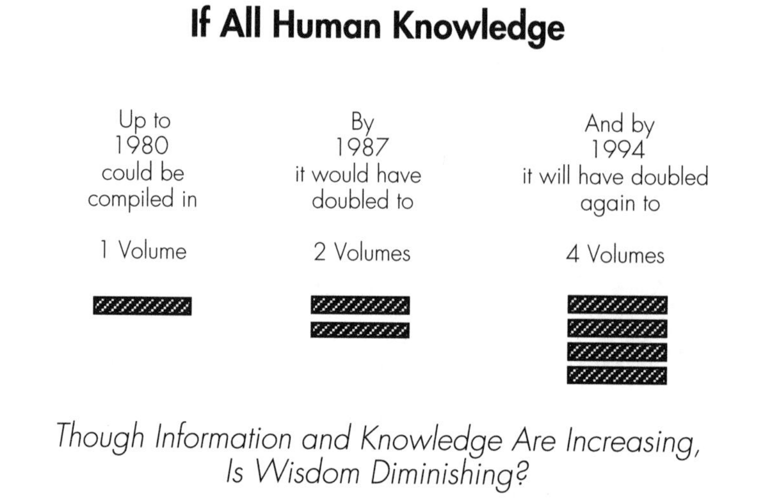

If All Human Knowledge

Up to 1980 could be compiled in	By 1987 it would have doubled to	And by 1994 it will have doubled again to
1 Volume	2 Volumes	4 Volumes

Though Information and Knowledge Are Increasing, Is Wisdom Diminishing?

Figure 1

In recent centuries, humanity has learned much about the path of innovation and technological development. Yet, as the momentum of material development has escalated, we have lost touch with the path of insight and wisdom so necessary to guide our development and keep our world in balance. Though human knowledge and power is doubling at an exponential rate, we are more vulnerable than ever before. Our lives are so busy, and our neurological circuits so jammed now, that most of the information that floods our lives is ignored or only partially assimilated. Observing the state of the world, it would seem that the qualities of mind and relationship that are essential to learning and survival appear to be increasingly rare amidst the accelerating complexity and pressures of our modern lives. Rich in information, we are lacking in wisdom.

The Challenge

With increasing intensity over the past few hundred years, humanity has launched a myriad of initiatives that have changed our world for generations to come. Seldom were the far reaching consequences of many "advances" thought out or tested from a systems perspective. It seems that we have much to learn from indigenous wisdom cultures that would first ask, "What will the consequences of this decision/course of action be for my children and their children out to the next seven generations?" or simply, "Is it good for the people?"

We have inherited an unmanageable world. Our businesses and our lives are far more interdependent, complex and rapidly changing than any of our formal training or learning has equipped us to handle. In the face of this far reaching learning crisis, many people in business today experience anxiety, some retreat into denial, and others, in an attempt to do something or to feel some control over things, opt for shortsighted, reactive courses of action that often breed even more confusion and problems for stakeholders downstream.

Wisdom at Work

Wisdom at work is reflected in how successfully we learn, how consistently we can tap our deepest creative intelligence, and how effectively we develop the raw material of our inspiration and systems thinking into the insights, concepts, communications, and innovations that can be embodied and translated into action.

There are many dimensions of human learning necessary to build a truly change-resilient and generative learning organization. We would like to offer you, the reader, a series of insights, models, and sets of lenses to stretch your thinking about the learning organization, and help you inquire more clearly and deeply into these dimensions. As you read this essay we encourage you to continually ask yourself:

- What opportunities and challenges do these ideas offer to me, as a learner, and to my organization?
- Which of these principles are currently being used to support the emergence of greater business effectiveness and learning in my life and the life of my organization?
- Which of these notions/principles are new to me, and which do I personally find most compelling and worth learning more about?

If you are serious about building a learning organization, remember: *Learning begins with yourself* and with other "yourselves."

The principles and insights offered in this essay are distilled from nearly 50 years of our cumulative cross-cultural, medical, and laboratory research, and from our work as change agents with more than 150 leading organizations. The unifying theme throughout this work has been what we call "higher order learning," and high level individual, team, and organizational performance. We have been asked to expand on this theme here, as a complement to the other organizational learning strategies offered in this volume, and to speak specifically to the personal paradigms for weaving higher order learning and creative intelligence into the fabric of organizational learning. In particular, this essay will explore: higher order learning, the Learning Wheel, multi-state learning, creative intelligence, and expanding the scope and complexity of consciousness.

These themes are rich in practical value for individuals and organizations who are struggling to survive and thrive in modern times. In this essay you will gain a glimpse of an extensive frontier of specialized and expanded human learning that has been well scouted and meticulously mapped by the "inner scientists" and "psychonauts" of our world in both modern and ancient times. It is our hope that you will be inspired by what you encounter here to look more deeply into these realms of learning and discover the value of creating a context within your life, and within your organization, that encourages wisdom to emerge at work. Let's now look at each of these themes in more depth.

Higher Order Learning

In our work with organizational learning, we have found the following distinctions of "higher order learning" very helpful.

Higher order learning understands that:
- The human *mindbody* is a multidimensional information receiving, processing, and generating system of incomprehensible complexity;
- The human *mindbody* has access to a virtually infinite spectrum of information and experience;
- The fluid, dynamic nature of the *mindbrain* makes it highly responsive to learning; the scope of its functioning, awareness, and performance potentials can be radically expanded through disciplined use of effective training protocols.

The three primary powers of higher order learning are:

- Direct access to an expanded spectrum of experience/information;
- Increased capacity for complex thought, such as dynamic systems thinking, and ability to use language and other symbolic abstractions with greater fluency;
- Increased ability to link direct experience to symbolic abstraction (i.e., language, mathematics, etc.) and effective interpersonal communication.

The resulting capabilities associated with higher order learning include:

- The ability to attend, to think, and to respond with an extraordinary quality of depth, sensitivity, wisdom, responsiveness, adaptability, precision, energy efficiency, power, grace, compassion, joy and sense of accomplishment;
- Greater ethical integrity and enhanced quality of relationships.

Higher order learning equips an individual or organization to produce enduring and sustained benefits that are widely shared, rather than a narrow, short-lived radius of impact that breeds more complications and problems for the next shift or for generations to come. In our work with organizational learning, we have found the distinction of "higher order learning" very helpful.

The Learning Wheel

The Learning Wheel is a powerful tool in our learning organization work. It is comprised of two complementary paths (see Figure 2):

- The Path of Innovation & Development, and
- The Path of Insight and Discovery.

Viewed in detail, these paths can be applied to organizational learning by addressing the potentials for insight and development across nine interrelated domains of learning.

These nine domains can be viewed as follows: Every human being has a deep yearning for a quality life. To realize such a quality of life, we rely largely on ourselves and others to provide quality goods and services by doing quality work. In an increasingly interconnected world, doing quality work requires building

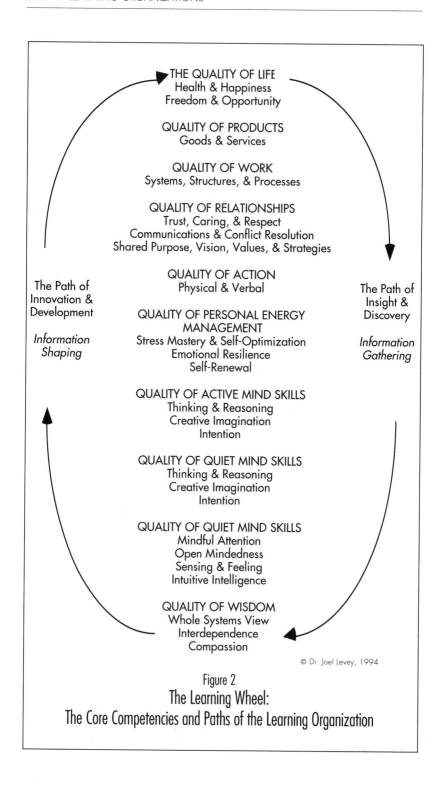

THE QUALITY OF LIFE
Health & Happiness
Freedom & Opportunity

QUALITY OF PRODUCTS
Goods & Services

QUALITY OF WORK
Systems, Structures, & Processes

QUALITY OF RELATIONSHIPS
Trust, Caring, & Respect
Communications & Conflict Resolution
Shared Purpose, Vision, Values, & Strategies

QUALITY OF ACTION
Physical & Verbal

QUALITY OF PERSONAL ENERGY
MANAGEMENT
Stress Mastery & Self-Optimization
Emotional Resilience
Self-Renewal

QUALITY OF ACTIVE MIND SKILLS
Thinking & Reasoning
Creative Imagination
Intention

QUALITY OF QUIET MIND SKILLS
Thinking & Reasoning
Creative Imagination
Intention

QUALITY OF QUIET MIND SKILLS
Mindful Attention
Open Mindedness
Sensing & Feeling
Intuitive Intelligence

QUALITY OF WISDOM
Whole Systems View
Interdependence
Compassion

The Path of
Innovation &
Development

*Information
Shaping*

The Path of
Insight &
Discovery

*Information
Gathering*

© Dr. Joel Levey, 1994

Figure 2
The Learning Wheel:
The Core Competencies and Paths of the Learning Organization

and maintaining quality working relationships. These in turn reflect the quality of the performance, efficiency, thinking, attention, and the depth of wisdom and compassion that each individual brings to their life/work.

Wisdom works its way into the world from the inside out. The inspired action of a single individual can change our world for better or for worse. The power of this influence increases as we improve our ability to gain insight, inspire, and communicate with others.

Along the Path of Insight and Discovery we access and gather information. On this path we live with questions, and engage in the process of research or inquiry that offers progressively deeper and deeper insight into the nature of things. Through penetrating systems analysis, deep inquiry and attention, insight illumines many important patterns of relationship that were previously mysterious and unknown. Along this path insight deepens to unfold into innovation. Our ability to walk this path is determined both by the quality of our analytical and our attentional skills. These equip us with the ability to look, think and intuit systems dynamics that are so vast, subtle and complex as to evade our ordinarily superficial and distracted attention. The fruit of this path is the wisdom, insight, inspiration, and joy of discovery which, as it matures, inspires and guides us through the next generation of innovation and development.

The Path of Innovation and Development provides a complement to the Path of Insight and Discovery. Along this path we give meaning to information by shaping it into images, ideas, communications, and actions. This path unfolds along a spectrum ranging from the most subtle idea or intention on through the progressively more tangible stages of formulation, communication, and action necessary to put an idea into action. The fruit of this path is the joy of accomplishment and the affirmation of seeing the fruits of our insights and labors. Following this path provides an individual, team, or organization with a sense of mastery and control that is balanced by the path of discovery's sense of mystery.

The Synergy of Innovation and Insight

Turning together, the two paths form The Learning Wheel. Turning this wheel generates the momentum of continuous learning and development necessary for any change resilient individual or organization.

The Path of Insight and Discovery taps the wisdom necessary for continual renewal, inspiration, and innovation in our work. When brought on line in service of organizational learning, the Path of Innovation and Development assures continuous improvement, adaptation, integrity, service and responsiveness to the changing needs of the customer and the environment. Learning involves simultaneously traversing both of these complementary paths. The systems integrity of this bimodal learning process demonstrates a way for us to access, organize, understand, and express our deepest wisdom through our work.

In this way we participate in the natural cycles of discovery and development, insight and innovation, wisdom and work, that serve as the in-breath and out-breath of the creative learning process.

Multi-State Learning

Conventional approaches to learning have traditionally assumed a single-state and state-specific approach. This means that complex learning tasks are generally approached with only the power and narrow perspectives of a single, ordinary state of consciousness. This accesses only a limited spectrum of brain-mind functions and is limited to a narrow frame of temporal and spatial reference.

By contrast, a multiple state approach to learning relies upon the systematic cultivation and optimization of an expanded repertoire of extraordinary mindbrain states and capabilities. Mindstates commonly involved in multi-state learning include: extraordinary mental stability, vivid clarity, concentration, perceptual acuity, accelerated response time, lucid dreaming, connectedness or nonduality between observer and the observed, intuition, empathy, joy, peace of mind, love and compassion. Neurologically, each mindstate can be correlated with a state of brain activity. Most commonly, the mindstates noted above could be correlated with brainstates exhibiting extraordinary energy efficiency, cortical specificity, unusual qualities of hemispheric coherence, very high amplitude or very low amplitude activity, ease in locking into or shifting between various modes of brainmind functioning.

While single state approaches to learning assume that humans wake up in the morning and maintain the same state of consciousness throughout the day, the multi-state approaches used by most cultures are more realistic, energy efficient, and brain-friendly. They optimize mental and physical performance by honoring and harnessing the cyclic fluctuations in biochemical, neurological, and psychological functioning that occur naturally throughout the day.

Creative Intelligence

Learning, be it personal, team, or organizational, is a dynamic process involving both active (information shaping) and receptive (information gathering) qualities of mind and behavior. The creative intelligence necessary for innovation and learning excellence is determined by the quality of our skills in building a dynamic synergy of both the abstract, analytic, and symbolic capabilities of the Active Mind functions, and the receptive qualities of attention and intuition that offer unbiased, direct experience—the Quiet Mind skills. In order to better understand these different modes of mental function, let's examine the nature and synergy of active and quiet mind skills and their relationship to learning.

Active Mind Skills

Active Mind Skills (AMS) are the tools of our intellect and reasoning. They include intention, thinking, and creative imagination. These skills help us to shape information through the power of *intention,* and give meaning to the complexity of our inner experience through the power of thought. AMS are vital to organizing and expressing our thinking, and to communicating our inner thoughts, feelings and intentions through tangible action.

What is the role of each of these important skills in learning, and how can they be developed in our own life and work?

Thinking and reasoning are creative acts of making or discovering meaning. Thinking gives us the leverage to experience and analyze our actual situation in order to go beyond the limitations of our thoughts and awaken the insight essential for learning, innovation, and self-renewal. It is helpful to distinguish between *thinking,* which means something active "is going on," and *thought* which refers to a mental model that "has gone on." Thought is rooted in memory and past experience. It is abstract and representational. Thought is the basis of the mental models, assertions, and internal conversations that we mistake for actual reality. Thinking and reasoning are power tools for shaping the flow of experience in the moment.

Creative imagination and visualization refer to modes of thought that are primarily non-verbal and often highly graphic. Utilizing the faculties of our mind's eye, mental imagery is experienced in a "high density format" that proves that one image is worth a thousand words. When intentionally focused, creative imagination becomes a potent tool for systems thinking, mental modeling, simulating complex systems and analyzing possible futures. Equipped with these tools, we are able to engage in "thought experiments" and "mental simulations" that can provide multiple perspectives while saving considerable time and expense at work.

Interestingly, creative imagination is the primary control language by which your mind communicates to your body. The body responds equally strongly to emotionally-charged mental and visual images. If you have any doubts about this, just think about something that excites or frightens you, and notice how your body responds. For example, just imagining biting into a sour lemon is enough to create a measurable change in your physiological state.

Intention, or will, is the organizing principle that keeps our focus of attention and action "on purpose" and in line with our desired outcomes. Intent holds the fulcrum position at the meeting point of active and quiet mind skills. Intention plays a critical role in the creative process. Intention focuses and directs attention, and organizes and shapes thinking, imagination, communication and action. Acting like a magnet or organizing principle, intention determines "selective receptivity" to the emergence of intuitive insights from subtler levels of the mind.

Quiet Mind Skills

The Quiet Mind Skills (QMS) represent a domain of powerful mental functions that are complementary to and essential for the effective use of the Active Mind Skills. QMS are primarily receptive mental functions that gather information through the faculty of *attention.* Multiple continuums can be used to map the quality of attention in QMS. For example, attention can be panoramically open or narrow in its focus, momentary or continuous in duration, or superficial or multidimensional in depth. Attentional versatility is essential for the integration and assimilation of information, and is vital to the success of any work requiring learning, creativity and innovation.

QMS involve the quality of "being" or presence, in contrast

to the "doing" nature of AMS. QMS determine the quality of attention and the subtlety and power of mindbrain states that we are able to bring to our life and work. Because the mental functions associated with QMS are more subtle and less "visible" than AMS, they are rarely recognized, and seldom fully developed. By way of analogy, AMS are like the forms and patterns of clouds that we can touch or see, and the wind or forces that shape them. By contrast, QMS are more "transparent" mental functions that are vast in scope, clear, and open like the sheer presence of the sky.

At work, QMS determine the coherence and power of all other mental functions. The QMS also provide access to the subtle revelations of intuitive insight so vital to breakthroughs in creativity and innovation. They allow us to reduce mental and emotional turbulence in order to focus our attention more deeply on the work at hand. In this way they enable us to access a deeper, more fundamental wisdom that reveals the authentic insight into the nature of our innermost being and the world in which we live. Consciously or unconsciously, all the great scientists and sages of the world have tapped QMS as the access states necessary to discover the "universal organizing principles" that have inspired and guided the development of humanity throughout the ages. QMS also awaken within us a sensitivity to the "life giving forces" that we experience as universal values such as wisdom, compassion, wonder, and heartfelt appreciation. Let's look more closely now at the primary QMS and some strategies for developing these qualities:

Mindful attention is the quality of lucid presence that enables you to know what you are attending to and how you are attending to it. Mindful attention, or mindfulness, gives power and precision to where and how you deploy your attention. With mindfulness you are lucidly present and aware of current reality and of the intention or direction that you intend to move toward. Mindfulness is the quality of mind that makes attention and action a conscious activity. It gives you the power to see clearly and deeply what is really going on here and now, within you and around you. Mindfulness can be contrasted with mindlessness— the habitual, reactive, unconscious and dysfunctional state of mind that is the cause of so many costly problems and accidents.

Open-mindedness is a quality of mind that is open to the flow of experience without bias or editing. The open-mind is free from the compulsive need to "know the answer." It is respectfully tolerant of chaos and ambiguity. This quality of open-mindedness is essential to learning and to working in and with any complex system. Open-mindedness allows us to encompass a more global, systems view of a situation, to honor diversity, and to recognize complex and dynamic patterns of relationships. These often overlooked patterns are frequently the source of inspired insights that can save incalculable amounts of time, resources and human suffering.

Sensing and feeling provide us with direct, embodied experience of our world. While our ordinary sensory systems (sight, sound, smell, touch, taste) provide a glimpse of a tiny spectrum of the information that bombards us, the body as a whole registers a virtually infinite spectrum of information. This is subjectively registered as a generalized "felt sense" of experience. What is commonly referred to as intuition is simply the conscious experience of subtle sensing which falls outside of the spectrum of ordinary perception. As we learn to refine our attention we are able to bring many previously unknown dimensions of subtle sense data to conscious awareness. This is the key to developing our intuitive intelligence.

Integrating Active and Quiet Mind Skills

In order to "make sense" of and give meaning to the chaos of direct experience we learn to describe our experience to ourselves and others in terms of various perceptions, emotions, moods, or feelings. Our ability to link our direct experience to our abstract, conceptual, linguistic capability creates a critical bridge for integrating AMS and QMS functions.

The importance of this linking is illustrated by a series of landmark studies conducted at the University of Chicago which concluded that the most important variable in maintaining high level physical and mental health is the degree to which a person has learned to pay attention to the "felt sense" of themselves. Further research identified a condition called alexythymia, derived from the Greek "alexy" (no words), and "thymia" (for feelings). This subtle, but dangerous condition is actually a learning disorder of epidemic proportions that many researchers believe is a primary cause of most stress-related and chronic illnesses.

People with alexythymia have little "felt sense" of their aliveness. They "live in their heads" mistaking their abstract, self-generated thoughts for actual objective reality and are generally unaware that they have a problem. Fortunately our vulnerability to this dangerous condition can be reversed by learning to bring greater mindfulness to our felt sense and learning to communicate our felt sense more effectively in words. This results in an increased sense of control, balance, and an improved quality of health, relationships, and job performance.

Control Follows Awareness

The cornerstone of learning is awareness. Seldom do major breakdowns in health, work, or the quality of relationship happen without warning. Most often they occur due to habits of inattention to the "whispers" (i.e., warning signs) that eventually become "screams" (i.e., real problems) calling for our attention.

Such inattention can have staggering implications for an aspiring learning organization. First, the medical bill for the United States exceeds $1 trillion each year and organizations pay the bulk of the costs. Second, as much as 95% of all illness is estimated to be stress-related and preventable. Third, individuals who are "out of touch" or "unfeeling" are dangerously at risk and ill-equipped to work effectively under pressure in today's world. While discernment is necessary, people who scoff at "touchy feely" disciplines may well be revealing their own vulnerability. Thus, learning that integrates active and quiet mind skills is a wise investment that provides vital assets to any learning organization.

The Quiet Mind at Work

A compelling case study of the effectiveness of QMS at work was brought home to us recently when we were working on a year-long corporate Learning Expedition with the change strategy teams from five major oil companies, a large utility company, a university medical center, and an international construction company. At the invitation of one of the engineers, a time was set aside before breakfast for "focusing and centering." A critical mass, about 40%, of the participants attended on a regular basis. We were asked to facilitate the sessions by offering a brief set of suggestions for how people might organize their attention for optimal results during a time of quiet reflection. Each person used this forum according to their own inclination. Some used this quiet time to focus and clear their minds, others for silent prayer or to organize their thoughts. Following the quiet time we briefly discussed insights that emerged that might inspire or direct our work for the day.

One evening, after a day of multiple difficulties and break-throughs, one senior vice president approached me on the way to supper. "You know," he said, "The members of our team who've been attending those morning sessions are really the source of some of the best thinking on our team. Their insights, questions, and contributions to our work have been worth their weight in gold. I'm not really sure what you're doing in those morning sessions, but keep up the good work. We need all the clear thinking and creative inspiration we can get to complete our work on schedule."

Creative Intelligence at Work

An inspiring example of the "applied wisdom" of these approaches can be drawn from a pioneering project we worked on at Weyerhauser in the late 1970s. For two years the members of the Creativity Engineering Team met every other week to search for breakthrough ideas to the myriad of special research projects going on within various departments. Representatives from different divisions participated, and each session a different research challenge was addressed. Here is an excerpt from one of the participant's journals:

> Over the past two years our team has learned about how the roots of creativity and innovation lie in the dynamic synergy of active mind skills (thinking, intention, and imagination) and quiet mind skills (concentration, attention, intuition). We have learned to seed the active mind with information and images about a problem or creative solution, and then to allow the quiet mind to reveal intuitive insights regarding possible answers or avenues for further inquiry. Over the years, each person has developed the individual skills necessary to focus and quiet their mind, to mentally simulate complex experiments, and to think in terms of complex systems.
>
> As a team we have developed the team protocols necessary to access states of deep intuition and awareness together, and to bring back and communicate our insights with each other. Our work together involves a dynamic flow of inquiry,

quiet reflection, imagineering, and animated discussion. It seems that any question we ask draws
forth a wealth of creative insights and revelations.
People are inspired and excited by the consistency
of our results and by the implications for reliably
accessing breakthroughs in creativity and innovation here and in other similar research settings
around the globe. Often we talk about what it
would be like to set these individual and collective
skills loose in service of solving some of the really
big challenges facing humanity. We know that our
collective experiment is creating a story that will
provide inspiration and guidance for other teams
for decades, or perhaps generations to come.

Expanding the Scope and Complexity of Consciousness

Implementing the evolutionary imperative of continuous
learning requires an ever-expanding complexity of consciousness. The glory of yesterday's hard won achievements quickly
pales as the needs of the customer or the realities of the environment change. As change and challenge increase, anxiety grows
and individuals, teams and organizations are motivated to discover and rapidly learn new skills. After these new capabilities
are mastered, however, the danger of relapsing into boredom or
complacency often occurs. There are four interrelated forces that
currently support the emergence of higher order learning in our
organizations:

First, there is an increasing interest in extraordinary human performance stimulated, in large part, by the interests of
military, medicine, sports, and more recently business concerns.
The 1990s have appropriately been declared by the U.S. Con-
gress as "The Decade of the Brain."

One of the most striking examples we can offer comes from
our experience designing and delivering the Ultimate Warrior
Training Program (aka, "Jedi Warrior Program") for the US
Army's Green Berets in the mid-1980s. Described by West Point
logisticians as "the most exquisite orchestration of human technology we have ever seen!" this project was motivated by the
enormous grief of the war and the tragic finding that more than

Results of the Ultimate Warrior Training Program for the U.S. Army Green Berets

The "Ultimate Warrior Program" was designed and delivered to the U.S. Army Green Berets in 1985 and 1986 after four years of intensive research and design. Listed below are the enhancements over the course of training on the Army's targeted outcomes for physical, mental, team and mission performance of the participating individuals and teams. PLEASE NOTE: The greatest gains are in the areas that they had had the least prior training. Baseline (i.e. skill level before training) is equal to zero. The enhancements listed below are percentage increases from that level.

	Percent Increase From Preprogram Baseline
MENTAL ENHANCEMENTS	(Baseline i.e. "before program"=0)
Mental development (summary)	88 % increase
Ability to manage stress	92
Ability to work with visualization/mental rehearsal	84
Clarity with regards to personal values	83
Familiarity and use of holistic methods	98
Access to extraordinary states of awareness	82
Access to extraordinary perceptual abilities	201
Confidence in ability to control mindbody	25
Ability to learn and integrate new ideas	109

PHYSICAL ENHANCEMENTS

Physical enhancements (summary)	110
Ability to manage energy	86
Understanding of the effects of diet/nutrition on performance	174
Ability to control pain	47
Ability to fine-tune physical performance	127

TEAM ENHANCEMENTS

Team Cohesion	40
Sense of confidence/bonding with team	30
Ability to blend effectively with team	43

MISSION ENHANCEMENTS

Mission Effectiveness	49
Ability to remain alert and motionless	70
Ability to extend sensory awareness	72
Ability to quickly relax and rest	120
Control of circulation and temperature	87
Personal Energy Management	120
Ability to optimize physical abilities	92
Confidence in using holistic methods	50
Acceptance of other cultures	45
Reduction of effects of shock/trauma	30
Confidence in own leadership abilities	50

Figure 3

twice as many veterans died of suicide upon return to the States than died in combat in Southeast Asia. This intensive six-month program was delivered to teams of men whose mission put them in a likely position to start or stop World War III under the old Cold War scenario.

After three years of research and design the program delivered a highly synergistic blend of sophisticated multilevel, multistate, learning technologies including: extensive "biocybernautic training" using biofeedback, meditation, intuition, and martial arts; high performance fitness and nutrition; team development; special operations skills; and work with the soldiers' families (see Figure 3).

In recent years we have adapted this multistate approach to learning into "corporate warrior training programs" producing similar enthusiasm and results with leaders, R&D and project teams in a variety of organizations.

Second, cognitive and neuropsychological research regarding the nature, functions and capacities of the human brain/mind are nascent sciences of at most one hundred years in the West. The meticulously systematic and replicated research of traditional "inner scientists," equipped with fantastically advanced "inner technology," has refined and recorded findings in exacting ways with millions of subjects over thousands of years. As a result, for the first time, Western culture has ready access to these ancient and time honored cross-cultural global treasuries of consciousness research, experience and technology.

Thirdly, until recently modern Western psychology and medicine have been primarily concerned with the stages of human development culminating in "normalcy." By contrast, the world's great inner science traditions have, for millennia, utilized sophisticated methods for expanding the spectrum of human learning and insight into a more whole systems, multidimensional scope.

Finally, as global travel and communications have become easier, we are witnessing an explosion in the diffusion of information on higher order learning. There is clear consensus on two key discoveries:

1. All human beings have the potential to tap into a greater level of intelligence capability than is usually encouraged or fully developed.

2. The higher order learning methodologies necessary to

bring a full spectrum of human intelligence on-line in service of improving the quality of life and work are readily available for those individuals and organizations motivated to expand the scope of their learning.

Closing Thoughts

It is humbling for us to reflect on the state of our world and our positions and freedoms within it. Those of us writing or reading this book likely belong to a tiny minority of people who have adequate, or even luxurious, living conditions compared to most of humanity. We live with relative safety and peace of mind, free from much of the frightening unrest and danger in the world. We are educated and possess many freedoms that others will never know. Many of us have the privilege and power to affect the lives of thousands of people and to help create the conditions for them to achieve a greater quality of life. We also have the privilege to develop and improve ourselves. If we choose, we can give time and attention to the disciplines of higher order learning and work with others who share our freedom and inclination to build healthier organizations and a better world for all.

In closing this essay, we ask that you take this good fortune to heart. We hope that your insights will ripen over time, and inspire an inquiry that continues to open a deeper kind of wisdom and wonder to your life and work.

PART THREE

Infrastructure

**Learning Communities:
An Alternative to the "Expert Model"**
Stephanie Ryan

Learning Out of Context
Eric Edwards Vogt

**Vitalizing Work Design: Implementing a
Developmental Philosophy**
Carol Sanford

Development Strategies for the Knowledge Era
Linda E. Morris

The Faster Learning Organization (FLO)
Bob Guns

**Managerial Practice Fields:
Infrastructures of a Learning Organization**
Daniel H. Kim

**Learning as an Organization:
A Journey Into Chaos**
David R. Schwandt

In this segment, we will explore structural models and forms for developing people and organizations. With the help of seven authors, we will take an excursion into history, looking at some of the traditional ways we have thought about and structured our worklives and our workplaces. We will then examine new approaches—ways that are more appropriate to developing real learning communities.

Stephanie Ryan offers an alternative to the "expert model" which has acquired much tenure in modern management theory. Eric Vogt helps us see how much of our "intelligence" has been out of context and presents a new architecture. Carol Sanford advocates the implementation of a developmental philosophy in organizations, revitalizing work design.

Linda Morris addresses developmental strategies for knowledge-value companies while Bob Guns reveals his model for faster organizational learning. Daniel Kim offers a comprehensive description of "practice fields" for managers in a learning organization, while David Schwandt focuses on the social system aspect of learning organizations.

*A long winding road
becomes the shortest distance
between two ideas.*

—William Warriner
101 Corporate Haiku

Stephanie Ryan is a facilitator of organizational learning and founder of In Care, a Massachusetts-based consulting company. She helps clients to see, understand, and improve the systems they are a part of by exploring the assumptions which influence their ability to produce results. Her primary focus is on creating learning communities, particularly exploring the kinds of relationships across traditional boundaries which are the fertile ground for collaboration. Her preferred clients recognize the emerging need to serve their communities and are willing to experiment with new ways of thinking and operating. She regularly delivers speeches and workshops on the disciplines of systems thinking, team learning, and mental models.

Prior to founding In Care, Ryan worked for a management consulting firm, Innovation Associates, Inc., for six years, where her work involved the design and delivery of management training programs focused on the disciplines of organizational learning discussed in *The Fifth Discipline: The Art and Practice of Learning Organizations*, by Peter Senge, co-founder of Innovation Associates.

18

Learning Communities: An Alternative to the "Expert" Model

Stephanie Ryan

How might our conversations be different if we experienced the "dance" of learning together? What ways of sensing and relating to one another support our learning together? Where can we find the practice fields to "learn in relationship" with others? I invite you to ponder these and other questions with me as I explore learning communities as an alternative to the "expert" model of instruction.

By "expert" I am referring to people who "know" the "right" answers to our questions. "Learners" in this model are generally assumed to be ignorant, passive, empty vessels who can be effectively filled up by the expert expounding knowledge. This "either/or" approach to learning, (either you know or you don't) assumes a linear cause and effect relationship, leaving little room for feedback. It also implies a one way flow of information which precludes an opportunity for the "expert" to learn from the "learner" or, more importantly, for the "learner" to learn from their own inner-knowing. This model of instruction persists as long as those seeking to learn assume that what they want or need to know exists outside of themselves in the form of an "expert."

Learning communities are essentially "communities of inquirers." Hence, the roles of "expert" and "learner" become

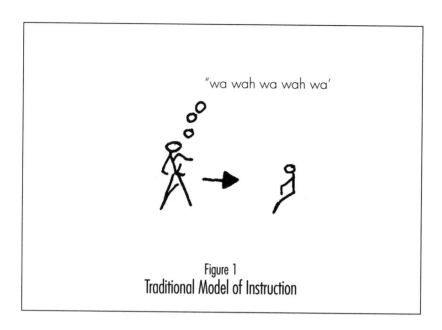

"wa wah wa wah wa'

Figure 1
Traditional Model of Instruction

arbitrary delineations. Everyone is asked to venture into the realm of curiosity together. With this invitation comes the challenge to suspend certainty and the need for answers outside ourselves. As an initial definition, learning communities value the collective process of discovery and people within them value living with their questions. These communities are sustained by a continued commitment to share this journey of exploration with one another on matters people care deeply about.

An Experiment

Publishing an essay about learning communities raised a dilemma for me because of the traditional, implied relationship between "knowing" author and "ignorant" reader. I wanted to consciously experiment with a new relationship, one that is more consistent with my image of learning in community where there is freedom and space to give voice to both what I know and what I do not know. I am writing this essay on a personal level, similar to the way I write to myself in my journal. I share my concerns, passions, and curiosity with you. Perhaps by publishing what I typically hold private I can model the vulnerability I so value in the learning process, creating the possibility for us to begin learning together.

Exchanging Curiosity in Our Conversations

The tendency to write of what we know rather than what we are curious about is also true of how we typically speak with one another. *How often has your response to someone else's questions furthered their curiosity and learning? When have you shut it down?* My curiosity has flourished in relationships with others who respond to my questions with their questions. I am often amazed at the insights we arrive at together when I am in conversations of *mutual* curiosity. These conversations have a rhythm of their own; they are characterized by high energy, periodic silences, and the willingness to venture down various lines of inquiry, dancing back and forth as needed. I contrast this with the times my curiosity is met with another's certainty. I feel my energy wane when I am being pulled outside myself and led down the path of another's alleged knowledge. *What is lacking in our exchanges that we do not value the dance of learning together more often?* I sense a partial answer to this question is a lack of appreciation and skill with inquiry.

In assessing an organization's culture for learning, I often look for the ability and freedom to inquire within the environment. I encourage clients to pay attention to the frequency and quality of questions in their conversations. In working with clients from business, education, and healthcare, I have been puzzled by the glaring void of inquiry and virtual avalanche of advocacy in meetings, memos, and other forms of communication. I wondered how people conversed on what they were curious about if it wasn't through the exchange of questions. I began to pay attention to what was at risk in these cultures for those asking questions. What I discovered was a stack of labels and judgments like: ignorant, incompetent, naive, trouble-maker, and the classic "not a team player." In one organization, asking questions of senior management was considered a "CLM"—career limiting move. These very same cultures rewarded those who answered questions, labeling them as knowledgeable, competent, and experienced. These rewards seemed to ensure that whenever a question did land on the table it did not last long before someone gave the "right answer" and others accepted or argued for "their right answer." *How long can a question go unanswered in your organization? What has been your experience of labels placed on the people who ask questions and the ones who answer them? What is the reward for asking a question in your organization?*

What has led us to generate these labels and judgments about people who ask questions? I sense part of the explanation lies in the "domain of intent." Questions which carry "excess baggage" beyond curiosity increase the probability of labels, judgments, and defense. *Yet if there is more risk than reward for posing a question, what kind of practice fields exist for us to improve our ability to ask and receive questions that promote learning?* On page 300, Eric Vogt references the grading system in an unusual high school that weighted half the grade on the quality of students' questions, not their answers.

Hurdles to Exchanging Questions

The first hurdle to learning how to exchange questions is erected by the virtual absence of questions. Taped conversations of executive meetings revealed hours passed before a question was asked. A classic example of this is the conference session where the designated time for "questions and answers" is at the end and the speaker usually runs late. *What if we valued the questions we hear as much as the answers we worship in our allocation of time?*

The second hurdle I consider more deadly. When the infrequent question does surface, it is typically framed as a yes/no question or someone's opinion disguised in the form of a question! Despite no formal training in law, managers appear quite skilled in asking leading questions. A good clue to such questions are ones that begin with "Don't you think....?" There is a difference between a question which invites the listeners to ponder and a question that demands an answer. For example, "What does the loss of this client tell us about the way we are doing business?" and "What's your explanation for losing such a major client?" Too often questions asked feel like an attack, like being knifed in the conversation by the hidden intent behind the seemingly innocent words. Questions which carry blame or judgment can cut or reopen old wounds and justly raise defenses in the bodies of the listeners.

As I have listened more intently to questions asked of me, I sense the questioner is often:
- trying to lead me somewhere
- testing me

- attempting to make me wrong
- asking me to fix something or someone
- wanting me to take on their frustration
- challenging me to prove the worth of something or someone

Questions asked with a seemingly hidden intent break down our sense of relatedness because they trigger in the listener a need to erect walls and defenses. Despite our best attempts to hide these intentions, they leak into our conversations. *Why is a question asked out of genuine curiosity so rare? In your conversations, how often do you or others ask a question when you do not already have the answer nor expect anyone else to answer it?* I believe questions which carry the spirit of curiosity behind them unleash the desire for learning. When asked, these questions hold the key to unlock an innate and often dormant curiosity. The courage to ask these kinds of questions lies with the willingness to be vulnerable, to admit to another in asking what "I don't know." The ability to leave these questions unanswered is the capacity to live with the unknown and to live in that vulnerable space until new meaning and understanding emerges.

The third hurdle to learning with others arises in the way a question is received, or our capacity to live with another's questions. *On the rare occasion that curiosity shows up in the form of a question, how do you receive it?* I catch myself resisting the ambiguity that unanswered questions create. This resistance often appears in the form of an answer rather than another question, or an acknowledgment of the unsettling nature of the question. *What is the average life span of a question in our minds and organizations? What understanding is there of the question itself before the answers spring forth? What questions do you let stand, unanswered? Where does the impulse to immediately answer come from?*

The most challenging questions to *receive* in curiosity are the ones I sense are not being *asked* of me out of a sense of curiosity. I find the wisdom of Aikido offers me an alternative way of relating to this unseen, yet strongly felt energy of attack I sense coming from another. Aikido encourages me to fully receive the energy and redirect it to help achieve a desired outcome. Rather than resist, which is often my unconscious response, I can consciously choose to stay open, listening fully with my curiosity, aware enough to test my assumptions about their questions.

This practice embraces rather than braces against the question and questioner, working with and not against the forces. It requires me to be conscious of my choice in that moment to "learn in relationship" with another. Meeting the challenge of receiving questions, regardless of how they are asked, by embracing both the questioner and question more often than answering prematurely or defending, takes compassionate practice. The ticket of admission for this practice field is vulnerability, in the form of intimacy, a willingness to be in relationship with myself and another.

Entering and Staying on the Field of Learning

I have come to appreciate that there are variations of "not knowing" that require more vulnerability than others. Perhaps the most vulnerable time is when an understanding arises (the insight into how our own thinking and subsequent actions are perpetuating our problems) without a simultaneous answer as to how to fix it. When this systems insight is reached, the ingrained habit of blaming our problems on external causes, which absolves us of responsibility, is rendered useless.

The first realization that, if there is an enemy, "the enemy is me," can be a real moment of truth. For some, this is an unbearable and fleeting moment followed by denial and other sophisticated defensive routines. For others, a second realization occurs—that there is no need of an enemy, externally or internally, setting them on a path of leading the change from within. *Why? Why do only some people simultaneously recognize and believe the solutions or answers also reside within? Why, if this realization is reached, do still fewer people accept the responsibility to begin the change by changing themselves?*

I suspect the amount of time I have spent in expert models of instruction (such as schools and training programs) has ingrained a belief that "right" answers reside outside myself. This belief can render me powerless in these moments of truth. The time I have spent being judged for asking questions and the pain I have inflicted in blaming myself and others when ready answers are not available, has buried the spirit of curiosity and the inherent potential for learning in me and perhaps many other people.

Letting Go of Answers as a Defense

How can I welcome the vulnerability that is created by living with unanswered questions? What would it take for me to let go of my need for answers, especially those found outside myself, and stand undefended? I have often wondered about the link between my need for certainty and my tendency to think of the world in terms of "either/or" (right-wrong, win-lose, good-evil). It appears as if "either/or" thinking created the need for my defenses, my need to know. To admit "not knowing" in this world of right-wrong, win-lose...was too threatening. If I did not know with certainty that I was right, the only other alternative was I could be wrong. Being wrong often means "I lose." In order to protect myself from losing I would appear certain, at least on the surface, to know.

My appearance of knowing is like a winter stream, snow and ice covers the surface giving the illusion of solid ground. Yet underneath these protective layers the water flows, like the current of curiosity which is so often buried in me. *To what extent are we all like frozen streams? How often does your curiosity lie hidden, unseen, unshared with others?* At times I feel I am so thickly insulated that my curiosity has become inaccessible—even to me. I am living out of sight, out of touch, out of relationship with myself. In an effort to defend myself from others, I have inadvertently prevented myself from knowing myself. Unknowingly, I have deafened myself from listening to the wisdom and instincts that live within my body.

When, if ever, am I undefended? When am I fully in touch with my deepest desires and living from them? When does the spring thaw allow the river of curiosity to flow freely? In moments of solitude in nature, in prayer, and during creative expression I am in a quality of relationship with myself I would characterize as undefended. I used to think passion (intrinsic motivation) was the only thing that prayer and creative expression held in common with learning, I sense the absence of defense links them as well.

Questioning the Value of Knowing

I wonder how much one person's knowing or their certainty every really matters to another? Too often I have witnessed in "experts" this tendency to spew forth "knowledge" in ways that rarely translate into the learner's capacity to act differently. The underlying assumption operating in these interactions is the attitude that the "expert" knows what is right and the learner does not. *What if the learner* does know, *yet knowing is not enough?* So many times I have "known better" and yet still acted in ways that do not serve me or others.

Having been trained in "systems thinking," I have known for nearly ten years how ineffective "either/or thinking" can be to foster a learning environment. Yet, my habit persists. This dichotomy between my knowledge and my behavior led me to ask a wise elder woman why this tendency for either/or thinking seems so prevalent in me and our culture. She succinctly replied "Either/or thinking allows us to avoid the whole." *I wondered, how can we ever really avoid the whole? When and why is my sense of the whole obscured?* It occurred to me when I am caught up in either/or thinking it is because I want to believe in the illusion of separateness and the illusion of control this offers. Now when I find myself thinking in either/or terms, I ask myself *"What or who is it I may not want to be in relationship with; what or who might I be defending against?"*

The responses to these questions are more readily accessible with the help of my body, not simply my intellect. My senses inform me and compliment my knowledge of a situation. The ability to sense, to perceive, and to understand demands an intimacy with myself that is not encouraged in expert models of instruction. On the contrary, expert models seem to divorce the learner from themselves, fostering the illusion of separateness, and undermining one's confidence to trust one's instincts.

Appreciation of Inter-Relatedness

The illusion of separateness in which many people live their lives—believing in and acting out of—is dispelled by an appreciation of inter-relatedness, a sense of the whole system. "Systems sensing" means I am a *part of,* not *apart from,* the beauty and disease of the world. Chief Seattle captured the essence of systems sensing in his address to the US. Government in 1854:

> *All things are bound together. All things connect. What happens to the Earth happens to the children of the Earth. Man has not woven the web of life. He is but one thread. Whatever he does to the web, he does to himself.*

The recognition that everything is connected and constantly changing frustrates some people because there is no singular "right answer;" you can never "figure it all out." I find great freedom in this realization; if no one knows, then it opens the door to experimentation. When we appreciate our interrelatedness, there is enough space to embrace the whole of life, including its mystery. A systems perspective offers a means for going beyond "either/or" thinking; it is an invitation for inquiry and experimentation. The phrase "systems sensing" is not yet widely spoken. I would like to believe the publication of this essay will awaken a curiosity about what is means and how it is different from the more familiar phrase of "systems thinking."

Systems Sensing

Systems thinking is often seen as an analytical tool for dealing with complexity. Managers are seduced by the promise of being able to "figure things out" and advocate their favorite solution in more sophisticated language. Systems analysis is only a small part of what a systems perspective has to offer. The discipline of systems thinking is far more powerful at generating shared meaning and insight when applied as a process for collective inquiry.

I believe the phrase "systems sensing" can serve to remind us that perceiving a system is not merely an intellectual exercise; it involves giving validity to intuition, people's senses and instincts, as well as measurable data. Systems sensing is about following hunches and curiosities. A wide variety of systems whisper to us everyday, requiring our keen sensitivity and attentiveness to their signals. Systems typically do not start screaming until they are in crisis. At that point, desired adjustments require far more time and money.

Systems sensing involves feeling, naming, and exploring the dilemmas we find ourselves in daily. These dilemmas are typically entered into unintentionally and unknowingly. Unearthing and inquiring with compassion into these dilemmas, over time can cultivate understanding. Holding a systems perspective means recognizing that apparent opposites can be true, staying curious and patient with inquiry until the whole system in which these opposites can "make sense" is revealed. Helping people discover and learn about the systems they perpetuate involves practice—asking, and receiving questions in ways that value the relationship with the learner—exchanging questions from the heart as well as the mind.

> *A human being is a part of the whole, called by us "Universe," a part limited in time and space. We experience ourselves, our thoughts and feelings as something separate from the rest—a kind of optical delusion of our consciousness. This delusion is a kind of prison for us, restricting us to our personal desires and to affection for a few persons nearest to us. Our task must be to free ourselves from this prison by widening our circle of compassion to embrace all living creatures and the whole of nature in its beauty.*
>
> —Albert Einstein

A person can not develop the discipline of systems sensing without practicing compassionate and passionate inquiry of themselves and others. *What if the inverse of this is also true, to the extent there are few questions exchanged in care in our conversations, there is little understanding of the systems we live in and the consequences of our thinking and actions?* I fear this is the case in most of our organizations today. Perhaps our habits of communicating have become a kind of prison for us. Our "skilled incompetency" in asking questions maintains the very defenses we need to eliminate if we are to learn together. In the absence of questions exchanged in genuine curiosity, our ability to generate shared insights and meaning is undermined.

To the extent that expert models persist, systems sensing, which requires going within as well as outside for answers, cannot be realized. Systems sensing values everyone's contribution because everyone has a unique perspective from living in the system. A system can never be fully perceived with just one pair of eyes and ears. One person's biases tend to filter out vital information. It is only with multiple, often divergent perspectives that the rich diversity of a system can be adequately represented. The ability to accept different points of view is present in community and desperately needed for us to develop the collective organs of perception which can more adequately represent a whole system.

If the doors of perception were cleansed,
everything would be seen as it is, infinite.
—William Blake

Questions carry the power to illuminate the web of inter-connections we depend on every day to accomplish our desired results. How questions are exchanged determines whether they mobilize the inherent creative energy of groups or further the fragmentation and isolation of our lives. *Where can I find a "safe space" to live with my questions? When does the curiosity of the unknown outweigh the fear of exploring it with another?* I have found myself willing to venture into this unknown territory when I am amidst people who respect and value our relatedness. This spirit of relationship has been most apparent to me in community building experiences. The sense of community—where an appreciation of our inter-relatedness, our wholeness, allows for differences to be expressed and transcended graciously—offers fertile ground for learning and collaboration. Living with this sense of relationship, with the question of my relationship to the whole, is the path of learning how to sense systems.

Boundaryless Learning

The words "learning" and "community" are commonplace in our vocabulary, yet the way I think of this is far from common in my experience. In my experience, learning communities are rare and sacred. One measure of their existence is if the quality of relationships honors both the individual and their questions.

Learning communities are distinct from our common inter-pretation of communities because they are not bound by geogra-phy, industry, profession, sex, race, religion, or age. Learning communities have the power to transcend these artificial bound-aries, binding us together with our shared humanness, curiosity, and creativity. Learning communities are more likely to arise when a few critical ingredients surface, including but not limited to: curiosity, commitment, and a desire to act collaboratively with a spirit of experimentation. I've written about this more extensively in my essay, "The Emergence of Learning Communi-ties," for the anthology, *Community Building: Renewing Spirit & Learning in Business.*

My image of learning communities is distinct from most organizational cultures by its circles of compassion, courage, wisdom, and forgiveness. Compassion is called for in recognizing

Learning communities are places where:
- invisible fabric of relationships are tended to and cared for
- vulnerability & diversity are welcome
- curiosity reigns
- experimentation is the norm
- inquiry is practiced with compassion
- questions can go unresolved.

The people within learning communities:
- communicate with each other honestly and openly
- offer themselves and others honor and respect
- value and seek feedback
- are challenged to see themselves and others with new eyes
- encourage each other to sense, see, listen to, and speak of the whole system,
- are free to be completely themselves, with no masks.

Figure 2
Learning Communities

the dilemmas people find themselves in, unwittingly and unintentionally. Courage is required to take a stand for the long-term health of the system and its people, when the culture predominately rewards short-term, political behavior. Wisdom is needed to let go of the need to know, fix, control, blame, or defend in the face of problems or resistance and to meet these challenges openly with curiosity and reflection. Forgiveness is the gift offered to transform perceived failures into opportunities for learning.

The quality of listening in the community elicits people's true voices and inner wisdom. I know I have touched this sacred space with a group when my inner voice ceases to chatter. I feel like I am standing on a bridge over a stream witnessing the past as the water flows to me, the present as it passes under the bridge, and the future as it flows away. I am able to connect what has been said with what is just about to be said. It is as if we have begun to communicate with each other beyond our words. Dialogue is one way to name this stream of conversation, where meaning flows between us, as Sherrin Bennett and Juanita Brown point out on page 178.

Meeting the personal, organizational, and societal challenges that face us today will require us to go beyond traditional, hierarchical, and linear ways of learning, beyond the "expert" model. Our tendency to create artificial boundaries between those who know and those who don't, have cut us off from ourselves and each other. Our impatience with unresolved questions coupled with our need to control has driven us to pretend we know the answers when we don't—to begin fixing problems we have yet to define properly. These artificial separations and lies are dehumanizing and undermining our ability to learn together. Learning communities can be a means to connect the fragmented thought and actions that perpetuates the dis-ease in our society.

What if there are no answers "out there" that can sustain us in the long-term as well as the ones we discover for ourselves? Rainer Maria Rilke wrote in *Letters to a Young Poet:*

> Here where I am surrounded by an enormous landscape, which the winds move across as they come from the seas, here I feel that there is no one anywhere who can answer for you those questions and feelings which, in their depths, have a life of their own...." "...have patience with everything unresolved in your heart and try to love the questions themselves as if they were locked rooms or books written in a very foreign language. Don't search for the answers, which could not be given to you now, because you would not be able to live them. And the point is, to live everything. Live the questions now. Perhaps then, someday far in the future, you will gradually, without even noticing it, live your way into the answer.

How do we arrive at the collective wisdom to let the questions answer themselves? What if I trusted that people already know and no amount of my telling them what I believe I know will really ever help them to discover their answers and learn to trust themselves, their own inner knowing? How might I or others act differently if we believed this were true?

I believe questions exchanged out of a sense of curiosity are the real "currency" of learning together. If the questions I have asked evoke a desire for us to further explore a conversation I hope you will take the time to contact me. I welcome the opportunity to learn from you.

Eric Edwards Vogt is an entrepreneur, educator and author with a depth of experience in the field of corporate learning. A former faculty member at the Harvard Business School, he is founder and president of MicroMentor, a professional learning design firm which has developed Desktop Learning, an interactive multimedia software.

Early in his career, Vogt was a consultant with The Boston Consulting Group where he led projects in both corporate strategy and industrial policy. He now serves as vice chairman of the Board of Bay State Skills Corporation, is a member of the Board of Overseers of the Boston Museum of Science, and a trustee of the Massachusetts Software Council. He holds an MBA from the Harvard Business School.

Vogt has been keynote speaker and featured presenter at The Research Board, The Conference Board, and the American Society for Training and Development, among others. In addition to numerous articles, his book publications include *A Framework for Swedish Industrial Policy* (with Ira Magaziner).

19

Learning Out of Context

Eric Edwards Vogt

"Why can't my organization learn? We spend six percent of payroll on training and development. Our catalog of courses is twice as large as our competition's. We use all the proven methods of Instructional Systems Design. Our corporate institute is filled to capacity. Every employee religiously completes a minimum of ten days of training each year. In addition, nearly all our executives have attended advanced programs at Harvard, Wharton, and Stanford. We have built competency models for every job classification. And we have just completed a series of accelerated courses in systems thinking and mental models. Yet nothing seems to be different," complains the CEO of TechnoCorp. "Our capacity to learn and innovate as an organization is nowhere. New product ideas appear at a dismal rate, relative to our competition. And meetings produce a lethargic sense of 'déjà vue all over again.' Why can't we learn here at TechnoCorp?"

Do these symptoms sound all too familiar? TechnoCorp is suffering from the same ills that many corporations now experience. Simply put, TechnoCorp is unconsciously applying the learning techniques and work skills of the Industrial Age to the learning challenges of the Knowledge Era. Continuing this tool mismatch will lead to a workforce incapable of achieving the learning rate and idea generation rate required to survive. Learning in today's Knowledge Era requires continuous attention and the ability to change direction with little advance notice. One reason that TechnoCorp lacks positive results is that they are using the equivalent of a *sledgehammer*, when what they actually need is a *windsurfer*. The context of work has changed from the predictable, repetitive single-purpose hammering of the Industrial Age to an ever-changing landscape of wind and water with no fixed reference points. Their learning is *out of context.*

How can we place learning in context? One approach to understanding this phenomenon is a simple yet powerful model. TechnoCorp's approach to learning with courses, a large catalog and a corporate institute reflects their Industrial Age mindset, with a focus on *content.* I might represent their view of the learning world as:

$$\text{Content}$$

This view of learning naturally leads to the sledgehammer approach to organizational learning. The apparent recipe for success is simple: identify everything that needs to be learned, build a course with Instructional Design principles, and when everyone has taken all the courses, then you will have organizational learning. This time-honored approach represents the ultimate outcome of Taylorism applied to learning. Twenty years ago, in a more predictable Industrial Age, the sledgehammer might have worked. Yesterday, work was more definable and the half-life of critical knowledge was closer to fifty years rather than five. Today, a strict content focus leads to a catalogue of courses which describe outdated work practices and yesterday's knowledge.

A Context and Process Lens of Learning

Today's expanded lens of organizational learning might be better represented as:

This view of organizational learning suggests that surrounding the *Content* of learning is always a *Process* of learning. Similar to the current activities in total quality management and reengineering, which focus on work process, there is a critical need to redesign our traditional learning processes. Indeed, in the Knowledge Era, *how* individuals learn (the process) and *why* they learn (the context), may be more important than *what* they learn (the content). To survive, TechnoCorp and today's corporations should focus considerable attention on the process of learning and upon the technologies which offer dramatic improvements in the learning process. Instead, most corporations use learning technology from 1904, as they unconsciously recreate their mediocre schooling experience in the corporate classroom. In addition, since the half-life of content knowledge is now roughly five years. Knowledge Era corporations must emphasize enhanced learning processes and skills of learning rather than focus solely upon traditional courses and knowledge transfer.

Early Corporate Innovators

There is some evidence of this new lens currently emerging in the form of leadership courses. Most of these corporate offerings require the development of more enduring process, mindset and thinking skills, as opposed to technical knowledge. Another example of a focus upon the learning process is occurring at the Chase Manhattan Bank. Chase's Professional Development Group has undertaken an experimental six-month learning experience to convert their corporate trainers into "learning designers."

This conversion of trainers into designers begins with an important change in mindset from training event to learning process. Chase's professional development objective is not training, but learning—defined as a process which enhances a person's capacity to take effective action in a particular domain. The learning process is best viewed as a complex set of interacting elements, not a simple sequence of events. Chase's professionals learned by doing—applying eight principles of learning design to their ongoing work at the bank. This process was facilitated by a coach and supported by their learning teams. At the same time, a series of learning experiences outside the context of banking, including juggling and dancing, provided the opportunity to explicitly reflect upon their own learning process.

The motivating philosophy is that Chase might achieve a higher return on investment by improving the learning process rather than by adding more courses. Perhaps TechnoCorp could benefit from the current thinking at Chase Manhattan.

A second corporate innovator provides another example of applying a process lens to corporate learning. During 1994, Kraft General Foods began experimenting with their first "content free" learning experience. Kraft aspires to shift their internal practice of static competitive analysis to a continuous competitive thinking loop. To accomplish this, they have designed a learning experience which focuses upon the participants' thinking processes, rather than content. For instance, during one section of this experience, both interactive multimedia software (*Desktop Learning* and *Team Learning*), Kraft managers improve their capacity to articulate powerful questions and compose scenarios in order to weave a wider fabric of perspectives and alternatives for the future. The Kraft and MicroMentor team has designed the learning process. Relevant content is supplied by the participants as needed, or obtained just-in-time through electronic sources. The learning experience itself is content-free in traditional terms, but process rich.

The DNA of Business Learning

"How can we focus upon the 'process ring' of this model of organizational learning? How can we redesign business learning?" the leadership of TechnoCorp asks. One useful first step is to think in terms of the DNA of business learning. The DNA model of business learning suggests that virtually all learning happens as a combination and recombination of three kinds of distinct learning events (see Figure 1).

Coaching is the art of observing, asking questions, and designing effective interventions. Coaching in this DNA model of business learning can also include short bursts of lecture, as long as the interaction takes the form of storytelling or clearly responding to the concerns of the learners. *Team Learning* is the art of establishing trust, framing motivating questions, and engaging in the generation of new perspectives through the art of dialogue. *Desktop Learning* is the practice of learning through interactive multimedia experiences designed to accommodate various learning styles and engage the learners' attention at a

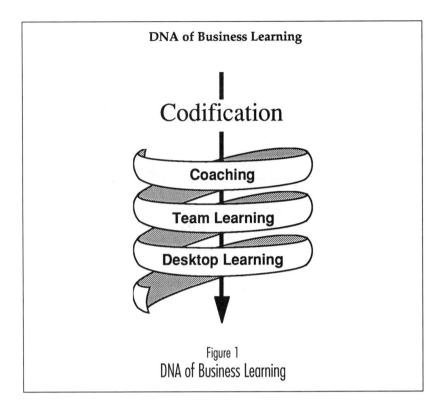

Figure 1
DNA of Business Learning

much higher level than traditional classroom.

The structure of any learning experience can be redesigned at a high level by simply combining the elements of coaching, Team Learning, and Desktop Learning to match the natural pattern of human learning. For example, one enduring pattern of natural learning is the "discovery learning loop" which comes to us from John Dewey, via Kurt Lewin and David Kolb. The discovery learning loop argues that all human learning experiences follow a process which may be best described by the four-step cycle shown in Figure 2 on the following page.

For example, consultants at Boston Consulting Group learn to diagnose companies for large reengineering projects by first listening briefly to a *Coach* speak about the principles of time-based competition (Abstract). This is followed by a *Desktop Learning* experience where they practice diagnosing the dysfunctional cycles of a hypothetical client company (Experiment). Young consultant *teams* work together to synthesize their views (Observe) and create a presentation for senior management

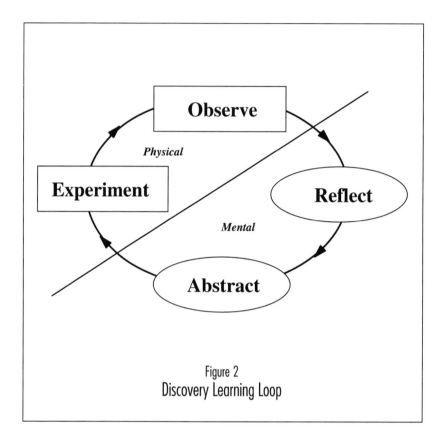

Figure 2
Discovery Learning Loop

(Reflect and Abstract). The result of this process change which blends an understanding of the DNA of learning with an appreciation of natural human learning, is more effective learning in less time at lower cost than the traditional corporate classroom alone.

Redesigning Business Learning

This approach to redesigning business learning has also been successfully applied recently for learning financial instruments at JP Morgan; audit methodology at Ernst & Young; total quality at Polaroid; medical benefits at Aetna; rate and inventory management at Holiday Inn; and procurement procedures at the World Bank. Using this model in practice requires that the aspiring learning designer, segment the intended learning into coaching, team, and desktop learning. This partitioning may be guided by several factors:

- The level of codification of the material.
- The importance of verbal practice with an observer.
- The importance of learning through team interactions.

This perspective will begin to inform the learning designer which segments of learning are best delivered through coaching, team learning, or desktop learning.

The second critical step in redesigning the learning process is the application of "learning design principles," as opposed to "instructional design principles." As the focus in corporations moves from repetitive training courses to just-in-time learning experiences, the school of thinking about learning design is making a similar adjustment. The emerging school of learning design focuses more upon the learner's experience, addressing intrinsic motivation, variable challenge levels, adjusting to learning styles, and learning-by-doing. A full elaboration of this school of learning design is beyond the scope of this chapter—interested readers are directed to Tom Malone's "Toward a Theory of Intrinsically Motivating Instruction" and MicroMentor's "Learning Design Principles." Applying Team Learning and Desktop Learning to existing courses designed with yesterday's instructional design concepts does not necessarily produce an effectively redesigned learning process. A change in design thinking from instructional design to learning design must accompany the change in learning mode in order to create learning processes suitable for the Knowledge Era.

So What is a Learning Context?

In this lens of organizational learning, the learning *Context* surrounds and informs the learning *Process*. For an understanding of learning context we might start with Webster's definition:

> **con•text** *n* [ME weaving together of words,
> coherence] **1** the parts of a discourse that
> surround a word or passage and can throw
> light on its meaning **2** the interrelated conditions in which something exists

A learning context can be best described as a combination of the definitions offered by Webster's—the definition of context suggests, a learning context will be partly constructed by weaving together words to support the corporate discourse which creates the interrelated conditions for learning. Since that is a mouthful, let's consider some examples of a learning context. While the specifics will differ for each organization, certain characteristic building blocks will always provide the foundation for a learning context in any organization.

The building blocks of a learning context are:
- a continuous learning mindset
- an architecture of learning
- cultural and emotional support for learning

Continuous Learning Mindset

When was the last time you saw an advertisement in an airplane magazine for a motivational poster saying "WELCOME IGNORANCE"? We apparently value TEAMWORK, CHALLENGE, SUCCESS, INTEGRITY. And yet while we claim to value learning, we don't value a critical pre-condition for learning: ignorance. In most organizations today we are more highly prized for having the answer than, for having a question and admitting ignorance. This is no great surprise, given that rewards are handed out in our educational system for knowing rather than searching. Ironically, the demands of the Knowledge Era require a mind which welcomes ignorance, as a chance to learn continuously, not as a verdict on your intelligence as a whole person.

The nature of this continuous learning mindset is distinct from the Industrial Age. Before, "learning" could be adequately viewed as transferring knowledge from the expert to the learner. Now, learning must be viewed as the process of idea generation, the creation of new perspectives, and the social construction of these new perspectives to ensure that they become codified and shared. How well do our schools prepare the new workforce for these skills of continuous learning? In contrast to the typical Western education, the distinguished Chilean biologist, Humberto Maturana, was recently asked how his schooling influenced his innovative thinking. He replied that he had attended an experimental high school in Santiago where half of their grade was based upon the quality of the student's questions, not their answers. This is an example of a continuous learning mindset.

Now you begin to see how TechnoCorp is trapped in its own mindset of learning as an event, rather than a continuous process. The fact that the CEO and senior management team of TechnoCorp pride themselves on filling the corporate institute and achieving a quota of training days each year is an early warning sign that their learning context is flawed.

An Architecture of Learning

It is difficult to take a journey without a road map. Organizational learning is the journey. *Learning architecture* provides a road map. At the highest level, an organizational learning architecture provides insight for the questions:

- Why should we learn?
- How should we learn?
- Where does learning happen?

Competency models, provided they are adaptable to changes in the business and linked to assessment and development plans, are an example of an organization's learning architecture. Chase Manhattan's Private Bank has innovated in this domain, linking competency models to an automated "Competency Builder" software which facilitates manager and peer assessment, leading to the creation of an individual learning plan. These plans point to the learning that needs to happen on the job, new skills which require additional learning, and opportunities to mentor and help others learn.

But a robust learning architecture must address the why and how of learning in social terms as well as technological terms. To what extent can work teams also be learning teams? Is there a mentor who is separate from the performance management/appraisal process? How do professionals come together to reflect on their experience? How are new perspectives spread throughout the organization? How do we maintain our organizational memory? How can we build our intellectual capital? This domain of learning architecture will witness much innovation during the next ten years.

Ernst & Young, a Big Six professional service firm, is one of the leaders in this field. In addition to their sizable investments in interactive *Desktop Learning* to disseminate new professional practices, they are actively researching new road maps in the form of metrics to measure learning and intellectual capital. If you can't measure it, you can't manage it. In 1994 IBM has tied their performance compensation to customer satisfaction. One result is that an elusive concept is going to be closely studied and measured. How could IBM and TechnoCorp measure the strength of their learning context?

Cultural and Emotional Support for Learning

How many times have you simply created a safe space for a child and watched her blossom and learn? How often have we forgotten that employees are people too? Does your culture tolerate ambiguity long enough to discover something new? How forgiving is your culture with "mistakes?" On a one to ten scale, how would you assess the level of trust in your organization and why? When colleagues are just chatting in your organization, how do they talk about their learning? Do they ask for help?

These diagnostic questions might be among the most important in creating the context for learning. Think of something physical you learned to do recently. There was probably a sense of anxiety or fear associated with the experience. An organizational culture can vary quite widely in its ability to deal with fear and insecurity towards learning. IBM is legendary in their commitment to training. At the same time, they might also be characterized as an organization which does not encourage experimentation and exploration for learning. Nor does Big Blue tolerate much ambiguity. You might contrast that culture with Intel's or Apple's, where experimentation and learning are part of the corporate ethic. And if you are not certain about the impact of a strong learning context on the marketplace, consider the market to book ratios of IBM, Apple, and Intel:

	1992	1994
Intel	3.34	3.88
Apple	3.22	2.11
IBM	1.04	1.55

Another way of understanding the power of cultural and emotional support in building the learning context is shown in Figure 3.

The learning motivation is almost always present. To achieve positive forward movement of learning in the organization it is often more effective to work to remove impediments from the right hand column. This is an arena where the new leaders can start to work. Alan Webber writes, "The work of the new economy occurs in conversations, and the leaders' role is to build trust." The stage is set for us to view leadership as a verb rather than a noun. Those who practice leadership in the Knowledge Era will engage in non-judgmental conversations which eliminate fear, build trust, invite ambiguity, and weave new perspectives into a

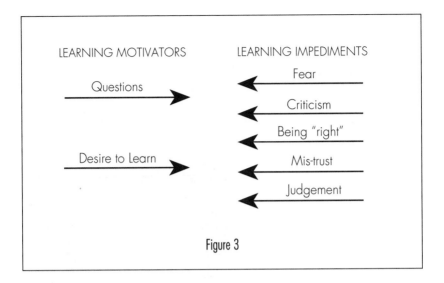

Figure 3

fabric of meaning. In this fashion, the learning context will become more robust, and the natural desire to explore and learn will emerge.

Learning Out of Context

Looking at TechnoCorp from this new vantage point we see that there is a play on words which defines both their problem and a potential response. I observed earlier that they were using Industrial Age learning tools in a Knowledge Era. In this way, TechnoCorp's learning is out of *context*. At the same time, I assert that effective organizational learning must redesign the learning process and most importantly, must come *out* of context. That is, learning is a natural human phenomenon. And, all learning occurs within a context. Establish and nurture the learning context, and organizational learning is the likely next result. TechnoCorp's approach to learning is *inside out*. Their well-intentioned focus upon content effectively prevents them from operating on their learning context and learning processes. Investing resources and attention instead from the *outside in*, building a context for learning and redesigning learning processes will reap much higher rewards in today's Knowledge Era.

Carol Sanford works in North America, Western and Eastern Europe, Africa, and Asia with global corporations who seek to access untapped potential in their people, product offerings, technologies, and raw material transformations. For over 15 years, she has worked as a resource for business, organizational, and human development, helping business teams design developmental work systems and businesses, develop strategic leadership capability, and integrate the business with all its stakeholder constituencies.

She is co-creater in research, development, and learning processes at the Center for Developmental Systems and Spring Hill Publications. Her work, which has been translated into ten languages, emphasizes continuous development of the intellectual capacity and thinking capability of individuals and teams, and of their ability to realize a meaningful contribution. Its theory base is drawn from interdisciplinary research in science, philosophy, systems theory, and psychology.

20

Vitalizing Work Design: Implementing a Developmental Philosophy

Carol Sanford

As I communicate with business leaders around the world, I never cease to be amazed at the faith and courage with which they leap into a new approach to improving their businesses. I am equally shocked at how little understanding they have of how to assess any particular approach and the potential it may offer. Many programs are adopted in the name of Learning Organization, Continuous Improvement, etc. which suggest new improved results and improved work environments. Many of these are really only repackaged or redecorated versions of traditional methods these leaders are seeking to escape. It finally occurred to me that leaders do not have a set of guidelines for assessing whether the method they have chosen has a sound base in its design. This article offers a structure for assessing the likelihood of a given approach taking an organization toward becoming more "developmental," i.e., more capable of continual evolution toward higher-order capacities and results.

There is a common set of principles among most so-called new work designs that is likely to lead an organization away from becoming more developmental in its approach to work. These principles cause limitations from the outset in many of the same ways that traditional work systems do. The traditional as well as most new designs are rooted in behaviorist philosophy. Behaviorism itself has a limiting set of principles and methods when applied to business environments. Behaviorism is the branch of psychology associated with Pavlov's finding that dogs salivated when the feeding bell rang and with B.F. Skinner and his study of rats in mazes. This legacy offered us a psychology that is based on the study of lower animals. Despite this, much of this body of work has found application in the workplace. This would be fine if our organizations were operated by rats and chimpanzees.

Exploration of a few of the tenets of work designs based on behavioral psychology can help us to understand the limitations of the principles offered and why so much potential cannot be realized through these designs. As a means of contrast, we will examine the principles underlying a developmental philosophy. The developmental philosophy is based on open systems designs and works on the development of whole persons. A developmental philosophy starts from seeing people (and businesses) as having open-ended potential to develop themselves and their capacities to *do* and to *be*. The tendency however is to become static in our work and our approach to work, especially when we are part of a large system. A Developmental Philosophy leads to work designs that continuously evolve the way of working and expands the potential of value-adding processes and the potential of organization members to evolve that potential.

Six Improvement Targets of Work Design

As a way to compare the different underlying principles, we will compare six universal arenas in which businesses seek to be successful in work design. The first three, Interaction, Concentration, and Freedom, are related to particular outcomes or results that are sought from a work redesign or design. The second three, Expansion, Identity, and Order are related to capabilities that must be built among the members of the organization for the work design to be effectively realized.

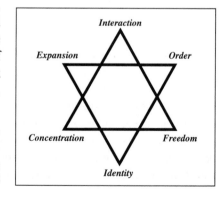

1. Expansion

The expansion of opportunity for individuals to contribute to the organization is one of the objectives of any new work design. It is now widely accepted that employees have been underutilized in most work settings, and most new work designs introduce systems in which employees have enormously expanded opportunity to use their skill and knowledge. People are able to develop themselves within the new system and to the full extent of the system. A common example of this is a skill-based pay and progression system which creates a thorough listing of the skills and/or knowledge that is to be developed by the workers, along with a system for certification of competence for each block.

A developmental philosophy sees the capability of people and their ability to contribute as open-ended. (Any pre-specified system of development, such as a Skill Block System, by its very nature provides a barrier to the very development and contribution that is sought from people placed within it.) Using a developmental philosophy, the design of the work and the development of work systems unfold, and with this unfolding, each person discovers new potential in self, product offerings, and markets as development occurs. Each individual is always working from a developmental plan with an interactively developed yet self-determined business contribution goal and a unique set of capabilities to be developed. The system that enables this development is not a matrix of cells, each with pre-specified skills and knowledge. Rather, it is one of guidelines regarding the nature of work arenas which, given the evolving values of stakeholder constituencies, serve as appropriate areas of contribution. This approach provides boundaries that ensure appropriate thrust toward business objectives is maintained even as individual creativity is nourished.

On the surface, these may not seem so different. Philosophically, however, they come from very different paradigms. One sees development as occurring *within* a *system*, with the system as the starting point of development. The other sees individual development as the means of evolving the system and each person is the starting point of their own development and the evolution of the system. The behavioral philosophy of designing a universal set of skills and knowledge through which each individual progresses, tends to homogenize the skills and knowledge of all persons within the system. Skill Block Systems and knowledge-based pay and progression systems or any system with predetermined standards tend to work to limit the possibilities of truly tapping and developing the full *potential* of people, businesses, and markets. Such logic is flawed because the business environment in which people work is dynamic and changes more rapidly than any prescribed system can allow for. Predefined systems can only be based on yesterday's ideas of needed skills and knowledge. Open-ended systems provide choice for working on the future.

2. Identity

Leadership in new work designs seeks to have people in the workforce identify with work and activities that are more conducive to increased flexibility, increased skill level, and increased accountability. The primary means in a behavioral-based system is one of establishing role models and of reinforcing behaviors that most closely approximate a desired behavior. Examples from such systems include evaluation procedures that specify desired behaviors, rating and ranking systems that honor those that achieve higher levels of frequency in being appropriate, and reward and recognition programs to single out those individuals or groups who most exemplify desired behaviors.

A developmental philosophy eschews role models as the very antithesis of what is needed for success—the unfolding of uniqueness. Attention is given to helping everyone in the organization increasingly discover their own uniqueness and to embed that uniqueness into the organization, its product offerings, and processes. No energy is put into comparing people as individuals, groups, shifts, or other collectives. Systems or processes that assume people should pursue modeling themselves after someone else are disassembled. There are no "low" and "high" performers, no "difficult people," no behaviorally-based categories at all. No tests are provided to help people discover what "type" of learner or manager they are. Emphasis is on the uniqueness of each individual and finding more ways for that uniqueness to be embedded into the life and outputs of the organization.

In behavioral-based work designs, it is also common to form teams out of crews that can rotate shared assignments. One result of the rotation design of teams that are based on shared shifts and work functions is that the individual's *will* tends to become subordinated to the collective or team or organizational *will*. The *will* we are speaking of here is that force or motivation that makes each of us unique—that causes us to be drawn to pursue particular interests and causes. It is the source of tenacity, creativity, and diversity. Most businesses have no idea how to maintain individuality while developing teams, so they unintentionally create work designs that effectively obliterate individual identities or essences—often more than traditional work designs do.

This collectivizing of *will* is accomplished through team building, consensus building, and by rewards for team and organizationally valued behavior, and by condemnation or punishment of undesirable behavior. This subordination of the individual to the whole is fundamental to most team designs where multi-skilling processes seek to gain uniformity and flexibility of performance. Unfortunately, this process is also a source of loss of individuality in terms of questioning of procedures, expression of uniqueness possibilities, and innovation regarding processes of work.

Another example of how this occurs is through the use of one of the numerous typologies for assessing personality style that exists today. The Myers-Briggs analysis is one example. These typologies focus on the surface or functional aspects of a person, moving people away from exploring their uniqueness as individuals and their own inner processes. The categorizing of students in schools and the classifying of people in workplaces has tended to cause us to see ourselves as static (as being of a particular type) rather than as evolving persons. These same processes cause us to see ourselves as common and definable by externally determined standards. When these assessment models are used in organizations they contribute to a field of external judgments whereby we see people as types—one of a limited number of categories. The life of a person is thus reduced to a box or a rank. These models are the thieves of developmental processes.

The philosophical starting point is fundamentally different. In one, there is a set of "desirable" behaviors based on profiles of "successful" behaviors. In the other, there is only a desire to better unfold the potential of each unique individual. This difference shows up in behavioral-based systems when there is an attempt to get individuals to move from identifying themselves with a narrowly-defined job to identifying with a whole task. With a developmental-based system, identity is not developed from a job or any other phenomenon that is internal to the organization. Rather, it is developed in terms of uniqueness, brought about through a connection to something that needs serving beyond the organization itself, and to the way in which the individual and the organization can most uniquely serve. Teams formed with a developmental philosophy are organized in ways that integrate all functions in the business with the only meaningful identity—with constituent stakeholders (e.g., customers, communities surrounding the site, the Earth) who invest in them by purchasing their products and providing the resources needed to run their business.

3. Order

Whether to meet legal and regulatory mandates, or for reasons of human relationships, there is a desire to have processes that provide order to work, and to ensure fairness in dealings. In a behavioral-based work design, order is developed and maintained through standardization, proceduralization, and classification. As mentioned above, people are placed relative to one another within a system and there is an attempt to treat everyone using the same procedures. Additionally, work is standardized and proceduralized in an attempt to ensure adherence to specifications. Over time, however, such routinization tends to invite a loss of meaning and creativity in all who engage in the work.

In a developmental-based system, order is maintained by connecting everyone in the organization to the marketplace and the stakeholders who seek a reciprocal relationship with the company—e.g., investment dollars for a return, public services for a tax base. Each individual is connected in an intimate way with these stakeholder parameters, and is involved in designing work to best achieve the collective effect sought by stakeholders. Such a system is a very powerful organizer of work and one which every entrepreneur understands well.

In a behavioral model, as exemplified by a socio-technical system, the ordering emerges from structuring of the organization that is imposed on the individuals. In a developmental model, the order continually emerges from individuals through their living connection to a dynamic and evolving environment. One is a closed system, that pauses every so often to allow in new information—then to restructure the standards, procedures, and classification. The other is a living system, with a constant and immediate lifeline between the sought value and the work of the employees who are the source of those values being realized.

4. Freedom

New work designs are most frequently initiated from a desire to have a business that can extend the arenas and timeframes over which they can successfully exert influence. This may be stated in terms of increased markets or market share, new customers in new categories, improved relationships with regulatory agencies, or even better relationships with the workforce directly or through their representative unions. In a behavioral model, this freedom is sought through increasing the understanding of the realities with which they must engage through improved exchanges of information and measurement systems. Examples of this are increased availability of competitive information, customer information, and technological knowledge. All the senses are put to work in the search for better, more current, and more accurate data and information which can be distributed to the organization in a usable form.

Organizational designers are always looking for ways of instilling more degrees of freedom that enable people to conceive of and "go for" the impossible. The limitations that traditional organizations have placed on performance of work have also placed the same limitations on the working of the mind. As a result, people working in traditional organizations tend to apply their creativity to endeavors outside of work. In behavioral work redesign, there are attempts to overcome this "tunnel view" by increasing participation. Employees are encouraged to contribute ideas and to become involved in creative solutions to problems. In a developmental model, freedom is seen as coming from the development of other intelligences that are no longer a part of our educational, societal, or professional training. Freedom comes from moving from what Edwin Abbott calls a "Flatland" or two-dimensional view of the world to a perspective that sees the dynamics of the world from escalating levels of complexity and significance.

A simple example is understanding that our actions can be understood and even influenced or improved more readily if we explore *what* we are thinking about that causes us to take particular actions. The thinking behind our actions or words might be described as a different plane of understanding. Exploring further into our thinking processes, we can increase our self-managing ability or improve the predictability of our achievements if we can see *how* we are thinking as well as *what* we are thinking. For example, many athletes have found they were blocked at improving performance by self-defeating thoughts. In order to change these thoughts, they had to have a process for changing how they were thinking. "Visioning" is one such example that has been used to successfully change *how* one thinks different thoughts, and ultimately has different behaviors. Educating ourselves regarding mental processes is fundamental to development and improvement—and to a developmental philosophy of work design.

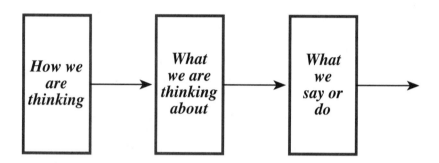

There are many different schools which offer ways to view the world from different levels of reality. Peter Senge points to the idea that structure generates pattern which leads to particular events. For example, the way we structure highways generates particular traffic patterns which result in particular events for individuals and groups. In human systems, the structure comes from corporate cultures and operating procedures. Nobel Laureate and physicist David Bohm offers a deeper three-level system which moves from what we can detect with our senses to that which cannot be sensed. He proposes a first level that he calls an *explicate order*. This order is the perceived world, based on physical phenomena which are "explicated" or made explicit through our life experience. Behind or beyond this world, however, is an *implicate order* which is the formative source of power regarding what can and does emerge in the explicate order. Joseph Chilton Pearce uses a metaphor of a hidden projector to clarify this relationship between implicate and explicate order. The hidden projector displays lights on a screen. If we want to see the light show, we look at the screen (explicate order) and its display, and not at the projector (implicate order). To change the images on the screen we must change what is within the projector itself, not what is on the screen. The analogy does not hold exactly in our world since the implicate order cannot be found by walking backstage. It is a "non-localized" order. Bohm then carries the worldview to a third level by pointing to a vastly more powerful ordering which produces the implicate order—a "supra-implicate order." Bohm describes this as that which represents the information that guides and organizes the movement of fields or patterns of reality.

Pearce further describes the relationships among these three levels of reality. An explicate order gives rise to our lived experience—that which is in front of us everyday. The implicate order gives rise to our personal consciousness or our inner-world experience. The supra-implicate order gives rise to and guides the implicate order. In our projector metaphor, the supra-implicate order is the very source of the projector—creator, power source, and operator.

Each higher level of worldview reduces the restraints we experience in being able to understand or come to terms with very complex phenomena and the workings of complex systems. The technologies that emerge from a developmental philosophy contribute to a capability to understand all the levels of reality that are creating physical world dynamics. This capability provides the base from which we can create more whole solutions to problems and more creative product offerings to the stakeholders of our businesses.

Behavioral philosophy work designs have incorporated the behavioral tenet that *reality* is something that is universal for all persons. All reality is seen as observable by the senses and can be experienced directly. This view of reality tends to exclude the inner workings of the mind and emotions and, therefore, excludes work human beings can do in regard to management and development of self beyond functional aspects. The sense-based form of reality also tends to make it difficult for us to see the "reality forming" processes that go on in our minds—unobservable by others and ourselves without the development of the skill to do so. Recent research has demonstrated a "reality" that is highly interpretative—one which is at least partially constructed by the filters and mental models through which we view the world.

Another Nobel Laureate, Ilya Prigogene, described the experience of reality this way: "Whatever we call reality, it is revealed to us only through the active construction in which we participate." Without understanding this we are at the mercy of forces we can not see.

We get so accustomed to looking at everything with the same set of eyes that we don't see anything different; we are only looking at the objective world, and all realities look pretty similar. When we have an insight, we say to ourselves, "I never looked at it that way before," which is the same as "I was able to take a new perspective and, therefore, see something from a different level." To continually awaken development of ourselves as persons, we need to continue to shift our perspective or worldview. We have the mental capacity to do that. In a developmental model, the inner *and* outer world views are nurtured and seen as giving the individuals and the organization the ability to see more possibilities.

5. Interaction

New work designs seek to provide for significantly improved communication among and across work groups. With communication there comes a better alignment between individual and organizational goals. These interactions include performance feedback among peers or between levels, task forces between departments, or the collection of additional customer feedback. In a behavioral organization, interactions are designed to improve the ability of individuals and teams to better understand how they are viewed by others, and to provide motivation for improvement based on external reflection.

Behavioral-based designs seek to create motivation through the use of external or environmental reinforcement. Achievement is seen as something people do to maintain inclusion by their peers and superiors. In behavioral psychology, there is no concept of a larger system in which the smaller system exists and with which the smaller system acts reciprocally. As a result of the emphasis on external evaluation, it has become increasingly difficult for persons to be accurate about appraising their behavior, even in such physical and functional arenas as whether they are on time for a meeting.

There is a culturally-derived tacit assumption in most organizational settings that human beings can *not* be self-governing or self-auditing because they can not be objective about themselves. This is partly true, but not innately so. With humans, if this ability is not developed in us from childhood, the capacity to be self-reflecting (self-observing and self-remembering) steadily diminishes. This is particularly true when our primary source of reflection is external (e.g., from others' interpretation of our actions). It is particularly true if the feedback focuses on elements that tend to pull us away from that which feels intrinsically self-integrating. As humans, we have a desire to realize a sense of integrity between our values and our behavior, even when we have to learn the "hard way." Individuals, through self-governance, can engage in a process of self-reflection and move themselves, over time, toward a pattern of behavior they consider to be more in line with personal values. This cannot be achieved through external manipulation. Only the individual can tell what is uniquely integrating for him/her self. This is a core life exercise in development of self-accountability. The behaviorist model works against creating self-accountable behavior through institutionalizing reinforcement and external feedback to create "other accountability."

In our Western education and parenting world, there are few processes for building capability and accountability for one's own reflective processes. One research study found that, by early school age, children could no longer correctly interpret whether they were performing accurately in a research exercise instructing them where to place their arms in relation to their body. Moreover, they would defend their answer as accurate even when shown photos of themselves performing inaccurately. However, within a few short weeks of being asked to reflect on the accuracy of their response to the same exercise, without any external input, they became increasingly accurate at assessing their own performance. Self-observation is a capability that has systematically been eroded in our culture. With practice we can regain it.

In Western culture, we have systematically instilled a culture with values that tend to erode self-accountability. First our parents, then our teachers, and now our employers/bosses tell us what to do. Our performance and our grade or rank are determined by others. We are told to what degree our behavior is correct. This is so embedded in our way of operating that it is difficult to see how pervasive it is and how much it works against creating self-accountable human beings.

From a developmental philosophy, the foundational element in effective work systems is self-reflecting, self-correcting, self-accountable, and self-evolving behavior. Energy spent on monitoring and attempting to affect the behavior of organizational members or collectives of persons from an external source is energy wasted—energy that could be better put to improving the business and the capability of people. The critical element is to increase self-governing, self-evolving capability.

6. Concentration

New work systems are based on the hope of producing products and services with the least possible waste, the fewest errors, and with the most effective return or yield from our efforts. In an effort to gain the highest efficiency in the early years of industry, much effort was put into breaking down the work into smaller and smaller units. New work designs have made an attempt to re-aggregate the work into more meaningful units called "whole tasks." An example of this attempt is seen when a person on a machine will do all the jobs related to the machine including beginning to plan the work itself or maybe even ordering some of the materials that are needed to do the work. All this, however, is structured within what can be managed by a team in the same physical location and usually on the same shift. Work is not redesigned; only the people who do the work are simply redesignated. The same work and same nature of work is done.

The thinking processes employed for doing the work are not changed. The thinking now only covers a larger number of tasks which are still seen as functionally divided from the work of other functions. The primary mental process that is utilized is one of the elemental mind. An elemental view emanates from the paradigm that presumes only parts exist—not wholes—and works to understand phenomena exclusively by reducing wholes into parts. In an elemental view, any summary of the whole is seen as accomplished by adding up of the parts. Parts tend to be viewed as fixed and unchanging. We describe what they are, not what they could be. Most feedback processes, goal setting, and measurement systems are based on an elemental view of the world. The initiatives to be acted on and measured are studied and implemented in a largely fragmented way. Organizations divide feedback forms into each type of behavior, and goals by target areas. This segmentation sounds reasonable, but it leads to the illogical conclusion that there is no difference between a comfortable house and a pile of building materials, or between a frisky mouse and a test tube full of chemicals.

The difference, of course, between the molecules in a mouse and those in a test tube full of chemicals is organization. The molecules in a mouse are organized in a precise and complex way, while those in the test tube are just sloshed together. Most leaders realize that it is important to understand how the pieces fit together, at least in their own field; but they are still mostly concerned about the "parts" rather than about the "pattern."

Behavioral philosophy work designs do not manage to overcome the reductionist view or elemental view of the world inherent in the modern culture and organizational operations.

In behavioral philosophy, there is a search for the causes that produce the effects as though cause and effect moves in a linear path. In the physical and non-physical world, the causes for any effect emerge from many interacting elements occurring simultaneously, as well as from the anticipation of events not yet in existence. In order to bring change to an element of a system, we must consider the dynamics of the whole and work in a holistic way. This systems view enables us to design change from an integrated perspective, but requires that we let go of the security of programs that focus on specific functions, classes of people, and classes of problems. Isolated measures must give way to whole systems measures that track the overall progress of the system.

In a developmental philosophy, just as there are different levels of reality from which we can gain understanding of the dynamics of the world, there are different types of work to be done. At a minimum, there is the work that improves what already exists. This is different from the work necessary to create a new existence—raw materials, technologies, and product offerings that do not now exist. In traditional organizations and even newer work design systems, these are divided among different functions and levels of the organization. In a developmental organization, all are working on both of these as well as on other types of work, without regard to their level or function.

Assessing your Work Design or Process

No matter what the work design or improvement program is called—High Commitment, etc.—you can tell what potential it has by reflecting on which foundation the design is built. The fundamental differences can be discovered by asking:

1. **Expansion:** Are people expected to expand their contribution and develop their capability from within a pre-set system? Or, are the work systems designed to evolve as a result of the ongoing development and contribution of people?

2. **Identity:** Are people expected to identify with a set of acceptable behaviors that are exemplified by role models, with evaluation systems, and with a work unit that shares a rotating set of tasks? Or, are people developed for their uniqueness, and

as an opportunity to contribute their essence to the business?

3. **Order:** Is order maintained by creating increasing numbers of procedures, standards, and classification systems around which people are expected to organize their work, and to which they are to match their performance? Or, is order developed through having all members of the organization connected by the nature of synergy, and to the self-organizing and symbiotic relationships that need to be maintained between the organization and its stakeholders and a mutually desired future?

4. **Freedom:** Do attempts to gain freedom from surprise come from multiplying data and information across the organization? Or, do they come from enabling people to view reality from different levels of understanding that make complexity and rapid change the source of challenge, creativity, and innovation?

5. **Interaction:** Are interactions and communication sourced from a desire to provide external motivation and reinforcement for organizationally-approved behavior? Or, are they sourced from increasing capability to be self-managing and self-evolving in the context of the emerging values of the stakeholders with which the business transacts?

6. **Concentration:** Is work based on using a reductionist view of the world that breaks every whole into its parts to work on it, organize it, and evaluate it? Or, is capability built to work from an understanding of wholes and how different wholes relate to one another?

A Learning Organization is Not Necessarily a Developmental Organization

I would be the last to disparage the pursuit of a learning organization—it does move many people away from the shortcomings of the behavioral era. However, I do not believe it has a philosophical or technological base that can ensure that it naturally evolves to a developmental approach for the creation of work systems. The capabilities triad of Expansion, Order, and Identity is not carried out in a learning organization in a way that would lead to this result. The technology that springs from a developmental philosophy is fundamentally based in the development, not just the use, of intelligences. To be able see life and reality through the ascendancy of different planes of thinking or mental frameworks, as I discussed in the *freedom* giving element, is fundamental to our becoming different beings and different organizational entities. Otherwise we view everything the same as everything else with no higher-ordering influences from which to make sense of the world. If this capability is not developed, the nature of *interactions* used to move toward self-evolving, self-organizing processes does not have sufficient power for people to transform their worldview or paradigms away from the two-term models with which we view most of the world (e.g., right/wrong, good/bad).

The systems thinking models normally utilized in learning organization processes are drawn from a cybernetic system framework. This framework was developed for creating artificial intelligence in computers, but has insufficient diversity and complexity to transform human consciousness or even for the understanding of human consciousness. To enable evolution to the levels of spiritual and intellectual capacity needed for a developmental approach, a more extensive step is needed toward building the capability of all the intelligences necessary to understand and utilize transformational and evolutionary systems thinking processes. Learning organization theory and practice contains the vision, but not yet the science and technology required to actualize the vision.

Summary

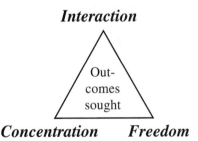

If organizational leadership continues to be hypnotized by the functional changes that can readily be produced with behavioral models, business enterprises and, therefore, society run a risk of losing the potential of several more generations of workers beyond those we have already lost. As you contemplate this summary, I suggest you consider my words from the level of an individual, a business organization, and at the level of society, or even the Earth. As Joseph Chilton Pearce says in his book

Evolution's End, we lose the freedom that comes from a grander framework for understanding the field of life when we do not develop the capacity of the total brain—maybe even lose the human race if he is right (Freedom).

Without the faith that comes from seeing others as capable of being self-reliant, within the context of the whole, we tend to see a need for some of us to teach, judge, and reinforce appropriate behaviors in others, thus creating a need for more disciplinary means and institutions. With an intellectually developed, self-managing society, even the prison inmates can help evolve the systems that govern them into ones that are developmental (Interaction).

An undeveloped mental capacity leaves us seeing ourselves, as humans, being something separate from all other living systems. We cannot see the essence of the role of each life form and the intricate role it/he/she plays in the web of all life, thus, too often inadvertently or even intentionally obliterating the physical life or at least the spirit and potential of that life, thereby reducing the possible futures for all (Concentration).

When the above capabilities are insufficiently developed, we ensure the very outcomes we seek will not be realized. In the

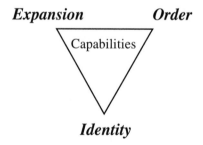

immediate as well as distant future, we lose the innate *will* human beings have to make a difference with their lives through expansion of their contribution and the means of contributions (Expansion).

We foster an entire society which is driven from our lower nature (e.g., defensive and egoistic), which is exemplified in succumbing to peer pressure rather than drawing from an internal sense of what is right and ethical (Identity).

We diminish the diversity and creativity that results from tapping the uniqueness of each person and may even be robbing ourselves of the sacred possibility that each human life brings. When any entity can not walk the path for which it was intended and can not make the difference it uniquely is capable of making, the whole does not become in totality what it could (Order).

These are the outcomes we lose—contribution to the greater scheme of things, the internal response to what is right for all, and the evolution of the whole that comes from the uniqueness of the part.

Linda E. Morris is a director in Ernst & Young's Professional and Organization Development Group. She is extremely interested in theories and practices on the cutting edge of learning and business management. She writes a quarterly column called "Research Capsules" for *Training and Development*, and has authored a variety of articles including "Learning Organizations: Settings for Developing Adults" that appeared in *Development in the Workplace* in 1993.

Morris is a leader in the American Society of Training and Development. She is also a founding trustee of the World Business Academy. She holds a BA degree from Regis College and an MS and EdD in adult education with a specialty in human resource development from Virginia Polytechnic Institute. She and her family reside in Reston, Virginia.

Development Strategies for the Knowledge Era

Linda E. Morris

This essay points out the strategic importance of moving toward a learning organization for firms that provide value by generating, developing, or distributing intellectual capital. It focuses on why successful organizations in the knowledge era will be learning organizations, advocates the adoption of a "development strategy" for their members, and describes three different strategies to consider. In conclusion, it examines some key conditions organizations can put into place, no matter which development strategy they choose.

I want to initiate a dialogue around the notion that merely constructing learning-efficient organizations will not be enough to create the type of generative, self-renewing, and reflective organizations needed to carry us forward into the next century and beyond. Rather, each organization will need to take a proactive stance to establish the conditions and pathways for its members to continuously develop. Taking such a stance will be central to success. No one specific people-development approach or strategy will fit all organizations. Implementation plans will vary based on organizational purpose and context. The organization's values, mission, product or service, industry, size, knowledge and skill requirements, stage of development, and location are all factors that will influence strategic and tactical choices for people development.

Crucibles for Individual and Organizational Development

As a new lens on organizational purpose and structure, the concept of a learning organization —an organization that consciously and intentionally develops its members and transforms itself—may provide a critical framework for shaping the successful businesses of the knowledge era. While some see learning organizations as the heirs of the total quality movement, others, like Michael Ray of Stanford Graduate School of Business, posit that they may be the embodiment of organizations acting in the new business paradigm. Indeed, business leaders such as Ray Stata, former president and chairman of Analog Devices, are beginning to believe that "the rate at which individuals and organizations learn may be the only sustainable competitive advantage, especially in knowledge-intensive industries."

Management's interest in learning organizations stems from a deep-seated conviction that businesses need to reorganize to retain a competitive position in the global marketplace. This interest is driven by the same environmental factors which are now focusing attention on Total Quality Management, Business Process Reengineering, and other recent initiatives aimed at revamping products and services. These factors include: the continuing shift from the Industrial Age to the Knowledge Era and the concomitant emphasis on intellectual capital as a source of wealth; the increasing complexity in all parts of life and business; globalization; an increasingly diverse workforce; and heightened attention to quality and client satisfaction. These factors affect both individuals and organizations.

For example, in an international professional services firm such as Ernst & Young, individuals are expected to master their technical discipline (i.e., audit, tax, actuarial services), to acquire expertise in an industry (i.e., electronics, health care, insurance), and to employ interpersonal and leadership skills to manage work and to serve clients. Moreover, the prevailing client-centered approach requires the professional services worker to focus on identifying the client's problems and to bring to bear the firm's capability to help the client—no matter what the service need is or where in the world the capability to provide it resides. Thus, somewhat strikingly, the individual managing the client relationship can be viewed as a node through which the collective knowledge and wisdom of the firm's 70,000 plus practitioners reach the client's operations.

The firm, on the other hand, is challenged to study, codify, and disseminate information and knowledge that affects its diverse clients, the problems those clients face and, most significantly, the resources available to serve clients. Additionally, it needs not only to exchange existing information among its members, but also to generate and document new knowledge on such things as environmental factors affecting clients and the resulting implications, whole new methodologies developed to provide services to clients, experiences in one situation that might be applied to another, and insights or creative ideas that break new ground for clients, practitioners, or the firm.

Organizations and their people are constantly challenged to work beyond their experience in situations and on issues or problems never before encountered. Moreover, to be able to perform tomorrow's work as capably as today's, organizations must continually build the performance capability of both the individual and the organization. Therefore, adopting the philosophy and practices of a learning organization benefits individuals and organizations alike by increasing knowledge and skills, thereby fueling current and future performance.

In learning organizations, learning is conscious and intentional. People not only make sense out of the anticipated and unanticipated results of their actions, they also plan to learn and learn from planning. Determining what and how to learn are viewed as key parts of discovery and problem solving processes. Knowledge building is collaborative and intelligence is collective. Business challenges provide opportunities to learn, strategic goals establish directions, and business results provide feedback.

People and organizations develop. Individual, team, and organizational learning and development are core values, linked to the fulfillment of the organization's vision, mission and the attainment of strategic goals. Values and value creating are important. In addition to classroom and individual self-development activities, learning strategies include coaching, team learning, computer-based instruction and, for some, computer conferencing.

The dialogue around learning organizations contains the seeds of transformative change. Its members consciously and intentionally take charge of personal and organizational learning and direction. People not only perform different tasks, but also speak differently, assume different roles, and see themselves in different relationships with one another. Personal and organizational emphasis shifts from knowing to learning; from objectives to outcomes and processes; from testing to goal attainment; from information dissemination and recall to pattern recognition, action and knowledge generation; and from evaluating to "valuating." The organization and everyone in it considers learning a primary, expected task and this is reflected in organizational culture, language, structures, and values.

Learning organization programs are being adopted to one degree or another by organizations such as AT&T, American Express, IBM, Hewlett Packard, Motorola, Herman Miller, and Federal Express. One could argue that by incorporating these learning organization approaches, these companies can regenerate themselves to be competitive in the year 2000 and beyond. Yet, for long-term sustainability and continuous renewal it may be that organizations will need something more than a strategy for *learning*. They also need a commitment to a *development* strategy.

Commitment to a Development Strategy

Deciding to become a learning organization holds the possibility of enabling companies to create new visions, and to initiate and implement new or "reinvented" business processes. However, to gain the high ground and the greatest long-term competitive advantage, an even greater shift is required. Organizations need to purposefully move through the stage of being a learning organization to committing to a development strategy. The world is moving quickly; in many cases organizations do not have time to codify and share knowledge rapidly enough to take advantage of advancing technology and meet clients' expectations. Instead they must develop and position their professionals to do so. Therefore, the type of learning organization needed is one that *consciously and intentionally develops its people and constantly transforms itself*. In such an organization the concept of development is central to its identity and pivotal to purpose and strategy. Key organizing principles include: recognition of the dynamic open state of business conditions, organization services, and ourselves as human beings; collaboration and integration of all types of efforts among all organizational members, levels and units, and with customers, suppliers, and even competitors; the creative and extensive use of technology; a future orientation; and the development of new measurement systems to map directions and monitor success.

A development strategy focuses on enhancing the development of and investment in people. Development strategies can be seen as natural responses to the change from making economic decisions based on the distribution of scarce natural resources to making those decisions based on choices among similar services, differentiated by perceived values created by knowledge. For example, Willis Harman and John Hormann suggest that when it no longer makes sense for an economically successful society to have economic production and consumption as its central focus, learning and development can become the society's central project. In their book *Creative Work: The Constructive Role of Business in a Transforming Society*, they argue that our society has reached this point and that employment's real purpose is self-development (e.g., fundamentally we work to create and only incidentally to eat). Moreover, development strategy is consistent with the increased understanding that adults develop over their life spans.

There is growing recognition that adults not only acquire more information over time, but that their capacity to act also changes. Indeed, from a developmental perspective, the "learning organization" may be critical to adulthood. Perhaps, for example, an entity that supports and enhances continuous growth and learning and development for individuals is the only type of organization in which a self-actualizing individual will grow and be happy.

The shift from production of goods, to delivery of services, to generation of knowledge as the core business activity requires a fundamental reassessment about what organizations need to do to ensure that they have the capacity for tomorrow's, next week's, or next year's "production." It is more and more apparent that capacity is resident in the organization's people and processes. Old "buy or build" and "up or out" human resource philosophies simply undervalue the breadth and depth of organizational as well as functional and industry knowledge required by, for example, a professional services firm. Interestingly, the market (current and future employees) is likely to demand this shift to a development approach: 1) our flattening, maturing population is at the age where self development is likely to be perceived as a major goal, particularly if there is no organizational place to go; 2) younger employees, devoid of career certainties, need to prepare themselves for their next jobs or positions while working at their current ones.

Learning organizations are important because they provide meaning to work and reflect the beginnings of a fundamental restructuring of the purpose of business and of society. Constructing them with a development strategy will provide the internal focus to link individual fulfillment and organizational attainment and to galvanize both.

Alternative Development Strategies

As with learning organizations the word *development* conjures up a variety of different meanings. What follows are three different development strategies to consider. They are alike in that they are based on a commitment to creating an environment that will allow people to develop skills, knowledge and capabilities over time. They differ in the intensity of the linkage between individual and organizational development, the emphasis placed on members' development by the organization, and the alignment between business strategy, human resource strategy, and stage theories of adult development.

Enhancing Individual Potential

With this approach, organizations realize and acknowledge that employees' expanding potential knowledge and skills are central to organizational success. Organizations modify processes and practices to enhance people's abilities to be in a learning mode, and to focus on continuous learning and self-development. One key basic assumption is that work and learning are two sides of the same coin—we work when we learn and we learn when we work. We focus knowledge, experience, and insight on clients' problems and our "solutions" are learned ones. An organizational climate that highlights the integration between work and learning, and connects and promotes the sharing of learning, will be positioned to build expertise and improve processes.

A related basic assumption is that personal or self-development (i.e., balancing one's life, identifying and achieving personal goals, interpersonal skills, etc.), is connected to workplace capability and is supported by the organization. This is based on the premise that we bring to every situation all that we are and have learned. Therefore what one learns in any domain is applied in all. Moreover, we consciously or unconsciously learn something in every exchange. Thus, experience increases or expands knowledge rather than diminishes it. Our task is to help people consciously and intentionally drive this process so that they and the organization increase benefits, and leverage what is learned.

Of the three strategies this may be the most diffuse from an implementation point of view. In concert with career counselors, individuals determine their most appropriate learning and development paths in their current and future roles. The organization creates a supportive learning environment with an emphasis on development. (It provides content and experience.) Supported by the organization, individuals then carry out short- and long-range learning and development activities, intentionally and consciously, alone, and in teams, sharing learning with others as they proceed.

Linking Individual and Organizational Development

Some organizations may wish to more actively link the development of members to the pursuit and attainment of specific strategic goals. With this scenario, organizations clearly identify specific individual competencies (knowledge, skills, and attributes) that practitioners and clients believe are required to meet objectives. Career development planning, assignments, and learning activities, in formal and informal settings, are then designed to help practitioners move through different levels of expertise or capability until they reach that level appropriate for each competency for their current role. Practitioners have a clear picture of what is and will be expected of them so that they can target the learning that occurs each day towards specific goals.

Organizational actions to support linking individual and organizational development include the identification of competencies that are aligned with organizational goals—and a reorientation of systems and processes to support development along these lines.

Leveraging Stages of Adult Development

The term "development," as used here, has a special, focused meaning—adults' passage through defined states or stages of thinking and being where they gain increasing capabilities to structure and create their environments. As humans develop, they continuously operationalize or bring to fulfillment new capabilities while retaining use of the ones they already have. To leverage this progression, organizations can create an environment or context that encourages rather than inhibits this natural expansion process.

In Table 1, Tom Boydell has expressed the stages of adult development within a framework that allows human resource developers to better understand development and to build learning activities, and perhaps even new human resource processes and systems, that will enhance it. For example, younger personnel or persons beginning a new role are apt to prefer to adhere to set standards, and to respond to changes by adapting the ways they operate. More senior and experienced personnel can also develop a "feel" for new situations, better work things out for themselves, and learn more from experience. Over time, people also become more attuned to thinking systematically, and consciously experiment with their behavior, monitoring the processes they follow, and using feedback from the results they obtain. Older and more senior personnel have additional and increased capabilities to recognize linkages, and work across whole fields of activities. They may be more prone to act on the basis of meaning and purpose.

Each of these stages or modes is distinct and as we move from one to another, we increase our repertoire of skills. Then our perceptions—or mental models—shift and we are able to view the world in different ways. And, our worldview influences everything we do (See Table 2). It frames our basic orientation towards experience. According to Boydell, operating in Modes 1 to 3, we see ourselves as acted upon by the world. It is only when we can act fully in Mode 4 that we view ourselves as actors. In Modes 5 and 6 we act upon the world and can function as director and producer.

Recognizing that these stages of development exist, organizations can make a concentrated and comprehensive effort to create human resource systems that support progress along these paths. Thus, learning for newer or younger employees might most appropriately focus on the content of knowledge; learning for slightly older or more experienced personnel might address integrating experiences and emphasizing processes; and learning for more senior and very experienced personnel emphasize making connections and linkages and creating or reshaping contexts.

Boydell posits that although people shift their basis of operations as they develop, they always have the capacity to act from any of the modes—and in fact do. Thus, when considering the development of an individual, it is appropriate to think of a person exhibiting a range or focus of actions rather than being in a particular stage. The individual can operate from all stages at once, although, at any one time, some modes provide a greater

	Table 1 Modes of Being and Learning
MODE 7 DEDICATING	Having a sense of the task (of the times) in front of me—and my part in it. Being able to see through things to the essentials—to sum this up in a word or an idea. Having a deep conviction and sense of purpose. Finding meaning in what I am doing and the way it is done.
MODE 6 CONNECTING	Realizing that things are somehow connected, are inter-dependent. Seeking wider overviews, bringing things together. Widening my outlook, my perspective; looking at the consequences and implications. Being able to work across a whole field of activity.
MODE 5 EXPERIMENTING	Needing to find out things, experiment and try out. Taking active steps to discover more to increase my understanding. Planning how to carry out experiments. Having a deep urge to discover; seeking, striving. Developing new ways of doing things for myself and others.
MODE 4 EXPERIENCING	Learning from experiences—and using this as a basis for action. Noticing what is going on and how I am affecting it—and how it affects me. Having my own ideas and theories which work for me. Being independent and working things out for myself. Doing things "my way"—expressing myself through what I do.
MODE 3 RELATING	Being sensitive, aware and in tune with what is happening. Understanding at a deeper level what is going on and be able to explain this to others, in terms of established ideas and theories. Having a "feel" for the situation, relating to it in an appropriate manner—as defined by the norms, customs and practice. Tuning in to the situation and responding in a skilled and effective way.
MODE 2 ADAPTING	Responding to variations from the routine by adapting the way I operate. Recognizing patterns of information and noticing the effects of changes. Desiring to make procedures work well, making modifications to bring things back into control. Putting together a series of skills and behaviors, making slight modifications to the way I have been taught.
MODE 1 ADHERING	Working to set standards or ways of operating that have been previously set down by others. Operating from memory, thinking in terms of rules, checklists and set procedures. Feeling insecure if there is no "correct" answer provided for me. Carrying out prescribed routines, implementing them "to the letter."

* The modes are nested. For example, the person operating from Mode 5, 6 and 7 has the capacity to act from all modes and does so in different situations.

Table 2
Summary of Some Key Dimensions of Mode

Mode	Prime Influence	World is...	I seek...	"Trade"
7. Dedicating		Living, in need of help	Purpose	Visionary
6. Connecting	My self on outer world	Magical, awesome	Connections, wholeness	Artist
5. Experimenting		Interesting	Insight	Scientist
4. Experiencing	My self	Exciting	Experience	
3. Relating		Attractive	Membership	Craftworkers
2. Adapting	Outer world	Dangerous	To conquer it	Manipulator
1. Adhering		Dangerous	Protection	Operation

Reproduced with permission. © Transform 1990

foundation for activity, behavior shifts based on situations, experience, and maturity (see Figure 1).

Moreover, the development process is iterative. When faced with new situations or contexts, individuals, intentionally or accidentally, rely on their capabilities to adhere and adapt and then move to another mode (for example, experimentation).

Our understanding of human development is still emerging. It has not yet been intentionally integrated deeply into learning programs and practices, organizational practices, or business and human resource strategies of any organization. However, tying adult development, to business planning and organizational development and supporting this approach with technology and knowledge of systems theory, would be a powerful long-term strategy.

Whatever the development strategy, choosing one is appealing; these approaches fit the nature of our work in the Knowledge Era, the development progression human beings experience, the demographics of the marketplace, the dynamic business conditions faced by organizations and their clients. Table 3 provides a comparison of the three strategies.

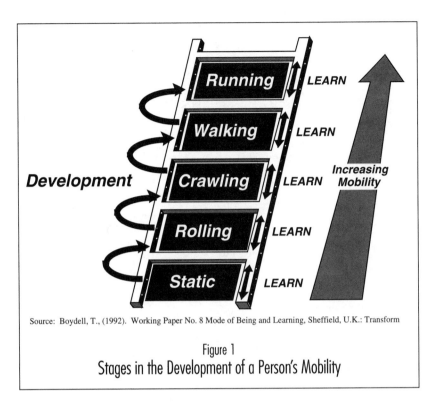

Source: Boydell, T., (1992). Working Paper No. 8 Mode of Being and Learning, Sheffield, U.K.: Transform

Figure 1
Stages in the Development of a Person's Mobility

Forging the Future

Currently, most organizational structures, processes, and procedures do not take into account the transitions and transformations of adulthood that impact feelings, motivation, thought, and behavior in intellectual, emotional, social, and moral domains. By incorporating what is known about adult development into the purpose, vision, and values of learning organizations, we may develop organizations that consciously recognize human beings' passages, as well as encourage and assist people through them.

There is no single path, approach, or strategy that will ensure that any organization will meet the goal. Indeed, we are only beginning the exploration of the organizational forms of the Knowledge Era. Moreover, because such a significant shift is required, movement will not be easy.

Futurist Don Michael's perspective on the type and depth of changes required of us is comprehensive and compelling. He posits that what's required is a society in which people self-

Table 3: Development Strategies Compared

Strategy	Situational Factors	Pros	Cons	*Methods/Approaches
ENHANCING INDIVIDUAL POTENTIAL DEVELOPMENT: Individuals create development plans with supervisors based on roles and short and long term assignments.	New, small companies Fluid business climate Diverse knowledge requirements Single practitioners Highly autonomous workforce Information rich environment	Enhances individual development Directed towards specific goals/situation Very flexible Quickly changed Takes advantage of external programs	Individual plans may not be systematically tied to one another or companies. Plans may not take into account company's longer range strategic needs.	Climate/time for learning Education subsidies/company sponsored learning activities Self-development centers Feedback and coaching Information/knowledge rich environment Measuring and rewarding learning time
LINKING INDIVIDUAL AND ORGANIZATIONAL DEVELOPMENT: Individuals create development plans with supervisors based on roles, long- and short-term assignments, and specifically articulated competencies which highlight knowledge and skill progressions, and which link to business strategy.	Larger global organization Systematic bodies of knowledge/skill required and able to be spelled out Providers of service, products where consistency is important.	Human Resources planning can be linked to strategic planning Diverse populations can be linked through competency attainment.	Requires "maintenance" of competencies to ensure flexibility Requires systemic thinking about learning and development.	Learning activities and assignments linked to competencies and business strategy Individuals encouraged to move through progression Data on personnel progressions available for Human Resource Planning Activities
LEVERAGING STAGES OF ADULT DEVELOPMENT: Learning activities and assignments developed to enhance individuals' targeted operating modes of being, learning.	Practitioners in a range of age groups. Companies with substantial investments in formal learning activities. Organizations with their own HRD personnel developing learning activities.	Links organizations' business strategy and HRD efforts to stages of development Reinforcement among all learning activities targeted at helping people operationalize skills related to a specific stage of development.	May be hard to sell; concept of stages of development now well known. Developing common reinforcing models of thinking/operating and linking them throughout HRD activities may be very complex.	Link business strategy, HRD strategy, and adult development stages A common core of explicitly stated thinking/operating models is shared throughout organization. All assignments/learning activities enhance development as well as addresses content/process objectives.

*Methods and approaches used in succeeding stages build on those used in previous stages.

consciously question premises as well as actions, accept uncertainty, and measure leadership competence at all levels by the capacity to acknowledge ignorance and uncertainty as prerequisites for change. He contends that leadership and organizational success in the future will focus on resilience rather than control, will include boundary spanning and the use of metaphors among key competencies, and will incorporate a proactive-future orientation that focuses vision and provides a basis for goal-setting.

Organizational leaders and human resource developers may find that these conditions provide a framework to address the significant underlying psychological issues involved in moving towards learning and development organizations. These conditions include:

1. Live with and acknowledge great uncertainty.

2. Embrace error.

3. Seek and accept the ethical responsibility and the conflict-laden interpersonal circumstances that attend goal-setting.

4. Evaluate the present in the light of anticipated futures, and commit to actions in the present intended to respond to such long-range anticipations.

5. Live with role stress and forego the satisfactions of stable, on-the-job, social group relationships.

6. Be open to changes in commitments and direction, as suggested by changes in the conjectured pictures of the future and by evaluations of on-going activities.

Acknowledging uncertainty allows individuals, organizations, and governments to see what still needs to be learned, and which activities need to be monitored to reveal the consequences of policies, decisions, or actions made in uncertainty. Personal, organizational, or societal processes or systems designed to detect or "embrace" error provide feedback to shift directions or realign behaviors.

While they are not a blueprint for building Knowledge Era organizations, these perspectives and processes provide a ground for action. And the rewards may be inestimable. As future-oriented learners spending the days of our lives in organizations that enhance, build, and perhaps even urge development, we are poised to take responsibility for realizing and bringing forth the people we are. It is an exciting time!

Bob Guns received his PhD in Organization Development from the University of Oregon in 1979. Since then he has headed up his own firm, Probe Consulting Inc., in Vancouver, British Columbia, Canada. Guns has also lectured in the University of British Columbia's Faculty of Commerce.

Through his consulting and leadership training practice, he focuses on creating faster learning organizations and developing key leadership skills such as facilitating and coaching. His clients include IBM, Fletcher Challenge, Motorola, Entertainment Publications, Canadian Imperial Bank of Commerce, BC Hydro, Merck Frosst, and MacMillan Bloedel.

Guns has developed an executive electronic network focused on creating a faster learning organization. He is currently writing a book entitled *The FLO Strategy: Corporate Speed Learning for Competitive Advantage.*

22

The Faster Learning Organization (FLO)

Bob Guns

Arie de Geus, former head of strategic planning for the Royal Dutch Shell Group, says the only way to sustain competitive advantage is to ensure your organization is learning faster than the competition.

The ability to learn faster becomes more significant as our corporations become more knowledge-based. If two 'knowledge' corporations have the same intellectual potential, the primary differentiating feature then becomes which corporation can learn faster.

The first step is to develop a strategy that creates a stimulating climate for faster learning. That strategy will focus on breaking down opposition to learning within the corporation in order to compete more effectively in the marketplace. Nothing is more depressing or intimidating than encountering a seemingly intractable resistance to learning.

Openness to learning is a necessary condition for faster learning. Unfortunately, being closed to learning is only too prevalent in North America. What is needed is a stimulus. The FLO (Faster Learning Organization) Strategy is just such a stimulus.

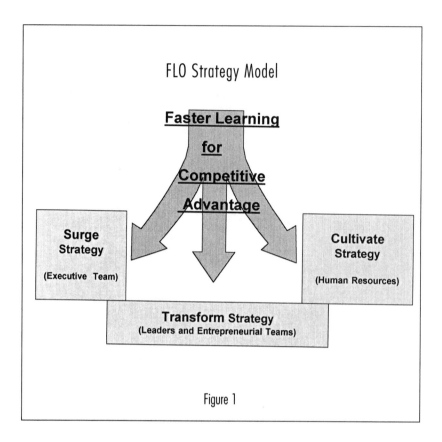

Figure 1

Three different but complementary strategies are encompassed within The FLO Strategy (see Figure 1).
- The Surge Strategy
- The Cultivate Strategy
- The Transform Strategy

The Surge Strategy is the most focused, short-term strategy. Through strategic analysis, one to three key leverage points are identified where, if learning is accelerated, it will allow the organization to surge ahead of the competition.

The Cultivate Strategy entails creating a profile of a faster learner, and then hiring and developing people according to that profile. The Transform Strategy, with the longest time horizon, focuses on a range of methods to accelerate everyone's learning in the organization. When properly implemented, the Transform Strategy creates the greatest impact on organizational learning.

The Surge Strategy

The Surge Strategy is developed at the executive level of the corporation. It can evolve out of the regular strategic planning processes in which the corporation engages. However, this strategy clarifies the corporation's near-term strategic focus for accelerated learning. Accordingly, the planning group must believe that learning provides the path to improved performance.

The first step in crafting the Surge Strategy is to identify those few key leverage points in which to accelerate learning. A simple strategic planning methodology might illustrate the point. The major opportunity and major strength or competency of the corporation are first identified. The overlap between opportunity and competency defines the critical area in which to exploit competitive advantage. It is this area in which learning needs to be accelerated.

A promising application of the Surge Strategy is related to value constellations. In their 1993 *Harvard Business Review* article, Richard Normann and Rafael Ramirez put forward a different view of strategic positioning: building the organization around a unique configuration of values shared with both customers and suppliers. The challenge, then, is to offer to both customers and suppliers exactly what they want in exchange for what the corporation wants. At least three kinds of faster learning can be applied to this type of strategic configuration:

- learning more quickly how to assess and configure the value constellation
- learning more quickly how to apply the value constellation
- learning more quickly how to reconfigure the value constellation as the marketplace changes

The Cultivate Strategy

The Cultivate Strategy can be generated at any point or level of the organization. It can be an organization-wide strategy or an individual team-based strategy. Its focus is on *hiring and developing* people according to a faster learning profile.

In developing that profile, the first question that has to be asked is: What does a faster learner look like around here? In other words, what are the characteristics of a faster learner? Those characteristics are then analyzed within the context of the organization's strategy.

What kinds of learning have to be addressed? Consider the following:

- **technical/task learning** - related to specialized (functional) expertise and how to perform and improve those related tasks assigned to us in the organization
- **systemic learning** - understanding the basic business systems and processes of the organization, how they are developed and implemented, and how they can be improved
- **cultural learning** - learning the myths, values, beliefs, and attitudes that underpin the way work gets done in that particular organization so that work gets done more productively
- **group/team development learning** - learning how to function effectively in a group or team to foster its learning, growth, and maturity
- **leadership/management learning** - learning how to better lead and manage individuals, work groups, teams, and business units
- **business learning** - learning the basics of a business or a high performing team configured as a micro-business, and how to make that business run
- **strategic learning** - understanding the basic business strategy of the organization, how it is developed and implemented, and how it can be improved
- **reflective learning** - how to think about and question assumptions, mental models, positions, and paradigms regarding the business
- **transformational learning** - how to bring about significant and needed change in individuals, teams, and the organization as a whole

Two dimensions of faster learning need to be taken into account: importance and application. That is, how important to our organizational unit is each of these types of learning? Secondly, to what degree is each of these types of learning being successfully applied? In considering both of these dimensions, a faster learning profile can be developed that will guide the corporation in both its hiring and development practices.

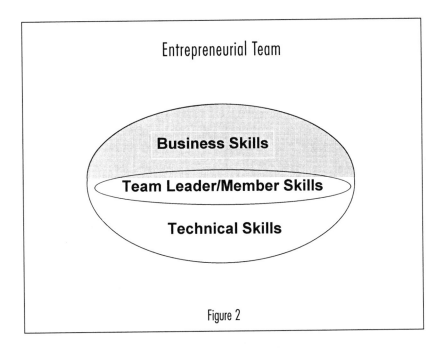

Figure 2

The Transform Strategy

The Transform Strategy is the most inclusive of all the FLO strategies. It creates a stimulating climate for faster learning through leadership of entrepreneurial teams. This strategy focuses on a kaleidoscope of accelerated learning methods. Combining these ten methods could dramatically impact organizational learning.

Stimulating Leadership

Leadership holds the key to creating a stimulating climate for faster learning. Two leadership dimensions are fundamental: challenge and support. Leaders need to actively and continually challenge their people, particularly teams, to achieve their visions and goals. The FLO leader also needs to provide all the support necessary for the team's achievement by supplying resources, removing obstacles, recognizing small successes, and picking the team back up after it has been knocked down.

The Entrepreneurial Team (see Figure 2)

The crucible of faster learning in an organization is the entrepreneurial team—a micro-business that is 'bottom line' driven. The entrepreneurial team is viewed as one that comprises three critical skill sets: technical skills, team leader/member skills, and business skills.

Technical skills are related to functional expertise. They need to be continually refined and honed. However, individual members of the team also need to become skilled as team leaders and members. For many, this presents a difficult leap in learning.

Added to this second skill set are business skills—how to run the team as a micro-business. These skills involve such things as strategic assessment, financial analysis, business and marketing planning, and so on. The sense of the entrepreneurial team truly controlling its destiny, and being significantly responsible for delivering a 'profit' is an incredibly strong motivator for learning. In the design and development of an entrepreneurial team, learning is accelerated in a number of ways. Learning accelerates through:

* moving the team to learning two new skill sets—team leader/member skills and business skills
* continually refining the three different skill sets
* 'seeing' the team as a micro-business
* moving the team from better serving internal customers to eventually serving external customers

Learning Levels (see Figure 3)

A third way to accelerate learning is to help learners move to a new level of learning. The first learning level is Awareness and Acquisition of information, knowledge, and skills necessary to do our jobs.

The second level is Application. We engage in this kind of learning every day as we do our work. Reflection forces us to slow down, to clearly focus on the key goals that will really make a difference.

In Reflection, we engage in strategic and systemic thinking, dialogue, change management, building stakeholder consensus, etc. At this level, we learn individually or collectively in groups or teams.

The highest level of learning is Transformation. Our views of ourselves, our work teams, our leaders, and our organizations are significantly, if not radically, altered as a result of this learning. Our most dearly held values and assumptions are challenged.

At this level of learning we need to be most open and courageous. It usually requires our breaking through both per-

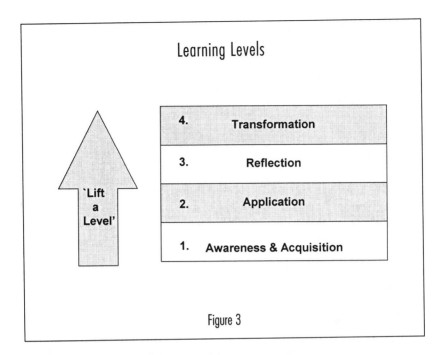

sonal and organizational barriers. Transformational learning is often an outgrowth of prolonged reflective learning.

Learning Stages (see Figure 4)

Learning is not sequential. However, there are learning stages that help us to better understand the components of organizational learning. I have developed an acronym, DIFPAT, that identifies different learning stages.

DIFPAT stands for:

DEVELOP an idea, concept or insight

INVESTIGATE the idea, collect more information or data to determine the validity or value of the idea

FIGURE OUT, analyze, and make a decision based upon the data collected on the idea

PLAN for action if the decision made warrants doing something with the idea

ACT upon the idea plan

TRANSFER the learning from the action taken to others who could benefit from the learning

DIFPAT is also an abbreviated version of 'differentiate the

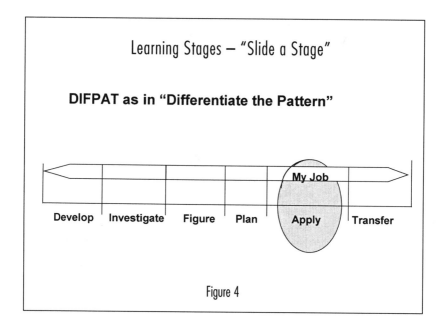

pattern.' Most of our learning comes from making finer and finer distinctions among things we experience; as we mature we become more sophisticated in differentiating these patterns in our lives.

Most learners have been caught in the A mode—in action. The whole thrust of empowerment has been to move people out of the pure action mode into other modes such as planning (P) or transferring (T). As learner leaders we need to help people 'Slide a Stage' in order to accelerate their learning.

Accelerator Effect (see Figure 5)

The Accelerator Effect brings "naturally" opposing groups or individuals together to confront their differences. The idea here is to create something new through the appreciation of the differences, not necessarily to resolve their differences.

I call this kind of learning "catalytic. " It requires a skilled facilitator, acting as a catalyst, to work the interface between these opposing forces. For example, a pulp and paper mill wanted a more `humane' downsizing process. This necessitated union and management formulating a common vision (initially thought impossible by management), and ground rules for how they were going to work together. Within this catalytic framework, union and management were able to hammer away at one another while

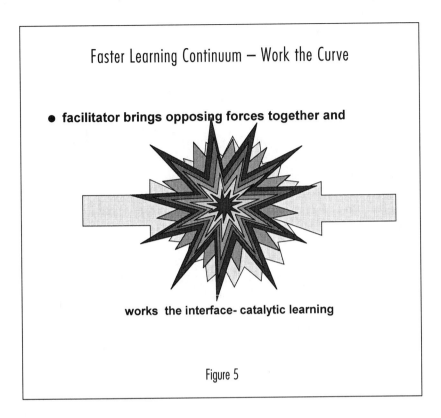

Figure 5

groping toward a new future together. The learning was deep, and was constructively applied in other arenas in which union and management views had been opposed.

Collapsing the "Learning Float"

"Learning float" refers to those times when there is either no learning or unfocused learning. In minimizing these times, we collapse the "learning float"—we bring a little more efficiency to the process. In effect, we try to reduce the gaps or redundancies in learning development.

A project team could plan its learning ahead of time, (using the DIFPAT Learning Stages model) by specifying what it needs to learn, assigning accountabilities, providing resources, and establishing timelines at, and between, each stage of learning. Moreover, the team could monitor its learning process to ensure it is maintaining its projected learning path. In this way, the project team collapses its "learning float" by planning its learning, assigning accountabilities, and monitoring its learning.

Transfer of Learning

Organizational learning can also be accelerated through three principal means of transferring learning:

* benchmarking
* flying squads
* technology.

Leibfried and McNair, in *Benchmarking*, define this first means as "*an external focus on internal activities, functions, or operations in order to achieve continuous improvement*. Starting from an analysis of existing activities and practices within the firm, the objective is to understand existing *processes*, or activities, and then to identify an external *point of reference*, or standard, by which that activity can be measured or judged."

Benchmarking transfers learning from an 'outside' organization to one's own organization. If the people responsible for the process being benchmarked are the ones who actually do the benchmarking, learning will accelerate. This early involvement in the transfer of learning builds stronger commitment to making it work.

In *Liberation Management*, Tom Peters cites FI Group's "flying squads" as a unique means of capturing and transferring learning. These people have one responsibility—to find out, in a widely dispersed organization, the significant things people are learning that can be quickly transferred to other parts of the organization that can benefit from it.

Technology can also be used as a quick transfer method through capturing and communicating significant learning from one part to other parts of an organization. Peters cites his former employer, McKinsey & Co., as a leading example of this kind of learning capture and transfer.

Work-Outs (à la GE)

Jack Welch's "Work-Outs" are widely known as a means of initiating significant change throughout GE's operations. Employees constructively confront their managers with issues important to them. On average, managers respond immediately to 80% of these suggestions. The other suggestions are responded to within 30 days. Accelerated learning takes place in these settings—learning about the manager/employee relationship, about change, about the meaning and value attached to work, about collaboration, about how to create a better operation and company.

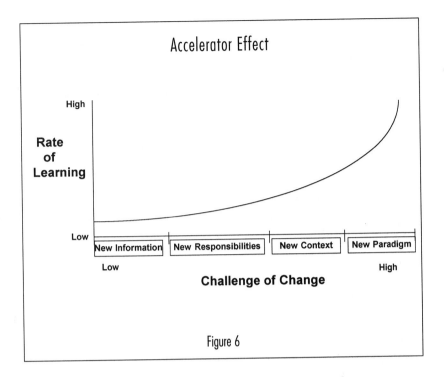

Figure 6

Counterpoint Learning

Each of us needs to test our ideas out with others—leaders, team members, mentors, associates, members of our 'community of practice' (from the Institute of Research in Learning), etc. Multiple exchanges in which ideas are freely shared, traded, and constructively confronted need to be encouraged.

The Faster Learning Continuum

The Faster Learning Continuum is based on the notion that we learn "off balance". Margaret Wheatley describes this phenomenon as learning "at the edge of chaos." Learning entails exploring the unknown. To do that, we abandon our safety or comfort zones. We need to be confronted by increasingly difficult sets of challenges. What is common to all these challenges is 'newness'.

At the least challenging end of the Continuum is "New Information." New information could include a memo announcing a new product launch, results of new technical research related to your work, training in leadership skills that are new to you, etc. As a learner in your organization, you need to process the information and see how it might apply to your work.

More challenging are New Responsibilities. Included in new responsibilities are such things as a promotion, assignment to a project team, or training somebody else in your job responsibilities. What is required of the organization learner in these instances is learning new responsibilities, tasks, and skills in carrying out a different assignment.

A New Context presents an even greater challenge. Examples of a new context could be appointment of a new CEO, embarking on a significant change effort such as TQM, or the installation of a new system or process that affects the way you do your work. These challenges are more complex because they impact a number of people other than yourself. How each of these people, individually and collectively, reacts to the new context will influence your own learning related to it.

Accelerated Learning Methods
Stimulating Leadership
Entrepreneurial Team
Learning Levels
Learning Stages
Accelerator Effect
Collapsing 'The Learning Float'
Transfer of Learning
Work-Out
Counterpoint Learning
Faster Learning Continuum

A New Paradigm is the most challenging of all. It confronts a set of significant assumptions held by the people in your organization about the way business has been traditionally conducted. For example, increasing globalization and competitiveness have forced us to reconsider the traditional roles assigned to management and employees, and how power is to be distributed between them. New paradigms present change and learning of the most profound kind: learning new values, beliefs, and attitudes.

The Faster Learning Continuum suggests that if we wish to accelerate our learning, we need to move individuals, teams, departments, divisions, and our entire organizations as close as we dare to the right of the continuum. The implication, however, is that our organizational learners will need to be open and competent enough to embrace the faster learning required of them.

In Summary

Individual and team learning in organizations demands competence, reflection, and transformation that can thrive only in a faster learning atmosphere stimulated by challenging and supporting leaders and entrepreneurial teams.

However, the most critical first step in creating a faster learning organization is reawakening an interest in learning. If each person is more open, then it becomes much easier to move everybody at least "one notch" in their learning development. That one notch, multiplied by all employees, represents a profound performance leap for the corporation.

Daniel H. Kim, PhD, is an organizational consultant and public speaker who is committed to helping problem-solving organizations transform into learning organizations. He is co-founder of the MIT Organizational Learning Center where he is currently the director of the Learning Lab Research Project.

Kim has worked with numerous companies including DuPont, Ford Motor, Harley Davidson, Hanover Insurance, Healthcare Forum, CIGNA, Life Technologies, Ameritech Services, Brigham & Women's Hospital, and General Electric. He has an SB in Electrical Engineering and a PhD in management from MIT Sloan School of Management and is co-founder of Pegasus Communications (Cambridge, MA), publishers of *The Systems Thinker* newsletter.

23

Managerial Practice Fields: Infrastructures of a Learning Organization

Daniel H. Kim

In the early 1980s, Royal Dutch/Shell's planning group uncovered some startling statistics: one-third of the companies listed in the *Fortune* 500 in 1970 had vanished by 1983, and the average life span of most companies was only forty to fifty years—roughly half that of a human being. Many young companies fail to develop succession rules, remaining too dependent on certain individuals. But long-established companies also die or weaken to the point that they become easy prey for predators. What causes their demise, and how can such an outcome be prevented?

According to Arie de Geus, former director of planning at Shell, a company's survival depends on its ability to detect and adapt to critical changes in its environment. Managing internal change by foresight, rather than by crisis, is only possible if the change in the environment is seen in time. At Shell, "managing by foresight" took the form of scenario-based planning, in which managers chart out their responses to alternative future scenarios.

Transitional Objects

Play is a key element of the scenario planning process. In a corporate setting, merely explaining your view of the world to someone else will not have a big impact on them. You need to provide a "transitional object" that the other person can work with and develop their own understanding of the issue, much in the same way a child plays with a doll and learns about social interactions.

The introduction of computer models into the corporate setting has been a significant advancement in this area. Using system dynamics models in the planning process at Shell, for example, has shortened the learning cycle. The insights from these "play sessions" are usually so graphic that no one needs to write the conclusions down. The result is that people find more options—more time paths into the future.

Learning: The Key to Corporate Longevity

Some time after its *Fortune* 500 research, Shell planners conducted another study. This time they searched for companies that would inspire Shell—companies that were older, were relatively as important in their industries, had experienced some fundamental environmental changes (like the oil shocks of the 1970s), and had survived with their corporate identity intact. They came up with only a handful—companies like DuPont, the Suez Canal Company, and the Hudson Bay Company. Their ages varied from 200 to 700 years, many times the average life expectancy of a person. These companies demonstrated that it is possible to see the signals of change earlier than most companies do and that, when it comes to corporate life expectancies, there is considerable room for improvement.

Shell concluded that an important key to corporate longevity lay in an organization's ability to adapt to its changing environment. A common characteristic among many of these "elder" organizations was their active experimentation at the fringes of their knowing. They had, in effect, institutionalized a process for constantly pushing the boundaries of their learning edge. The planners at Shell realized that the plans resulting from their scenario planning process were not nearly as important as the process itself. They realized that learning was an essential factor in corporate longevity and that their planning process was, in fact, a learning process.

What Shell had stumbled on was that their planning process was, in effect, the beginnings of a learning infrastructure that would help them continually enhance their capacity to adapt to their changing environment. For most organizations, however, such learning infrastructures do not exist. Yet they may be the single most important factor for sustained competitive advantage.

New Infrastructures for Learning

Imagine you are walking across a tightrope stretched between the World Trade Towers in New York City. The wind is blowing and the rope is shaking as you inch your way forward. One of your teammates sits in the wheelbarrow you are balancing in front of you, while another perches on your shoulders. There are no safety nets, no harnesses. You think to yourself, "one false move and the three of us will be taking an express elevator straight down to the street." Suddenly your trainer yells from the other side, "Try a new move! Experiment! Take some risks! Remember, you are a learning team!"

Sound ludicrous? No one would be crazy enough to try something new in a situation like that. Yet that is precisely what many companies expect their management teams to do—experiment and learn in an environment that is risky, turbulent, and unpredictable. Unlike a high-wire act or sports team, however, management teams do not have a practice field in which to learn; *they are nearly always on the performance field.*

An Infrastructure for Working "on" the System

To facilitate and accelerate learning, we need to design in opportunities for making mistakes. In addition to designing fail-safe systems to ensure smooth operations, we also need to create "safe-failing" spaces to enhance learning. Building infrastructures for learning requires a parallel process that takes us out of the day-to-day pressures into a different kind of space in which we can practice and learn. With learning infrastructures, we are able to step out of the system so that we can work "on" it and not just "in" it.

There is an ongoing learning cycle that creates a bridge between the performance field (working in the system) and practice fields (working on the system). The learning cycle of Observe-Assess-Design-Implement (O-A-D-I) links the two processes together: "Assess" and "Design" are more emphasized in the practice field while "Implement" and "Observe" are more emphasized in the performance field (see Figure 1).

Perhaps the most important link in the learning cycle lies in the "Observe-Assess" step, because our designs can only be as

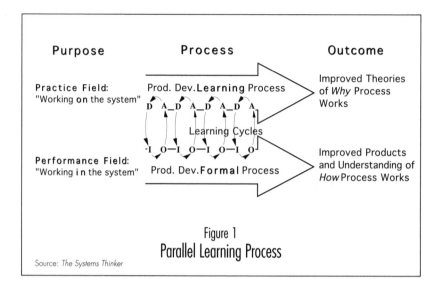

Figure 1
Parallel Learning Process

Source: *The Systems Thinker*

good as the assessments on which they are based. In turn, if our assessments are not grounded in actual observations, but in previously-held mindsets, then we are on shaky ground. The O-A-D-I learning cycle helps us continually reflect on what we think we know and how we know it—in essence, to challenge our prevailing mental models.

This parallel process can be likened to a manager's equivalent of a practice field which enhances his or her ability to perform on-line by creating an environment that is safe for experimentation and failures. Like a sports team, this practice field provides the tools and the appropriate arena for trying out new "plays" or strategies that may be a radical departure from standard procedure.

Designing Meaningful Practice Fields

A "learning laboratory" can be viewed as a manager's equivalent of a sports team's practice field (see Brian Kreutzer's essay on page 217). The goal of a learning lab is to provide a "real" enough practice field so that the lessons are meaningful but safe enough to encourage experimentation and learning. In the tightrope example, a practice field could be a rope stretched across two pillars six feet off the ground. There may be mats below to cushion the fall as well as a large fan to simulate the kinds of winds you would encounter in the actual setting.

A managerial practice field should also have its own set of

equipment and tools for making the practice sessions meaningful. The purpose of a learning lab is to provide an environment in which managers can experiment with alternative policies, test assumptions, and practice working through complex issues in a productive manner. It should allow managers to practice working together as a team on issues of real significance to them. To be effective, the learning lab must provide:

1) a safe learning space, i.e., an environment that is conducive for learning,

2) a way of surfacing mental models, our deep-rooted assumptions that affect the way we think and act,

3) tools for understanding systemic interconnections and the systemic consequences of our actions,

4) a management flight simulator that will allow us to speed up or slow down time, experiment with different strategies, and see the long-term consequences of our actions.

Creating a Safe Learning Space. Learning usually involves making mistakes because we are trying things we have never done before. It requires us to approach things from a place of "not knowing." It involves risk. How, then, can we create a safe space where people feel free to learn? There are some ground rules that can help create such safe spaces. One ground rule is to hold each person's viewpoint as being valid. That requires taking the position that "if I could stand in the other person's shoes, I too could see what the other person sees." It does not mean you agree or disagree with that person's view; you simply acknowledge the right of that person to hold that view. A second rule is to suspend one's own assumptions and the other person's and hold them equally in our minds, without judging ours to be superior or "right." Creating such a learning space also means engaging in dialogue rather than discussion—operating in a spirit of inquiry rather than one of advocacy.

Surfacing Mental Models. Along with the proper environment, we need tools for helping people surface and share their assumptions. For example, the "Ladder of Inference" (see Figure 2) developed by Harvard's Chris Argyris, distinguishes between directly observable data, shared cultural meanings, judgments, conclusions, and beliefs and assumptions. Argyris uses the ladder to illustrate the "leaps of inference" that occur when people take a little bit of observed data (person walks into a 2:00

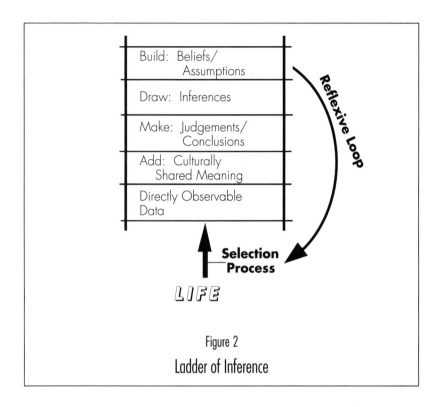

Figure 2

Ladder of Inference

meeting at 2:15) and go straight up the ladder to the level of values and assumptions (he's late and doesn't care about the project or the other players) without even being conscious of it. The ladder provides a useful framework for helping people "walk back down the ladder" to understand what is really happening and begin managing by facts, not opinions.

Understanding Systemic Interconnections. Systems archetypes provide a powerful set of tools for mapping out a person's understanding of a problem or issue in a form that invites others to inquire and clarify the picture together. An archetype embodies a storyline or theory about system behavior that illuminates the structures that are driving the behaviors. In a "Shifting the Burden" archetype, for example, a problem is often resolved with a quick fix which alleviates the symptom in the short term, but results in a systematic erosion of the fundamental capability of the system. Over time, quick fixes continually have to be applied as the system's capability to correct itself weakens.

Having one's assumptions captured in terms of archetypes and causal loop diagrams helps to depersonalize the issue and focuses energy on the diagram, not the person. These diagrams can also make the assumptions behind the connections explicit, clarifying the points of agreement or contention.

Management Flight Simulators. When practicing a concerto, an orchestra has the ability to slow down the tempo in order to practice certain sections. Through Management Flight Simulators (computer models that have been turned into interactive decisionmaking games), managers can accelerate time to see the long-term consequences of decisions or slow down the flow of time at each decision point. With a simulator, a manager can test out new strategies and policies, reflect on the outcomes, and discuss pertinent issues with others in the team.

By providing quick and accurate feedback, the computer simulator can facilitate learning by shortening the delay between action and outcome. Managers can chart a strategy and implement it over a simulated number of years in a matter of minutes. They can try scenarios that might bankrupt the company or lose market share without risking a single dollar or a single job. As they explore the systemic reasons for their results, managers can begin to understand the underlying forces that produce a given set of outcomes.

Management Flight Simulators (MFS) provide a simulated environment in which managers can "learn from experience" in a controlled setting. The simulator captures the interconnections between the different parts of the system under study and provides a computer interface which allows managers to interact with the model through a familiar "lens" (reports, graphs, and spreadsheets).

Similar to a pilot's flight simulator cockpit, an MFS puts managers in control of a realistic environment where they are in charge of making key decisions similar to the ones they face in their actual work settings. MFS's are particularly useful for getting away from the details of day-to-day operations and focusing on the long-term dynamics of managerial decisions.

MFSs can be most useful for understanding situations in which causality is distant in time and space or when the inherent time lag is particularly long (on the order of months or years) and organizational complexity is high. Learning from experience in those situations can be fraught with pitfalls. An MFS allows you to leverage your ability to learn from experience in a complex environment.

Managing vs. Learning

There are two fundamentally different uses for an MFS—managing and learning. MFSs designed to support decision making in a real operational setting must focus on capturing the operational reality precisely. The accuracy of the numbers is important because operational or strategic decisions will be based on those numbers.

MFSs that are designed for learning, on the other hand, are much more concerned with surfacing the tacit mental models which drive managers' decision making. Accuracy of specific numbers is not as important as the relevancy of the issues and concepts captured in the simulator. In other words, simulators for learning are idea-rich versus data-rich.

There are several different design criteria to keep in mind when designing an MFS:

- A Clear, Real-World Context provides a real operational focus that engages line managers in greater learning about their own issues.

- Face Validity: Make the MFS real enough so the simulator "grounds" people in their own real-life experiences.

- A Strong Conceptual Framework helps make systemic sense out of the complex dynamics (e.g., systems archetypes).

- Conventional and Unconventional Information Systems provide a familiar information environment, as well as an opportunity to explore and experiment with new ones.

- Surface and Challenge Mental Models to break through individual "mental straightjackets" and corporate sacred cows, thus advancing team learning.

Designing MFSs as Transitional Objects

Designing an MFS for learning requires an interface that maintains a careful balance between realism and comprehensibility. It needs to be real enough to serve as a transitional object which, according to Seymour Papert, in his 1980 book *Mindstorms*, allows managers to "play out" a scenario and learn not only about the system, but also about how they interact with that system. However, it also needs to be manageable. If the model tries to

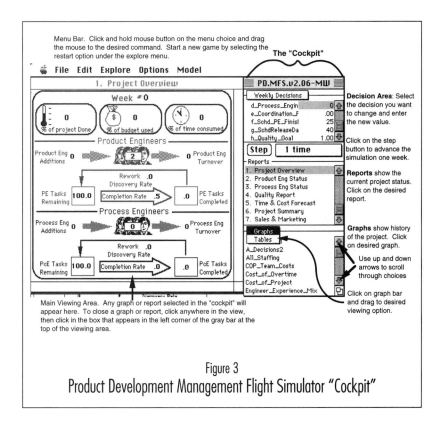

Figure 3
Product Development Management Flight Simulator "Cockpit"

capture every little detail of reality, it can become just as complex and incomprehensible as the real system.

In a learning setting, it is also important to position the model as an exploratory tool for gaining a better understanding about one's environment, not as an "answer generator." The MFS acts like a mirror that reflects mental models in a way that helps us to understand current reality better.

There are three major elements of an MFS: decisions, reports, and a management information system (see Figure 3).

Decisions. The kinds of decisions that must be made in the MFS should be those the participants would either make themselves in real life or those someone else in the organization would make that affect them. These decisions should be directly relevant and easily transferable from the simulator to the workplace. If the decisions are too far removed, the MFS becomes more of an academic exercise or a game, even when a meaningful context is built around it.

Even though the participant might not be the one who makes hiring and staffing decisions at his/her level, for example, those choices can be included in the MFS because they are still part of the real environment in which they manage. In fact, putting that manager or supervisor into the decision-making role can be an illuminating experience, showing them what role they play in the system and the challenge of managing from the level above.

Reports. As far as the actual physical design of the simulator interface, there are some general guidelines. The reports should look similar to what people typically receive—they should only provide data that is normally accessible. If additional variables need to be included, they should not be as prominent as more typical day-to-day data.

Information Systems. Designing the information system provides a lot more flexibility in reporting variables that are normally inaccessible. A chosen critical variable like "time pressure" can be made available so you can experiment to see how people may manage differently when provided with such information.

Outcomes from the MFS

Once participants work with the MFS and understand the theory behind it, they can more easily make connections between it and their real work situation. Participants can also explore what interventions they might make in order to better manage the process: What kinds of adjustments need to be made? What controls do they need to monitor?

Theories in Use. The MFS can be a powerful tool for surfacing tacit assumptions, since it reflects the participants' understanding of the system. When someone makes a decision and then explains it with data or information that is not in the model, they make explicit their own theories and understanding of what's going on. For example, in an MFS created for insurance claims managers, participants assumed settlement dollars were rising because of inflation. However, when they discovered that inflation was not included as part of the MFS, they had to rethink their own understanding of what causes settlement dollars to rise.

As they write in their book, *Organizational Learning*, Argyris and Donald Schön, believe that people operate with a gap between their espoused theories (what they conceptually believe is the right course of action) and their theories-in-use (what they choose to do, given the surrounding circumstances). Failures to recognize and close those gaps impede organizational learning. The MFS can help reveal and close such gaps. For example, in a session with a product development flight simulator, the participants all agreed that investing in coordination and communication between upstream and downstream activities was important. But when they were placed in the simulator and given the objective of meeting timing, quality and cost, most of them actually chose to invest very little in coordination. Instead, they focused on trying to get the tasks done in each of the respective areas.

Team Learning. An MFS can be even more useful if used in groups. The interplay between the participants, as they propose new strategies and explain their reasoning, helps them to surface and clarify their assumptions. In order to encourage team learning, the MFS can be structured to require participation and coordination among a group of people. For example, in a product development case, the team could be made up of a product and a process engineer. Each one would be responsible for staffing and workweek decisions for his or her particular function. Together they would decide on a program completion date and manage the coordination between the two functions. The use of the MFS can provide a richer practice field for a team of people.

New Theory-New Learning

Creating learning infrastructures such as practice fields or learning laboratories is an important part of becoming a learning organization, but alone it is inadequate. It is too easy for such structures to become "training" infrastructures. There is nothing wrong with training per se, but training involves teaching a new twist on a well-established body of knowledge or disseminating that body of knowledge itself. Learning, on the other hand, requires a shift in the understanding of the base of knowledge itself. One is acquiring new information that fits into a current theory and the other involves developing a new theory altogether. Learning infrastructures should help organizations build their own ongoing theories about how they work as a system.

The word theory is too often viewed as an esoteric word that has no practical meaning. In fact, theory is of utmost practical importance because theories are distillations of our knowledge and understanding of the world. Theories represent the general principles drawn from a body of facts and observations. Without them, we could not learn because we would have no means to provide a coherent structure to our observations.

Given today's pace of change and organizational complexity, managers need to be competent in applying the research skills of a scientist to better develop theories about how their organizations work as a system. The old paradigm of feeding experiments from organizations into research institutions that then feed the results back is no longer adequate. Schön points out that a major disruption occurred when the pace of change crossed into the intragenerational state—lessons learned became obsolete within the same generation. Intragenerational change means that the research cycle must be done within a much shorter time frame, otherwise solutions (in the form of research results) will be stillborn—the problems which they were addressing will no longer be relevant.

Managers' New Roles: Researcher and Theory-Builder

Managers need to become theory-builders within their own organizations. They must create new frameworks within which they continually test their strategies, policies, and decisions to inform them of improvements on the organization's design. It is no longer sufficient to apply generic theories and frameworks like band-aids to one's own specific issues. Managers must take the best of the new ideas and build a workable theory for their own organization. As theory-builders, managers must have an intimate knowledge of how their organization works as a whole. They also require some guiding theory and methodology to make sense of their experience and learning.

There is no "golden formula" that will hold for all time, or even for one's tenure in a present position. Companies who lived by the learning curve theory almost died by the learning curve theory, as in the case of Texas Instruments and their personal computer debacle—the TI 994A in which they had to write off about $600 million! Those who followed the Boston Consulting Group business portfolio theory also had their share of problems by either giving up entire markets or not taking full advantage of synergies among their different businesses. Theory building should not be done as an academic exercise but as a process grounded in reality which continually helps provide a framework for interpreting one's competitive environment.

Collaborative Research/Practitioner Model

The research partnership at the MIT Organizational Learning Center is, in part, a mutual mentoring process. It is a consortium of eighteen partner companies—Ford, Harley-Davidson, Federal Express, Intel, Motorola, AT&T, and Herman Miller among others—who are committed to advancing organizational learning. This type of partnering and collaboration requires significant immersion into both corporate and academic worlds, producing results that can be interpreted in each other's culture and language rather than each being sufficient only to its own separate community. It is necessary for researchers to move away from the detached, purely rationalistic perspective and recognize the inherently chaotic nature of organizations.

In this kind of research, the messenger has to be consistent with the message. The work would not be as effective if the researchers were not always, in their best efforts, trying to model the principles and practices that are part of the process. Anselm Strauss has his own reflections on the relationship between the researcher and the research which resonate with my own:

> We should add that while much research involves routine operations and can at times be boring, assuredly also at its most creative it is exciting, fun, challenging, although sometimes extremely disturbing and painful. This means that researchers, as workers, *can and should care very deeply about their work* [emphasis added]— not being simply possessive about its products or jealous of their research reputations, but find deep and satisfying meaning in their work.

It is to that spirit of deep caring that a learning organization should be dedicated to creating.

David R. Schwandt, PhD, is an associate professor of human resource development and director of The Executive Leadership Doctoral Program in HRD at The George Washington University. His research and practice are in the areas of organizational development, strategic thinking, organizational learning, and performance management.

Schwandt has published work in management development, performance management systems, and has delivered papers at the Academy of Management and the Systems Development Conference, University of Stirling, Scotland. Before joining the university he was the Director of Organizational Development at the U.S. General Accounting Office.

24

Learning as an Organization: A Journey into Chaos

David R. Schwandt

Managers and researchers are engaged in a struggle to understand the complexities of organizations in a changing environment. For many, this struggle is perceived as being between order and chaos. Our understanding of organizations is increasing arithmetically. Unfortunately, the complexity of our environments is increasing geometrically! The theories and models we employ in our understanding of this struggle are limited to narrow sets of conditions and singular frames of reference. Organizational life has become dichotomized into sets of "either-or" choices such as "compete or collaborate" and "performance or learning." We have tried to reduce the complexity of these choices into simplified checklists of cause-effect relationships that, when put into practice, fall short of their advertised promises. Managers are led to the use of processes and interventions that have limited usefulness and merely become the latest "fad." The concept of organizational learning is at a critical junction. It may also become one of these short-lived fads if we can't integrate it with the dynamic behaviors of people in organizations.

This essay deals with both theory and practice. In the past, most managers have dismissed theory because of their pragmatic action orientation, they are beginning to understand Kurt Lewin's statement that "there is nothing more practical than good theory." Theory helps in our understanding of the relationships between concepts such as performance and learning. We must understand these concepts as patterns of social change. At times they are familiar and simple. Other times they are strange and complex. This is the nature of the journey into social chaos.

The purpose of this essay is to present a model of organizational learning that has evolved from the application of the concepts of open systems thinking and chaos theory to the theory of social change within human collectives. I hope to present the model in a way that demonstrates the dynamic nature of social systems and, at the same time, provides an additional lens through which we can observe and understand the complex functions and actions required of the collective to learn. The first sections of the essay provide: a discussion of the assumptions that form the basis of the model, a brief review of organizational learning, and present the model and an explanation of its associated organizational learning patterns. The last sections provide case scenarios depicting the use of the model and its implication for practice, management and future research.

The Crisis of Failure and the Paralysis of Success

It is not uncommon to hear stories of significant organizational change in response to a crisis or critical event that threatens the survival of an organization. When we examine these stories, we attribute the end result (either positive or negative) to factors of leadership, culture, environment, structure, or strategy. In most cases we identify a specific factor that has made a difference in the performance processes of the organization. Very seldom do we carry out this critique with respect to the existence of, or differences in, the learning processes employed by the organization.

It is more uncommon to hear stories of "successful" or profitable organizations grappling with change. For example, a large health insurance agency has been, and still is, enjoying large profits and control of its market. The changes in the health care financing industry are the focus of almost every conversation with in the organization. Some managers and employees see the need for organizational change, however, most do not. They feel that their performance has been successful and that there is no need to "over react" to an uncertain environment. They are in a state of paralysis reinforced by their successful performance.

Again, the focus is on organizational performance, not on organizational learning. Actually, this organization is in a crisis and doesn't know it; a crisis of diminished capacity to learn.

All change is important for both successful and unsuccessful organizations. However, it takes on different meanings that are rooted in the complex mixture of organizational performance and learning. To understand the dual nature and consequences of these conditions, managers and researchers are turning to a "new science" that provides additional windows through which they can observe existing anomalies and new emerging phenomena.

When we examine organizations and their environments through multiple frames of reference, using concepts such as chaos theory and open systems, we are better able to understand new phenomena and to reexamine existing knowledge. Margaret Wheatley's 1992 book, *Leadership and the New Science*, provides us with an example of this reexamination. She makes an argument for the advent of chaos theory in the applied behavioral sciences using as an analogy the introduction of quantum theory to classical physics and the subsequent shift away from the Newtonian view of physical dynamics.

In the context of organizations, the new science must deal with the human collective and the patterns associated with its social structure and culture. This requires simultaneous focus on both organizational performance and learning so that we can better deal with changing environmental conditions. It is this dual focus that makes organizational learning a fundamental prerequisite for understanding the complexity of modern-day organizational life.

Assumptions Concerning Contemporary Organizations and Change

Organizational learning assumes that systems of social actions are non-linear and open, and inherently evolve toward higher states of complexity. This in turn requires more complex constructs to aid in our understanding of social systems.

In the past we have dealt with organizational complexity through reductionism processes. Now we are meeting the challenge with concepts of chaos theory, duality, spirituality, and self-organizing systems. Organizational science is only in its infancy concerning this shift in world view. With the advent of concepts such as "organization configuration," managerial and organizational cognition, and organizational learning, we are embarking on a new era in research and practice, just as our colleagues have in the physical sciences.

We must consider multiple variables simultaneously. These are seen from one perspective as chaotic, yet if focused on with a different lens appear to manifest patterns. Organizational learning is a process manifested in patterns of actions and attributes of changing social systems rather than causal relations between isolated variables.

Organizational Learning

In spite of the agreed upon importance of organizational learning, there are divergent conceptions of what constitutes organizational learning and how organizations learn. Many of the organizational theorists' efforts appear to be directed at descriptive typologies.

Knowledge structures—their formation, usefulness, and limitations—are becoming a major path to the investigation of collective sense making—a pattern of culturally-based assumptions that the collective uses as a reference in the interpretation of actions within the context of the organization. Sense making is used to assign relative value and shared meaning to behaviors and events.

Much of the empirical research is centered on the mental models that managers bring to their position, their actions, and organizational renewal. The role of the organization as an interpretive system has been seen as being dependent on organizational differences in environmental scanning, equivocality reduction, strategy, and decision making.

A Dynamic Organizational Learning Model

The Organizational Learning Model discussed in this essay provides a synthesis of many of the earlier theoretical works and employs the General Theory of Action posed by T. Parsons, R. Shils, and E. Bales in 1953.

Parsons' social action system theory suggests that both performance and learning processes have the capacity to change or disrupt the equilibrium in the organization-situation relationship. However, change in the "social system" itself occurs only through the learning process, not the performance process. It is related to the basic assumptions held by the organizational

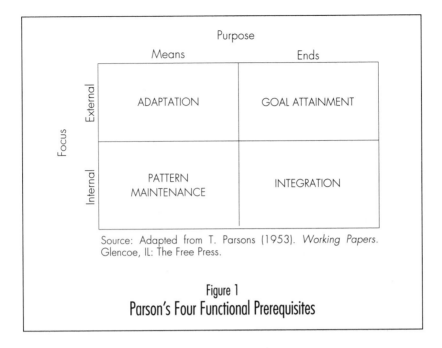

Source: Adapted from T. Parsons (1953). *Working Papers.* Glencoe, IL: The Free Press.

Figure 1
Parson's Four Functional Prerequisites

culture. This concept is identical to that put forth by Ed Schein in his 1993 discussion concerning the importance of cultural patterns and basic assumptions and the role they play in organizational change.

Parsons describes four sets of system responses to four critical problems associated with its survival. The actions are directed toward the environment inside and outside the system itself. Based on the purpose of those actions, they can be characterized as either instrumental actions (means), or as goal-oriented actions (end results). Parsons' actions of a social system are interrelated with respect to their "focus" and their "purpose," as shown in Figure 1.

As a collective of actions, organizational behaviors may be viewed as dynamic patterns of acts to adapt to, or to try to shape, its external environment (Adaptation), to attain organizational goals (Goal Orientation), to integrate or re-integrate all parts of the organization (Integration), or to reinforce the prevalent behaviors and the organization's cultural patterns (Pattern Maintenance).

Grounded in the Parsonian theory, the Organizational Learning Model focuses on the learning aspect of an organization as a social system. It provides a way of viewing organizational behav-

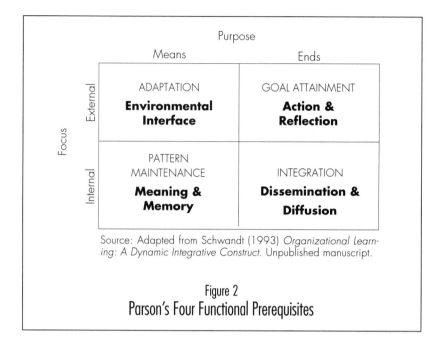

Source: Adapted from Schwandt (1993) *Organizational Learning: A Dynamic Integrative Construct.* Unpublished manuscript.

Figure 2
Parson's Four Functional Prerequisites

ior that can explain how people in an organization collectively engage in the dynamic social actions associated with learning. Organizational learning here is defined as "a system of actions, actors, symbols, and processes that enables an organization to transform information into valued knowledge which, in turn, increases its long-run adaptive capacity." Learning is focused on the system's ability to adapt to its environment, not just through a performance orientation, but rather through a creative capacity that influences the cultural values of the collective.

My colleagues and I postulate four learning subsystems that carry out these functional prerequisites for the learning system. They are: Environmental Interface (Adaptation), Action and Reflection (Goal-Attainment), Dissemination and Diffusion (Integration), and Meaning and Memory (Pattern-Maintenance), as depicted in Figure 2.

Theses subsystems are defined as follows:

The Environmental Interface Subsystem functions as the informational portal for the organizational learning system. It consist of a collection of interdependent activities and actions that responds to signals from both the inside and outside the organization determining the information it seeks and disperses. This subsystem includes acts directed at survey-ing customers, public relations, research efforts, lobbying, and other means of scanning the environment. It also includes activities that provide screening of information and data, such as monitoring news broadcasts and printed literature.

The Action-Reflection Subsystem creates valued knowl-edge from new information. It defines the relationship between the organization's actions and the examination of those actions which enables it to assign meaning. This subsystem functions as the nucleus of the organizational learning system. The processes in this core function are heavily dependent on variables associ-ated with the dynamic operation of the organization. These processes exist at two levels of action: 1) the level of routine actions that characterize the day-to-day operations of the organi-zation, and are governed by standard operating procedures; and 2) the level of major actions which are perceived by the organiza-tion as having significant impact on its adaptive capacities.

Reflection exists at both levels of action in different forms and intensity. The organization can reflect on its actions from three different perspectives: the processes used in the action, the content or results of the action, and the underlying premises of the action. Each of these reflection perspectives combines with a level of action to create knowledge, which is the goal of the learning system.

The Dissemination and Diffusion Subsystem exists to transfer information and knowledge among the subsystems. It includes acts of communication, networking, management acts of coordination, and other roles supporting the movement of information and knowledge. The technical processes include electronic data transfer mechanisms and audio-visual means.

Dissemination processes are those that are more purpose-fully directed and are governed by formal procedures and poli-cies. Diffusion techniques represent more informal processes such as rumors and informal communications.

The Meaning and Memory Subsystem provides the foun-dation from which the other subsystems draw guidance and control. It maintains the mechanisms which create the criteria for the judgment, selection, focus, and control of the organiza-tional learning system. Also included are those acts directed at sustaining and creating the cultural beliefs, values, assump-tions, and artifacts of the organization. The premise upon which this subsystem is based is that learning is dependent on some

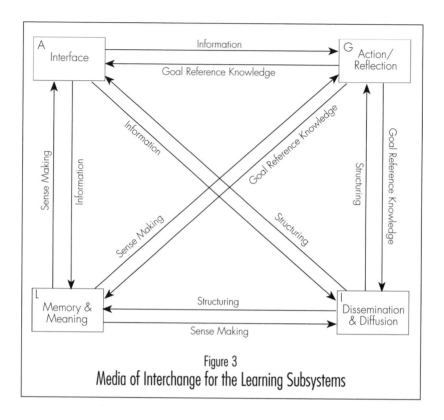

Figure 3
Media of Interchange for the Learning Subsystems

shared understanding. The memory portion of the subsystem contains a series of storage mechanisms, each with its own retrieval schema. These storage mechanisms are the individuals, the culture, the ecology, the transformations, and the structures. This subsystem's operation includes both human and technical processes, for example, records, data bases, routines, and people. Human processes include collective and individual remembering and the use of consensus to construct the collective history.

These learning subsystems are not independent: dysfunction in one learning subsystem will jeopardize the effectiveness of the whole system. Each learning subsystem requires inputs from the other subsystems. This interdependence is accomplished through the exchange of concrete patterns of traditional organizational variables. It is important to recognize that we are not talking about the variables themselves, but the patterns that these variables form. These patterns we call "media of interchange." The learning subsystems' interdependence on the media of interchange is graphically illustrated in Figure 3.

Table 1
Variables Associated with the Media of Interchange for the Learning Subsystems

Interchange Media	Variables*
New information	Internal and external data Customer feedback Employee survey
Goal Referenced knowledge	Results of an experiment Evaluation results Decision-making processes Knowledge structures
Structuring	Organizational roles Leadership Policies Organizational structure Group norms
Sense making	Schemas/scripts Language and symbols Values/basic assumptions

*This list of variables is not meant to be complete, only representative.

We have named these media of interchange New Information, Goal Referenced Knowledge, Structuring, and Sense Making. Organizational variables traditionally used in singular cause-effect relationships are the elements that make up the media of interchange and create the patterns that enhance or inhibit the capacity of the organizational learning system. Table 1 provides examples of the traditional variables as they relate to the media of interchange. The media of interchange (patterns) allow us to operationalize the model, both in research and practice. To illustrate this facet of the model, the next section presents two case scenarios that depict the use of the organizational learning model.

Organizational Learning Scenarios

The following scenarios provide more concrete examples of the subsystems and their media interchange. They were derived from in-depth descriptive case studies conducted in actual operating organizations. The data used were primarily qualitative in nature and were collected and analyzed using recommended procedures for ethnographic research.

Each of the scenarios emphasizes one of the organizational learning subsystems. However, it must be noted that the discussion of an isolated subsystem automatically distracts from the systems nature of the model. Also, it is not presupposed that the organizational learning model should be an alternate explanation to any performance model descriptions of the organization as it adapts to its environment. Rather, it should be in addition to these other frames of reference. Lastly, these studies were designed to determine whether the model could be used to describe organizational learning from a sociological systems perspective. They were not designed to determine cause-effect relationships among the variables that comprise the patterns. The first scenario is based on 1994 research conducted by F. O'Neal and discusses the Environmental Interface subsystem.

Case I – Inside-Outside Implications

Situation

A small unit of seven people form a customer liaison group for a large, highly competitive computer hardware firm. The unit's mission is to provide services to the customer and to act as an "on-line" feedback mechanism for obtaining information concerning customer needs, product performance, and future sales leads. The firm felt they were not gaining any new information from the unit, thus little goal referenced knowledge was being generated. The firm conceptualized the problem as a unit performance problem.

Analysis

Each member of the unit was individually very capable in the job they were doing. However, the firm was not getting the performance from the unit that they expected and needed for survival. This poses the question "How can all the members of the unit be performing, but the unit not be meeting its objectives?" The answer lies in the complex relationship between organizational performance and learning. When we frame all organizational problems in terms of performance only, we will always arrive at short-term performance solutions and not address the long-term learning capacity of the organization.

If we examine this case from an organizational learning perspective, the unit's objective with respect to the firm was to provide a service to their customers, but also to provide the Environmental Interface function for the firm's learning system. That is, they were to provide the firm's organizational learning system with New Information (media of interchange) from the customers. As we found from the data, individuals were highly competent in obtaining this information, however, when interviewed about where the information went and how it was moved we were told:

> I think what happens is when folks forward information, say to a particular manager, that particular manager may not listen to them because they already have it made up in their mind that they're going to do things their way. The person trying to forward the information will know that every time they try to do so, they will be shot down or rejected.

and

> Information is put out at a managerial level and it's not ... it's not passed down.

The information concerning customers was portrayed as not being Disseminated and Diffused because of the relationship associated with the manager's role as gate-keeper and controller rather than integrator. In realty these incidents reflect a very complex pattern that is supported not only by the role of managers in disseminating information, but also by the way this organization makes sense and assigns meaning to their internal operations.

When we probed deeper in our interviews with both people in the unit and people who interacted with the unit we were told:

> I might know something that somebody else thinks would be valuable, but I might not see it that way. So that's an example of [information] not flowing because I'm the one who's deciding whether or not the information is valuable and I might not make a correct decision based on somebody else's needs. I'm focused on my needs and what I perceive my task to be.

and

> Well, it's because it goes under their quota. I
> mean they have a goal that's a million dollars or
> whatever their goals are, and I have goals. If they
> can get the sale under their headings, they will.
> That's just the way the system is set up today in
> the firm.

Customer information was to be used to improve customer services and change the product design. Analysis of the interview data obtained from the unit members, customers, and other units within the firm indicated that the new information was indeed brought into the organization by the unit. However, when the sense-making media of interchange was examined, it was characterized as "noncollaborative" in nature. The highly competitive assumptions and cultural values of the firm that had kept them competitive in their external markets had moved inside the firm and were being used by the unit to make sense of their relationships with the rest of the firm.

We found deliberate mechanisms employed to retain and use new information for internal competitive reasons rather than for the benefit of the firm. Customer information was used as a commodity of exchange and was directed by the management of the unit to position themselves and their unit. The dissemination and diffusion subsystem was not distributing the information to all of the internal units that could use it to change their actions with respect to the customer. It wasn't a singular variable, nor was it a singular medium of interchange such as information from the customers, or the organizational structure, or the noncollaboration sense making. Rather, it was a combination of these media that contributed to an organizational learning pattern that inhibited the open flow of new information.

The actual organizational learning pattern is a configuration of all media of interchange. The new (customer) information, in combination with "noncollaboration" sense making and an organizational structure and managerial roles that were not supportive of the movement of information created a dynamic pattern that distracted from the firm's capacity to learn as an organization. As a result the firm suffered from an absence of goal-referenced knowledge about their customers.

Case II – Mixing Messages

The second case is based on A.M. Gundlach's research and provides a closer look at the importance of sense making as a medium of interchange and the functions of the organizational learning Memory and Meaning subsystem.

Situation

A large government agency has maintained an internal, centralized human resources unit for many years. The unit carries out all Human Resource Management/Development (HRM/D)-related activities for the agency. The changing external environment and the reinventing of government has provided new information for the agency and the unit. The information indicates a need to move the centralized HRM/D services provided by the unit to agency line managers as part of their responsibilities, with the central unit assuming a more consultative role. Two years after the announced change by the agency's top leadership, the shift of responsibility and functions have not yet taken place. The agency has portrayed this nonaction as a result of competing demands on the unit staff's time (i.e. the implementation of an agency-wide training program) and therefore, participation in the process has been lacking.

Analysis

Multiple in-depth interviews were conducted with the entire unit staff and management. The purpose of the interviews was to ascertain a description of what meaning was being assigned to their (eventual) role change and how that meaning was connected to the creation of (or lack of) knowledge in order to adapt to the change. This change in role was generally characterized by the staff as:

> Sounds like a fig leaf... it put a positive view on a negative situation.

and

> Here it comes again. We're still trying to define ourselves because we don't know who we are or where we're focused.

Comments such as these led the agency to a change intervention around goal setting and discussions about their "mission." Their insistence on performance meant "to change we must set clear performance goals."

The organization tried to intervene with traditional change strategies. It conducted large meetings to increase participation; they did "visioning"; and they even used external change experts to aid in helping their staff personally deal with this "transformation." However, none of this seemed to help; the staff still did not change, they didn't even understand what was going on. Or did they?

Most change strategies that are available to organizations have been designed to address singular variables that will increase performance. But if the culture is being driven by its memory, and it makes sense from its past experiences, then these interventions may be seen as manipulative and phony.

If change is seen as being accomplished through the organization's ability to both perform and learn, then we can expand the breadth of our analysis by examining sense making in the context of organizational learning.

All actions concerning the change, and any attempt by the agency leadership to promote the change, was interpreted using this sense-making medium of interchange in the organizational learning system. The "skepticism" influenced the overall learning capacity.

The skeptic medium of interchange was the only schema that was available for the action-reflection process of the unit's learning system. Thus any reflection resulted in a devaluing of the new information about the reinventing of government, which in turn resulted in unit actions and knowledge that were based on a "nothing new" frame of reference.

The leadership role was interacting with the skeptical meaning schemas to create a pattern that distracted from the learning capacity of the unit. This case reinforces the assumption that, in order for organizations to adapt and change, their members must develop and assign new meaning to organizational actions and events. The preservation of the unit's meaning schemas, in conjunction with the lack of integrating leadership roles, discouraged shifts in the unit's interpretational capacity and limited its response to the new information and environmental change.

The description of the agency's situation using the Organizational Learning Model provides a very different picture. It confirms our understanding of the extent of control associated with the sense-making processes within an organization's culture and their relationship to learning.

Implications and Conclusions

I have presented an Organizational Learning Model that has as its roots the sociological paradigms associated with social action systems. It incorporates the concepts of systems and the "new science" into a better understanding of collective learning. This understanding necessitates the characterization of learning as not only an outcome, but also as a systemic process that we can explain through the use of pattern descriptions. Two conclusions are provided to stimulate further thought about organizational learning:

1. The relationship between collective performance and learning is not well understood. Both functions seem to be needed. However, in application it appears we give much more credence to performance than to learning. In both scenarios discussed above, performance was seen as the initial concern. However, the learning description pointed to much deeper and longer term solutions to the problem. Each organization's learning patterns appeared to be critical to any change.

2. We must be careful that we don't oversell the concept of organizational learning and thereby allow it to become a fad or fashion. We must first understand the ideas of configurational theory and patterns. We must not jump to cause-effect relationships because we don't even know if cause-effect is a viable concept in the application of the new science.

With these implications and conclusions, I call on our fellow managers and researchers to continue to experiment with, and support inquiry into, the ideas associated with organizational learning. It is only through these actions that we will be capable of understanding our journey through chaos and truly become a learning society.

PART FOUR

Arenas of Practice

The Challenge of Stewardship:
Building Learning Organizations
in Healthcare
Alain Gauthier

Restructuring Education:
Designing Tomorrow's Workplace
John H. Wood

Transforming Mental Models through
Formal and Informal Learning:
A Guide for Workplace Educators
Robert Weintraub

Leadership, Quality, and the U.S. Navy
Robert L. Masten

Case Studies:

Organizational Learning:
Medical Metaphor and Corporate Practice
Alan K. Graham

Shared Values: Nutrients for Learning
Frank Hoffmann and Bill Withers

Creating a Learning Organization
by Accident
Mary Byrd

Beyond Ego to Wisdom:
The Eicher Experience
Dinesh Chandra

With a variety of applications and case histories, this concluding segment of this collection offers eight essays representing a rich array of experience.

In addition to commercial organizations in private enterprise, the fields of education, healthcare, and the military are included in these perspectives.

Alain Gauthier begins this segment as he examines the challenge of steward-like leadership in healthcare. John Wood—our education system and the need for it to become a true "learning" system. Robert Weintraub examines formal and informal learning from the perspective of the in-house educators of the workplace.

Robert Masten takes a rare look at the U.S. Navy and the challenges it faces as a learning organization. Alan Graham uses medical metaphor as he examines the transition to a learning organization by one medical manufacturing company.

Frank Hoffmann and Bill Withers build a strong case for shared values as "nutrients" for developing learning environments in organizational cultures. Mary Byrd describes her company's road to becoming a learning organization—as if "by accident." And, finally, Dinesh Chandra reports on one bank's experience in meeting the challenge of change.

The key to success for the organizations of tomorrow is not having the "right" answers but knowing which questions to ask—and asking them.

—John Renesch, editor
The New Leaders business newsletter

Alain Gauthier is a graduate from H.E.C. (Paris) and earned a Stanford University MBA. With 30 years of consulting, teaching and managing experience in strategic management and organizational rede-sign, he focuses his work on innovative approaches to leadership development and organizational learning. He has served a large variety of client organizations both in Europe and North America, first as an associate of McKinsey & Company, then as an independent consultant. He is currently Executive Director of Core Leadership Development in the San Francisco Bay Area, as well as Directeur-Associé of Athanor S.A. in Paris.

He supervised the French adaptation of Peter Senge's book *The Fifth Discipline: The Art and Practice of The Learning Organization* and recently contributed to *The Fifth Discipline Fieldbook* on the subject of strategic priorities. Gauthier's current clients include Alcan, Andersen Consulting, Hewlett-Packard, and a number of major healthcare organizations.

25

The Challenge of Stewardship: Building Learning Organizations in Healthcare

Alain Gauthier

We face a challenge in building learning organizations in a service industry which has to reinvent itself amidst drastic and multifaceted changes. This challenge calls for stewardship among healthcare leaders—the ability to see a broader picture and to take a long-term view. Peter Block defines stewardship as the willingness to be accountable for the well-being of the larger community by operating in service of those around us.

The First Trillion Dollar Industry

The healthcare industry needs to become more effective: already the largest industry in the country with over one trillion dollars in health outlays estimated for 1994 (i.e., 15% of the gross domestic product), it will double in size by year 2000 if the current growth rate of 13.5% per year were maintained. The cost per capita of the United States healthcare system is already twice the average of twenty-four industrialized countries and represents a growing economic handicap when competing on global markets. And yet, at least 15% of the American population do not have regular access to the system. These issues of cost and access have put healthcare reform in the limelight since the 1992 presidential election, and it is likely to remain one of the most controversial political issues over the next few years. However, enhancing health is a much broader societal issue than the reform of access and payment mechanisms. We need to build healthier communities. This will require a widespread sense of stewardship.

Over the last five years, I have become involved in healthcare as an educator and a facilitator, by teaching leadership development seminars for executives and by facilitating meetings and retreats for approximately thirty organizations. The focus of my work has been to help managers, physicians, and board members explore and apply—personally and collectively—the disciplines of learning organizations. Although healthcare reform has now undeniably become a powerful motivator for change, a number of these organizations took a creative approach to learning by committing to Continuous Quality Improvement (CQI) several years ago. Over the last two years some of them have chosen to collaboratively explore ways to accelerate their learning in a program called "Transforming Healthcare Delivery."

I still have a lot more to learn about healthcare and its organizations. I write this in a spirit of exploration and dialogue with other "change agents" concerned by this industry and the lessons it may offer for other components of society. I will first review the forces at work in healthcare and point to the key shifts in thinking and behavior needed to build a system that would work for all of its stakeholders—the vision. Next, I will share my perception of the specific obstacles to learning in healthcare organizations—the current reality. I will then illustrate the path followed by some organizations to move from current reality to vision, both individually and collaboratively, and emphasize the leadership challenge that these changes represent. I will conclude with some generic learnings for organizations in other fields.

Forces at Work and Basic Shifts Needed in Healthcare

I recently heard a physician executive tell his audience that healthcare is no longer going through white waters: it is already over the falls! This may be particularly true for hospitals and physician specialists in some exposed markets like large cities in California, Minnesota, Oregon, and Washington. But most other healthcare organizations may think they have a few years to prepare themselves for radical changes, depending on the speed and depth of both reform implementation and organizational consolidations.

What needs to emerge in the long run is a *new healthcare system which truly enhances the health of all concerned*—patients and providers alike. Health may be defined as the ability to function as close as possible to one's physical, emotional, mental, and spiritual potential. A number of basic shifts in thinking and behaving, all systemically interconnected, will be at the core of this transformation.

- The first major shift now under way concerns the payment base for healthcare providers: from *fee-for-service* (or full-cost reimbursement) to *contracted care* (services paid for at a discounted rate) and to *capitation* (annual or monthly fee per enrollee, irrespective of the services provided). It means that hospitals and physicians will become accountable for the health of a given population for a fixed sum of money. Most of them have already some experience of contracted care (e.g., with Medicare, Medicaid, and large employers), but only Health Maintenance Organizations (HMOs) such as Kaiser Permanente or Group Health Cooperative of Puget Sound have an in-depth understanding and practice of capitation. The gradual move to capitation—from less than 20% currently on the average to probably over 80% of total payments in a few years—will make most providers responsible for the quality *and* the cost of healthcare, instead of continuing to behave like the vendors to the Department of Defense who contract on a "cost-plus" basis. It will become impossible for them to shift the cost burden to other categories of patients, contrary to what they have done until now.

- The shift to capitation will accelerate another trend already under way: from mostly *inpatient*—acute care involving an overnight stay in the hospital—to more and more *outpatient* procedures which are much less costly. New technological advances in testing and surgery amplify this trend. Experts predict that more than half of the existing 900,000 inpatient beds will need to be closed or converted to outpatient facilities by year 2000. A number of the outpatient services may not be located on the hospital campus but in decentralized clinics, closer to where patients live or work. Ambulatory care (including mobile units), home care and other alternative services are also being developed and demand some radical rethinking about hospital boundaries, investments, and relationships for hospital administrators and physicians alike.

- A related shift already affects the *relative importance and status of specialists vs. primary care physicians.* Traditionally, specialists have been more influential and highly paid; thus, specialized medicine has attracted the vast majority of medical students. Now, primary care physicians are considered the key to success in capitated care, and their role as gatekeepers and care managers of the new healthcare system will be increasingly rewarded. In the more exposed markets, the oversupply of specialists and the high demand for primary care physicians are already forcing specialists to become generalists, move to another town, or retire early. Ultimately, both primary care and specialized physicians, who have behaved mostly as *individualistic* entrepreneurs, will have to practice medicine in a collegial way to offer the best quality care at an acceptable cost.

- An even broader shift will bring healthcare providers *from a production orientation to a customer-focused service orientation.* Hospitals and physician specialists have thrived by maximizing utilization of their facilities: filling beds, operating rooms, and elaborate testing premises. Most resources have gone to high-cost inpatient acute care, in hospitals that look like modern factories and that often compete with one another to attract the best referring physicians in the community with the latest piece of equipment. This "medical arms race" has left very little for prevention, education, and health maintenance; most administrators and specialists still expect the patients to come to the hospital rather than connect with them preventively wherever they live, study, or work.

- In the longer term, only a shift *from the "illness" to the "wellness" paradigm* will enable this country to afford its healthcare system. Education and prevention cost less than one-tenth of the price of a cure, as recently illustrated publicly with immunization programs for children. But, currently, the only access to healthcare by uninsured or indigent people is through the emergency room—a very costly access from all viewpoints. A new goal must be to help everyone feel responsible for their health and offer them guidance and incentives to use providers as resources and partners.

This is a far cry from considering the doctor's office or the hospital as a repair shop to take one's body when it suffers the consequences of one's lifestyle. Acute care will, of course, continue to be necessary for emergencies and unavoidable illness, but resource allocation will be more balanced between cure and prevention when we give up the addictive behaviors of today's healthcare system. The forward-looking healthcare organizations will take the lead in building healthier communities in collaboration with health and local government officials, employers, schools, and churches. Healthcare providers need to behave as stewards of people's health in their community. In the long run, they are likely to find that it is more satisfying and rewarding.

- The shift to the wellness paradigm will be accompanied by *a greater recognition of the effectiveness of alternative medicines and the self-healing capacity of the individual.* A 1993 article in the *New England Journal of Medicine* reported that Americans made more visits to providers of unconventional therapy (chiropractors, acupuncturists, homeopaths, massage therapists, etc.) than to traditional primary care physicians in 1990, although they had to pay for most of them out of their own pocket. A PBS television series with Bill Moyers entitled "Healing and the Mind" showed powerful and moving examples of how we can call on our inner resources, as well as on support groups, to deal with terminal illness and promote healing. A better balance between traditional Western medicine and "alternative treatments" will need to be achieved in a more effective system.

- Another set of shifts concern *the healthcare organization as a working environment.* It needs to become a healthy place for providers of care, giving up frequent addictive behaviors such as blaming, workaholism, excessive stress, and burnout. It should also move from a hierarchical and fragmented structure to a service-oriented, patient-focused, team-based, and networked organization. It needs to become a community of learners, living out shared values—including service and compassion—and valuing the contribution of everyone, rather than be run like a "business machine" emphasizing only efficiency and short-term financial performance. The organization as a whole should become focused on long-term results and stop rewarding quick fixes.

Key Learning Disabilities

Healthcare organizations differ greatly from one another, but most seem to have some learning disabilities in common due to the nature and the history of the industry.

- Most hospitals are *highly fragmented organizations*, where an extreme degree of specialization is compounded by different personal reactions to suffering and terminal illness. Most of the specialists—administrators, physicians, nurses, technicians, etc.—have been trained in their own disciplines and strongly identify with their profession, and there are very few "natural bridges" among them. For instance, physicians have not usually been trained in interpersonal skills or organizational dynamics, and administrators do not generally know much about medicine or the medical problem-solving model. Each specialist/person may also react differently to the suffering or death of patients and thus can feel even more isolated from the others (e.g., a physician doing research on terminally-ill children vs. the nurse in charge protecting them from painful procedures out of compassion).

- The increase in size and complexity of most hospitals has widened the *split between physicians*—MDs in charge of clinical care—*and administrators*—MBAs in charge of the rest of the organization. This split often materializes as minimal understanding of each other's issues and a lack of a common language (except when investing in clinical equipments that doctors want). Diametrically opposed incentives tend to reinforce this split, particularly as the proportion of fee-for-service payments begins to decrease; for example, multiple tests prescribed by a physician to reduce the risk of malpractice suits increase the cost of care. A vision shared by a hospital and its physicians cannot be successfully implemented unless most of these opposing incentives are realigned.

- *Other traditional polarizations* aggravate the lack of alignment and sound communication within a healthcare system: primary care practitioners vs. specialists, physicians vs. nurses, clinicians vs. support services, acute vs. non-acute care, personnel, and activities located on the hospital campus vs. disseminated "out there" in the community. Just as between administrators and physicians, these polarizations result from a lot of untested assumptions, attributions, and generalizations about each other.

- *The clinical and administrative habits* inherited from a long history of fee-for-service may also stand in the way of the new behaviors that are now required of the key stakeholders. The "medical arms race" between hospitals in the same community—which led to bed and equipment overcapacity in many cities—as well as ambiguous relationships between hospital and physicians, have generated a lot of distrust among parties that now need to contract and collaborate for their own survival and better service to the community. Board members who have been mostly driven by somewhat narrow financial considerations and have not consistently expressed the voice of the community must also renew their responsibilities and relationships with administrators, physicians, and other civic leaders.

- Many healthcare organizations have *a well-entrenched history of reactive behaviors*—"quick fixes" that become addictive when confronted with changes such as new regulations, inflationary costs, and increasing competition from HMOs. They have practiced cost shifting, across-the-board cost cuts, and discounting without understanding the longer-term consequences of their actions. When confronted by new challenges such as capitation and clinical outcome measurements, they may be tempted to look at reengineering, continuous improvement teams, and visioning as another wave of quick fixes, without realizing the underlying changes in the management philosophy that these approaches imply. Most healthcare organizations have been late adopters of CQI and several factors tend to limit the effectiveness of their efforts: a predominant emphasis on tools and techniques, a lack of early involvement of clinical staff and customers, as well as an insufficient number of managers retrained as facilitators.

- As in other industries, *the high turnover/instability of senior management* is a barrier to learning, particularly with the increasing need to build stronger relationships with the medical staff and within the community. It is aggravated in a number of cases by the boards' or parent organizations' focus on short-term results and a mounting wave of mergers, acquisitions, and nation-wide consolidations.

- *The lack of physicians willing and/or prepared to take on leadership roles* within their group practice, a new Physician-Hospital Organization (PHO), or the medical staff can hamper the growth of healthcare organizations that need to be increasingly co-led by administrators and physicians. Doctors have some strong points to build on as leaders, but most of them also need to experience some basic shifts in their ways of thinking and behaving due to their selection process, their primary training, and the conditioning of years of practice. But too few courses or seminars focus on the personal changes which are critical to the development of leadership skills that many physicians will need to demonstrate in the new healthcare context.

- Another obstacle is *the lack of deep relationships with the community as a larger health system.* Their community outreach is often limited to fund-raising, and very few have engaged in active collaboration with employers, health-related services, or other providers. When the organization's purpose and values-in-use do not reflect a concern for the larger system of which it is a part, it may experience a conflict between a public service mission and a business logic that is likely to be reinforced by managed competition in reform proposals.

- Finally, one of the main obstacles to generative learning may be *the level of fear that is now increasing among physicians, managers, and employees of hospitals* around the country. Several related factors tend to feed this fear: increased competition from large HMOs and hospital chains; large-scale consolidation and integration leading to change of ownership and hospital restructuring or closing; change in the respective capacity of health plans, hospitals, specialists and primary care physicians to capture and distribute the available healthcare dollars; reduction in specialists' income due to overcapacity and cost containment efforts; and uncertainties about the depth and speed of healthcare reform. Economic survival may become the main motivator for many providers, thus preventing them from learning through creative experimentation and making mistakes.

The Transformational Path

Moving to a more effective healthcare system will initially require some political intervention to change the rules of the game because the system has been unable to reform itself from within. In an article entitled "No More Band-Aids for Healthcare Reform," Kellie Wardman has used the systems thinking archetype called the "tragedy of the commons" to characterize the existing state of the system: As the early settlers abused the common pasture by blindly pursuing their self-interest and grazing more and more cattle, so have all healthcare stakeholders—patients and their families, physicians, hospitals, insurers, employers, federal and state governments—individually contributed over the years to the current breakdown of the healthcare system. Everyone has conspired through shortsighted or addictive behaviors to build a system that is not sustainable in its current form.

Fundamental change will only fully materialize if individual healthcare organizations take the lead in overcoming obstacles to learning, and help create healthier communities. A small number have already proactively started their journey on the path of self-renewal and transformation, without waiting for the threat and specific measures of political reform. They recognize that they need time to accomplish the basic shifts that will be required of them and their constituencies; some of them are stimulated by the rate of change already affecting their community. Here is a brief account of some of the most significant efforts already under way in the organizations I have worked with or known about over the last five years:

- A majority have started *building a shared vision.* Senior executives, leading physicians, and board members imagine what they would want to create together to best serve the needs of their community and the other stakeholders, three to five years from now. Community leaders are sometimes invited to reinforce the voice of the primary customer—the community.

  One or two "visionary planning" retreats usually provide the initial impetus for the vision-based process. Initially, participants reflect on their personal values and vision for their work life, before they share their views of what the organization would mean for its key stakeholders, and what measures of success would be appropriate in the future. In the same spirit of dialogue, they share their perceptions of current reality and identify the key areas of creative tension between vision and reality. The session concludes with a consensus on the key strategic priorities enabling them to bridge the gap; on the ground rules that will help them to dialogue, learn, and work most effectively together; and on the next steps needed to extend the vision-sharing process throughout and outside the organization.

  The main retreat is often preceded by shorter educational workshops. These give board members and physicians an opportunity to internalize some of the new external challenges and to reflect on the shifts needed in their respective thinking and behavior patterns. In most cases, the retreat is integrated into the overall strategic planning process in order to take advantage of the environmental and internal assessments that are normally included in that process. But the main difference with a traditional strategic plan is in the high level of individual and collective commitment to achieve measurable milestones that would lead to the realization of the vision.

- *The visionary planning process can be enhanced by "idealized design" sessions* involving one or several stakeholders—administrators, physicians, board members, patients, payers, or community leaders. In these sessions, participants are asked to imagine that the existing system has been destroyed. They are invited to envision a new system that will best meet the combined needs of all stakeholders in the current or most probable environment. The absence of current constraints and the playfulness participants bring to this exercise generates creative insights and bold proposals that are later integrated into the vision and the redesign of the organization. One proposal was a "healthcare mall" integrating outpatient services, primary care physicians and nurse practitioners, social services, and a wellness center.

- In several organizations, managers and physicians have been *introduced to the concepts and language of systems thinking in conjunction with vision sharing.* These sessions enable them to acknowledge their part in creating current reality and to empower themselves to modify structures at their level in order to move toward the vision. The application of systems thinking in mixed teams on critical issues also allows them to challenge mental models that stand in the way of breakthrough thinking and solutions; for example, some realized that health plan enrollees and primary care physicians, not the hospital, would need to be the primary focus of the new system; others were able to see the long-term vs. short-term trade-offs involved in investing more consciously in health education and prevention.

- At least two of these multiple hospital systems also *explored the practical links between idealized design, systems thinking, and process reengineering.* They realized that many of their continuous improvement team efforts could lead to costly duplication of efforts between units without addressing some of the key leverage points for the system as a whole. They reframed their priorities through a customer-idealized design that led to the reengineering of patient care across the multi-hospital system and to the streamlining of the corresponding CQI projects. Another organization—an HMO—used idealized design to rethink and streamline its strategic planning process, from the internal users' perspective.

- In a few communities, *an ongoing dialogue* has been initiated by one of the local healthcare providers *to enable local leaders to surface, inquire into and remove underlying barriers* to a more affordable, high-quality and coherent healthcare system for the area. Participants include representatives from competing providers, dominant payers and employers, health and local government officials, and other major providers. After six to nine months, they have gained critical insights about the nature of the current system's incoherence and have built a safe enough climate to start dealing with major issues and tensions that had been historically undiscussable. The next steps should allow them to design some new solutions and guide pilot projects within the community.

- Finally, most of these organizations have begun to *invest consistently in the development of their leadership teams*—board members, leading physicians, senior and middle managers—realizing that learning must start at that level. The visionary planning retreats mentioned earlier were usually a first step in that direction, because they included work on personal mastery, as well as team building and team learning activities.

  Three years ago, to go further and accelerate their learning, eight healthcare systems decided to join a learning collaborative which has proven to be very worthwhile for all participants, as described below.

In all of this, the dedication of senior leadership to personal and organizational learning, and their "consistency of purpose," have been critical for the transformation of the organization; this will be the subject of the last part of this chapter.

Collaborative Learning

The learning collaborative entitled "Transforming Healthcare Delivery" was created in 1992 by the Healthcare Forum to offer participants similar benefits to those enjoyed by the members of the MIT Organizational Learning Center: access to specialists of the learning disciplines, pooling of resources to pursue action research, opportunities for exchange of experience, benchmarking, and stimulation. In addition, the industry-specific nature of the collaborative enables it to address generic healthcare issues and to jointly develop new learning tools at a crucial point in the evolution of the healthcare system.

As it approached the end of its grant from 3M, the *collaborative truly became a learning community* for the twenty-four participants from the eight systems. This group met for three days every three to four months in a different city, with each meeting hosted by one of the organizations. The members, called "bridge builders," were introduced to practical applications of the five learning disciplines and particularly to the complementarity of visioning/idealized design, systems thinking, and total quality approaches. They experienced having a dialogue around complex issues, where everyone takes the time to inquire into the quality of their thinking; this activity was even more worthwhile as they represented a wide variety of organizations in size, management philosophy, and market conditions. Participants shared some of the applications and experiments they conducted at their sites. They also contributed to the development of two learning laboratories and tested an organizational learning assessment tool. The learning labs, called "Mastering the Transition to Capitation" and "Strategic Management in an HMO," enable the bridge builders— trained as facilitators—to expose a number of managers and physicians in their organization to practical applications of systems thinking and to challenge prevailing mental models, thus increasing their alignment around a shared vision.

Highly satisfied with these results, collaborative members have decided to continue learning together in a modified format, but with the help of the existing core facilitators. Some of the participants have volunteered to help facilitate learning labs and other sessions in organizations other than their own, recognizing the value of cross-organizational experiences and of learning by teaching. Three organizations with similar interests are now joining the original group to further increase the diversity and richness of the collaborative.

These first three years have also underlined *a few conditions for the success of collaborative learning across organizational boundaries:* It is helpful to have organizations with a similar maturity level on the learning continuum (e.g., with some experience of CQI and vision building); senior executives and line managers need to commit to a multi-year program and to involve themselves personally in the learning sessions; non-competition between members creates a safe environment for sharing all relevant experiences; a core team of facilitators combining general and specialized skills should be involved in and between the meetings to help structure a cumulative learning experience and increasingly involve the participants in designing and co-leading the sessions; there must be a willingness to experiment in content and format from session to session, and a commitment to dialogue and collaboration (i.e., to public reflection on the experiments and learnings); participants should also be encouraged to take the time for exchanges through computer networks and site visits between the general sessions; finally, a focus on personal development and on challenging one's mental models should be adopted from the beginning and sustained throughout the multi-year program.

The Less-traveled High Road

My experience with individual organizations and learning collaborative members confirms that, not just learning, but also stewardship needs to be demonstrated by leaders in order for these two operating principles to permeate the entire structure. Senior executives, leading physicians, and board members should set the tone by challenging their own mental models, self-concepts, roles, and behaviors, and by developing new leadership skills. These times of drastic change for healthcare require courage to stay the course in the quest for self-mastery and deep learning, especially with all the pressures for short-term performance that come with highly visible positions.

Administrators, trustees, and physicians alike need to *experience some of the following shifts in their role and self-concept:* from a driver of change to a "gardener of people" who sees the potential in others and helps create the conditions for them to grow and reveal themselves; from *appearing* learned—someone who is supposed to and therefore pretends to know—to *being* a learner who doesn't hesitate to admit "I don't know;" from behaving as a problem solver or a "turn-around expert" to acting as an architect or designer who discerns the emerging patterns and gradually transforms the various structures that condition human behavior; from being perceived as an authority figure and a charismatic visionary to becoming a midwife of others' visions and a custodian of the shared vision, particularly when times get tougher; from being ego- or image-driven to becoming a servant leader.

Taking the high road of stewardship first means to commit to the path of self-mastery which includes: being in touch with one's deeper values and aspirations; understanding one's own deeper dynamics and self-limiting patterns; being open, vulnerable and compassionate; accepting ambiguity and some discomfort as part of the learning process; "walking the talk"; being capable of detached involvement (i.e., being passionately committed to the path without getting too attached to the outcomes); managing one's energies to achieve results with an economy of means; and living a balanced life which includes time for exercise, family life, community involvement and self-development.

It also means *developing new skills* such as recognizing different patterns of human dynamics and the deeper capacities that exist in everyone; engaging in and facilitating dialogue by being mindful and present; seeking and building on diversity; taking time to build relationships; thinking systemically; helping others gain a broader perspective; and continually testing theories and challenging mental models.

My work with individual organizations and with the learning collaborative has enabled all of us to experiment with some *new methods of helping leaders* who want to accelerate their own development and that of their associates:

- Dr. Sandra Seagal's Human Dynamics approach offers a deep and practical awareness of the different patterns of learning, communicating, and working with others, as well as of the deeper capacity that exists in each of us and can be developed. Coupled with work on personal vision and values, this approach enables leaders to venture safely onto the path of self-knowledge and to engage in dialogue and team learning on a much sounder basis.

- Dr. Joan Kenley's work on developing human capacity opens new avenues for leaders who want to explore and use more of their internal energetic resources to be more present to their experiences and achieve results with greater clarity, ease, and inner strength. As the

CEO of a leading-edge healthcare system puts it: "With the help of this work, I feel more integrated and more at ease with myself as I meet my daily challenges."

- Dialogue groups and learning networks, through meetings and computer conferencing, such as the Healthier Communities Fellows of The Healthcare Forum, also offer great opportunities to develop and practice the mindfulness which is so critical for true inquiry and communication. They are complementary to the new learning labs or management practice fields that help uncover and challenge mental models associated with the key shifts needed in healthcare and service activities in general.

- Finally, a few leadership development seminars— including a new program designed to enhance collaborative leadership among administrators and physicians—focus on the practical exploration of the new stewardship qualities. An expanded version of these programs will be offered in a new center located in the Sierra Nevada—the Montreux MetaResort. Scheduled to open in 1996, the center will combine physical, emotional, mental, and spiritual regeneration for individual leaders, their teams, and their families.

Concluding Lessons

In conclusion, some key lessons emerge from dealing with change in an industry that is undergoing fundamental shifts:

- Organizations that commit to investing in their own gradual transformation—while facing radical challenges and budget restrictions—are more likely to succeed in the long-term than those addicted to quick fixes and heroic turnaround efforts.

- Leaders at all levels must be *willing to anticipate* and address important but less urgent issues in spite of short-term pressures; they need to allocate time and resources to a transformation process which doesn't yield immediate results; they *demonstrate their courage* and determination by "staying the course" over several years; they proactively address the stewardship challenge by *investing significantly in both personal and organizational development.* They understand that self-transformation enables organizational transformation and community development which, in turn, foster further personal development in a upward spiral.

• These leaders are also *willing to experiment* with new approaches and tools which help challenge prevailing mental models and habitual behaviors, without falling into the trap of the management "fad of the year" (which generally breeds cynicism throughout the organization).

• Learning collaboratively with other institutions can accelerate an organization's progress toward meaningful change, particularly when a number of industry-specific issues can be best addressed in common, and when a safe environment is created which encourages public reflection and thorough sharing of experience among participants. It enables organization representatives to reach a much deeper level of understanding and insight than what is commonly referred to as benchmarking.

• Finally, stewards recognize the need to *transcend the boundaries of their organization* and to include other stakeholders *in creating a learning community.* They gain a sense of what needs to emerge for the greater good, realizing that not all visions are created equal.

When leaders become stewards, acting in service of their organization and their community, they inspire others to do the same, and can tap both the personal dedication and the collective intelligence that are needed to deal with changes as complex as those faced by healthcare organizations, schools, businesses, and governments in our society today.

John H. Wood is a founder and president of the Center for Developmental Organizations, based in Portland, Oregon. The Center's focus is on enabling the strategic effectiveness of business and educational organizations through the development and application of systems principles.

Wood has consulted with large and small corporations in the US and Europe for the last seven years. Prior to that, he was a division manager in a large international company. He has served as an officer in many community organizations, including president of the board of education.

He holds an MS in Operations Research from Stanford University and a BS in Engineering Physics from the University of Oklahoma. He is currently working on his PhD in Human Sciences under Dr. Bela Banathy at Saybrook Institute in San Francisco, as well as continuing studies and research at the Institute of Developmental Processes in Carmel, California, founded by Charles Krone.

26

Restructuring Education: Designing Tomorrow's Workplace

John H. Wood

In America, education is the critical limit to the development of the workplace. Since the workplace is the instrument for society's development, our educational systems are limiting our society.

It is natural for work to be an integral part of a person's life and for work to be a source for the development of one's life force and vibrancy. Children know this from their beginning. Children learn life's first lessons through play and they seek new opportunities to work and learn more. They make no distinction between work and play. They rebel when the opportunity to learn has been exhausted or taken out of their hands.

By the time children graduate from high school, they have learned that "work sucks." They have learned "their place" in the workplace and they are resigned to earning a livelihood as replaceable units in a workplace isolated from their lives (personal, home, and community). Attempts to design new kinds of workplaces, which improve work life and bring a greater integration to their lives, are, therefore, strongly suspect.

In a real sense, tomorrow's workplace is being structured in today's classroom. The fundamentals of organization life—thinking and interaction, roles and relationships, learning and work habits—are being modeled in the way the schools' are organized.

Deeply-held beliefs about workplaces are being formed early in the minds of our youth as they attend school—beliefs society wishes to transcend.

Small wonder that society is so intent on restructuring education. Educational restructuring must look beyond just resolving the public outcry for better academic performance, lower dropout rates, etc. Reacting to the outcry's content is the strategy that has been used by education unsuccessfully for decades. A larger more systemic perspective is needed. Education must take leadership in co-evolving with the restructuring efforts in the other parts of society: business, health and communities.

Businesses are restructuring, laying off thousands of workers to the detriment of communities' social health but to the betterment of the business's financial health and survival. Schools are restructuring due to diminishing support from the community. Business is critical of education for not providing the knowledge workers business now wants, but ignores the fact that education has, for decades, been structured to meet business's demand for compliant, functioning units. On the other hand, business is not providing, nor are education and communities demanding, workplaces of sufficient quality and stability to support the higher aspirations of youth.

Too many young people have unhappy family experiences resulting from their parents' working conditions. The young people want no part of what they see happening in their parents' worklives. Youth see no hope for a better life in what they see reflected in the school workplace, which forms their view of their future worklife.

The educational community is professionally vested, by experience, training and success, in their beliefs of what is right and wrong. The characteristic ongoing turmoil of change in education, the frenzy to enact the latest theory, is a re-application of their deeply held tenets in different forms. The process drains energy and recreates what has always been.

Change in education is like a thin layer of stratus clouds, ever changing with the wind but always the same. What is needed is a bank of air-cleansing thunder clouds—fresh leadership with new concepts from outside the educational community.

The Direction of Restructuring

Restructuring education's workplaces must be guided by society's evolution, current trends in workplace design, and new discoveries in science.

Society is moving beyond the current period of proliferation and diversity generated by the successes of the physical sciences, reductionism and analytical thinking, toward integration, incorporating the new science of the mind, synthesis and systems thinking. Trends in workplace design are moving away from behaviorist models toward developmental models, and toward involving the whole person, teaming, and participation. New discoveries in science support these trends such as those described by Margaret Wheatley in her book *Leadership and the New Science.*

In light of these trends, three deeply-held beliefs which are structuring the educational workplace must be challenged and transcended. These assumptions, which concern the individual, relationships and the organization, may be stated as:

- People are fixed, knowable quantities, capable of only limited learning, each having their own separate place, role, and job. People are a market commodity, expendable and replaceable.

- In organizational relationships, there must be a dominant person with superior knowledge, ultimate authority, and the power to reward and punish. Others comply and "do" their assigned tasks accordingly.

- The organization is master of its domain, focused inwardly on efficiency and simplicity of function. The organization meets boundary conditions and outside demands when seen in its best interests.

There are, of course, other articulations and expansions of these underlying assumptions (for instance, see Ken Murphy's essay on page 197). The qualities expressed are: fixed and expendable; limited job descriptions and compliance/dominance; and efficiency and self-interest. These are hardly ideal qualities for a rapidly changing world, struggling with increasing violence and courting environmental disasters.

These qualities are common to most other workplaces outside of education, including many of those being designed for the future. Educational restructuring must leapfrog the current workplace designs to regain education's natural leadership role in extending the limits of society. Quick fixes and programmatic responses will not do. Only deep restructuring at the level of beliefs, and a complete reinvention of educational workplaces, can hope to advance society's development.

Transcending these assumptions poses a huge challenge which may take decades. Many experts in the field of organization effectiveness believe that the systems sciences are the only way to meet this challenge.

Before examining the challenge of transcending the assumptions underlying the educational workplace, which limit the further development of all workplaces, a common understanding of some systems concepts is in order.

Systems Thinking

There are different levels of systems thinking that are important to the job of re-structuring education. System dynamics models, described in *The Fifth Discipline* by Peter Senge, enable the organization to see below the level of activity and events to discover the causes of recurrent patterns. Thus, systemic causes can be isolated and corrected.

From the more comprehensive perspective of systems design, Bela Banathy, a leading systems designer in the field of education, believes that education must be totally reinvented, not "fixed up." He believes we must create a new language. Words such as "school" and "classroom" carry so much baggage we are unable to truly reinvent. Design must come from the outside in: from what is of value to society, to the internal functioning that provides those values.

During the 1960s, John Bennet, a British scientist, mathematician, and philosopher, led the development of another level of systems thinking, called "systematics." Systematics is about the ongoing development of the "systems mind." It involves thinking about thinking with the intent of developing self-mastery. Charles Krone, a leader in organization theory and practice, integrates systematics into the design of innovative organizations. In these organizations, developing a systems mind becomes an integral part of analyzing, designing, and evolving the organization.

Common to each level of systems thinking is an effort to get at the essence of what drives or motivates the activities, patterns and forms observed as "the system." In practice, restructuring is more often re-forming, because the word "structure" is thought to refer only to the observable form.

In systems thinking, particularly as it relates to human activity systems or organizations, structure refers to what gives rise to form—the underlying laws and principles. Unfortunately, these structures are not obvious. Discovering these structures is like a fish discovering it's in water. The fish doesn't know it's in water until it's thrown out.

We can change form but not the underlying structure. The tendency in restructuring is to consider current forms and activities in light of unfavorable situations or results. From that perspective, re-forms are made and new activities introduced to improve the situation or result. You may have a local improvement, but, systemically, things can get worse.

Regardless of the amount of change, unless the thinking involved in the system is developed or evolved, the underlying structure, including the mind, remains unchanged. The use of sophisticated systems techniques does not ensure a change of mind. The mind learns to use the techniques to further its ends.

Restructuring human activity systems begins with developing the systems mind. The following sections discuss the developing mind and new organizing assumptions for education which can enable it to leapfrog current workplace designs and regain its natural role of leadership.

The Triune Brain

Research has yielded a model of the brain composed of three distinct neural systems. These three brains are remnants from different evolutionary stages and are correspondingly referred to as the reptilian brain (r-system), the old mammalian brain (limbic system), and the new mammalian brain (neocortex). The three brains are integrated, but can operate separately to some degree. Each has its own set of distinct functions and related mind aspects, motivations, concerns, and aims.

The r-system governs the moving centers and presents the physical world to us through the senses. It stores learnings and experiences and governs automatic, patterned behavior. It is characterized by simple distinctions, i.e., light-dark or this-that, and behaviors that are reactive and two-fold such as aversions-attractions. The mind aspects of this r-system are concerned with issues related to maintaining the individual's own state or status with self-preservation as an aim. Its motivations are to search for security, freedom, rights, and a sense of place or ownership.

The limbic system adds feeling, desire, and emotion to the r-system. Together, they provide a more powerful intelligence with richer experiences and more flexible responses. With the addition of the limbic system, the simple responses of the r-system are elevated to experiences containing feeling tones radiating from polarities such as likes-dislikes, pain-pleasure, and affirmations-denials. The mind aspects of the limbic system are concerned with issues related to the future welfare of the individual and have an aim of increasing personal potency. Its motivations are to search for personal identity, involvement, recognition, and influence.

The neocortex adds thought, intellect, creative thinking, computing and, if developed, compassion, empathy, and love— thus completing the possibility for a systems mind. The neocortex has concerns beyond self-interests including wholeness: felt concerns about all to which the individual can relate and connect. The neocortex's aim is the overall improvement in the integration of a three-tiered whole. This whole has three levels of concern—those of the individual, the individual's proximate environment, and, more universally, that which significantly affects or is affected by the results of the actions and interactions of the individual with its proximate environment.

The degree to which the neocortex is developed is the degree to which individuals can self-manage their own states. Self-management enables a person to self-generate motives which attract the higher natures of the mind. Self-managing is always in the context of achieving personal aims in the fulfillment of a higher purpose.

In the undeveloped brain, when a threat or crisis is perceived, the r-system commands the attention of the higher brain, but uses only a small portion of it. Thus, if a person is in a state of crisis (perceived or real) over long periods of time, the neocortex is underused and atrophies. Because we can operate well with only a small portion of the neocortex, there is danger of underutilizing it and losing its power. A conscious effort is needed to continuously develop the neocortex, which has enormous unused capacity and untapped potential. Developing the mind is humankind's evolutionary duty.

Developing the capacity to self-manage develops the higher mind qualities of the neocortex. Thus, when the reptilian brain calls on the neocortex, the developed neocortex manages the situation. If the threat is urgent, the alarm is handled by the r-system which can operate many times faster than the neocortex. If the threat is not urgent, there is time for compassion and empathy to enter the situation and the individual to become creative about the situational context, its meaning, possibilities, and values. The neocortex is developed also through integrating the three brains.

The three brains are integrated through imagery, produced by the higher neocortex. This is a key to continued development and evolution of the mind. The neocortex is developed by rising above the polarities of the lower minds by appreciating the arts, music, literature, and poetry; deeply understanding someone as they would themselves; taking on challenges beyond one's capability; fully visualizing and considering others' propositions. Engaging the mind in systemic thinking transcends likes and dislikes and opinions of right and wrong, avoiding the tempting demands of the lower brains.

The developmental principle for restructuring education, raised by the above learnings, is suggested by Joseph C. Pearce's statement, "Nature's imperative...and her over-arching developmental rule,...is that no intelligence or ability will unfold until or unless given the appropriate model environment."

Educational organizations, like most other workplaces, are structured around principles that appeal to the lower brains or keep the lower brain in a perceived state of crisis, threat, or fear. The need for self-managing individuals and organizing forms which develop the self-managing capability is overridden by organizational forms such as power hierarchies, functional and reductionist distinctions, and even physical structures, such as classrooms and office buildings. Neither evolution of societies nor their development are being modeled by these forms.

Rather, education organizes its work around the principles of standards and procedures and efficiency. Even time and space are organized for functional efficiency. Space is organized into classrooms for efficient teaching environments and where learning can be contained. There is a preordained time for work, a time for learning, and a time for play.

I recently asked a 10-year-old, "What do you find interesting about school?"

The reply: "Recess! We get to play."

I asked, "What if your classrooms were like recess?"

The reply: "I'd hate that. We would have to learn all the time."

"So what?" I asked.

"Learning makes my head hurt."

"What do you learn when you play?"

"Nothing."

What the organization was modeling and the student was learning is that learning is work, work is drudgery, and we get to play after.

An organizing model in which everyone—students, teachers, administrators, and classified employees—are developing self-managing skills, and in which everyone is both teacher and learner, has a greater possibility for developing society than principles focusing only on efficiency, standards, and procedures.

Behaviorist Models

The typical educational workplace is based upon behaviorist principles which limit potential. This is not to say that behaviorist models do not work; they do. Behaviorist models appeal to the same brain that is used in the behaviorists' laboratory experiments—rat brains.

The behaviorist techniques of rewards and incentives or punishment and consequences create the perception of a threat in the r-system. They become motives which invite negative motivations of self-interest, fear of losing livelihood, and recognition. In this excited state, the r-system commands the undeveloped, higher brains to join it in trivial pursuits of aversion and attraction. Concern for the organization or those it serves are absent or diminished.

The behaviorist models are limiting to the development of human potential and to individuals' contributions. So, why do these ideas persist? An historical perspective may help answer this question.

Role-to-Role Relationships

The development of psychology as a study of human potential was sidetracked by American psychologists nearly one hundred years ago. Psychologists had to justify themselves to business people, their appointees, and politicians for university appointments, research funding, and professional opportunities. Psychologists were in positions of social power and were interested in techniques of social control and of tangible performance.

K. Danziger, a professor of psychology at York University, Toronto, writes, "American psychologists responded to this opportunity with a promise that was totally innovative. This promise involved nothing less than the claim that experimental psychology would supply the fundamental laws governing all human activity, irrespective of context." The goal for psychology became "the prediction and control of human behavior."

Danziger's point of view is that the concept of control is implicit in the experimental model. The experimenter controls the object in the experiment and its environment. This implicit quality of external control is a limiting factor in workplace design.

In the behaviorist concept of workplace, one group of people has superior knowledge and "super vision" and is vested with ultimate authority. They decide what is best for others and intervene with manipulative shenanigans, which appeal to the lower brain. The concept produces predictable tangible results, as well as unintended social consequences, and lost potential.

Organizations based on behaviorist principles rely upon role-to-role relationships which are dominant-compliant, e.g., boss-subordinate, teacher- student, expert-client. In role-to-role, there is often the use of reward/punishment. For example, in a teacher-student relationship, the teacher decides what to learn, when to learn it, how to learn it and how to behave while learning it. If the student fails to comply, there is an external consequence. This dominant role-to-role relationship is not conducive to learning.

Self-to-Self Relationships

A markedly different organizing concept is the concept of self-to-self relationships. In a self-to-self relationship, each party speaks for himself and remains open to a change in direction. Each person is always making a unique contribution toward the development of each other, the workplace, and the organization. The contribution is toward the higher purposes they serve.

Relationship Power

The current direction of workplace design recognizes the unnatural power imbalance in role-to-role relationships. New workplaces attempt to alleviate the effect of this inequality with techniques like empowering, teaming, skill-based pay, appreciative inquiry, participation, etc. The new workplace designs—socio-tech, TQM, learning organizations, are improvements, but more reformations than restructuring. They tend to work inside the relationship, improving the interactions and performance, but do not focus on developing the aim, work, and capacity of the relationship. Further, technique will never overcome the loss of potential where imbalance of power is used for manipulation. Only by giving up the concept of power as an organizing principle and embracing the concept of development can full realization of value occur in the workplace and society.

In developmentally-focused organizations, self-to-self relationships exist within a hierarchy based on increasing value, complexity, and scope, not on control, power, or status. Each level of the hierarchy is distinctive and additive to the pursuit of a shared vision and mission. Each higher level of the hierarchy, is developing and providing motives of higher, more encompassing value which enliven the work. These motives invite motivations of the higher self, stewardship, contribution, and adding value.

In an early educational case, Socrates provided motives to his students, in the form of challenging questions which attracted the students' motivation for discovering their own hidden knowledge and capacity to learn. The students would reveal their learnings so that, in time, Socrates came to know and understand their motivations, qualities, and limitations and was enabled to continue the development of the learning process. All became more knowledgeable and capable.

Evolving Complexity

The social institutions of community, education, health, and business are systemically intertwined. The effectiveness of one is dependent on the effectiveness of the others. Yet, each attempts to chart its own course independent of the others. Evolving the whole is thought to be too complex.

However, the increasing level of complexity marks a society's evolution. The more complex a society becomes, the more evolved it is. Education is the institution which must provide the leadership and that begins with changing the way it organizes to deliver education—changing the structure of its workplace.

But first, what is complexity and how does it occur? Complexity is a psychological process or state of being—an individual's state of mind in regard to what is knowable and understandable.

Without the human mind, nature is just nature, doing its thing. But, it is human nature to want to know, so humans study nature, including humankind. We learn, or make up, a lot of facts about nature. A list of facts is not so complex; it may be long, but it is not complex.

There is another part to complexity that humans need to understand in order to know about things at a higher level than just a growing list of facts. Humans want to be in charge, to control and predict. Thus, there is a need to bring some structure or integration to this list, to discover meaning, usefulness, and relatedness. Now things start to get complex.

Mihaly Csikszentmihalyi, author of *Flow,* observes in his book, *The Evolving Self,* that complexity is the coalescence of two mental processes—diversity and integration. Diversity is the mental process of expanding knowledge or science. It manifests in the world as goods, causes, interests, niches, theories, etc. Integration is the mental process of structuring these distinctions and refinements into more meaningful and useful concepts—bigger, more manageable and complex facts. Integration manifests in the world as increasing order.

Complexity is an expanding container holding these two processes. It works like a ratchet. When diversity exceeds the capacity to integrate, there is a call for more integrative capacity, a transformation of the mind. When there is more integrative capacity than facts, there is a void to learn more and to make finer distinctions.

When things get out of balance, we experience disintegration: things fall apart; we can't get it together; or things are just too complicated and we feel the need to simplify. We experience this as "increasing complexity," but that experience is caused by diversity and integration being too far out of balance.

In education, subject matter as mere knowledge increases diversity without increasing integration. Studying literature, mathematics, art, and music to understand the underlying structure increases our ability to integrate structure, and experience meaning, imagery, and emotions.

In workplace design, the reductionist tendency to further simplify work into smaller more easily controlled functional units increases diversity without increasing integration. A developmental approach develops work *and* the individual's capacity to manage greater complexity. For example, in an educational workplace that was developmental, you might see an ongoing practice of developing the capacity of cooks, bus drivers, and maintenance people to educate students in: nutrition, buying, and meal planning; transportation and bus maintenance; security and increasing the value-adding capacity of physical assets. Imagine what needs to be developed for that to happen and imagine what will develop from that.

At the level of societies, we appear to be at the end of a long period of increasing diversity: endless discoveries of infinitesimal facts about the universe, the information explosion, and product proliferation. We are exceeding the capacity to integrate. Disintegration has begun to occur—witness the break-up of the communist countries, the damage to the environment, and the diminishing ability of governments to maintain order.

In America, witness our inability to integrate our diverse communities into an evolving society. Education has an inability to provide a safe, orderly learning environment in our schools. There are many similar problems: the failure of our health care system; the inability of businesses to provide secure, meaningful and profitable employment; the increasing numbers of special interest groups and gangs making demands without regard to the whole of society; our overloaded courts, civil and criminal; and ever-increasing rules and regulations. Each problem compounds the other problems. People and institutions are managing complexity by collapsing inward, from societal interests, to special interests, to self interests to small interests. In short, we are "honoring diversity" in lieu of evolving complexity.

New Organizing Beliefs

The following three new organizing beliefs might be used by education to replace the current beliefs:

1. People are passionate about contributing their ingenuity to shared visions of higher value. They value stewardship, involvement, cooperation, and under-

standing. They have the capacity for self-managing within environments of increasing complexity and scope.

2. Greater potential is developed and higher values are realized in self-to-self relationships contained within hierarchies providing motives of increasing value-adding capacity that promote the continuous development of self, the organization, and society.

3. Organizations see themselves as an integral part of a stream of users/suppliers in which each reciprocally maintains the other in pursuit of adding greater value to society and the environment. All such streams are consciously co-evolving with each other toward a continuously developing society.

With new assumptions in place, we might see all elements of the educational community demanding that society provide better working and learning opportunities for students. Students are fully themselves in making their contributions and, at the same time, seek new opportunities for further development.

We might see an educational workplace in which every one is a learner and teacher; where students are involved in developing their own curriculum; where bus drivers enable students to know and understand safety, mechanics, and scheduling; where cafeteria workers help students learn nutrition, cooking, and kitchen management; where students are engaged in improving school property.

We might see a learning place in which every one is engaged in designing: where students are engaged in designing their classrooms and curricula; where students are designing effective interactions between themselves and their families, friends, and different communities; where students are designing the day after tomorrow's learning-places and workplaces.

If that is to be:

Who must we become? How must we think? What must we sacrifice? Why?

Robert Weintraub is a senior consultant in IBM Education and Training. He has spent ten years in workplace education, focusing on executive education, marketing education, education technology, education strategy, and, most recently, education for transformation. He helped create, communicate, and implement IBM's worldwide education vision, directions, and strategies. He has helped over 50 organizations establish their education strategies and harness education technology.

In 1993, Weintraub created and began implementing an education plan to help transform the way IBM's North American Marketing and Services division does business, to increase its value to customers as well as shareholder profit. He also helped revamp IBM's leadership development programs. Most of his current work focuses on improving human performance through cultural change. Weintraub is a doctoral candidate in adult education at Columbia University Teachers College.

27

Transforming Mental Models through Formal and Informal Learning: A Guide for Workplace Educators

Robert Weintraub

Perhaps the most significant learning that can take place in adulthood involves changing what Peter Senge calls "mental models—deeply ingrained assumptions, generalizations, or even pictures or images that influence how we understand the world and how we take action." It also can be the most difficult kind of learning. Most people avoid it and only attempt it when faced with a crisis, or what Jack Mezirow calls a "disorienting dilemma." When the attempt is made, it often involves long-term interventions, such as psychotherapy.

The mental models of an organization constitute its culture. It is what Edgar Schein calls the "pattern of shared assumptions that the group learned" over time because the pattern worked well for the organization and, therefore, got passed on to newcomers "as the correct way to perceive, think, and feel...." It, too, tends to remain intact until the organization faces some crisis. It is especially difficult to change in a large organization that has been extremely successful—where cultural habits were learned and honed over decades and were continually reinforced by increasingly significant business accomplishments. The mental models then maintain a firm hold over the psyche of the organization. And, even if we wanted to, we couldn't put the organization on the therapist's couch!

This is the imposing situation that many workplace educators have been asked to confront. They have generally focused on instrumental learning, in which clear objectives can be set and measurable competencies can be achieved. How, then, are they to take on the transformation of the organization's mental models?

They cannot do it alone. Whatever they do must be accompanied by other interventions—e.g., organizational development initiatives, changes to the measurement and compensation systems, changes to the human resource policies and practices, supporting communications, and outside change agents. In some cases, old leaders must be replaced with new leaders who already possess the needed mental models, and who can model the needed behaviors.

However, there is a lot that workplace educators can do to facilitate the required transformation—through a variety of formal and informal methods that will be discussed in the remainder of this chapter. The methods are gleaned from business, organizational development, and adult education literature and from practice within the IBM Corporation.

Formal Learning Provides the Framework

Most large organizations of the "industrial era" defined the process of learning as they defined their business processes— i.e., learning is a process that can be scientifically managed to produce predetermined behavioral outputs. As Victoria Marsick and Karen Watkins point out, this "'formal learning' is typically institutionally-sponsored, classroom-based or highly structured." It is based on the assumption that educators can define clear, causal relationships between structured educational activities and the knowledge, skills, and attitudes required on the job.

The question is, how can such a systematic approach be used to foster a learning organization; or, more specifically to the issue at hand, how can it be employed to help change mental models? It is my contention that formal learning can, and should, establish the *framework* for the transformation of mental models within an organization.

The Role of Principles and Processes

As individuals in the pursuit of "personal mastery," we must challenge our unique mental models, and the assumptions upon which they rest, in order to move closer to our personal visions. So, too, must the organization challenge its existing mental models and assumptions. But, it must do so within the context of the "shared vision" it needs to build and the mental models it needs to possess. For the most part, these come from the organization's leadership—how they interpret the environment and how they believe the organization must respond to it. The vision and mental models they fashion provide a foundation for learning and action. As Senge suggests, without that foundation, "empowering people will only increase organizational stress and the burden of management to maintain coherence and direction."

Educators cannot simply teach the new foundation. The propagation of new mental models does not lend itself to formal learning. However, today, in many organizations, those mental models become tangibly revealed in stated *principles* and *processes*. The principles defined by leaders tell us the fundamental assumptions we must accept, and how we must fundamentally behave, if we want to participate in the refashioned organization. Once they are established, business "re-engineers" can delineate consistent processes that serve as guides or maps to the needed behaviors. In Russia, for example, the vision and mental models of *glasnost* and *perestroika* are defined by the principles of democracy and capitalism much as we know them. Now, legal and market processes must be established to help the society work within the boundaries of those principles.

In IBM, a set of principles defined by its relatively new chief executive demands that the organization's members act as entrepreneurs in highly productive teams that urgently strive to satisfy customers, and yield profits for shareholders by providing technology-based products and services of the highest quality. The processes, then, provide ways of acting entrepreneurially and with teamwork, of satisfying customers, of efficiently developing and delivering products and services, and of maximizing quality and profitability. They also provide a tangible basis for challenging our existing mental models.

Process Workshops

Once these principles and processes are defined, education must be developed that helps people see how their ways of acting have become outmoded and how they can adopt and customize the new ways of doing business. As a first step, educators can implement formal "process workshops."

A process workshop may be built using a systematic approach, which workplace educators generally call an instructional systems development process. Initially, a needs analysis is performed in which the principles and attendant behaviors, and the rationales behind them, are gleaned from the organization's leaders and the documents they have produced. The key facets of the processes, along with the rationales behind them, are gleaned from the re-engineers and their documents, and from those in the organization (or, if necessary, in another organization) who have successfully piloted the processes. The focus of the analysis should be on how people need to act and interact differently. The prospective audience is analyzed to determine the current *modus operandi*, how willing and able people are to implement the new ways of doing business, and significant obstacles and issues. Then, the workshop is designed and developed to give people a *framework* for filling their knowledge, skill and attitudinal gaps, as well as to deal with the obstacles and issues.

Generally, the workshop itself revolves around cases or scenarios, each of which focuses on a major process or group of processes. Teams of learners play roles and interact as they would on the job but are guided to do so as the new processes prescribe.

It must be emphasized that the processes are not procedures. They are guides to doing business and making individual and team judgments in accordance with the principles of the organization and the field in which it functions. They are tangible outgrowths of mental models which must change for the organization to change and grow. So, in essence, we are not trying to help people learn new steps, but new perspectives and behaviors that will allow them to take steps in the direction the organization must go. In a learning organization, the processes are, first and foremost, tools to change mental models.

Each role-playing exercise is followed by a discussion in which the educator must be a facilitator who enables learners to respond to such questions as: what's different in the new way of doing things, why should we do things that way, why is it important to the organization, why is it important to my "customers" and "suppliers," why is it important to me, what's wrong with the old way, what's wrong with the new way, why am I so uncomfortable with it, what problems does it bring, how can we overcome them, and how can I make it work? This "critical thinking" is the most important element of the workshop. As Stephen Brookfield asserts, "it involves calling into question the assumptions underlying our customary, habitual ways of thinking and acting and then being ready to think and act differently on the basis of this critical questioning." Such critical thinking involves "dialogue" and "systems thinking," and what Donald Schön calls "reflection-in-action." "We think critically about the thinking that got us into this fix or this opportunity; and we may, in the process, restructure strategies of action, understandings of phenomena, or ways of framing problems."

I am not under the illusion that this "process workshop" will change mental models. However, by using the tangible representations of the needed mental models, the principles and processes, as a basis for critical dialogue and reflection, workplace educators can create the *framework* for the subsequent change of those models (see also Mezirow, bringing out and examining critically the presuppositions upon which one's beliefs and feelings are derived). If people can continue such dialogue and reflection as they implement the processes back on the job, mental models will change.

An IBM Example: Customer Value Management

IBM has struggled to change its mental models. It suffers from years of success that reinforced perspectives and behaviors that have become obsolete. As a result, it has too often neglected its primary mission as a business organization—to provide value to its customers and ensure a commensurate profit for itself.

IBM's North American Marketing and Services division determined that to correct the situation it would re-engineer its business. It did so within a schema known as "Customer Value Management" (CVM) whose principles outline a new way of doing business for the division—from how it chooses markets and the ways it will serve them, to how it manages opportunities, works in teams, prices transactions, accounts for its costs, designs and delivers solutions and ultimately satisfies customers. Each of these aspects is delineated through processes that, when combined with supporting information systems, form a closed-loop system for continuously improving business decisions and activities.

CVM represents a mental model that is not commonly held by IBM personnel. No matter how logical its principles and processes may be, and how easy they may be to understand, there are too many ingrained assumptions and habits that hold sway. But, in part, it was up to me and fellow educators to foster the change.

We generally followed the instructional systems process outlined above, as delineated in IBM's "Systems Approach To Education." Fortunately, CVM had been piloted successfully in IBM's Indiana Trading Area, so much of the workshop content, and many of the obstacles and issues, could be culled from leaders and participants in that pilot.

The workshop was conducted by facilitators from *outside IBM* to help counter the influence of outmoded, yet deep-seated, IBM mental models. These facilitators also had the ability to continually challenge the perspectives of the learners. There was frustration and antagonism and relatively low ratings—which initially disheartened the *IBM educators,* who were used to receiving high praise for their offerings. Yet, more significant measurements revealed that the participants better understood CVM and its importance to IBM and themselves, began to develop skills needed to implement CVM on the job and, overall, held a more accepting attitude towards the new ways of doing business.

It was also clear to the educators that these gains would be lost if they were not supported and increased when the learners returned to their work environments. This meant changes to human resource management systems and information systems and supporting communications. It also meant formal "complementary courses" and a lot of "informal learning."

Complementary Courses

One of the negative comments that often appeared on feedback sheets was that individuals did not have the necessary knowledge and skills in specific areas of the business, or with specific processes or information system tools, to implement their parts of CVM in an efficient and effective manner. Therefore it was imperative that IBM educators provide formal courses to fill the specific gaps.

Some new courses had to be developed to deal with radically new roles and responsibilities. However, many of these "complementary courses" had already been developed but without the "CVM twist." So, it was necessary to modify them to incorporate the new principles and processes and focus on what's different. For example, since the way we plan and price and account for costs is different, much of our finance curriculum needed elements of that CVM twist. A specific course in pricing now has to deal with a new process, a new information system tool, and their relationship to the other CVM processes and tools, emphasizing how they all work together in a closed-loop system.

In essence, educators need to place their other formal offerings within the context of the mental models they are trying to propagate. As with the process workshop, this can be tangibly executed through the use of the principles and processes that represent those mental models, along with their rationales. In the complementary education, they will take on the flavor of the particular discipline—e.g., marketing, engineering, finance—but they will remain consistent with the needed mental models. And, as before, the gains of this formal learning need to be significantly supplemented on the job with larger doses of informal learning.

Informal Learning Makes It Happen

According to Marsick and Watkins, informal learning "is not typically classroom-based or highly structured, and control of the learning rests primarily in the hands of the learner….(Such) learning is experience-based, non-routine, and often tacit." It occurs when a new member in an organization observes the behavior of experienced members and it occurs when someone turns to a colleague for help with a problem.

Most American organizations have paid little attention to this learning. In fact, in many ways, their cultures have thwarted it. How often have we been critical of people who have stopped "work" to reflect on something they observed; and, how often have we avoided helping a colleague with a perplexing problem because it does not pertain to our work at hand. It seems that the first organizational assumption we need to change is the one concerning the use of time for teaching and learning.

A few years ago, I worked with an IBM colleague who was in the U.S. on assignment from Japan. One day he told me that he was rather shocked that people worked in separate offices as much as they do, because they miss the opportunities to learn from overhearing colleagues' conversations and watching them in action. A study done at Xerox, in their service division, showed how the "war stories" that the service representatives brought back to their colleagues at the end of a day served as indispensable lessons. And the Institute for Research on Learning (IRL) speaks of "communities of practice" that develop in organizations and that cross departmental and functional boundaries . The communication that occurs across these informally established communities is a major source of individual, group and organizational learning (conversation with Etienne Wenger at IRL, 1992).

Research in adult education increasingly shows that adults are more likely to learn in an informal manner. More and more, workers assert that they do not have the time to leave their work and take structured courses. They also argue that much of the formally taught material is material that they already know or that is irrelevant to their on-the-job needs. Combine that with the increasing rate of change and you arrive at a situation that increasingly demands informal learning.

But this is not the paradigm of most workplace educators. The needs, objectives, methods and evaluation of the learning are, to a large extent, determined by the learners, not the educators. So what are they to do? It is my contention that informal learning can be, and often needs to be, facilitated by educators as part of the development and maintenance of a learning organization. Watkins and Marsick assert that educators "can extend their impact in almost exponential fashion by working with all employees to make self-managed learning more effective and by creating ways for people to share what they learn." Experience in general is a good teacher; but, experience that is appropriately selected, planned and/or managed for learning, and that incorporates critical dialogue and reflection, is much better.

For the most part, mental models will change as people experience success with the behaviors that are the outgrowths of those models and as those behaviors become more habitual and tacit. It is an iterative process involving understanding and action. People will begin to act in a desired fashion as they apply what they absorbed in the formal learning events. But the obsolete behaviors will reassert their dominance unless a variety of informal learning experiences follow. Many of these cannot be orchestrated by educators. "Modeling," for example, is an essential informal learning intervention that is the responsibility of leaders at all levels (and by leaders I mean those people, managers or not, who others tend to follow). Unless the organization's leaders are continuously exhibiting the desired behaviors, it is unlikely that most members will. However, educators can help leaders become better models.

Feedback Analysis and Coaching

As in the process workshops, to help transform mental models, the informal learning interventions must get people to take hard looks at their own perspectives and behaviors, see what is inconsistent with the new principles and ways of doing business, pose and consider viable alternatives, and begin to incorporate or practice those that are most needed.

Educators can facilitate this process through the use of instruments that provide individual feedback. Such instruments can be generic, such as the Myers-Briggs Type Indicator, and help people see the strengths and weaknesses of their personal styles. But the task at hand more than likely requires a rather powerful challenge to a mind-set that will "fight like the devil." Therefore, it may be necessary to design an instrument that specifically focuses on the organization's principles and attendant behaviors and that garners open and honest criticism from associates with different work relationships and perspectives. Furthermore, educators need to ensure that the feedback is the basis for critical dialogue that works towards personal change.

IBM created a "principles assessment" tool that helps individuals see how their behaviors match those required by IBM's guiding principles—based on input from themselves, their managers, their managees, their peers and, potentially, their customers. But it is clear that the instrument would fail to do its job unless it was followed by individual and group analysis. Group analysis allows people to share their "shock" in learning that they are not living the principles they regularly espouse and to get some different perspectives on what needs to be done. It is led by a facilitator or coach skilled in drawing out honest and open criticism, as well as dealing with the consequences. Individual analysis is done with a coach who is also willing and trained to be properly challenging and critical, and to help individuals think critically and develop personal action plans.

These kinds of coaches are sorely needed in most organizations. They are critical to the transformation of mental models and, thus, to the development of a learning organization. As individuals and teams attempt to re-engineer the business, implement radically new processes and, more importantly, make judgments and practice within a new and changing framework, they need coaches who can help them increase their ability to do so.

On page 198, Ken Murphy, referencing James Flaherty, describes these dimensions of coaching as changing the "structure of interpretation" through "language" and "practice" or through what Chris Argyris refers to as "double-loop" learning. As Murphy suggests, these take very different "skills and qualities" than we find in most organizations today. Yet, these are the skills and qualities that workplace educators need today. And they are the skills and qualities that workplace educators must propagate throughout their organizations.

"Walk-Throughs"

An informal learning intervention that a coach or facilitator might use to build on formal learning is a "walk-through." Once people understand the new principles, processes and behaviors and begin to interpret and customize them for themselves, they will try to implement them on the job. Most likely, this implementation will be clumsy and will be met with numerous obstacles and frustrations. These include: misinterpretations, conflicting messages, insufficient skills, poor communications, lack of teamwork, inconsistent measurements, and outmoded or underdeveloped information systems. Depending on the circumstances, any of these may be enough to thwart change; however, understanding and dealing with the problems as a team can often surmount the obstacles.

A walk-through allows just that. Whether planned or *ad hoc,* a walk-through involves a role-play of a process or business activity. People on the team play the roles of all the people who might have been or will be involved in such activity. As the play goes on, the obstacles are encountered and, with the help of a facilitator or coach, the team determines ways to deal with them. If an issue arises that cannot be immediately handled, it is put on an issues list with someone assigned to respond to it. The responses are published and widely distributed.

In IBM's CVM example, the walk-throughs were a primary learning vehicle. First practiced in IBM's Midwestern Area, people representing many segments of the business periodically came together in Chicago to walk through difficult facets of the new way of doing business. There the "coach" would create an atmosphere of mutual respect and good humor, which permitted critical dialogue and creative solutions. The representatives then went back to their organizations armed with ways to surmount the obstacles and a richer grasp of the new mental models—and greater energy to spread the word.

The Role of Information and Communications Technology

In a large organization, spreading the word is not an easy task. By the time learnings are communicated, they often have lost their immediacy and meaning. Information and communications technology may provide the vehicles to bring informal learning to the "desktop."

In many organizations, the technology applications needed to facilitate informal learning are already in place, but these organizations have only thought of the applications in terms of data processing and communications. If one looks at the literature on "groupware," for example, it is clear that the focus is on improving work and productivity, with very little mention of learning. Cannot the following be learning vehicles: help-screens, on-line tutorials, database searches, electronic bulletin boards, electronic mail, computer conferences, electronic performance support systems, help-lines, phone-mail and conference calls? In fact, they can be if they are developed and used in a fashion that promotes informal learning. And it is up to workplace educators to make that happen.

Research I performed in IBM's Northeastern Area revealed that the most significant technology-mediated informal learning came from dialogues, whether through computers or phones. The degree of learning often depended upon the skills of the users in conducting or participating in dialogues through electronic media. And I learned it is possible to have the kind of critical dialogues necessary to help change mental models through such media. The research also showed that it is quite possible to have a coaching relationship through the use of both computer and telephone applications. In many cases, it is acceptable to conduct the needed dialogues in an "asynchronous" manner, i.e., where the participants give and receive input at different times, as with e-mail and phone-mail. Technological factors, such as ease of access and use, also affected learning; but, again, the most significant factor was skill in using the applications as informal learning tools.

The Japanese colleague I mentioned earlier doubted these conclusions. He told me that in Japan people avoid using phone and computer communications as much as possible, for too much is lost when people are not face to face. With this in mind, I would suggest that different combinations of technology-mediated and non-technology-mediated interactions are warranted, depending on the learning needs. But as the technologies advance and interaction through them becomes more like face to face encounters, they will provide even better vehicles for informal learning—vehicles on which workplace educators will have to help their organizations capitalize.

The Best of Both Worlds: Action Learning

Over the past couple of years, I have learned about a process that logically combines formal and informal learning approaches and benefits in the quest to transform mental models. The process is often referred to as "action learning."

Action learning seems to mean different things to different people. To me, there are three key ingredients that provide its power. First, it involves a team of relatively diverse people working on a project to deal with a significant organizational or business problem. The problem should be systemic so that it arises from and affects multiple facets of the organization, should be complex so that it cannot be solved easily or quickly, and should be ambiguous so there is no clear or right answer. The team should have the power to implement whatever solution they develop.

Second, when the team comes together to work on the project, they should be joined by an action learning facilitator—another new job for the workplace educator. The facilitator most often observes the group in action but, periodically, he or she intervenes and pushes the group into critical dialogue and reflection on the ways they have worked and behaved as a team and as individuals. The dialogue calls into question the assumptions that each person brings with him or her and forces each person to view the world through different glasses.

Third, as the group progressively reveals various learning needs that are encompassed by particular bodies of knowledge, the facilitator or a team member arranges relevant formal learning events.

The project work goes on continually, when the team is together and when the members are back on their jobs. The problem solution is the most tangible product of the process. However, the learning is the most significant product. If successful, the process yields noticeable transformations in mental models, along with team learning, more advanced systems thinking, and steps toward personal mastery. A marketing executive from a major manufacturing company told me that he went into an action learning program with his own agenda and goals, "holding my cards close and only showing what I needed to. But the facilitators forced us to open up and see that the old ways of working won't work....The reflection process allows you to get back on course with agreement....And we were able to assimilate what we learned into the way we work....The process affected my personal life, my relationships; and, actually, that's how we do business anyway, through relationships." When such participants go back to their jobs and model new behaviors based on their learnings, additional informal learning occurs and changes ripple through the organization.

Transforming the Mental Models of Workplace Educators

Action learning is a powerful example of how formal and informal learning can be combined to help change mental models. But, given the direction of the business environment, it is clear that the weight must increasingly be on the informal side. And that's a big change for workplace educators. Most are not prepared to be learning facilitators or coaches. Most are not used to unstructured situations, where needs, objectives and methods change quickly and are often ambiguous. Most are not used to challenging people's perspectives and forcing critical dialogue. Most are not used to using technology to facilitate informal learning. Most are not used to getting people to learn on their own as a primary goal. And, most are not used to changing mental models.

It appears that the next most important task for workplace educators, then, is to change their own mental models about workplace learning. They need to challenge their own assumptions and perspectives. They need to learn about different informal learning methods. And they need to experiment with these methods in bold ways. Workplace educators have a key role to play in forging learning organizations; but, they can only play that role with new mental models of learning.

Robert L. Masten is a retired captain in the Navy and founder of Masten Consulting Group. Masten spent one-third of his Naval career as the chief executive of three diverse businesses: a research and development laboratory, an internationally operating service organization, and a manufacturing company. Building on those experiences, he spent his final tour in the Navy as an in-house Total Quality Management consultant for the U.S. Atlantic Fleet. Masten is now the chief executive of Masten Consulting Group, a leadership and management consulting firm based in Norfolk, Virginia.

28

Leadership, Quality, and the U.S. Navy

Robert L. Masten

"Man overboard! Man overboard, starboard side!" cries the stern lookout into his headset. Instantly, the phone talker on the ship's bridge echoes, "Man overboard, starboard side!" Without altering the step of her stride to the starboard bridge wing, the Officer of the Deck (OOD) brings the ship to action, "Hard right rudder! All engines ahead flank!" "Boatswains Mate, pass the word throughout the ship: man overboard, starboard side; boat crew to the motor whale boat, report when ready to start the engine and lower the boat; lookouts, report when sighting the sailor in the water! Captain to the Bridge!"

Within moments, Captain Martha Miceli arrives on the bridge. Calmly she surveys the situation, and satisfies herself that Lieutenant Commander Peggy Caughlin, the OOD, has the unfolding events firmly in hand. Quietly, she makes her way to the Captain's Chair, and settles in to observe her crew in action.

The ship builds speed and heels to port, as the 8,700-ton destroyer responds to the actions of her crew, and makes her turn to the right. Commissioned in 2004, USS Wainwright optimizes the best of 21st Century technology and the constraints of the 1998 federal budget. As the ship's head crosses 60 degrees to the right of the original course, the OOD barks to the helmsman, "Shift your rudder!" And the mighty man-of-war, now knifing through the water in excess of twenty knots, heels sharply to starboard as she strains against the force of the water. As the ship approaches 180 degrees opposite her original course, the OOD reduces speed and eases the ship into her earlier wake.

"Officer of the Deck, Sir," the bridge phone talker calls to Lieutenant Commander Caughlin, "the port lookout reports: sailor in the water, fifteen degrees off the port bow, 500 yards distant. In addition, Sir," the phone talker continues, "the boat coxswain reports the motor whale boat is ready for lowering." "Very well," responds the OOD, "start the engine while lowering the boat."

Shortly, the bridge phone talker again breaks the silence, "Officer of the Deck, Sir, the boat coxswain reports the boat won't start!"

It takes Captain Miceli only a moment to react, "What do you mean the boat won't start? I told the First Lieutenant I would have his hide if that boat ever failed to start again! Boatswains Mate, pass the word for the First Lieutenant to report to the bridge on the double. Commander Caughlin, maneuver the ship closer to the sailor, and get a life ring to him."

Had It Been a Learning Organization

Would this story have unfolded differently had Wainwright been a learning organization—an ensemble of Systems Thinking, Personal Mastery, Mental Models, Shared Vision, and Team Learning, as described by Peter Senge in *The Fifth Discipline*, evoked throughout the organization so that it continually creates its own future? The answer depends on the specific person and situation. If the ship had been a learning organization of long standing, the sailor might never have fallen overboard in the first place. But life at sea is hazardous and accidents happen, so that assumption is probably not a good one.

Lieutenant Commander Caughlin's execution of the Williamson Turn, designed to return a ship to her wake proceeding in the opposite direction, was flawless. She was well trained, practiced, and took charge of the life threatening situation expertly. A learning organization environment probably would not have markedly influenced her performance.

Ensign Hank Tobias is the First Lieutenant, the officer responsible for boat readiness. He is also responsible for a myriad of other things related to the exterior of the ship, from maintaining the anchor windlass and various winches, to keeping most of the ship's exterior painted, to lashing the rat guards to the lines which hold the ship to the pier in port. He supervises 47 mostly junior male and female sailors, including those who maintain and operate the ship's three boats. As an Ensign, he is new to the Navy and has been aboard Wainwright for seven months. He has received no formal boat training, and what he knows about boats he has learned mostly from observation. To have learned the ropes as First Lieutenant within a learning organization would have dramatically changed the way Ensign Tobias went about his business.

Captain Miceli was selected as the first Commanding Officer of Wainwright because of her proven ability to meet commitments. Naturally inclined to be an authoritarian leader, she has been sufficiently schooled in the Navy's Total Quality Leadership program to recognize the value in making that paradigm shift. For Captain Miceli to make the transition from authoritarian to Total Quality leader is a continuing and painful process, as it demands major changes in her thinking and behavior. To make the transition further to a learning organization mentality is not something she is prepared to do. Had Wainwright been a learning organization at the time of the overboard, the environment in which the boat was launched and the sailor recovered would have been considerably different.

How does Wainwright, or any other Navy command, become a learning organization? By staying on the course of Total Quality Leadership on which the Navy has already embarked, and to the degree it makes sense, evolving into a learning organization from there.

Lessons from Total Quality Leadership

The course the U.S. Navy set for Total Quality Leadership is basically one of Total Quality Management tailored to fit the needs of Navy. The emphasis is on leadership rather than management in recognition that the Navy is manpower intensive and that people enhance their productivity through leadership more so than through management. With 900,000 employees, the Navy is one of the largest organizations in the world implementing TQM.

Since its implementation in the early 1980s, the Navy's TQL initiatives have been meandering and successful: Meandering, because one cannot make a straight line out of hundreds of starting points, and because the vision of the Navy's future has not been clearly articulated at all levels; successful because, in an organization of so many individuals, almost all progress is good, and because the Navy has made numerous changes with beneficial outcomes. What is important in these experiences is the enhanced understanding of TQL implementation, and how these lessons may be applied toward becoming a learning organization.

This essay will review some of these TQL lessons and the application of these lessons to the development of learning organizations. The lessons are drawn from my Navy leadership and consulting experiences. They are equally applicable to any business or academic institution which has embarked on TQM implementation and now desires to become a learning organization.

Lesson: The Typical Strategic Planning Model is Flawed.

The Navy's mission is provided in Title 10 of the U.S. Code: "be organized, trained and equipped primarily for prompt and sustained combat incident to operations at sea." That mission is meaningfully translated for each individual command. The commanding officer of a submarine knows why he is in business, and it does not include, for example, the option of going into the business of launching aircraft. He also knows that, at the end of his tour, he is to leave his command more capable of carrying out that mission than when he arrived. Generally speaking, that is his vision. These things understood, the typical commanding officer ensures the currency of the command's mission, vision, guiding principles, and strategic goals, and then puts his or her focus on TQL implementation. Each successive commanding officer modifies these efforts to fit expected operational taskings, available resources, perceived readiness shortfalls, and personal leadership and management desires.

The typical private sector business does not have some outside entity doing its strategic planning, and can't afford to leave the future to chance. Accordingly, it needs to earnestly grapple with why the company is in business, and how it is going to create the future which actualizes that purpose. This is heady and demanding work, particularly as it relates to making the future actually happen.

Differences in strategic planning methods aside, it is my observation that the typical strategic planning model is flawed. The model reads well on paper (broad objectives, broken down into ever smaller goals, as illustrated in Figure 1), but commonly

Mission

Vision

Guiding Principles

Strategic Goals

Objectives

Accomplishments

Actions

Figure 1
Nominal Strategic Planning
Model

fails to cause the described events to occur. What is supposed to happen is changed behavior by the work force consistent with the executive's vision of the future. Failure typically results from an inability to accurately forecast the future, the bureaucratic distance between the executive and the worker, the lack of a vested interest by the worker in the executive's vision, and limited grasp of the complexities of TQM and learning organization implementation.

What needs to be added to the model to help one focus is illustrated in Figure 2. After the leaders have determined the purpose, vision, guiding principles, and strategic goals of the organization, they need to identify the processes which are critical to customer satisfaction. These are the processes which demand executive attention. They are also the processes in which sailors have a vested interest. Get

Mission

Vision

Guiding Principles

Strategic Goals

Customer Supporting Processes

Process Improvement

Customer Supporting Behaviors

Figure 2
Customer-Driven Strategic Planning Model

the sailor focused on improving the processes which the leader knows yield satisfied customers, and the command will benefit. With a strategic and operational focus on customer satisfaction, the leadership can see the linkage between worker performance and customer satisfaction, and is positioned to optimize each. This relationship seldom develops using conventional strategic planning.

Lesson: Continuous Process Improvement, Not Problem Solving, Yields the Real Fruit of Successful TQL Implementation.

Rear Admiral Kevin Delaney tells a story from his days as the Commanding Officer of the Naval Air Station at Jacksonville, Florida. From his frequent visits to work centers around the command, he learned of recurring potholes in a high usage parking lot. Initially, he made a casual remark to his public works officer (PWO) who said he would get it fixed. A few weeks later at a meeting with other work center personnel, the Admiral was again asked if he could get the lot repaired. When queried, the PWO reported he had already repaired the holes, but would do so again. After this sequence cycled five times, Admiral Delaney and the PWO recognized they didn't understand the process confronting them. They were trying to solve the pot hole *problem:* the Admiral said fix the potholes and that is what the PWO did. Their behavior was driven by a reaction to symptoms rather than by a real understanding of what was wrong. Instead, their focus needed to have been on the parking *process,* collecting data and analyzing why the process had broken down. Had the command done so, analyzing the causes behind the sailor's complaints or the frequency of pothole repair, they would have discovered, amongst other things, that it was time to repave the entire lot. Not understanding one's processes can be expensive. And doubly so in this case, as the cost to repave the entire lot was only slightly more than responding to the repeat trouble calls.

The problem with being a problem-solver is that it has one operating in a reactive mode, where the objective is to recreate that which had existed. It is not the path to the future. It enables an environment overflowing with daily crises. It is burnout territory with the bodies of the least enduring littering the path to the present. Bottom line: When the problems aren't simple and the solutions aren't known, it is a dumb way to manage!

The better approach is captured in Dr. W. Edwards Deming's

Point Five: "Improve constantly and forever the system of production and service." Instead of the negative and reactive "solve problems," it is the positive and proactive approach of improving processes continuously. By adopting a systems perspective and working toward system stability and the reduction of system variation, one is able to predict and reduce or eliminate problems before they occur. It is a much better way to manage.

Continuous process improvement is not a new lesson, but it is a lesson which is sufficiently contrary to the routine practice of problem-solving that it merits repeating—often.

Lesson: People Don't Understand the Power in Data Analysis.

Hank Tobias is so busy fixing his boat problem, and fending off the anger of Captain Miceli, that he gives no consideration to the boat readiness process. "I'm too busy to collect data!" he is quick to say. "But Ensign," responds Chief Petty Officer Burnsville, Wainwright's Total Quality Coordinator, "how are we ever going to know how long it takes to start each boat engine if you don't have data?" Ensign Tobias listens blankly. Undaunted, Chief Burnsville continues, "Tomorrow, have the boat crew plot on a run chart how long it takes between their arriving at each boat and each boat reaching its operating temperature." Respectfully, the Chief then inquires, "How long does it take to plot a few data points, a second or two?" He continues, "Do that, and, in a couple of weeks, you'll have enough data to tell with predictability if starting the engine on time, every time, is a reasonable expectation. The data will also help you pinpoint if there is something wrong with the boat, or the boat readiness process." Ensign Tobias looked relieved. "That would certainly be useful information to pass on to the Captain," he said. Ensign Tobias' cooperation was assured when Chief Burnsville volunteered his direct assistance. "Ensign Tobias," he offered, "I'll be at the whale boat in the morning to give your crew a hand."

Understanding the reason why data varies provides the power in analyzed data. Take a coin and flip it. Flip it again, and again, and again. At what point in that process do you become suspicious of the coin when each flip results in a head? Six times? Seven times? The number isn't the issue. What is important is the use of data to indicate that things are not right, and the subsequent, "Why?" The data, the keeping track of the number of flips and the number of heads and tails, provide the rationale for decisions which follow. Such an approach is a much better and more informed manner on which to base decisions. It is also a much better and informed way to assess and improve one's processes.

Once it registers that significant variation is the enemy of good leadership and customer satisfaction, as it did with Ensign Tobias, gains follow quickly. The leader soon recognizes that reducing variation in processes is the avenue to continuous process improvement. Reduced variation means improved quality and productivity. It means less time and cost to have reports written, inventories provided, products completed, and customers serviced. It is the leader's tool for determining which worker is performing at a standard above or below other workers in the same process, and for deciding when and who merits recognition for superior performance or when and who needs help. It provides the rationale for when training should occur and who should receive it. It tells the leader when to intervene in a process and when to leave it alone.

Captain Miceli hasn't yet conditioned herself to routinely ask for data. When she does, and she will as her TQL understanding increases, she will see any unusual patterns in the data. Those insights will make her a better leader as she will better understand the nature of the ship's processes.

Lesson: Fear of Math Gets in the Way

Fear manifests itself in other ways as well. If I'm the Commanding Officer and I say to my department heads that I want everyone to wear purple bandannas tomorrow, that order will get carried out. In today's Navy I'll be questioned as to why (as well I should) but, ultimately, if that is my desire, I can make it happen. But if I say to my department heads that I want them to start collecting and analyzing data on one of their critical processes, my success rate will be much lower. Why? A multitude of reasons certainly; but central among them is a fear of numbers (from simple measuring, to data compilation, to number crunching). It is a built-in resistance to things mathematical. What a shame our education system doesn't instill glee for what numbers can tell us.

To eliminate fear of mathematics, an organization must demystify the data affecting its processes. That requires a culture which sees data as a component of decision making. It takes training and practice to build math knowledge and confidence.

The requisite training and practice do not have to be extensive nor expensive. For the sailor, it is elementary data collection and analysis—a tick mark in a box or a point plotted on a chart, for example. It has to be relevant, participative, and thought-provoking. It needs to be provided just-in-time, and include discussion as to why one collects data—why you are measuring what, and the nature of systems and processes. It needs to include lots of opportunities to actually play with numbers. To stay focused on driving out fear, the training also needs to be based on the underlying principle of "knowledge is confidence." Confident people have less reason to be fearful.

Getting the sailor to use the newly acquired statistical training remains a challenge. One successful approach has been to identify a simple process important to the sailor for which data already exist or are easily collected, ensure that the process boundaries are clearly defined, and task the sailor to flow chart it. Typically, these efforts build ownership, and the application of statistical techniques is the obvious next step.

Lesson: Learning is a Natural Process.

I'm a Navy-trained diver. I was in a 500,000 gallon swimming pool recently, recertifying my diver qualification. At one end of the pool were initial diver trainees undergoing pool harassment. This is underwater confidence-building training where an instructor snorkels down from the surface and pulls off the trainees mask and/or mouthpiece. These are safe evolutions which train the novice in what to do when such an event occurs during an actual operation.

At the other end of the pool were trained and experienced mine clearance divers who were being trained in one of the Navy's latest mixed gas SCUBAs. They were responding to directions written by an instructor on a slate to describe equipment failure conditions. At one point the instructor, who was wearing an air filled SCUBA, voluntarily removed his mouthpiece because his air bubbles were hindering his ability to see what he was writing. After writing the message, he replaced the mouthpiece. His next action was to raise his face mask to allow rising air bubbles to force out the water which had collected inside the mask. For the instructor, removal of his mouthpiece and mask were routine.

Observing from the pool bottom, I was struck by the contrast between the trainee and the already-trained, and learned again that transition from one to the other was a natural progression. It is like learning to hit a ball, ride a bicycle, or become a Naval officer. If one gets proper training—formal or informal—and practices sufficiently, learning is the natural consequence.

The Navy has learned this lesson reasonably well in its technical courses. From pipe fitter to aircraft mechanic to sonar technician, schools are provided throughout one's career. Where appropriate, the training occurs both in the classroom and practice area. Once a sailor reports aboard a command, the better supervisors maintain the momentum of a learning environment.

The Navy is changing its approach to leadership training. It intends to implement formal leadership training at critical points in a sailor's career. Instead of a single course in leadership fundamentals, it will provide a leadership continuum over a sailor's career which matches leadership knowledge and practice to anticipated leadership requirements.

The difficulty in providing leadership training manifests itself in practice as the increasing discomfort associated with leading people up Maslow's Hierarchy of Needs. Naval personnel are not specifically trained to do that. Intuitively, the leadership understands the necessity of satisfying the individuals physiological and safety requirements. They are fairly obvious and can be accomplished with programs and money. Hence, the Navy provides acceptable working and living conditions both afloat and ashore. But programs that facilitate increased belonging, esteem, and self-actualization are not so easy to conceptualize, or orchestrate, and the Navy doesn't do them so well. Nonetheless, learning is a natural process, and leadership practices need to be taught. If the Navy were to emphasize what it means to lead up Maslow's hierarchy in its leadership training, the quality of leadership would get even better.

Integration of Authoritarians, TQL, and Learning Organizations

A dichotomy exists between the Navy's fundamental business—fighting wars—and its evolution through TQL to being a learning organization. To fight wars the Navy needs authoritarian leaders, trained and practiced in making life-threatening and life-saving decisions. The heat of battle is no time for ambiguity or "group think." It is a time for clear-cut authority and decisive action.

Nonetheless, the Navy spends most of its time preparing for

war, not actually fighting in one. That fact has provided ample rationale for the Navy to honor less authoritarian leadership styles, and support the implementation of TQL. Over time, the Navy's culture should evolve to a workable blend of war fighting leadership, and TQL.

That workable blend includes authoritarian leaders who develop the strategic plan, define the operational environment, and tell subordinates what to do. Desired learning is defined by the organization. Hence, the Navy goes to sea in ships, sailors do the jobs they are assigned, and professional training is the hallmark of learning.

What is important in a learning organization is learning. It begins with the individual, and multiplies with the team. As individual team members learn to develop vision, values and mental models which they share in common, they become better able to harness their collective wisdom. As they bring their expanded understanding of themselves and the team to the organization, they become better able to actualize the organization's future. There is a place in the Navy for both approaches.

There is a Genie in the Dialogue Lamp

I am reminded of an experience as a junior officer sitting around a table in Puerto Rico discussing the hull design of diving boats we were evaluating. I now recognize that what made it an extraordinary and productive event was our operating as a learning organization. We had a common purpose, feelings of community, shared vision and values, and a willingness to suppress egos and suspend personal and professional assumptions. Each person brought competencies and mutual respect to the table. It was a time for the sharing of ideas and opinions. It was not a time for seniority or the convincing of others. What was right worked its way to the forefront, in a natural and easy-flowing manner, as ideas were offered and developed. The boat which resulted from that evening led to a replacement craft which was used for years by the bomb disposal community as its principal diving boat. It is still widely used by the Navy in a variety of applications.

What went on around that table was team learning. The boat which resulted was more than anyone of us alone could have developed. What happened in that "learning organization" was a generative conversation—a dialogue—in which we had connected at a level far deeper than usual. Operating at that level, where the "noise" of the typical conversation wasn't a factor, productivity just happened. It is this spontaneous interlocking of ideas which is the magic of dialogue, and a key to successful learning organizations.

There is a genie in the dialogue lamp. We just have to figure out how to let him or her out. For the Navy, it is going to take recognition that generative conversations happen among sailors working in teams, under circumstances where such dialogue is part of the normal course of business. Acquiring that increased understanding will demand continued questioning of the assumptions which call for authoritarian leadership, and greater clarity about when authoritarian leadership is the appropriate style. The leader testing assumptions might ask, "When is fear an acceptable form of leadership?" or "When does collaborative leadership get in the way?" or "When is the leader's vision more important than customer needs?" Obtaining *the* correct answers to these questions is not the reason for asking them. It is to create opportunities for dialogue, which will, in turn, create other questions and more dialogue opportunities. Suspend enough assumptions, and ask enough questions, and the genie will be let out of the lamp.

Apply dialoguing teams to a command where sailors and teams are valued as process and system components, and the value of each worker to the organization becomes clearer. With that orientation, the individual becomes a knowledge asset worthy of continued optimizing investment on all fronts. Allowing for its authoritarian needs, the Navy is evolving its way to that orientation, one individual, one command at a time.

Not Likely; Not Fully; Not Anytime Soon

I think it is highly unlikely and mission-defeating for the Navy to ever fully become a learning organization. War fighting is the height of competition. It is about winning and losing. It is about death and destruction. These are not learning organization ingredients. In addition, the Navy's authoritarian leaders, both senior and junior, are successful because they have been good problem solvers; not necessarily because they advocate dialogue, empowerment or continuous process improvement. To deliberately cast off the old approach and head off with a new, uncertain one is filled with career threatening risk and the pain of change.

Most won't venture forth without leadership at the forefront, and, at present, such leaders are still too few.

But TQL is the Navy's chosen direction, and the Navy is good at staying on the chosen course. Also, gains are continually being made. At some point down this path, sailors will be operating as knowledge workers and dialoguing team members. They will be honored as central to the Navy's success as a system. Such words may sound a lot like an operating learning organization, but don't be fooled. When TQL has blossomed almost everywhere within the Navy, there, on the high seas, will be the authoritarian leader the nation needs to defeat the enemy.

Alan K. Graham, PhD, is a Principal at Product Development Consulting, Inc. of Cambridge, Mass., which assists corporations in rapid improvement in new product development. Graham is a senior member of the IEEE, and has served on the board of directors of the Massachusetts Council for Quality, which administers the Armand V. Feigenbaum Massachusetts Quality Award.

Previously Dr. Graham was Director of Operations for the Center for Quality Management (CQM), a consortium he helped found of high-technology corporations that collaborate on quality improvement efforts. He implemented the CQM's well-regarded Six-Day TQM course for senior executives. Dr. Graham has also been an independent consultant, and a research staff and faculty member at MIT in System Dynamics.

Dr. Graham's publications include *A New American TQM: Four Practical Revolutions in Management* (co-authored). He has consulted to Pugh-Roberts Associates, Bose Corporation, Analog Devices, Cummins Engine, Booz-Allen, the Institute for Defense Analysis, and Apple Computer.

He has a BS, MS and a PhD in Electrical Engineering and Computer Science from MIT.

29

Organizational Learning: Medical Metaphor and Corporate Practice

Alan K. Graham

Organizational learning as a concept in business management circles has enjoyed unusual longevity. This longevity may in part come from the difficulty companies have in defining or implementing it. Therefore, few or no companies are able to debunk it as a failed fad! Herein lies a marvelous opportunity to use the concept in an un-fadlike way.

I plan to use the organizational learning concept purely as a metaphor, which sheds some light on a case study of successful corporate "learning." The case focuses on an area where organizational learning of any kind has traditionally been extraordinarily difficult to achieve: Research and Development (R&D), specifically new product development. As an added bonus, the metaphor offers a resolution to the perpetual battle between two arch rivals—the proponents of standardization and the protectors of creativity.

An Enduring Metaphor

The parallels between individuals and organizations have been built into the English language for centuries. We speak of organizations, that is, of entities created by becoming *organ-ized*, i.e., acting like *organs* in the body, forming linkages and relationships to make the whole *organism* productive. The metaphor was fruitful for Thomas Hobbes as far back as 1651 in *Leviathan*, where he analyzes the functions of government in terms of an artificial being.

In the 1970s, Russel Ackoff, in his book, *Creating the Corporate Future: Plan or be Planned*, used biological metaphors extensively to tell corporations how to create systems to adapt proactively to changing circumstances. Peter Senge, in *The Fifth Discipline*, and others also have recently revived the metaphor, examining explicitly the structures that create behaviors and introducing the concept of a corporate learning disability. By the time of Ackoff and Senge, management scientists had not only the power of verbal analogy, but of mathematical models to understand how complex systems, including biological organisms, respond dynamically to their environment. Part of that mathematical infrastructure is the field of System Dynamics, a field in which I practiced and published for many years. This field gave rise to what is now known popularly as systems thinking, which can be thought of as one means of enhancing organizational learning.

The discussions of organizational learning are now being augmented by Total Quality Management (TQM) viewpoints. TQM can be thought of as a body of empirically-validated practices for institutionalizing company-wide improvement activities, both evolutionary and revolutionary. As such, TQM probably offers the richest collection of documented examples of real corporate organizational learning. For example, David Garvin's "Building a Learning Organization" in *Harvard Business Review* gives a very high-altitude survey of what the practice of organizational learning looks like. The book I co-authored with Shiba and Walden, *A New American TQM*, describes a generic architecture for corporate learning systems, albeit largely in TQM terms. By contrast, this essay uses fewer specialized terms to detail a narrow slice of both the metaphor and the corporate practices to which the metaphor corresponds. All of the tools and practices described here, however, are detailed in *A New American TQM*.

To make the journey from organizational learning as a metaphor to actual practice, we begin with the most basic question: What is it that is being learned in organizational learning?

What Is Being Learned?

Individuals learn both knowledge and skills. A person acquires knowledge and can present facts based on that knowledge, or acquires skills and can perform those skills. The difference between knowledge and skills is the difference between art history and art. Knowledge is talking the talk; skill is walking the talk.

By contrast, most corporations need only aim at learning and using skills—to acquire the ability to perform processes such as creating and delivering products. So how can we distinguish between an *organization* learning a skill, in contrast to a few of the *people* within it having learned that skill?

There is a continuing tension between a focus on individual learning skills and organizational learning skills embedded in the structure of business processes. For an example in this book, contrast the "individual-centric" exposition in Jayme Rolls' "The Transformational Leader" (see page 101) and the "system-centric" exposition in David Schwandt's essay (see page 365).

One distinguishing test is a thought experiment that might be called the "missing persons test." Imagine replacing people in an organization with others who are equally competent, but ignorant of how the organization works. Then assess the level of skill in the execution of corporation tasks. Does the "basic physiology" (the analogs of digestion and metabolism) still work? Is production running smoothly? Are orders being filled? Will the "analysis skills," such as perceiving new markets, creating new products, and deploying new organizational forms, remain intact?

This experiment implies that long-term memory of needed skills rests not with individuals, but with explicit and implicit business processes (including the processes that hire the individuals and their skills). These processes include reporting patterns in the organizational chart, formulas for budgeting, programs and practices that acquire and maintain skills, and procedures defined either on paper or implicitly on computer systems. The fundamental medium of organizational memory—skill retention—is business processes.

If organizational memory lies in business processes, what are the individual learning disabilities that correspond to corporate difficulties? I would suggest (1) poor study habits and (2) impairment of long-term memory. (Robert Dilworth, in effect, identifies this same pair of issues in his "The DNA of the Learning Organization" on page 243)

We probably all remember from high school being urged to study with the television off, pre-read material, take notes while reading, and outline before writing. So most of us can understand being disorganized or being ignorant of tools that help in understanding and digesting information. We also probably recollect examples from corporate life of fact-gathering performed with inconsistent thoroughness and improvised, ad hoc methods.

But the second disability, impairment of long-term memory function, is probably less familiar and requires more background.

Corporate Confabulation

There is a neurological impairment known as Korsakov's Syndrome, in which long-term memories suddenly disappear. Its victims retain full cognitive and expressive abilities, but are not only unable to form new long-term memories, but lose some or all of their previously-accumulated memories.

Neurologist Oliver Sacks, in *The Man Who Mistook His Wife for a Hat, and Other Clinical Tales,* has detailed his observations of one patient with Korsakov's Syndrome—a forty-year-old man with long term memory only through the age of 21. Though 21 in spirit and memory, the individual wakes each morning in the body of a man twice his remembered age, bewildered and terrified.

Corporate analogs to Korsakov's Syndrome spring to mind. There are corporations in which every business cycle downturn is the end of the world, and if heads roll and some people's jobs are sacrificed (often including the President's), all will be well again. This happens every three to five years during business cycle downturns; this has been called the "Bum-Hero Cycle." Behavior is very much different in those companies that have formed "long-term memory" embedded in an effective business planning system that accommodates to the uncertainties of the economy.

Some patients afflicted with Korsakov's Syndrome constantly lurch from one identity to the next, improvising identities and explanations as they go along. The clinical term is "confabulation"—making up and believing stories or "fables" about who they are and what they're doing.

Corporations confabulate during management-by-crisis and management-by-fad, continually changing organizational identity and purpose. For instance, such "loss of memory and identity" often strikes companies that reorganize their sales force. Suddenly, neither customers nor the sales force knows how to get things done efficiently, and both lurch through one improvisation after another.

A less extreme example of impaired long-term memory formation is the analog of students who cram for an exam the night before, pass the test but then soon forget the material. Companies will enroll workers in a one-shot training program. For a time, the individual may behave differently due to the training. But there are the pressures of everyday business to contend with, and people just forget the skill over time, or they will often move on to tasks or jobs that no longer call for those skills. The ability to behave differently goes away; the long-term memories were never formed.

At this point, we have traveled from the overall metaphor of "organizational learning" to two specific "syndromes": poor study habits and difficulties with long-term memory to specific corporate behavioral problems. We are now ready to see how one company avoided these difficulties and enhanced its skills as "a learning organization." The case holds a particular interest because the process and methods were completely explicit, known, and reproducible.

The Medrad Story

Medrad is the dominant maker of automated vascular injection systems and related products for various types of medical imaging (X-rays, CAT scans, and magnetic resonance). To enhance image quality, doctors inject the patient with radioopaque liquids; Medrad products let medical technicians do that in a very controlled way. Between the spring of 1989 and the spring of 1994, this $70 million company has increased revenues 15% per year and profits 38% per year. Part of this success is due to Medrad's Quality for Life (QFL) program, a TQM-style initiative involving problem solving and quality improvement methods modeled after Xerox's processes, and strong programs to encourage individual employee involvement through suggesting new ideas and participating in Quality Improvement Teams (QITs).

To accelerate improvement in new product development,

Medrad formed a cross-functional steering committee, with leadership through participation of three vice presidents (Committee chair Ken Grob, Executive Vice President, Operations; Joe Havrilla, Vice President, R&D; and John Friel, Executive Vice President, Sales and Marketing), with guidance from Product Development Consulting (myself and John Carter). The committee worked toward four goals that had been defined at the corporate level: cycle time, quality, new product investment productivity, and predictability. They worked as a group three to four days per month during the six months or so of the most intensive effort, which began in the Spring of 1992.

They undertook a systematic diagnosis of weaknesses in new product development. In addition to more usual types of data collection, product development teams were tasked to reflect on the history of a completed project to identify very specific instances of weakness and their root causes.

What was the steering committee to do with this detailed information? Rather than rely solely on reports written by the teams or the consultants, the steering committee devised an integrated method to analyze and act on the project histories.

Interlocking Teams

We didn't know it at the time, but what the steering committee did is exactly what Ackoff advocates for his system of *interactive management*. Fundamentally, we arranged participation on the various teams so that the membership overlapped. Figure 1 illustrates.

The steering committee selected the projects to be analyzed partly on the basis of whether members had direct contact with projects under consideration. When the teams formed to examine the project history, a steering committee member was on the team and attended the day-long session.

The transmission of factual information from the project history team to the steering committee took three forms: written presentation, oral presentation, and the presence of someone on the steering committee who had been through the whole analysis. So the committee as a group had very in-depth knowledge of the sample projects, as a result of the structure of interlocking teams.

After a process of synthesis and prioritization based on factual evidence, the steering committee arrived at a small number of improvement projects. A similar scheme was used to

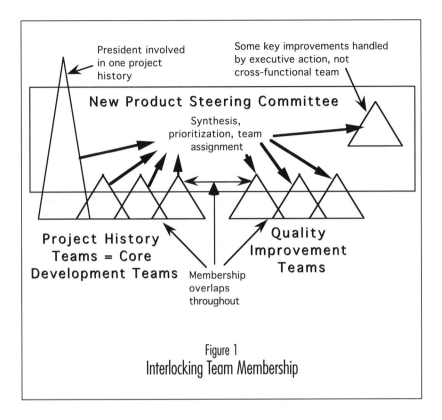

Figure 1
Interlocking Team Membership

enact those improvements. For the areas that were attacked by teams, each team contained at least one, and often two, members of the steering committee. (Some areas required only executive-level actions, which the executives on the steering committee followed through on, without the need to form further teams.) So newly chartered teams still started off with in-depth knowledge of the problem and best practices that address it, by virtue of interlocking membership with the steering committee.

In other words, Medrad used interlocking teams to make information transfer more reliable. This "good corporate study habit" is analogous to an individual making notes or working examples to make information transfer from text to mind more reliable.

As a second example of good corporate study habits, we return to a practice only briefly described before: gathering and analyzing data about product development projects.

Project Histories

Good students in a college science lab take complete notes, keep them all in a lab notebook, and tabulate the results to form fact-based conclusions. Likewise good corporate learners gather comprehensive evidence and follow a visible process to reach conclusions. One such process is the project history method.

The project history method represents a compromise between a broad view (which takes as inclusive a look as possible to seek out lurking problems) and an expedient approach (which tries to get at some kind of answer as quickly as possible). Rather than rely on extensive collection and analysis of one type of data, such as the root causes for engineering change orders, three separate sources of readily-available data are used. Figure 2 shows how Medrad collected and synthesized these three types of data.

One type of data, depicted along the bottom of Figure 2, came from functional organizations, such as marketing, engineering, and quality. The data included headcount (e.g., the number of design engineers), length of experience, use of standards for processes and tools (e.g., phase gate reviews and software repositories), and budget components (e.g., fraction of revenue spent on capital equipment for new product development). This data was compared to benchmark data that we provided as consultants.

The other two types of data came from an analysis of eight representative projects. Basic numerical information about each project (the second of the three data types) was collected (as shown along the left edge of Figure 2). These data included: (1) staffing over time by discipline; (2) complexity of the project measured by part count and lines of software code; (3) risk factors rated on a pre-defined scale; (4) planned versus actual financials, including total project cost, product sales, and product cost; (5) planned schedules versus actuals; and (6) priority given by management to the project.

The third type of data was verbal, descriptive information. The core members of each selected project's development team, including a steering committee member with relevant experience, spent a day together analyzing the project's history.

First, they detailed a timeline for the project, and for significant events did a "fishbone diagram" (also known as "cause-and-effect diagram" or "Ishikawa diagram"). This tool, one of the standard "Seven Quality Control Tools" standardized

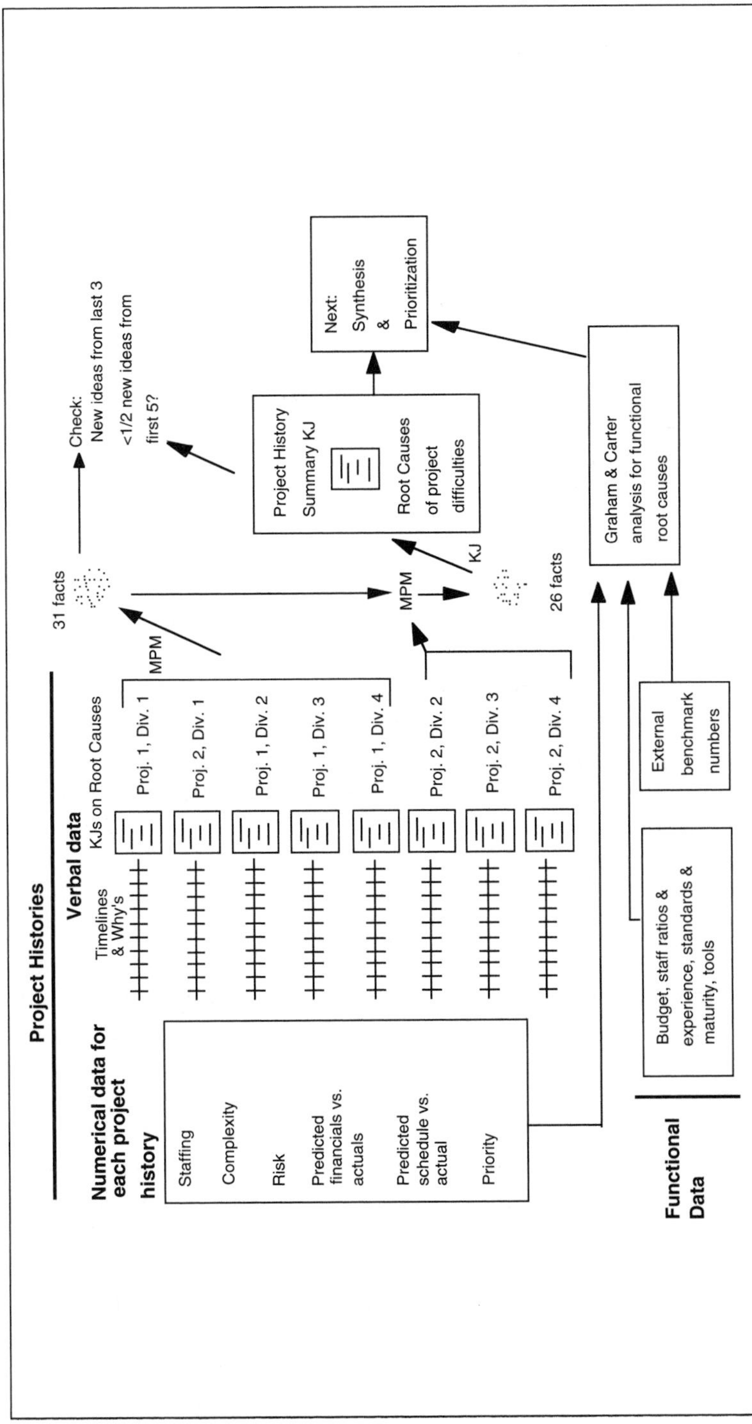

Figure 2   Project Histories

in Japan in the 1960s, has team members brainstorm causes of a condition, causes of those causes, and so on. The finished product looks somewhat like a fish skeleton. Then the team used the "KJ method" to draw a consensus conclusion from the fishbone diagrams. The KJ method is a variant of one of the "Seven Tools for Management and Planning" standardized in Japan in the 1980s. (KJ is named for its inventor, Japanese anthropologist Kawakita Jiro.) In contrast to brainstorming, the KJ method has numerous rules and criteria to guide a team through several steps. The team:

- Writes statements on Post-Its™ relevant to the problem at hand
- Assists the author of each statement in refining it to an unambiguous statement of verifiable fact
- Groups the facts to create a new conceptual framework
- Titles the groups to create concepts that have specific meaning for the team
- Prioritizes the concepts by cause-and-effect relation-ships and by vote

The KJ concluded each project history day.

Each project team presented the timeline, fishbone dia-grams and KJ diagrams of root causes to the steering committee, who then used a method called the "Multi-Pickup Method" (or MPM) to cull the common results from all of the projects. To synthesize the overall results, the steering committee used the KJ method.

The conclusions of the "KJ of KJs" were broad statements. But in contrast to the usual context in which such statements are made, there was a clear *audit trail* or *genealogy* from specific events, sometimes down to the meeting minutes on specific dates. Moreover, members of the steering committee had discussed all of the examples in detail with the teams during the project history sessions, so they knew the factual basis intimately.

We used a relations diagram—another of the seven tools for management and planning—a words-and-arrows diagram rather like causal loop diagrams drawn in systems thinking. The dia-gram showed cause and effect relationships among the various root causes. The diagram identified the causes likely to be the most fundamental "drivers," so that solving them would help with several other issues.

Then, the "Matrix Method" (yet another of the seven management and planning tools) was used repeatedly to prioritize the various possible root causes according to such criteria as alignment with overall corporate goals, commonalty among divisions, relative ease of improvement, and whether each was a causal driver of other problems. In using the matrix method, the team draws a large matrix on flip-chart paper, with the various problem areas down the left side and the criteria across the top (e.g. contribution to the corporate time-to-market goal, contribution to the corporate product quality goal, etc.). Then the team marches through each element of the matrix, ranking each problem (in rows) according to how critical it is to the criteria (in columns), stopping along the way to discuss initial differences of opinion. Finally, the team adds up a numerical score for each problem area, which guides ranking the overall importance and priorities of which problems to work on. The matrix method can be thought of as a form of discussion that organizes dialogue about each criterion applied to each alternative problem area.

The matrix enabled the steering committee to arrive at a consensus on the vital few problems that should be addressed. Finally, the committee plotted the root causes on a flow diagram of the product development process, to understand which problems were related and to avoid chartering teams with conflicting "territories." This was completed in the Fall of 1992.

With the "good study habits" described above, the Medrad steering committee had consensual, fact-based learnings on the handful of areas that could most use improving. From these followed several steps that are likewise good study habits: writing team charters and forming teams, doing detailed analysis of the areas, learning about best-in-class practices in those areas, and designing and testing solutions. What we will examine next is how Medrad incorporated the new practices into the institutional—"long-term"—memory of the corporation.

Forming Long-Term Memories: Making Improvements Permanent

What follows is a relatively high-level description of the changes Medrad made to make the improvements permanent. Remember that they arose not from a long laundry list of interesting changes to make, but from a handful of initiatives aimed at a few business processes. There are many changes because the teams needed to make several changes to really institutionalize doing the right thing in these few areas. The areas were:

> **Product definition.** Using knowledge of best-in-class practices, one Quality Improvement Team set out to define an explicit process for product definition that has become an extension of the overall product development process. They chose four tools for collecting information about customers and markets and acquired the necessary training sources. They instituted a system of tracking and reporting customer contacts conducted for the purpose of product definition, so that managers can see how much real contact and intimate knowledge lies behind a product definition. As of this writing in early Spring 1994, the new product definition process is being used extensively on products now starting development, and the team is finalizing the manual and training materials.

> **Product development process.** Another Quality Improvement Team undertook to streamline the product development process, focusing on making *phase gate reviews* and sign-offs add value and occur earlier in the development process. Phase gate reviews ensure that all the project's "ducks are in a row:" that resources and schedule are appropriate to the technological task, product features are in line with demonstrated market need, etc. They are cross-functional reviews by upper management. Dr. Ken Grob, the new product steering committee chair, says "The early reviews have been especially effective in getting management commitment and empowering teams during the subsequent stages."

> One important aspect of working on the product development process, almost a "tail wagging the dog," was initiating the widespread use of a best-in-class engineering practice, *design reviews.* Design reviews are examinations of technical matters by technical experts. Their purpose is to anticipate and reduce technological difficulties in development. As part of phase reviews, executives see that design reviews happen as scheduled.

> **Project leadership.** Steering multiple product development projects involves interactions among (1) project management (to manage resources, activities, and

schedules), (2) the product marketing that defines the product during initial development (sometimes called *in-bound marketing*), and (3) the product marketing that creates the materials and campaign to be used by the sales force (sometimes called *out-bound marketing*) Based on benchmark data, knowledge of best-in-class practices, and several specific issues, Medrad executives reorganized in a way that clarified these three roles and functions. This was not the common "if there's a problem with the way people interact, reorganize 'em." Such reorganizing without thorough benchmarking and analysis usually substitutes one set of problems for another. One group wins and another loses. By contrast, Medrad's actions were highly focused, fact-based, and consensual. Broadly, the changes were win-win. According to Grob, the steering committee chair, "The moves worked out well, and the individuals involved generally were supportive, because we were addressing their problems and frustrations."

Project management. A team standardized beefed-up project management practices and selected a standard training and standard tools. All project managers take the same three-day course. The team chose computer packages (and training sources) for work-breakdown structuring and project timeline tracking, whose use is now an expected part of managing a development project. A separate effort created a system to track time and expenses by project and report those to project managers, both for project tracking, and for realistically scoping future projects. Medrad also hired a full-time person to support project managers with project scheduling and tracking. Finally, Medrad implemented several changes to streamline their configuration management system.

"Good study habits." The New Product Steering Committee has gone on to use similar learning practices to tackle new issues. Chairman Grob says "we laid an excellent foundation and, as a result, we can continue to go after still more improvements." Moreover, similar practices have expanded beyond the steering committee. KJ diagrams and relations diagrams are used "all the time," according to Grob. A more standardized version of the overall process, known as hoshin planning or policy deployment, is now being taught widely in the company.

Hoshin is known additionally as management by policy and hoshin kanri. It is standardized throughout a whole company, so that multiple hierarchical levels and multiple functions can conceive of and execute improvements, often breakthrough improvements, simultaneously. The standardized practices incorporated in hoshin planning include several that were used by the steering committee and the Quality Improvement Teams, but were only alluded to here, including explicit goals for both intermediate and "bottom line" metrics, data analysis, deployment of goals through multiple layers of hierarchy, and explicitly planning and agreeing on the means of achieving the goals, to name a few.

These changes pass the "missing person test": If a new person were to be inserted into the company, there are that many more standard training programs, written procedures, standard forms, and automated tools to let a new person do the job well. This standardization leverages the effort put into the study and resultant changes (see Mary Byrd's essay on page 477).

Conclusion

Executives and engineers often express an aversion to standardizing creative processes such as product development. Yet the organizational learning metaphor has told us that standardization is not only good but probably necessary. Learning (increasing the capability for constructive action) consists of both studying and remembering. Studying without remembering the lessons is useless.

If we remember that all of Medrad's changes in standard operating procedure were systematically aimed at important sources of difficulties, it seems apparent that the changes should make life easier for the "standardizees." The fun part of being involved in product development is creating new and useful things. The non-fun part is misunderstandings, late changes to product specifications causing re-doing of existing work, uncertainty and unpredictability, conflicts among people, and conflicts over resourcing, to name a few. These are the issues that the new standards addressed.

To put this issue into another context, let me use the organizational learning metaphor one last time. Making the transition to well-supported standardization within an organization corresponds to making the transition from conscious skill to unconscious skill within an individual.

Most of us can undertake carpentry or sewing, but only with a great deal of concentration and effort, needing to figure out each step and to check carefully as we go. We can't apply much imagination or do very complex tasks because we're still consciously controlling the basics, often haltingly. I have to worry about holding the nail correctly before I swing the hammer; it's all one motion to a practiced carpenter. A professional carpenter or tailor moves almost continuously, is more relaxed, and incorporates more complex techniques as a matter of course. That's because they've become unconsciously skilled at the basics. They've had the "mind-share" to work on acquiring more advanced skills.

A project manager without a standardized process and tools has to worry about the basics. (Where does the data come from? How do I draw conclusions from it? How do I sell this to my boss?) Often, such a project manager often will not gather all the relevant facts, may synthesize them inconsistently, and can have difficulty marshaling them effectively for presentation to executives. So the plans must be negotiated with management and reworked several times. Soon, everyone gets tired of rehashing the issues and the project either stops altogether or proceeds with a still-flawed plan.

A project manager in a company with standardized program plans, tools, and preparation process can come close to completing a plan in one pass that is acceptable to executives and feasible for developers. There is opportunity to tackle more advanced issues, like creating synergy with other product development programs. There is no need for the organization to pay attention to the basics of program planning. This is the organizational equivalent of an unconscious skill, where again there is "mind-share" to tackle more advanced skills.

As one engineering director at Apple Computer (a company known for its individualism and creativity) told me, "I really don't mind following a standardized development process. It's like an automatic pilot that keeps me from going into the obvious traps. So I get to focus on the more creative and challenging parts of the work."

A Japanese product development guru, Kiyoshi Uchimaru, states the case even more strongly, asserting that professionalism in engineering in many cases requires cessation of creativity. This makes sense; professionals do standard things in standard ways and focus their energy and creativity on the greatest challenges and the largest opportunities for improvement.

To return again to Medrad, not only are better practices being practiced, but they are becoming routine skills. The formal and informal training materials are increasingly available, and the practices are becoming firmly embedded in the business processes. Benchmark metrics have been developed for Medrad's New Products Process and standard reporting is now in place. Significant improvements are apparent in some areas, and others need more time, as is the case in any improvement process. In the words of Ken Grob, "We recently reviewed our progress and there's no doubt that the changes have stuck. We've been weaving the changes into the fabric of the organization, and going after more issues."

In terms of the organizational learning metaphor, Medrad has nearly internalized one very useful set of skills, and now has the "mind-share" to acquire even more capabilities.

Frank Hoffmann (left) is the director of learning and develop- ment at Rosenbluth International, a company recognized for having one of "the ten best training programs in America" in *The 100 Best Companies to Work For in America*. Hoffmann also serves as the director of Learning Frontiers, a special venture of Rosenbluth that provides customized training services and programs to outside organizations. In addition, Frank has served on the Board of Directors for the North Dakota University System Foundation as well as the Board of Governors for the Philadelphia High School Academies, and appears in Tony Buzan's training video entitled, *"If At First . . . Overcoming the Fear of Failure."*

Bill Withers (right) leads Rosenbluth International's Learning Frontiers team in the creation, customizing, and marketing of the firm's successful learning experiences to organizations around the world. He has developed successful train-the-trainer and professional development video leader's guides in South Africa, implemented customer service training in Russia, coordinated a nationwide TQM roll-out for a client in Canada, and designed needs analysis instruments for a multilingual client in Hong Kong. He has presented at the Association for Quality and Performance, Department of Labor Office of the New American Workplace, International Alliance for Learning, and Seton Hall University Graduate School.

30

Shared Values:
Nutrients for Learning

Frank Hoffmann and Bill Withers

Learning happens constantly and continuously, regardless of the setting or the circumstances, influencing every aspect of our lives. It is as difficult for human beings to turn off and on as breathing. Whether *consciously chosen*, like the information imparted in the seminars we attend; or *unconsciously absorbed*, like the TV commercials we can repeat verbatim—we are learning machines. Sometimes learning takes on a life of its own, bursting openly and happily out of control, spreading like wildfire. At other times learning is forced underground, where it becomes dark, secret, and destructive. Lunchroom conversations may tell more about the *real* lessons learned in some companies than a hundred formal meetings may ever reveal. Regardless of the *nature* of the learning, however, one thing is clear: where there are people, there is learning. It is that pervasive, and that inescapable.

Learning is an autonomous, uncontrollable function of our "human-ness." It just happens. The culture in which this learning occurs—the framework, atmosphere, environment, set of circumstances—is the compelling determinant of the type or quality of the learning. True generative learning is more than the blotting up of information. It is the processing, transformation, and application of that information. The context heavily influences the outcome.

This is especially true in the corporate environment, where corporate cultures play an integral role in the quality of learning. Thanks largely to popular business books such as Craig R. Hickman and Michael Silva's *Creating Excellence*, and Terrence E. Deal and Allan A. Kennedy's *Corporate Cultures*, the idea of a corporate culture was introduced to many companies in the 1980s. We learned that a company embodies its own special culture, which manifests itself both on the level of official policies and plans and on the "human" level of attitudes, leadership styles, etc.

The Power of the Culture

In the corporate world, the culture of a company—"The way we do things around here"—either supports and steers learning or it does not. The concept of the "learning organization" is easily absorbed into the business jargon, watered down, sloganized, and devalued. Many companies profess to be learning organizations, but upon closer scrutiny, they fall considerably short of that ideal. In these companies, the learning organization is in danger of becoming the latest "flavor of the month"—packaged and launched as a pet management program, hitting or missing based on an insurmountable number of human variables as seemingly out of our control as the weather.

How do we manage the unmanageable in the context of corporate culture? Peter Senge aphorizes, "Don't push growth: remove the factors limiting growth." This speaks to all of us who have said (or at least thought at one time), "If they would just get out of my hair, I could figure this out myself."

A culture which minimizes fear and breeds innovation and the excitement that comes from shared ambition is what is needed for learning to flourish. Unfortunately, the culture at large rarely provides this atmosphere. Our educational system was originally designed, in part, to promote conformity, and often seems to stifle creativity. As working adults, most of us plunge to the bottom rung of Maslow's hierarchy every Monday morning at 9:00 A.M. For companies and employees alike, survival and competition routinely take precedence in most work places, and short-term thinking unfortunately takes over.

We must, then, mold culture where we can, within our respective spheres of influence, within the organizations which we create. Try as we might to control what, when, how, and why people learn, each individual's response will be different from the next, and may not reflect our intentions at all. In fact, the culture we create will spin its own web of interrelationships which will reach well beyond our "target audience". The medium is indeed the message. And consistency is key.

A boy of about ten jostled a stranger in a crowded store. His mother—mortified—apologized to the stranger, took the boy firmly by the shoulders, pushed him backwards into his sister, and shouted, "No shoving!"

"Talk about mixed messages," commented another shopper. But the message was really quite straightforward: "Those who can, shove."

How often is this story played out on the job? A mission statement touts opportunity in a company with a segregated board room. A corporate video preaches innovation in an organization that rewards conformity. The sign says, "Honesty is the best policy," but whistle-blowers see their lives and careers come apart at the seams.

In the final analysis, there are no "mixed messages." The culture will win every time.

Linear Learning

While most corporate executives would readily agree with the notion that learning, by its very nature, cannot be stopped, they would also move rapidly to put controls on the learning that takes place within their organizations. These controls dictate *who* needs to learn *what*, and often *when.* They take the form of a specific curriculum designed for each job title—courses that employees *must* take, and ones they *may not* take. They show up in the form of linear learning, a specific body of knowledge or set of skills imparted by one individual (a trainer or leader) to another. Linear learning is the unavoidable product of a culture that values control and places clear accountability (in the performance appraisal process) on leaders at every level for their employees' productivity, but not for their professional growth. It is also one of the unfortunate by-products of a culture that places significant value on "doing it right the first time." Of course, like the hidden message that accompanied "No shoving!", the controls themselves teach *other* lessons that will last far longer than the knowledge poured into employees in a traditional classroom.

Learning can and should be *the* most dynamic and exciting process taking place in organizations every day. We are not, however, advocating totally uncontrolled learning. *We ARE strongly advocating an environment that guides and encourages learning through the shared values defined by the organization.* Beyond the job skill training necessary for satisfactory performance, a strong corporate culture can provide all of the direction an organization needs to place on learning, *without the danger of predetermining the specific lessons that will be learned.*

A learning-friendly culture can open doors to unlimited learning while providing guidance for the application of lessons learned. For instance, a group of people united by the strongly-held belief that "honesty and integrity" are the foundation upon which all client interactions are based will routinely apply new skills and knowledge in ways that are consistent with that belief. In most companies, however, the sheer unpredictability of dynamic, unlimited learning throughout the organization is threatening to senior leaders who are disinclined to relinquish control and direct their focus away from the company's core objective of making money. In today's competitive marketplace, where a company's energies and resources are frequently consumed by efforts to simply survive, creating and nurturing a learning environment tends to be far down on the priority list.

The Rosenbluth Culture

Rosenbluth International is a company noted for, among other things, a strong corporate culture that emphatically places people first. In fact, *The Customer Comes Second* is the title CEO Hal Rosenbluth chose for a book he co-authored, describing the company's unusual approach to conducting business and his strongly-held belief that organizations have far too great (and, usually, far too negative) an impact on the quality of their employees' lives. He further believes that companies "owe" their employees the opportunity to grow, develop, and work toward both personal and professional goals. For this to be possible, a learning-rich environment is essential.

During the last ten years, senior leadership has taken large and daring strides aimed at making the creation of a "learning organization" one of their core objectives. Not coincidentally, the company has—during that same time span -grown from a 400-employee, eastern Pennsylvania travel agency to a 3,100-associate international provider of corporate and leisure travel services and technology, meeting services, and training programs. The company's astounding growth has been closely paralleled by the evolution of the company's training department. As the emerging culture was identified and embraced by company employees in the early 1980s, the training department accepted the added role of training all employees how to best serve *one another*, as well as how to best serve the client. In 1990, the company began to adapt the concepts of Total Quality Management for the service industry, in addition to the training programs it had previously instituted. Every employee—numbering over 2,000 at the time and now referred to as "associates"—attended mandatory classes in statistical process control and process improvement. Associates formed into natural work teams with peer advisors trained in quality techniques. Managers and supervisors—re-named "leaders" in official parlance—attended a pre-requisite one-day workshop called "Leadership at Rosenbluth" before registering in regularly-offered skill-based courses in subjects such as "Listening Skills" and "Time Management." This introductory session focused on a culturally-consistent leadership philosophy and stressed the need for compatible values in one's personal and professional lives.

Cultural Signals

Every lasting culture, whether familial, ethnic, religious, national, corporate, or what have you, is involved in the ongoing creation and evolution of "cultural signals." These signals are a means of group identification, communication, education, and reassurance. They allow group members to feel "safe at home" and contribute to interpersonal understanding and intergenerational continuity. Every corporate culture has signals. Some are more subtle than others. Communication styles, attitudes about work/family conflict, and work ethic are all "unofficial" but widely accepted signals. Others are more overt: slogans, mission statements, perks, and policies, for example.

At their most enduring, these signals take the form of symbols and rituals. One such "corporate ritual" that surfaced at Rosenbluth during its period of rapid growth is "Live the Spirit" orientation. Every new-hire flies to world headquarters for two days of "culture orientation" during which they are challenged to personally contribute to the further development of company culture. They are served high tea by CEO Hal Rosenbluth or another member of the senior leadership team as a symbol of our commitment to serve and support every member of the team. In small groups of twenty to twenty-five, the new associates are then invited to participate in an open discussion of their expectations and apprehensions and to ask Hal any questions they have about the company. This has also become a time for "tribal story-telling," when associates from around the company share stories of exceptional service, best practices, individual successes, and favorite experiences. As these stories are absorbed into the common experience, the culture and the company's ability to act and react as a cohesive unit are strengthened.

These early efforts were tremendously successful in pro-moting a culturally-consistent approach to every process and policy within Rosenbluth. Hiring and promotion practices, training programs, compensation programs, and the application of quality management tools were re-designed to both reflect and model the values and culture of the company. Job applicants were screened not only for skill sets and experience, but for "fit", often being interviewed by teams of their prospective peers. Associates were encouraged to share new ideas and to make their errors public so that others could avoid them. Classes were held in innovative thinking and teamwork. Training was designed for interaction and required the contributions of all participants. Leaders were no longer rated for productivity alone, but for their effectiveness as cultural role models.

From day-to-day examples, associates saw that leadership was committed to living and working according to certain core values: people focus, service, trust, teamwork, growth, excel-lence, sharing, and social responsibility. These values cut across social, ethnic, national, religious, and gender lines. As a result, a strong, supple work force with a positive view of its own potential began to emerge.

A Culture of Individual Responsibility

This centralized capturing, monitoring, and advancement of corporate culture has been the key to Rosenbluth's resilience and growth. It was also creating a dependency on the company to provide the initiative and direction for individual and team learning. As the culture moved inexorably in the direction of uncontrolled learning, it became more and more obvious that what had made it so wildly successful in the past had to change for it to move forward. Responsibility for learning had to be accepted by each individual associate if the organization was to create a learning organization environment. It had to let go of centralized control.

Corporate emphasis was shifted to providing multiple avenues for individual and collaborative learning, at increasingly accelerated rates of speed. Controls—other than those defined by shared values—would only stifle and redirect learning in ways that could ultimately prove fatal to the company. Management began to focus its energies on setting the cultural stage for "warp speed learning."

In January of 1993, Rosenbluth's training programs were listed among "the top ten in America" by Robert Levering and Milton Moskowitz in their book, *The 100 Best Companies To Work For In America*. Yet by April of that year, the training department chose to completely reconfigure itself into a centralized learning resource called "Learning and Development." Its new role was to spearhead a learner-driven philosophy of associate development, as opposed to the traditional company-driven training. This represented a fundamental change in attitude about corporate trainers—from "deliverers of training" to "learning consultants" (a new job title within the department). These individuals now help leaders at the business unit level determine how learning can be built into the daily functioning of their office or team. Human Resource consultants work with the learning consultants to prepare leaders for the implementation of 360-degree reviews: evaluations of each associate by peers, leaders, clients, and those who report to them. Fueled by this feedback, every associate then prepares an Individual Development Plan that guides them as they enhance their ability to support the achievement of the company's strategic objectives.

All of these successful learner-based programs are rooted in the organization's most basic values. For learning to flower and grow, the cultural soil must be prepared with at least four key nutrients: (1) trust and the reduction of fear, (2) teamwork and sharing, (3) leaders as champions of people and their ideas, and (4) the encouragement of constant change.

In studies conducted on leadership values or traits, writers such as James M. Kouzes and Barry Z. Posner in their 1993 book, *Credibility*, have found that integrity comes up consistently as the most desired one. People desperately want to trust their leaders. Career advancement opportunities, pay increases, and job security are most influenced by leaders' appraisals. Because the trust we have in the organization is most influenced by the trust we have in our bosses, leaders *must* understand that mistakes will result when we try new skills. The greater the stretch from our current job or our present set of skills, the greater the chance of error *and* the greater the opportunity for learning to take place! If a company's culture has rewarded mistake-free performance and frowned on those who stumble along the way, the degree of risk-taking necessary for warp-speed learning will be next to impossible. The reason: lack of trust in the organization to support the human-ness of making mistakes along the way.

Nutrients for Learning

For a learning organization to take root and grow, it must stop holding people accountable for mistake-free performance, and begin holding them accountable for learning from their mistakes.

There's a huge difference between these two approaches to performance management. The first approach encourages employees to take small, conservative steps and cover up the mistakes made "in practice." The learning organization approach encourages not only the making of mistakes but the *sharing* of them for the benefit of the organization. The key is in putting a clearly visible "safety net" in place and allowing everyone to see it work. This safety net can take the form of clear parameters for risk-taking and decision-making or in "real-life learning laboratories" that allow employees to try on new behaviors in a safe environment (see Daniel Kim's essay on page 351). At Rosenbluth, newly-trained reservation agents take their first "live" calls from clients in a controlled environment known as a Transition Learning Center. Here, they are supported by several coaches who provide immediate help and feedback. This learning safety net must ultimately be embedded in the very foundation of the organization—accepted as "something that is done around here" and safeguarded by every single employee.

The key to culture strength is consistency, and the key to consistency is having *everyone* "on board," sharing in the responsibility for the culture's health. This sense of teamwork and sharing is the second key nutrient in the growth and maintenance of a learning organization. Sharing the lessons we learn from the mistakes we make requires not only trust but a strong sense of teamwork and a belief that *"I benefit when my colleagues continue to grow and develop as well."* When the culture of an organization rewards individual performance only (or even primarily), it promotes a "survival of the fittest" mentality and sends a message to everyone that sharing can hurt your career. Internal competitions between individuals, offices, teams, divisions—no matter how friendly—send this same subtle message. Some companies have openly created a culture that rewards the individual genius of maverick contributors. But in so doing, these same organizations severely hamper their company's learning potential. We must build into the reward and recognition systems of our companies (and the succession planning systems as well) clear benefits to the individual for helping others succeed. Much like reducing the fear associated with making mistakes, this is no easy task—especially if it involves a 180-degree shift from a deeply entrenched corporate value. And then we need to deal with beliefs employees picked up previously—from other cultures in which they've been involved. After all, even our school districts have taught us to "do our own work and not look at others' papers."

Rosenbluth has identified *teamwork* as one of the core competencies that transcend all roles and levels of the company. In keeping with that, team incentives exist as well as individual compensation packages. These incentives are not competitive between groups; rather, they are set up against a standard that all groups can achieve. Buddy systems, "shadowing" programs, and mentoring relationships are both formally and informally arranged through Learning and Development. In addition, "best practices" are shared as a standard portion of general manager meetings and are communicated regularly through the learning consultants and their human resources counterparts.

The third culture nutrient critical to the creation and maintenance of a learning organization is the role and behavior of our leaders as champions of people. This begins with: (1) clearly defining the role of a leader, (2) communicating the requirements of that role to employees whose future aspirations may include leadership positions, (3) implementing succession planning and performance appraisal systems that are *consistent* with the values defined, and (4) eliminating misconceptions that employees may have about a leader's role. Leaders in a learning-rich environment must take less and less control, make fewer of the decisions that need to be made, and effectively alter their role

Traditional Training	Learning Organization
Teaching content	Learning processes
Classroom-focused	Workplace-focused
Teacher-centered	Learner-centered
"Belongs to" training department	"Belongs to" each associate
Activity-centered	Outcome-based
Training Specialist	Learning Consultants

Figure 1
Traditional Training vs. Learning Organization

from that of the "All Knowing One" to "Group Learning Facilitator." This change in role requires a completely different mindset and an entirely different set of skills (see Figure 1). It requires a very different approach to the preparation of future leaders and in the selection criteria and recruitment process for each and every employee, especially if the culture values "promotion from within." Reward systems must be built around leaders' abilities to build learning networks and promote the mental growth of the company, not on their individual contributions. We must prevent the egos and competitive nature of so many of our great leaders from becoming liabilities.

Trust and the reduction of fear, teamwork and sharing, and leaders as champions of people—set the stage for the final nutrient necessary in our cultural foundation: a belief that change must be driven. If learning results from challenging old ideas and processes, and trying new ways to do everything we're currently doing and more, then change must occur at a constant pace. But change cannot be something created or driven by senior leadership alone. It must be consistently and passionately embraced throughout the learning organization. For this to happen, a support system must be firmly in place—one that recognizes our often negative reactions to change. In other words, we must be able to trust the organization to understand peoples' natural aversion to the sheer pace and risk of warp speed learning.

In order to facilitate the process of shifting the responsibility for learning from the company or leader to the individual associate, the role of "Leader in Learning" was created within every business unit. These very important individuals serve as the critical link between Learning and Development and the field units. As the learning consultant's on-site liaison, they are learning (and teaching others within their office) to take responsibility for conducting skill and knowledge assessments, facilitating workshops, establishing a network of peer coaching, and organizing cross-training strategies.

The first Leaders in Learning project was the facilitation of an "Embracing Change" seminar in 1993. Learning Consultants collaborated with associates on a program featuring a series of interactive exercises that led associates through the expected emotional reactions to change, with discussions about coping strategies. The goal of the program was to help people through the rapid change taking place in the company and to reinforce the message that change becomes the status quo in an organization that learns.

The ongoing challenge at Rosenbluth International is for every associate to acknowledge and accept the fact that constant, rapid learning begets constant, rapid change. As the culture replaces traditional views of jobs and functions with newer and fresher ideas, we need to replace the fear of living in flux with a shared anticipation of future possibilities. This will only be accomplished by driving out fear of failure.

As organizations evolve from leader-controlled learning to leader-driven learning, to learning which is expected, supported, and celebrated by every person in the company, we may continue to step back, letting go of what we think we know, and know that by losing control we are speeding the growth of our people, our companies and our profits.

A Closing Metaphor

Like gardeners, those of us who influence the direction of organizational development must consider every element needed for a successful result. We know that as water flows irresistibly down hill, so learning travels through the organization. Our system of irrigation should be efficient and effortless, seamless, and unobtrusive. Our soil must be prepared for maximum yield, and our seeds must be healthy and compatible. Each and every one of our gardeners must understand and embrace a consistent approach to gardening. As designers and leaders, we must never forget that we are planting, nurturing, weeding, and reaping *values*—not programs, projects, or objectives. The success of our gardening will be measured by the extent that these values form the foundation for a culture that is supportive of learning. The more we believe that specific outcomes can be "grown" without properly "preparing the soil," the more we will be found setting boundaries, stifling creativity and imposing unworkable directives.

The real barriers to learning lie deep within the cultural soil of our organizations. Organizational realignments, new training programs, and modified job descriptions alone will not succeed in overcoming these barriers.

As has been learned at Rosenbluth, a strong, consistent culture grown from shared values provides all of the control necessary for directing learning. *True* learning organizations will grow from a culture that accepts the premise that continuous, uncontrolled learning is a necessity for future success. As leaders continue to focus on maintaining the strength of the culture and making sure that it is consistent, the culture will allow associates throughout the organization to learn at the rate of speed necessary to move forward.

Mary Byrd is manager of Education Services at Informix Software, a leading supplier of information management software. Her charter is to educate employees and partners on key Informix products, business processes, and technologies. In this role, she must leverage the knowledge of many experts to a worldwide network of employees, customers, and partners.

Prior to joining Informix, Byrd spent almost five years with Ernst & Young's Professional Development Group. She was responsible for managing Industry Education programs for internal employees and selected clients. She was also an instructor for Inner Quest, an experiential education company that used outdoor adventure as a medium for team-building, problem-solving, and self-discovery. She holds a Masters Degree in Human Resource Development from The George Washington University in Washington, DC.

31

Creating a Learning Organization by Accident

Mary Byrd

Informix Software did not set out to create a learning organization. Our CEO did not proclaim that we would become a learning organization. No corporate-wide programs were launched; no change efforts were put into place. It is quite by accident that we have created an environment that is naturally conducive to the learning and development of the employees.

Can learning organizations be created through formal programs, or are they a natural evolution of a company's culture, structure, and daily business processes? This essay describes the culture and business principles that allow learning to evolve at Informix Software. These principles provided the environment for learning to take root at Informix, just as the right combination of soil and fertilizer help flowers to flourish in a garden.

Although learning is taking root, I am not sure that we are a "learning organization," as described and characterized in recent books and business magazines. We are a technology company with energetic and motivated people. Because our core product is nothing more than intellectual property stored on magnetic tape, people are our most prized asset. We do not own any buildings and possess very little capital equipment. Instead we invest in recruiting and keeping highly knowledgeable workers.

While I do not claim that our company is a "text book" learning organization, something about this environment is naturally conducive to the learning and development of the employees. There are a few key principles on which the business is run that help to create this atmosphere:

1. There is the freedom to create.
2. We cannot do it all ourselves.
3. Learning is linked to the success of the business.
4. Managers are resource and process facilitators, not "experts."
5. Individuals manage their own careers.
6. Open systems provide knowledge freeways.
7. Success is shared.

There Is the Freedom to Create

Informix Software is a $350 million information management software company with 2,200 employees worldwide. Our industry is highly competitive and highly volatile. Companies in this industry constantly race to leapfrog each other with new technology and products. In this environment, speed, flexibility, and the ability to create new knowledge are keys to success.

Our executives set the overall direction and boundaries of the business, providing the control needed in our changing industry. However, they do not attempt to over-manage the chaos because they know that unneeded bureaucracy and tight controls stifle the creativity and flexibility of the company. Each department is given the freedom to decide how to manage its own way and to create its own processes to achieve goals.

Because paths are not always clear, and many groups have overlapping functions, this may make for chaos at times. However, this chaos is not always bad. It often serves as a creative lever to move the organization forward. Because there is very little structure, departments and individuals create the processes that work best for them. This freedom to create brings a unique energy and excitement to the workforce that makes up for the frustration caused by lack of structure. Most importantly, having fluid structures allows the company to respond quickly to customer preferences and market dynamics.

This type of freedom provides a wonderful background for the learning and development of all employees. Since there are no clear lines between the departments and their functions, much of the work is done in either ad hoc or structured teams that share existing knowledge and create new knowledge.

Departments and individuals feel personally responsible for the processes they create and the results they achieve. This drives employees' intrinsic motivation to continually learn new things to stay abreast of technology, and to look for ways to improve business processes. If something is not working, people learn what they need to know to fix it. The business needs and demands are the motivators for learning.

Although our environment allows a lot of freedom, it is not always easy to deal with. In fact, some employees who come from larger companies with structured environments find it disconcerting. It takes about six months for new employees to find their way in an unstructured environment or decide to leave the company. Although some people do leave, most stay and do so because they thrive on the opportunity to make a real contribution to the organization.

We Cannot Do It All Ourselves

Partnerships are critical to the success of Informix. Our business model is such that we can do more by partnering with others than we can by trying to do everything ourselves. Doing business through partnerships allows the company to leverage the knowledge and expertise of others to help our own company learn and develop. Many companies today are partnering with others; however, our approach to partnership is unique in that it has historically been part of our mission and business model. We do not view our partners as one-time business deals, but rather long-term relationships that are critical to our success, as well as theirs. As such, we have an ethic around partnerships that keeps our relationships strong and allows exchanges in knowledge, technology, and processes, with and among our partner companies.

At the heart of partnering is the concept of leverage. Webster's dictionary defines leverage as "an increased means of accomplishing some purpose." Virtually every department in the company leverages partnerships as a means of achieving business goals while, at the same time, fostering the development and growth of all members.

For example, the Marketing Department leverages partnerships with Value Added Partners who take our technology and add something to it to bring it to the marketplace. The Sales Department leverages partnerships with computer hardware vendors and other software companies that provide compatible products to bring the broadest range of solutions to our customers. The Education Services Department has partnerships with a few key partner companies to provide training to increase the level of knowledge within both companies. The Product Development Department leverages partnerships with all types of technology companies, both hardware and software, to develop, test, and create performance benchmarks on products.

One example of a Product Development partnership is our relationship with Sequent Computer Systems, Inc. to jointly develop our next generation of product. This joint agreement has allowed both parties to learn a great deal and to advance the technology to new levels. Our engineers worked side-by-side with their engineers to build hardware and software that would run faster and use less resources. Their engineers taught us about the physical limits of hardware and how to make software that uses the resources most effectively, and we taught them the intricacies of software and how to make hardware that will run the software with greater speed. This joint effort raised the level of knowledge of the engineers in both companies, and, at the same, time helped to produce a product that is being touted by the industry press as one of the leading database architectures.

Partnering in this fashion requires an emphasis on relationships and business ethics. We must treat our partners and each other with absolute integrity to ensure the ongoing success of the partnership. This maintains the trust that is needed when sharing knowledge and information with our partners. Integrity is a core value of our company and is considered in virtually every key business decision that is made. We will not knowingly enter into business situations that create conflicts with our business partners.

This integrity is part of our culture and provides an atmosphere of trust that is needed in a learning organization. Learning happens best in an environment that is open and full of trust.

Learning Is Linked to the Success of the Business

Because we are in a knowledge-intensive and highly competitive industry, learning is critical to our success. Not only must we learn new technologies to stay ahead from a product perspective, but we must also learn new business processes and ways of managing that help us to stay profitable. In this environment, time is a precious commodity; thus, structured learning activities in formal environments are too time-intensive to be a primary method for learning.

Instead, learning that occurs at Informix is similar to the learning that occurs with young children. It is not done in formal classrooms but rather on the job through experimentation, trial and error, and curiosity. Young children learn by being curious and interacting with their environment, with few rules or "right ways" of doing things. At Informix, our employees also learn a great deal through daily interaction with other employees, customers, and partners. This learning is usually tied to something they need to know to do their work or advance the state of our technology.

An example of this occurs during the introduction of a new technology or product. Teams with members from R&D, Marketing, Training, Public Relations, Advertising, and Sales work together to learn what the technology is, how it will best serve the needs of the customers, and where it should be positioned in the market. Once the team formulates their initial plans and assumptions about the product, they test them with industry experts, customers, and others to determine if they are accurate or if new knowledge can be gained from these outside sources. Once a final plan and positioning is created, the knowledge gained by the team is leveraged with the rest of the company, particularly the sales force, executives, and partners worldwide to ensure a successful product launch and the adoption of the technology by customers.

This leveraging of new knowledge begins with a formal training program that includes detailed product information and sales tools to communicate it to customers and partners. From this basic start, amazingly, the knowledge gets shared and leveraged out to all employees worldwide and our many and varied sales channels with few formal mechanisms or programs for doing so. It is because this knowledge is so valuable that it gets leveraged out almost on its own. Our employees, partners, and customers are hungry for the knowledge, and find ways to learn it to achieve their business goals.

As this example shows, most learning that occurs is self-motivated and driven by a business need, whether it be something related to technology or the more human aspects of our business. This on-the-job learning is supplemented by very focused formal training programs that serve to teach employees about new business processes, product features, or tools that they need to do their jobs.

The training functions in the company do not build large training curricula and try to keep seats filled, but rather, offer very focused programs to target audiences based on business needs. Examples include: advanced sales methodology training, new product training, desktop application software training, and software support training. Since training programs are related specifically to critical areas of their jobs, most employees enthusiastically participate in the formal programs that are offered.

Managers Are Resource and Process Facilitators, Not "Experts"

The managers at Informix, whether they are at a senior level or new to the company, are resource and process facilitators, not "experts." It is not uncommon to see younger, less experienced persons managing older, more technically experienced individuals. In many cases, managers are not promoted because they know the most about a certain discipline, but because they have the ability to acquire and manage resources, whether they be people, technology, or money, to produce results.

Because technology-driven companies require a multitude of very focused skill sets, managers are not always expected to be the experts in the group. However, they are expected to design processes and motivate teams of highly skilled workers towards achieving goals.

One example of this includes an executive marketing director, who has a variety of directors reporting to her, each highly specialized in a certain marketing channel (e.g., Value Added Resellers, Original Equipment Manufacturers, Third Party Suppliers, etc.). She is not as much of an expert in each channel as the people with direct responsibility; however, she is highly skilled at creating the big picture, helping the groups to leverage each other's work, managing time and resources, and, most importantly, creating a strong team environment to move the group forward.

This type of management structure leads an organization away from top-down bureaucracies towards more flexible and democratic work groups. Because the manager does not have to be the "expert," the best talents of the team can shine and be brought forth with very little jockeying for position or power.

Managers can be open to learning and set an expectation that the work group can learn together. This empowers the team, including the manager, to learn together without risk of ridicule from others. If the manager sets the example of being curious, reflecting on mistakes, and looking for ways to improve processes, this sends a strong message to the team that learning is desired and should be a natural outcome of every project, even if the ideal results are not always achieved.

Managers as resource and process facilitators are much less intimidating to all employees than the "know it all" manager typical in business for decades. Most managers inspire trust and confidence in their employees and provide an environment where risk taking is encouraged and failures are accepted as learning opportunities.

Individuals Manage Their Own Careers

In our rapidly changing environment, individuals at Informix are encouraged to manage their own careers. Unlike other companies, where career paths are clear and directly related to time in grade, career paths at Informix are loosely defined and built on opportunities provided by rapid growth. Employees can move freely within and between departments to learn new skills. Sometimes the path is straight up for super stars, but more often it is curved, allowing individuals to try many types of jobs—each of which round out the skill set of the employee.

Individuals must be proactive about managing their own careers. This keeps most employees sharp and wanting to improve their current knowledge base so as to be employable not only at Informix, but also anywhere else in the industry in case some unforeseen event occurs. This type of proactiveness serves both the company and employee well because individuals are motivated to learn and keep their skills current without an entitlement mentality which can weigh heavily on a company's ability to respond to change.

Managers can help facilitate the direction of their employees' careers by providing guidance, specific projects for learning opportunities, and formal training programs. However, it is up to each employee to be proactive in letting the manager know where their interests lie and what direction they want their career to take. In this proactive environment, employees are motivated to seek out their own education and project opportunities to keep their skills current and learn new things for future opportunities. The manager approves the education activities chosen by the employee and provides them with the time to attend. In most cases, especially if the education is directly related to a business need, the managers are fully supportive of these self-directed learning activities.

This type of self-directed career management can pose problems for individuals who are more used to formal structures and career paths. They may not be able to envision their own unique career paths, thus they do not take advantage of projects and education that will lead them forward. In addition, they may feel stuck in their current jobs if they cannot see the next ones. To counter these problems, our company needs to provide the managers with some more formal career development strategies, so they can assist individuals in mapping out their future directions.

Open Systems Provide Knowledge Freeways

Informix develops it core product line and runs most of its daily business on the UNIX operating system. UNIX is an open operating system that was developed by AT&T in the 1970s and shared with university computer science departments all over the country. Over the last ten years, it has become a commercial operating system, because it is very robust and allows many users to tap into shared file structures and systems.

At the heart of the open systems movement in the computer industry is the concept of being able to link any type of computer to any other type of computer and have them be able to talk to each other. Although Open Systems is still in its infancy, and not all computers can talk freely to each other, at Informix we have been able to use the central principles to link up a worldwide network of many types of computers (e.g., workstations, PCs, Macintoshes, dumb terminals, etc.).

This worldwide network provides e-mail to every employee. File server systems allow the sharing of files and applications among many different departments. In addition, there are several databases that are available to any employee with the proper permissions that provide instant information on customer calls, software development issues, customer and internal training enrollments, and many others.

This type of network provides employees with a vehicle for sharing and leveraging knowledge worldwide. Some examples of this include: the Marketing Department posting the latest graphic presentations for all sales offices to use with customers; the Training Department providing their training materials on-line for any office to use when training customers, distributors, or partners; Product Development engineers documenting software development issues and sharing them with other engineers, technical support, and field system engineers.

Although these systems are not always perfect, they do provide a backbone for sharing knowledge and information throughout the organization. In addition, our links to the Internet allow us to connect to our customers, partners, industry analysts, and many others to share knowledge. These links allow us to look beyond our own boundaries for both sharing and receiving information.

It is interesting to note that the changes brought forth by technology almost parallel changes called for to create learning organizations. For example, the move from large mainframes to smaller desktop computers and localized servers follows the trend in large organizations from top-down bureaucracies to flatter, leaner structures. Computer networks link companies and people worldwide, paralleling the trend of learning organizations looking outside of their own sphere for new knowledge and ideas. Graphical User Interfaces on computers parallel the trend toward symbolic language and pictures for synthesizing and sharing knowledge in learning organizations. The move from proprietary computing systems to open systems parallels the move towards openness in terms of diversity and global awareness in learning organizations.

Success Is Shared

The last few years have been highly profitable for Informix. In 1993, we had 24% growth in revenues with a 24% operating margin. We have been virtually debt free since October of 1992 and have generated sufficient cash to fund internal growth and to acquire new technologies and distribution channels.

This outstanding financial performance is due to many factors, but much of it is our ability to leverage resources, knowledge, and partners in a way that gives us tremendous productivity. Our annualized revenue per employee is one of the highest at $220,000. Another factor in the financial performance is a simple business financial model which is followed from broad departmental perspectives, but not over-managed at the individual line-item level.

This successful financial performance is shared with employees who are not on another bonus or commission plan. In the past two years, the profit sharing has averaged around 20% of annual compensation. This type of profit sharing system makes every employee feel accountable for the company's success and that they will be personally rewarded for a job well done. In addition, stock option awards are given annually to outstanding performers, directly tying their performance to sharing in the company's financial success.

Another example of sharing success occurred in late 1992, when we won a $26 million contract from the federal government. When the final payment came in on this contract, our CEO went into the lobby of Informix's headquarters and announced he was giving every single employee a check for $1,000 for their contribution to winning this contract. This type of spontaneous reward helps to make every single employee feel valued for his or her contribution to the organization's success.

Summary

The learning that occurs at Informix is not a result of large formal change efforts or proclamations by top executives. Instead, it flourishes as a result of the simple, yet highly effective business principles outlined in this article. These principles provide the right environment and culture for learning to flourish, just as the right soil and fertilizer allow flowers to grow in a garden.

With the right environment, learning will occur naturally. It does not need to be managed from the top down in a formal program. If Informix had set out to create a learning organization in a formal program, it would not have taken the shape it has today or provided an environment that is conducive to learning. Instead, departments would have debated the pros and cons of becoming a learning organization, resisted such a program because it is not part of their daily bottom-line responsibilities, and participated only half-heartedly with nudging from above. Perhaps an immediate change may have been seen, but as soon as the formal program was over the changes would not have lasted.

So how do organizations create an environment for learning when it does not happen by accident? I believe organizations should not focus on creating learning itself, but rather on creating structures and processes that allow human creativity, curiosity, and ingenuity to flourish. They should also create mechanisms to leverage the learning that occurs within and between organizations.

Each organization must find the structures and processes that work best for it. The most critical element in "creating" a learning organization is to encourage the natural learning that occurs with formal processes to capture and leverage the learning. Processes that are top down and bureaucratic stifle the very learning they seek to create. Processes that focus on what occurs naturally in daily business have a greater chance of promoting and leveraging learning. Companies that are able to create these processes will become learning organizations.

Dinesh Chandra is the president of Global Quality Associates, a firm specializing in organizational transformation—renewing the strategic planning process and developing the change strategy in an integrated manner—with clients around the globe. Starting with a technical background, he learned new philosophies, such as the key to successful implementation of new technologies, TQM, was the people using the new system. He proceeded to develop a keen insight into this human aspect. As director of productivity for Coulter Corporation, he served as internal consultant to their U.S.A., U.K., France and Brazil divisions for the implementation of JIT and TQC.

Chandra holds a BS in Mechanical Engineering, an MS in Industrial Engineering, and an MBA in Finance. He has served as Adjunct Faculty for the Graduate School of Nova and Florida International University. He is a frequent speaker for APICS, ASQC, ASTD and is the author of the upcoming book, *Aha, So This is Total Quality Management.*

32

Beyond Ego to Wisdom: The Eicher Experience

Dinesh Chandra

> *I have three treasures*
> *which I hold and cherish*
> *The first is known as compassion*
> *No compassion, no wisdom*
> *knowledge yes...*
> —Tao Te Ching

In today's global business world, there is no dearth of knowledge; yet true wisdom, the deeper knowing that forms the basis for continuous learning, remains elusive. Perhaps, as the Chinese philosopher suggests, what is missing is compassion. After decades of organizational development and team building, the business community is still largely uncaring. It's rare to see a top management team in which members are sincerely devoted to making each other successful. The bottom line continues to be the motivating force, under the assumption that "businesses have to be run this way."

The experience of the Eicher Group, a large manufacturing firm based in India, demonstrates that businesses do *not* have to be run this way to be successful. If people within an organization are able to move beneath each other's surface to experience deeper connection, learning ability improves—with positive implications for bottom-line health.

Organizations today are emphasizing the need to manage in a holistic, systemic manner, avoiding compartmentalizing people in functional silos. People are beginning to be seen not just as machines, or pairs of working hands, but as whole individuals—hands, brains (left as well as right), and bodies, with families and other considerations outside the job.

With the recent increase of the feminine presence in the workplace, companies are even beginning to acknowledge emotions and feelings. But the deeper issues, sometimes referred to as "spirit" or "soul," still seem to be confined to Sunday School. So fragmentation persists.

Although "soul" has recently become a popular concept (witness the success of Thomas Moore's book *Soul Mates*), it is ignored in the office and boardroom. Individuals in corporate functions interact with each other as though this aspect of the human being simply does not exist. This "nonexistent" soul makes its presence felt, with insistent and painful clarity, in the presence of the psychotherapist or the clergyman, but then is submerged again in the day-to-day functioning of the organization.

Eicher's story is of a company's struggle toward becoming a learning community by exploring the road to compassion. Eicher has consciously encouraged its employees to go more deeply within, and to acknowledge and synthesize the importance of "soul" in the workings of the company and their relationships with each other. The firm discovered that moving beyond the ego and escaping from the prison of intellect has provided an opportunity to be in touch with each individual's connectedness to others. Heightened trust has diminished nonconstructive conflict. Learning has become more natural, less of an effort. Memorizing and recalling mechanical rules has become unnecessary.

Eicher's Business Conundrum

India has always been a land of contrasts and complexity, and its business climate is no exception. During the last few centuries, the country and its industries were ruled either by feudal and religious or rigidly traditional bureaucratic creeds. Beginning in the early 1980s, however, the inexorable global forces of free enterprise have swept into the country and have begun to change the entire way business is done.

Reaction to these winds of change has, on the whole, been positive. A determined set of industrialists and entrepreneurs are supporting the change process, even in the face of short-term loss. They realize that the mechanical, horizontal technology transfer of yesterday no longer works; today's organization has to send down roots in the local community in order to function successfully.

Given this realization, one might think that the traditional Indian doctrine of *karma yoga*, a teaching of the *Bhagavad Gita* that emphasizes the selfless pursuit of one's duties while detaching oneself from the result, would hold sway over practical aspects of Indian life. But economic struggles and Western influence have drawn most business leaders away from the ancient wisdom; India is a land full of self-oriented, self-serving, and extremely competitive individuals. Because of the vast economic gap between managers and workers, anything other than token social mingling is unimaginable. In this respect, India mirrors other third-world countries where people operate from a paradigm of scarcity.

In such a situation, it is not easy to talk about teamwork, abundance mentality, and collaboration. However, a few organizations are experimenting with these ideas on their transformational journeys, as they explore Total Quality Management (TQM), re-engineering, and creation of learning communities. The Eicher Group is one of these companies.

Eicher has been producing tractors and other vehicles since 1960. With only a very few hiccups, the tractor industry basked in a solid seller's market until the beginning of the 1980s. Then, when the forces of global competition began to challenge Eicher along with other manufacturers, senior managers immersed themselves in anything to do with quality.

Quality orientation evolved from a narrow product quality focus to a much broader understanding of all the needs of internal and external customers. When Eicher entered into a joint venture with Mitsubishi Motors to manufacture state-of-the-art light commercial vehicles at a new plant, Eicher executives began to explore elements of the much-talked-about Japanese management system. One of these was TQM.

After some initial successes in TQM, Eicher ran into a major obstacle: intense internal competition—which prevailed even after a major overhaul of the performance appraisal system—did not encourage the team culture that is fundamental to a quality-based organization relying on empowerment. In addition, Eicherites resisted learning each new idea or model. After they had learned something, there was great momentum to move forward, but when time came to move on to a newer learning, tremendous resistance rose up again. For example, even as TQM was being accepted, the process of introducing new products was changing very slowly. Obviously, the organization had some learning disabilities.

The Transformation Begins

The breakthrough to beginning Eicher's transformation came when the group CEO acknowledged that he himself posed the single greatest difficulty in fully implementing TQM theories and systems. "I was apprehensive about the process for some time, even after we had begun," he said. "It is the mindset of the chief executive that poses the biggest problem."

This startling statement provided a wonderful role model, enabling others to search their own motivations. It launched Eicher's long, difficult, exciting journey beyond the ego—a journey that focused on creating a learning community, not merely manufacturing a change.

The first overt step in this journey was to replace an archaic operational review forum with a quarterly management conference committed to learning and dialoging—without specific decision. This conference consisted of about thirty senior managers and evolved over time.

In one of the early conferences, the concept of "dialogue" was introduced, as discussed in Peter Senge's book *The Fifth Discipline*. The purpose of dialogue is to go beyond any one individual's understanding. The group explores complex issues from many points of view; individuals suspend their assumptions yet communicate these assumptions freely.

The Eicher group chose its own topics for dialogue discussion, using Harrison Owen's "open space" style in which simple rules prevailed: everyone has a choice, whoever comes are the right people, whatever happens are the only things that matter, it starts and ends at the right time, people should honor the "law of two feet" (leave when they wish).

Those were turbulent times. Dialogue enables individuals to expand their view of reality, refining their perceptions and thinking patterns, deepening their level of inner wisdom, and

discovering their highest purpose. As a result, politically incon-
venient issues began to surface as members begin examining
their own and others' assumptions. Nothing was sacred, including the vision, mission, and core values. Authenticity of communication became a focal point.

Several skeptical managers discarded the whole idea of
dialogue as gimmick. In private conversations, they rated authenticity of communication as about 2 or 3 on a scale of 10,
opining that people simply say what top managers want to hear
and what will help them in moving along their career paths.

One of the first topics addressed was the notion of the
"leadership model" versus the "professional management model":
the flexible, inspiring, empowering leader as opposed to the
efficient, rigid, controlling manager. At first, the majority believed
that Eicher enjoyed a good balance between leadership and
management; results of several diagnostic questionnaires at-
tested to this belief. Finally, however, one senior member of the
group disagreed openly, suggesting that the company might not
really be in balance, and deep reflection ensued. That was the
day *authentic* dialogue was born.

The Soul Connection

Gradually, managers began to realize that if they were to be
serious about empowerment—the keystone of Japanese-style
TQM—they must listen to the aspirations and desires of all
employees and develop agreement on the direction of choice. One
issue that was generating intense heat was the question of how
to deal with surplus manpower in a company with which Eicher
had a strategic alliance. In the past, Eicher had made an un-
equivocal statement that productivity improvement would not
result in any reduction in permanent manpower, even in tough
times. But Eicher had limited control in the alliance, which was
now facing tremendous market pressures.

Here is where Eicher experienced its first encounter with
the issues of compassion and soul. In an organizational climate
where logic is dominant, it would be easy for managers to
conclude that, because the marketplace is changing, it is necessary to get rid of "dead wood" to cut costs and remain competitive.
But when people start to express themselves from deeply-held
personal values, the issue becomes much less clear-cut, as
comments in Eicher dialogues indicate:

"Eicher is facing an issue which is fundamental to our existence. Is profit our main purpose? I don't think so. I think in this company people are the purpose."

"If the worker was my brother, how would you deal with him? We are all human beings and the ancient Indian concept of 'Vasudhev Kutumbakam' [world is a family] reminds us that we are part of the same family. All our souls are connected."

The latter comment represented a profound shift in the Indian context, where workers are poles apart from managers in almost any respect. This led to an examination of the family prototype: what happens to a family if the income goes down; do we ask members of the family to move out? The answer was obvious: We don't; the sense of connection and compassion for each other enables us to go through tough times together.

Now the company was moving closer to true community—a sense of mutual commitment and a higher purpose than individual gain. The role of the ego in blocking the awareness of the soul was breaking down. In fact, the formerly unacceptable word "soul" was being discussed in a business setting. As a result, the approach towards the employees was one of caring and following up even after a voluntary retirement plan was implemented in one of the companies with which Eicher had a strategic alliance. This was a new approach to dealing with the turbulence that generally follows the implementation of a voluntary retirement scheme.

At Eicher, as in other Indian businesses, management and workers did not socialize, managers did not take an interest in each other's family affairs nor attend each other's social ceremonies. Trying to connect at the level of the heart seemed reasonable to begin with. But as the company began to organize structured programs for executives and their spouses, the company experienced an uneasy sensation of venturing too far into the realm of the intangible in its desire for interpersonal connection.

Serious questions arose about whether people have the ethical/moral right, in an organizational setting, to try to influence each other's beliefs about being, life, and other soulful matters. If they don't, though, how can they discuss, with authenticity, the concept of shared visioning and its place in changing the destiny of the organization and its members?

Among the poignant comments were:

We all come to these quarterly dialogues like

souls (Atma) and the energy here is like a great spirit (Paramatma). It re-energizes us, but will the great spirit be with us when we go back?"

"Are we not going too far into this venture? Isn't this too spiritual for an organization to get involved in, and should we back off?"

"How could we talk about a whole view of organization and yet take a fragmented view of the human being?"

The journey via dialogue was not an easy one. At first, dialogues occasionally died a sudden death. Over time, however, people realized that it was not as important to find the "right" answer as it was to understand that individuals operate from different mental models about life and destiny, and that these models affect the decision-making process, leadership styles, and interpersonal relationships. Acknowledging the deeper issues helps to clarify confusing issues.

The most interesting discovery the group made was the importance of childlike play in learning and in understanding different viewpoints. In one afternoon session, when the group was divided into subgroups, one subgroup decided to meet right in the swimming pool in their swimming trunks. The spirit behind the idea caught on, and soon people came up with further innovations.

Pictures, songs, poems—anything that enabled communication—began to gain acceptance. At these conference sessions, marked by laughter and playfulness, it was hard to imagine that this was a group of senior executives of a structured company known for its serious professionalism. Someone pointed out that Carl Jung had said that men change when they get back to their childhood; that's where they are in touch with their intuition and feminine side. At that, someone else mentioned—and others agreed—that increased female participation in management would be a welcome addition.

Benefits and Lessons

So the journey continues, and each quarterly dialogue is dedicated to ongoing inquiry into Eicher's learning system. The dialogue process has been dubbed the "Learning Laboratory." Although people tend to enjoy dialogue, some have questioned whether the organization has realized tangible benefits as a result. The believers have pointed out that outcomes and attitudes resulting from the Learning Laboratory were spreading to other parts of the company. It was no coincidence, for example, that Eicher's divisional management began listening to union members, with their mouths shut and hands noting down the comments on flip charts, for as long as the workers wanted to talk.

Trust began to grow between unions and management, resulting in contracts unparalleled in India. Individual and collective monetary incentives, traditionally used in setting target output levels, were abolished. The group felt that the high trust level made the connection between output and money unnecessary. The fixed salary was adjusted by the average bonus amounts of the past twelve months (a one-time increase), so that there was no loss of income for the workers.

A wider participation in the strategic planning process, initiated in the quarterly management conference, highlighted the lack of consensus regarding the corporate mission. Certain groups of executives wanted the firm to be known for engineering excellence, and preferred vertical integration focusing on the key technologies. Others wanted it to be a diversified business group, and preferred horizontal integration driven by core values. To the latter group, any business—ranging from leather to clothing to housing—was fair game.

Dialogue on mission led to an understanding of the fundamental differences of assumption regarding the firm's core competencies, and finally resulted in further decentralization, which is more conducive to a diversified business. This helped to create an environment where both groups of executives can pursue their dreams in alignment with the corporate vision.

Today, all of Eicher's seven plants, the Research Center involved in the design and production of vehicles and components, and other corporate functions—involving, in total, more than seven thousand employees—have reported significant progress on the TQM path. Eicher has also launched a thriving consulting enterprise serving the needs of other companies.

Creating Dialogue

Eicher has learned that the following elements are important in using dialogue to create a learning community:
- The chairman or key person in the group has to be

deeply committed to the process, and be willing to relinquish his (or her, but in Eicher's case it was a male) position of authority. In the early stages, self-restraint in holding back his ideas encourages others to open up and express themselves freely.

- The group must be very clear about the intent behind community, empowerment, and other "soft" issues. Is the dialogue a management strategy aimed primarily at increasing productivity, or is it a search for deeper meaning, not only of work but of life itself? If the latter, the group must agree, up front, that it is okay to explore the uncharted waters of spirituality in business, and that it is within the corporate domain to examine the deepest beliefs held by members of the group.

- The group has to be just as committed to re-engineering relationships as to re-engineering organizational procedures. To this end, it must seek authenticity in communication.

- A broad spectrum of top managers—not just one or two individuals—must choose and support the consultant who facilitates the process of creating the learning community. To increase credibility with the team, the consultant should be willing to expose his or her own vulnerability.

Continuing Dialogue

These issues are ripe for continuing dialogue:

- Should we take the risk of bringing the "soul" out of the closet? How do we do this?

- What can we do to bring about a shift away from the short-term-profit mentality?

- Should we expand our learning community to include the major stockholders?

- What are our beliefs regarding commitment to people versus commitment to the bottom line? Are the two really incompatible?

- Are we learning from global sources or are we still caught in our own local models?

- How do we strive for a balance between what we admire

in a manager (transactional) and in a leader (transformational)?

- How can we satisfy the various result needs of the organization's stakeholders?
- How can we create awareness in individuals about their egos? How can the acknowledgment of the whole human being enable us to move forward along the path of learning?

If people are not to be considered machines, the reality of choice cannot be ignored. Change can be forced on a machine, but humans must make the choice to change. As Gary Zukav points out in "Evolution in Business," an essay in *The New Paradigm in Business*, "As more and more humans begin to see themselves and others as immortal souls involved in a learning process that entails the experiencing of consequences that each has chosen, they begin to choose their actions and responses to the actions of others more carefully, and hopefully more wisely."

Compassion is directly linked to organizational learning. Systemic learning is not possible when part of the system—the "soul" part that transcends logic and ego, and acknowledges fundamental connection—is ignored. True wisdom depends upon the compassion that results from a sense of connection.

The Business Yogi

Although the typical Indian business person's focus on the bottom line is no different from that of business executives anywhere else in the world, certain spiritual and mystical ideas can modify this attitude. Especially appealing is that of Karma Yoga: the idea that we are not helpless victims of circumstances because we always have choices.

Karma Yogis truly enjoy what they are doing because they know they are making a choice. When they do their best to delight everyone who comes into contact with them, their behavior is not mechanistic but springs from a deep inner desire and conviction. At the same time, these Karma Yogis know they can perform their best only when they are not concerned with the outcome. The *Bhagavad Gita* states: "Therefore, without attachment, constantly perform action which is duty, for, by performing action without attachment, man verily reacheth the Supreme."

Duty is that which must be done whether or not it is in agreement with likes and dislikes. If likes and duty coincide, the action becomes spontaneous. Otherwise, the action is deliberate: a matter of choice.

In Indian tradition, life is divided into four phases, and the duty-bound (choice-making) human can practice four *ashrams* connected to these phases. The first quarter of life can be dedicated to *Bramhacharya,* meaning preparation while leading a simple life. The second quarter can focus on *Grahastha*— prosperity, career, and family. The third, *Vanprastha,* involves preparing to leave the worldly life and enter the fourth phase, *Sanyas,* a deep state of unifying with the universe.

A businessman performing his duty in the second phase might be called a "business yogi." Throughout his life, mindful of all four phases, a business yogi remains an enthusiastic learner with compassion for his fellow beings. In the second phase, success of his team becomes his success. Business yogis find that they are much more than an integration of their logical and emotional sides, and that alignment of their goals with those of others is not enough until they have experienced the gift of the soul: a sense of connection and accompanying compassion. Just as Indian businesses are learning from Western concepts, the Western world can learn from the concept of the business yogi—which transcends nation, language, color, and other such dividers.

When you are part of a top management group in a rapidly growing, successful company, you acquire a certain degree of confidence. However, no matter how successful you are, at some point in time the paradigm shifts and you are forced to reevaluate. Here is where a business yogi attitude is useful. Eicher is fortunate in having a business yogi as its chairman, Vikram Lal. This man keeps a very low profile and uses few words, but his actions speak a great deal. Recently, a leading magazine wanted to do a "Businessman of the Year" cover story on him, which he politely turned down. When I asked him to coauthor this chapter with me, he declined, adding:

"As far as I am concerned, I feel I have had my innings, and it is now for younger, braver souls to proceed further. Surprisingly, I also don't have a desire to author an article or write for a magazine. It simply embarrasses me!"

Here is a leader whose ego (although he is truly successful) does not get in the way of his compassion and wisdom.

Conclusion: Reflections of Learning from a Gathering

Sarita Chawla

In July of 1994, at the Mount Washington Hotel at Bretton Woods, in New Hampshire, a group of friends and colleagues interested in practices of creating learning organizations gathered. They were interested in exploring the natural phenomenon of collective learning and the creative process. The gathering was collaboratively designed with input from potential participants. It was not intended to be a conference where experts shared their expertise, but one where everyone learned from each other.

There was a request to leave our egos at the door.

As an experiment with learning in different modalities, not only academics such as Peter Senge participated, but poet David Whyte, musician Michael Jones, and Playback Theater West joined in to enhance the "learning edge." Sheryl Erickson, a colleague and friend, organized the conference and invited me to be one of its convenors.

In turn, I invited all the attending co-authors of this book to participate in a dialogue and held a vision that it might provide input for this conclusion. I imagined:

- participants including authors, line practitioners, staff practitioners, consultants, executives, and researchers
- possibly a seed question—shared by all to create a shared container, understanding, and initial inquiry

- collective exploration of possible paths and unintended consequences
- a generator of un-mediated, creative, intuitive insight
- a source of collective and individual action
- proceedings that result initially in a conclusion for this book that only the dynamic collective wisdom of this group could birth
- seeds of interconnectedness that could last a lifetime

Many of the authors of this book were present at the gathering. A two-hour dialogue had been arranged. I had invited some customers/practitioners to join us. Some of the authors had ideas for who to include. The intent was to model learning as a collective.

Mitch Saunders, of California Leadership and one of the dialogue facilitators of the MIT Organizational Learning Center, had agreed to facilitate the session. We started by providing the context of this book and the dialogue. In order to begin to create shared meaning and a starting point, each participant was asked to introduce themselves and share a question that was on his or her mind.

Here are summaries of their words:

Robert Masten (author): What I'm pondering, as I watch the frustration that goes with total quality and learning organization implementation, is making it happen.

Sherrin Bennett (author): How is the pattern of our minds, the neurons and their linking and their growing into one another, the dendrites and their connections reflected among us in community? What would the shape of our knowing be with one another? Because I think the pattern that's within us is similar to the pattern that's trying to grow between us.

Joe Sensenbrenner (practitioner): Very few public organizations are very far down this path. I'm also involved in TQM activities as a precursor way of breaking old patterns and establishing some analogous new path. I see learning organizations as a successor stage. I've never explicitly recommended these techniques in any organization I'm working with because I don't wish to risk any high profile public effort not to work out well. I'm trying to think of success factors that I can recognize and foster over time.

Paula Underwood (author): How can I help effectively, because I'm bridging from one tradition into quite a different tradition. I don't want to be in a position of running around saying "be a nice little Indian (American) and we'll get along fine." I want to be effective in helping any group, person or organization turn to options as far as learning ways are concerned. Perhaps a theme here has been that it's inherently good to become a learning organization. I suspect that for some it is not a really swift idea.

Leilani Henry (practitioner): My experience is that there is a lot of fear around education. So how do we develop the self confidence to use education as a tool, to then have that as a stepping stone to the larger issue of the learning organization, collectively learning from our experiences and really gaining personal mastery at the individual self?

Barbara Shipka (author): How do we change a tradition and long-held belief around businesses being responsible to themselves and extend the learning out to all the stakeholders that are involved in business and all the ways in which business is a stakeholder to the larger whole?

How do we learn in ways that transcend time so that we don't have to respond to urgency and we can do things that are really important—that have to do with me, with the unlimited resource of creativity?

Bob Guns (author): How do groups and teams learn? Teams are the crucible for future organizations and we need to find out how they do that. Someone suggested that perhaps one fruitful method would be to examine language and how that changes.

Ken Murphy (author): The chapter I'm writing about is called Generative Coaching, which is about re-examining the very assumptions that are inherent in most of the human systems in organizations and perhaps making new choices, moving away from behaviorist, manipulative models that almost all organizations are based on. In both the book and learning organizations in general, can this help us as a society to re-examine the very assumptions upon which we base the kinds of things we do? Not necessarily to choose new ones, but to bring them to the surface for re-examination? Sometimes we can get better and better and we can learn more and we can compete better, but we don't always ask the question, "To what end or why are we doing this?" Somehow the corporation becomes a bigger person than the actual people. There seems to be a little craziness in this. Can this work? If we resurface those assumptions will it allow us to make new choices?

Peggy Stich (practitioner/customer): How do we move ahead and be a learning organization and be thoughtful, thinking, and caring about what we're doing? How do we do this and move towards using consensus? How do we avoid a state of inaction and a state of constant questioning where we almost have non-empowered people because we can't decide what to do?

Dinesh Chandra (author): My dream was to be part of a team which is interested in making each other successful, and not only focusing on their own success. I've yet to find such a team. How can we create such a team?

Bill O'Brien (practitioner): I'm concerned that learning is becoming an amorphous buzz word. All organizations in my experience are learning organizations. If you intervene in the weakest and least effective corporation, you'll find that they learn like hell when you change the ground rules. They usually learn the wrong things. But they are good learners. So the question that I think about is, what is it that we want to learn? I focus less on process.

Bill Withers (author): What can we do to help insure that there is not a new hierarchy that forms—one of information, knowledge, understanding, and recognition—so that what happens is an organic unit and that leadership as we define it even in our best terms becomes a museum piece?

Joel Levey (author): How can we take the learning deeper?

Sarita Chawla (co-editor): It seems to me that some of the ingredients for an effective organization, including learning organizations, are creativity and coherence. The question that I'm holding is the paradox of knowing on the one hand that honoring, focusing on and really seeking out *diversity* enhances creativity and wholeness, as well as knowing when I focus on diversity I find that I add to fragmentation. How does one balance the two?

Michelle Levey (author): What are new ways, new core competencies about learning that have to do with honoring and increasing our ability to be comfortable with the edges and to really honor connections that enable us to be part of the whole rather than one chapter?

Eric Vogt (author): My question is about both small scale and macro level learning. How do individuals in Africa learn to learn in a way that their learning teams are effective? How do you connect that organic learning that I believe will happen in the next two decades to addressing global concerns? I think there is an interesting challenge of context and how do we develop those skills and those capacities in the next two generations.

Katrina Petrie (practitioner): There is a German saying—how can I know what I'm thinking if I don't hear what I'm saying? What do I really mean about learning organizations?

B.C. Huselton (practitioner/customer): We're just trying to do it! The search is fine but there's also...just do it. I'm appreciative that people go out into outer space and reflect, but the pressure of the question is: please come back and do something! When you go into outer space and come back, there is a whole group of people that look at everything that is being said here as mumbo jumbo. There is a very delicate balance needed here—to make sure that there is an appreciation for that, but still recognize that people can be confused in the moment yet need to find a way to act on it.

Bill Lambert (practitioner/customer): I ask myself, who is the customer and what does that mean? The question that I wrestle is: how can I get closer to the customer and potential customer and get closer to their deepest request? They're not asking for this stuff. Not where I come from. Can I help them create experiences such as dialogue and gathering some open space to think about and deal with their context?

Stephanie Ryan (author): What ways of seeing and relating to the world support us in living with our questions and how might I understand the distinctions between letting go, letting something happen, and letting it be?

Mitch Saunders (facilitator): What is it that keeps me contributing to things that I know in my heart of hearts may not need to continue?

Asking the proper question is the central act of transformation....

> *The key question causes germination of consciousness. The properly shaped question always emanates from an essential curiosity about what stands behind.*
>
> *Questions are keys that open secret doors...to swing open. What is behind the visible?*
>
> —Clarissa Pinkola Estes

A rich dialogue ensued after our inquiries. I have high-lighted capsules of it below, focusing on the questions them-selves and an examination of how we measure.

Regarding questions...

- Like a koan, a question on the surface sometimes seems insoluble. Continued reflection on it can cause one to re-examine the whole frame, causing it to dissolve. The question is no longer appropriate.

- There is not a lot written about the architecture of a powerful question.

- Asking questions is a way of learning.

- When our kids come home from school, what if we were to ask, what questions did you ask today?

- In personnel reviews, what if we asked, what questions did you ask this year?

- A very tactical model currently used: Weekly two-hour meeting with no agenda other than surfacing and reframing questions until we are certain that what we want to use is compelling.

- The executive function might very well be to discover the most important strategic questions that a corporation might need to address, while the work of others is to explore answers in the long and short term.

- Is it possible that answers just stop you, like decisions murder alternatives?

- It's not just the questions, but the assumptions beneath those questions.

- The power of questions is also to make assumptions more explicit.

- There is another very subtle dimension of answering questions and problem solving. We are so anxious to solve problems and in so doing create others that, in turn, have to be solved. We sometimes never get to the original goal that we set. We have a funny sense of time. We see an action arise from a problem solved as a short period of elapsed time, but there is often an infinite time between a tangible result and the original goal set out. Other ways, such as staying with the question, seem too long because we don't get to action fast. It may in fact be shorter if one looks at the total. We have a "funny sense of time" because we are trying to fragment into little problems. It might be worth going into the assumptions that we have about time.

- Questions organize our attention. The other part is our intention. What would mastery of attention and intention look like?

Regarding measures...

- If most breakthroughs occur with new measurement tools, *how* might we measure and *what* might we measure?

- We have come to regard the term "measure" in a way that is very different from its inception. Being of a western scientific mind, measure only means those things that we can move into numbers in some mechanical way. Back to the root of the word, it was referred to as things in "fair measure," not just about quantitative measure. Over time, we've constrained ourselves to just quantitative measures. Everything has boundaries within which it is useful, but it's important to know when you have crossed those boundaries. Keeping things in good measure initially had an implication of understanding within which frame is something useful and being careful not to go outside that frame and applying it. What does it mean to measure itself might be worth a lot of exploration.

- Questions open up a lens. Measures give us relevance or relational information as well as credibility to continue dialogue.

- What might be other ways of looking? If financial balance sheets are rearview mirrors, what might be "front view" windows? How can we look at other cultures and disciplines such as linguistics or anthropology?

- There are many ways of learning but we only measure a few. What can we learn from silence? Is there a way to learn without speaking?

After an invitation to tune into a possibly different channel through some silent reflection...

- My terror is that I don't know what a learning organization looks like, smells like, feels like.

- Is there an inner and outer circle? There is a sense of "I'm there and you are not." How can we include a diversity of different approaches?

- I don't know how to help myself become more open to learning. How can we find ways to open ourselves?

- At times it feels like the ego stops us from learning. I'm not able to stop it. Maybe it's not about the eastern concept of surrendering the ego but what David Whyte said to me on a walk one morning during the conference, "Can we be aware of when we are ego-ful and when we are soul-ful?" Learning occurs in soulful moments, because an ounce of compassion is worth a ton of rules.

The dialogue session concluded with all present sharing a word or phrase as closure. These included: Openness, junction in the road, power of communion, awareness of groupness, ambiguity, hope, listening, reflection and, like democracy, learning is a journey.

In conclusion, a wondering and an invitation....

I wonder what organizations and the world would be like if we could value learners and learning at least as much as we value knowers and knowing. My invitation: Continue the learning odyssey in two ways. Firstly, to share your reflections with all of us who collaborated in this collection. Contact information is provided later in these pages. Secondly, consider:

Today, like every other day, we wake up empty
and frightened. Don't open the door to the study
and begin reading. Take down the dulcimer.
Let the beauty we love be what we do.
There are hundreds of ways to kneel and kiss the ground.

—Rumi

Recommended Reading & Resources

Abbot, Edwin A. *Flatland: A Romance of Many Dimensions*. New York, NY: New American Library, 1984.

Abrahamson, E. "Managerial Fads and Fashion: The Diffusion and Rejection of Innovations," *The Academy of Management Review*, 16(3), 1991.

Acebo, S.C. & K. Watkins. "Community College Faculty Development: Designing a Learning Organization," *New Directions for Continuing Education*, 38, 1988.

Ackoff, R. *Creating the Corporate Future*. New York, NY: John Wiley and Sons, 1981.

Adler, E. *Everyone's Guide to Successful Publications*. Berkeley, CA: Peachpit Press, 1993.

Adler, P. & T. Winograd. *Usability: Turning Technologies into Tools*. New York, NY: Oxford University Press, 1992.

Alexander, C. & Langer, E. *Higher Stages of Human Development*. New York, NY: Oxford University Press, 1990.

Ancel, David. *An Interpretive Approach to the Mediation of Culture and Technology in the Global Workplace*. Doctoral dissertation, University of San Francisco, School of Education, (forthcoming 1995).

Andersen, D.F. & G.P. Richardson. "Scripts for Group Model Building." In *Proceedings of the 1994 International System Dynamics Conference*, Stirling, Scotland, 1994.

Angelou, Maya. *I Know Why the Caged Bird Sings*. New York, NY: Random House, 1969.

Angelou, Maya. *On the Pulse of Morning*." Inaugural Poem. New York, NY: Random House, 1993.

Apple, Inc. *Human Interface Guidelines, The Apple Desktop Interface*. Reading, MA: Addison-Wesley, 1987.

Argyris, Chris. *Overcoming Organizational Defenses: Facilitating Organizational Learning*. Needham, MA: Allyn Bacon, 1990.

Argyris, Chris. "Teaching Smart People How to Learn." *Harvard Business Review*, 69(3), May-June, 1991.

Argyris, Chris & Donald Schön. *Organizational Learning: A Theory of Action Perspective*. Reading, MA: Addison-Wesley, 1978.

Argyris, Chris, R. Putnam, & D.M. Smith. *Action Science*. San Francisco, CA: Jossey-Bass, 1985.

Bakken, Bent. "Learning and Transfer of Understanding in Dynamic Decision Environments." Unpublished Ph.D. dissertation, MIT Sloan School of Management, Cambridge, MA., 1993.

Banathy, Bela H. *Systems Design of Education*. Engelwood Cliffs, NJ: Educational Technology Publications, 1991.

Banathy, Bela H. *A Systems View of Education*. Engelwood Cliffs, NJ: Educational Technology Publications, 1992.

Bandler, Richard & John Grinder. *The Structure of Magic*. Palo Alto, CA: Science and Behavior Books, 1975.

Barfield, L. *The User Interface: Concepts & Design*. Reading, MA: Addison-Wesley, 1993.

Barr, P.S., J.L. Stimpert, & A.S. Huff. "Cognitive Change, Strategic Action, and Organizational Renewal." *Strategic Management Journal*, 13, 1992.

Barrett, William. *The Illusion of Technique.* New York, NY: Anchor Press/ Doubleday, 1979.

Bauersfeld, P. *Software by Design: Creating People Friendly Software.* New York, NY: M&T Books, 1994.

Beard, David. "Learning to Change Organizations." *Personnel Management,* Jan. 1993.

Beck, M. "Learning Organizations—How to Create Them." *Industrial & Commercial Training,* 21(3), 1989.

Beckhard, R. & Wendy Pritchard. *Changing the Essence: The Art of Creating and Leading Fundamental Change in Organizations.* San Francisco, CA: Jossey-Bass, 1992.

Bennett, J.G. *Deeper Man.* London: Turnstone Books, 1978.

Bennett, J.G. *The Dramatic Universe.* Charlestown, WV: Claymont Communications, 1966.

Bennett, J.G. *The Dramatic Universe: Volume II, The Foundations of Moral Philosophy.* Charlestown, WV: Coombe Springs Press, 1956.

Bennis, Warren. *On Becoming a Leader.* Reading, MA: Addison-Wesley, 1989.

Benson, Tracy. "The Learning Organization: Heading Toward Places Unimaginable." *Industry Week,* Jan. 4, 1993.

Bertalanffy, L. "The Theory of Open Systems in Physics and Biology." *Science,* 111, 1950.

Bethanis, Susan J. *Transforming Organizations: Understanding the Relationships Among Paradigms, Language, and Action.* Doctoral dissertation, University of San Francisco, School of Education, UMI Publications, 1993.

Birren, F. *Color and Human Response.* New York, NY: Van Nostrand Reinhold, 1978.

Bissonette, Douglas R. & Lisa A. Murray. *Learning Design Principles.* Cambridge, MA: MicroMentor, 1994.

Blanchard, Kenneth & Norman Vincent Peal. *The Power of Ethical Management.* New York, NY: Fawcett Crest, 1982.

Block, Peter. *Stewardship: Choosing Service over Self-Interest.* San Francisco, CA: Berrett-Koehler, 1993.

Bohm, David. *On Dialogue.* Ojai, CA: Ojai Institute, 1989.

Bohm, David. Unpublished address given at an MIT seminar, October 3, 1989.

Bohm, David. *Wholeness and the Implicate Order.* London: Ark Paperbacks, 1983.

Bohm, David & Mark Edwards. *Changing Consciousness.* San Francisco, CA: Harper, 1991.

Bolman, Lee & Terrence Deal. *Reframing Organizations.* San Francisco, CA: Jossey-Bass, 1991.

Bowers, C.A. "Curriculum as Cultural Reproduction: An Examination of Metaphor as a Carrier of Ideology." *Teacher's College Record,* Vol. 82, 1980.

Bowers, C.A. *Responsive Teaching: An Ecological Approach to Classroom Patterns of Language, Culture, and Thought.* New York, NY: Teachers College Press, 1990.

Bradshaw, John. *The Family.* Deerfield Beach, FL: Health Communications, Inc., 1988.

Bradshaw, John. *Healing the Shame that Binds You.* Deerfield Beach, FL: Health Communications, Inc., 1988.

Bridges, William. *Transitions, Making Sense of Life's Changes.* New York, NY: Addison-Wesley, 1980.

Brookfield, Stephen D. *Developing Critical Thinkers: Challenging Adults to Explore Alternative Ways of Thinking and Acting.* San Francisco and Oxford: Jossey-Bass, 1987.

Brown, John S. & Paul Duguid. "Learning & Improvisation: Local Sources of Global Innovation," draft document, 1989.

Brown, John S., Paul Duguid, & Susan Haviland. "Towards Informed Participation: Six Scenarios in Search of Democracy in the Electronic Age." *The Promise and Perils of Emerging Information Technology.* Washington, DC: Aspen Institute, 1993.

Brown, Juanita. "Corporation As Community: A New Image for a New Era." In *New Traditions in Business.* John Renesch (ed.). San Francisco, CA: Berrett-Koehler, 1992.

Buber, Martin. *I and Thou.* New York, NY: Charles Scriber's Sons, 1970.

Calvert, Gene. *Highwire Management: Risk-Taking Tactics For Leaders, Innovators and Trailblazers.* San Francisco, CA: Jossey-Bass, 1993.

Campbell, Joseph. *The Power of Myth.* New York, NY: Anchor-Doubleday, 1988.

Capezio, P. & D. Morehouse. *Taking the Mystery out of TQM: A Practical Guide to Total Quality Management.* Hawthorne, NJ: Career Press, 1993.

Capra, Fritjof. *The Tao of Physics.* New York, NY: Bantam Books, 1976.

Capra, Fritjof. *The Turning Point: Science, Society, and the Rising Culture.* New York, NY: Bantam Books, 1983.

Carroll, G.R. "A Sociological View On Why Firms Differ." *Strategic Management Journal,* 14(4), 1993.

Carroll, J. Designing Interaction: *Psychology at the Human-Computer Interface.* New York, NY: Cambridge University Press, 1991.

Casey, A. *A Study of the Content, Structure, and Transmittal of Collective Memory In An Organization.* Unpublished dissertation, The George Washington University, 1994.

Casey, Karen & Martha Vanceburg. *The Promise of a New Day.* Center City, MN: Hazelden Foundation, 1984.

Chijiiwa, H. *Color Harmony: A Guide to Creative Color Combinations.* Rockport, MA: Rockport Publishers, 1987.

Cory, Diane. *AT&T Teaching Tales.* Available from Diane Cory, 620 Sidelong Court, Sykesville, MD 21784.

Cox, K. & D. Walker. *User Interface Design (Second edition).* New York, NY: Prentice Hall, 1990.

Craig, R. (ed.). *Training and Development Handbook: (Third edition) A Guide to Human Resource Development.* New York, NY: McGraw Hill, 1987.

Cringely, Robert X. *Accidental Empires: How the Boys of Silicon Valley Make Their Millions, Battle Foreign Competition, and Still Can't Get a Date.* New York, NY: Harper Business, 1993.

Csikszentmihalyi, Mihalyi. *A Psychology for the Third Millennium.* New York, NY: Harpers Collins, 1993.

Csikszentmihalyi, Mihalyi. *Flow: The Psychology of Optimal Experience.* New York, NY: Harper & Row, 1990.

Culhane, S. *Animation From Script to Screen.* New York, NY: St. Martin's Press, 1988.

Daft, R.L. & K.E. Weick. "Toward a Model of Organizations as Interpretation Systems." *Academy of Management Review,* 9(2), 1984.

Danziger, K. "The Social Origins of Modern Psychology." Psychology in a Social Context. New York, NY: Irving Publishers, 1979.

Day, G.S. Learning About Markets: Commentary. Cambridge, MA: Marketing Science Institute, Report Number 91-117, 1991.

de Geus, Arie. "Planning as Learning." Harvard Business Review, Mar./Apr. 1988.

de Geus, Arie. Stockton Lecture. London Business School, May 3, 1990.

Deal, Terrance E. & Allen A. Kennedy. Corporate Cultures: The Rites and Rituals of Corporate Life. Addison-Wesley, 1982.

Deming, W. Edwards. Out of the Crisis. Cambridge, MA: MIT, Center for Advanced Engineering Study, 1986.

Deming, W. Edwards. The New Economics For Industry, Government, Education. Cambridge, MA: MIT, Center for Advanced Engineering Study, 1993.

DePree, Max. Leadership Is an Art. New York, NY: Currency Doubleday, 1989.

DePree, Max. Leadership Jazz. New York, NY: Currency Doubleday, 1992.

Diehl, Ernst. "Effects of Feedback Structure on Dynamic Decision Making." Unpublished Ph.D. dissertation, MIT Sloan School of Management, Cambridge, MA, 1992.

Diehl, Ernst. "Participatory Simulation Software for Managers: The Design Philosophy Behind Microworld Creator." European Journal of Operational Research, Amsterdam, North Holland, 1992.

Dilworth, R. Quotation included in material used by the Learning Organization Network of the American Society for Training and Development, 1991.

Dilworth, R. [Interview of Task Force member, Florida Power and Light], 1990.

Drucker, Peter. Management: Tasks, Responsibilities, Practices. New York, NY: Harper & Row, Publishers, 1973.

Drucker, Peter. Managing for the Future. New York, NY: Penguin Group, 1992.

Drucker, Peter. Post-Capitalist Society. Harper Business, 1993.

Dumaine, Brian. "Mr. Learning Organization." Fortune, October 17, 1994.

Echeverria, Rafael. Learning to Learn. San Francisco, CA: The Newfield Group, 1991.

Eisenberg, Dr. David et al. "Unconventional Medicine in the United States." The New England Journal of Medicine, Jan. 28, 1993.

Eisler, Riane. The Chalice and the Blade. San Francisco, CA: Harper, 1987.

Ernst & Young. Valuing the Learning Organization. Ernst and Young, Professional Development Symposium Journal, 1993.

Estes, Clarissa Pinkola. Women Who Run With the Wolves. New York, NY: Ballantine, 1992.

Filipczak, B. "I Am a Learning Organization." Training, Dec. 1993.

Fiol, C.M. & M.A. Lyles. "Organizational Learning." Academy of Management Review, 10, 1985.

Forrester, J. Industrial Dynamics. Portland, OR: Productivity Press, 1961.

Forrester, J. Principles of Systems. Portland, OR: Productivity Press, 1971.

Forrester, J. "System Dynamics and the Lessons of 35 Years." In De

Greene, Kenyon B. (ed.). *A Systems-Based Approach to Policymaking.* Boston: Kluwer Academic Publishers, 1993.

Frayling, C. *The Art Pack.* New York, NY: Alfred A. Knopf, 1993.

Galagan, Patricia. "The Learning Organization Made Plain: An Interview with Peter Senge." *Training & Development,* Oct. 1991.

Galen, Graham, et. al. "The Learning Organization: How Planners Create Organizational Learning." *Marketing Intelligence & Planning,* 1992.

Gardner, Howard. *Frames of Mind: The Theory of Multiple Intelligences, Tenth Anniversary Edition.* New York, NY: Basic Books, 1993.

Garvin, David A. "Building a Learning Organization." *Harvard Business Review,* 1993.

Gauthier, Alain. "Strategic Priorities." In Senge, Kleiner, Roberts, Ross, & Smith *The Fifth Discipline Fieldbook.* New York, NY: Doubleday/ Currency, 1994.

Gilligan, Carol. *In a Different Voice.* Cambridge, MA: Harvard University Press, 1982.

Glynn, M.A., F.J. Milliken, & T.K. Lant. *Learning About Organizational Learning: A Critical Review and Research Agenda.* Working Paper Series A, Number 88. New Haven, CT: Yale University, 1991.

Goodman, M. Study Notes in System Dynamics. Portland, OR: Productivity Press, 1974.

Greenleaf, Robert K. *Servant Leadership: A Journey in the Nature of Legitimate Power and Greatness.* New York, NY: Paulist Press, 1977.

Greenleaf, Robert K. *Teacher as Servant.* Indianapolis, IN: The Greenleaf Center, 1987.

Gundlach, A.M. *Sensemaking and Organizational Learning.* Unpublished dissertation. The George Washington University, 1994.

Hagberg, Janet. *Real Power: The Stages of Personal Power in Organization.* New York, NY: Harper Collins, 1984. Revised edition, San Francisco: Harper, 1994.

Hammer, Michael & James Champy. *Reengineering the Corporation.* New York, NY: Harper Collins, 1993.

Handy, Charles. *The Age of Unreason.* London, England: Hutchinson, 1989.

Handy, Charles. *The Age of Paradox.* Boston, MA: Harvard Business School Press, 1994.

Harman, Willis. *Global Mind Change: The Promise of the Last Years of the Twentieth Century.* Indianapolis, IN: Knowledge Systems, Inc. 1988.

Harman, Willis & John Hormann. *Creative Work: The Constructive Role of Business in a Transforming Society.* Indianapolis, IN: Knowledge Systems, Inc., 1990.

Harrison, Roger. "Strategies for a New Age." *Human Resources Management,* Fall, 1993.

Hawley, Jack. *Reawakening the Spirit in Work.* San Francisco, CA: Berrett Koehler, 1993.

Heckel, P. *The Elements of Friendly Software Design.* New York, NY: Warner Books, 1984.

Hedberg, B. "How Organizations Learn and Unlearn." F. Nystrom & W. Starbuck (eds.). Handbook of Organization Design. New York, NY: Oxford University Press, 1981.

Heidegger, M. *Poetry, Language, Thought.* New York, NY: Harper and Row, 1971.

Hertzel, B. *The Complete Guide to Software Testing.* Wellesley, MA: QED Information Sciences, 1984.

Hickman, Craig R. & Michael Silva. *Creating Excellence in Managing Corportate Cultures: Strategy & Change in the New Age.* New York, NY: Plume, 1984.

Hirsch, Gary B. & Jennifer M. Kemeny. "Mastering the Transition to Capitation." *Healthcare Forum Journal,* San Francisco, May/June 1994.

Hodgson, A. "Hexagons for Systems Thinking." In Morecroft & Sterman (eds.) *Modeling for Learning Organizations.* Portland, OR: Productivity Press, 1992.

Hodgson, Anthony M. *Thinking With Hexagons.* Eradour, Scotland: Idon Ltd., 1992.

Huber, G.P. "Organizational Learning: The Contributing Processes and the Literature." *Organizational Science,* 2(1), 1991.

Huczynski, A. & D. Boddy. "The Learning Organization: An Approach To Management Education and Development." *Studies in Higher Education,* 4(2), 1979.

Hyman, Sidney. *The Aspen Idea.* Norman, OK: University of Oklahoma Press, 1975.

IBM. *Object-Oriented Interface Design: IBM Common User Access™ Guidelines.* Carmel, IN: QUE Corporation, 1992.

Idon, Ltd. *Thinking with Hexagons: Users Manual.* Pitlochry, UK: Idon Publications, 1990.

Innovation Associates. *Visionary Planning.* Framingham, MA: Innovation Associates, 1987.

Institute for Research on Learning. A *New Learning Agenda, 'Putting People First.'* Palo Alto, CA. 1993.

Interact Healthcare Consortium. *An Idealized Design of the U.S. Healthcare System.* Bala Cynwyd, PA: Interact, 1992.

Isaacs, William. "Dialogue: The Power of Collective Thinking." *The Systems Thinker.* Cambridge, MA: Pegasus Communicatons, Apr. 1993.

Isaacs, William. "Taking Flight: Dialogue, Collective Thinking and Organizational Learning." *Organizational Dynamics, AMA Journal,* Fall, 1993.

Isaacs, William & Mitch Saunders. "Dialogue for Collective Learning & Inquiry: The MIT Dialogue Project." In *Healthier Communities Action Kit/Module 2.* San Francisco, CA: The Healthcare Forum, 1993.

Jaccaci, A. "The Social Architecture of a Learning Culture." *Training & Development Journal,* 43(11), 1989.

Janeway, Elizabeth. *Between Myth and Morning: Women Awakening.* New York, NY: William Morrow & Co., 1974.

Jones, Lauren. "We Need to Re-expand Our Organizational Brains." *Journal for Quality and Participation,* June 1993.

Jones, Michael. *A Conversation With Michael Jones.* Audio tape. Milwaukee, WI: Narada Productions, Inc., 1990.

Jones, Michael. *After the Rain.* Compact disc. Milwaukee, WI: Narada Productions, Inc., 1985.

Jones, Michael. *Morning in Medonte.* Compact disc. Milwaukee, WI: Narada Productions, Inc., 1992.

Kampmann, Christian E. "Feedback Complexity and Market Adjustment: An Experimental Approach." Unpublished Ph.D. dissertation, MIT Sloan School of Management, Cambridge, MA, 1992.

Kanter, Rosabeth Moss. *The Change Masters: Innovation & Entrepreneurship in the American Corporation.* New York, NY: Simon & Schuster, 1983.

Kanter, Rosabeth Moss. *When Giants Learn to Dance: Mastering the Challenges of Strategy, Management, and Careers in the 1990s.* New York, NY: Simon & Schuster, 1989.

Kanter, Rosabeth Moss. *Men and Women of the Corporation.* New York, NY: Basic Books, new edition 1993.

Kanter, Rosabeth Moss, Barry A. Stein, & Todd D. Jick. *The Challenge of Organizational Change: How Companies Experience It and Leaders Guide It.* New York, NY: The Free Press, 1992.

Kaplan, Robert D. "The Coming Anarchy." *Atlantic Monthly.* New York, NY: Feb. 1994.

Kaplan-Williams, Strephon. "Purpose." *Dream Cards,* card #55, Fireside, 1991.

Kauffman, D. *Systems 1: An Introduction to Systems Thinking.* Minneapolis, MN: S. A. Carlton, 1980.

Kearney, Richard. "Paul Ricoeur and the Hermeneutic Imagination." T. P. Kemp & D. Rasmussen (eds.), *The Narrative Path.* Cambridge, MA: MIT Press, 1989.

Kenley, Dr. Joan. *Voice Power: A Breakthrough Method to Enhance Your Speaking Voice.* New York, NY: Henry Holt, 1989.

Kiechel, W., III. "The Organization That Learns." *Fortune,* 121(6), 1990.

Kiefer, Charles. "Leadership in Metanoic Organizations." *New Traditions in Business.* John Renesch (ed.), San Francisco, CA: Berrett Koehler, 1991.

Kiernan, N. "The New Strategic Architecture: Learning To Compete In The Twenty-First Century." *Academy of Management Executive,* 1993.

Kim, Daniel H. "Learning Laboratories: Designing Reflective Learning Environments." In P. Milling & E. Zahn (eds.), *Computer-Based Management of Complex Systems: Proceedings of the 1989 International Conference of the System Dynamics Society.* Berlin: Springer-Verlag, 1989.

Kim, Daniel. "Guidelines for Drawing Causal Loop Diagrams." *The Systems Thinker,* 3(1), Cambridge, MA: Pegasus Communications, 1992.

Kim, Daniel. "Learning Laboratories: Practicing Between Performances." *The Systems Thinker,* 3(8), Cambridge, MA: Pegasus Communications, 1992.

Kim, Daniel. "Systems Archetypes at a Glance." *The Systems Thinker,* 3(4), Cambridge, MA: Pegasus Communications, 1992.

Kim, Daniel H. *Toolbox Reprint Series: Systems Archetypes.* Cambridge, MA: Pegasus Communications, 1992.

Kim, Daniel H. "Paradigm-Creating Loops: How Perceptions Shape Reality." *The Systems Thinker,* Cambridge, MA: Pegasus Communications, March, 1993.

Kim, Daniel H. "A Framework and Methodology for Linking Individual and Organizational Learning: Applications in TQM and Product Development." Unpublished Ph.D. dissertation, MIT Sloan School of Management, Cambridge, MA, May, 1993.

Kim, Daniel H. *Managerial Practice Fields: Infrastructures of a Learning Organization,* 1994.

Kim, Daniel H., & Peter M. Senge. "Putting Systems Thinking into Practice," *System Dynamics Review*, Vol. 10, No. 2-3, 1994.

Kolb, David A. *Experiential Learning*. Prentice Hall, 1984.

Korten, David C. *Getting to the 21st Century: Voluntary Action and the Global Agenda*. West Hartford, CT: Kumarian Press, 1990.

Kossleyn, S. *Elements of Graph Design*. New York, NY: W. H. Freeman and Company, 1994.

Kouzes, James M. & Barry Z. Posner. *Credibility: How Leaders Gain and Lose It, Why People Demand It*. San Francisco, CA: Jossey-Bass, 1993.

Kramlinger, Tom. "Training's Role in a Learning Organization," *Training*, July, 1992.

Kreutzer, D., J. Gould, & W. Kreutzer. "Designing Management Simulators" in Zepeda and Manchuca (eds.), *Proceedings International Systems Dynamics Conference*, Cancun, Mexico, 1993.

Krishnamurti, J. *On the Nature of the Environment*. San Francisco, CA: Harper, 1991.

Kuhn, T. *The Structure of Scientific Revolutions*. Chicago: Chicago University Press, 1970.

L'Engle. *A Wrinkle in Time*. New York, NY: Dell, 1962.

Lakoff, George. *Women, Fire, and Dangerous Things*. Chicago, IL: University of Chicago Press, 1987.

Lakoff, George & Mark Johnson. *Metaphors We Live By*. Chicago, IL: Univ of Chicago Press, 1980.

Langer, Monika M. and Merleau-Ponty. *Phenomenology of Perception*. Tallahassee, FL: Florida State University Press, 1962.

Lant, T.K. and S.J. Mezias. "Managing Discontinuous Change: A Simulation Study of Organizational Learning and Entrepreneurship," *Strategic Management Journal*, Volume 11, 1990.

Laurel, B. (ed.). *The Art of Human-Computer Interface Design*. Reading, MA: Addison-Wesley, 1990.

Laurel, B. *Computers as Theatre*. Reading, MA: Addison-Wesley, 1991.

Laybourne, K. *The Animation Book: A Complete Guide to Animated Filmmaking from Flip-Books to Sound Cartoons*. New York, NY: Crown Publishers, Inc., 1979.

Levey, Joel & Michelle Levey. *The Focused MindState*. Chicago, IL: Nightingale-Conant, 1993.

Levey, Joel & Michelle Levey. *Quality of Mind: Tools for Self Mastery and Enhanced Performance*. Boston, MA: Wisdom Publications, 1990.

Lindbergh, C.C. "On Organizational Learning: Implications and Opportunities for Expanding Organizational Development." In Woodman, R.W. and W.A. Pasmore (Eds.), *Research in Organizational Change and Development*, Volume 3, Greenwich, CT: JAI Press, 1989.

Lindgaard, G. *Usability Testing and System Evaluation: A Guide for Designing Useful Computer Systems*. London, England: Chapman & Hall, 1994.

Loeb, Marshall. "Editor's Desk." *Fortune*, December 14, 1992.

Mack, Alice. "The Missing Link in Leadership Development: How Hearts and Minds are Changed," *World Business Academy Perspectives*, Volume 7, Number 1, 1993.

Madison, G. B. *The Hermeneutics of Postmodernity*. Bloomington, IN: Indiana University Press, 1988.

Mandel, T. *The GUI-OOUI War: Windows™ vs. OS/2®: The Designer's Guide to Human-Computer Interfaces*. New York, NY: Van Nostrand Rheinhold, 1994.

Mander Jerry. *In the Absence of the Sacred: The Failure of Technology and the Survival of the Indian Nations.* San Francisco, CA: Sierra Club Books, 1991.

Marquardt, M. & A. Reynolds. *The Global Learning Organization:* New York, NY: Irwin Publishing, 1993.

Marsick, Victoria. "Learning In The Workplace: The Case For Reflectivity And Critical Reflectivity," *Adult Education Quarterly,* 38 (4), 1988.

Marsick, V. & K. Watkins. "The Learning Organization: An Integrative Vision For HRD," *Proceedings of the First Annual Academy of Human Resource Development Conference,* 1994.

Marsick, Victoria & Karen Watkins. *Informal and Incidental Learning in the Workplace.* London & New York, NY: Routledge, 1990.

Maturana, Humberto R. and Francisco J. Varela. *The Tree of Knowledge.* London: New Science Library, Shambhala, 1988.

Mayeroff, Milton. *On Caring.* New York, NY: Harper & Row, 1972.

McCall, Morgan and Michael Lombardo. *Off the Track: Why and How Successful Executives Get Derailed.* Center for Creative Leadership, Jan. 1983.

McKnight, C., A. Dillon, & J. Richardson (eds.) *HyperText: A Psychological Perspective.* New York, NY: Ellis Horwood, 1993.

Merton, Thomas. "The Sacred City." In *Preview of the Asian Journey.* New York, NY: Crossroads, 1991.

Meyer, A., A. Tsui and C.R. Hinings. "Configurational Approaches To Organizational Analysis," *The Academy of Management Journal,* 36:6, 1993.

Mezirow, Jack. Lectures and conversations, and *Transformative Dimensions of Adult Learning.* San Francisco & Oxford: Jossey-Bass, 1991.

Michael, Donald N. "Governing by Learning: Boundaries, Myths and Metaphors," *Futures,* 25 (1), 1993.

Michael, Donald N. "Leadership's Shadow: The Dilemma of Denial," *Futures,* Volume 23, Number 1, 1991.

Michael, Donald .N. *On Planning to Learn and Learning to Plan.* San Francisco, CA: Jossey-Bass, 1973.

Microsoft, Inc. *The Windows Interface.* Redmond, WA: Microsoft Press, 1987.

Miller, Alice. *For Your Own Good.* New York, NY: The Noonday Press, 1990.

Miller, Lawrence M.. *American Spirit: Visions of a New Corporate Culture.* New York, NY: Warner Books, 1984.

Minasi, M. *Secrets of Effective GUI Design.* Alameda, CA: SYBEX, Inc., 1994.

Mindell, Arnold. *The Year I, Global Process Work: Community Creation from Global Problems, Tensions and Myths.* New York, NY: Penguin Group, 1989.

Mintzberg, Henry. "The Rise and Fall of Strategic Planning," *Harvard Business Review,* Jan./Feb. 1994.

Morecroft, J. & J. Sterman. *Modeling for Learning Organizations.* Portland, OR: Productivity Press, 1994.

Morgan, Gareth. *Images of Organization.* Newbury Park, CA: Sage Publications, 1986.

Morimoto, Kiyo. "Notes on the Context of Learning," *Harvard Educational Review,* 1973.

Morris, L. "A Focus On Development," *Training & Development*, Nov. 1992.

Morris, L. "Learning Organizations: Settings for Developing Adults," in *Development in the Workplace*. Demick, J. & Miller P. Hillsdale, New Jersey: Lawrence Erlbaum Associates, 1993.

Nahser, F. Byron and Susan Mehrtens. *Executive Summary: What's Really Going On?* . Corporantes Business, 1993.

Nielson, J. & R. Mack. *Usability Inspection Methods*. New York, NY: John Wiley & Sons, Inc., 1994.

Nielson, J. *Usability Engineering*. Boston, MA: AP Professional, 1993.

Nonaka, Ikujiro. "The Knowledge-Creating Company." *Harvard Business Review*, Nov./Dec. 1991.

Norman, D. *The Design of Everyday Things*. New York, NY: Doubleday Currency, 1988.

Norman, D. *User Centered System Design: New Perspectives on Human-Computer Interaction*. Hillsdale, NJ: Lawrence Erlbaum Associates, Publishers, 1986.

O'Neal, F. *From Individual Knowing to Organizational Learning: An Analysis of Factors impacting the Organizational Utilization of Individually Valued Information*. Unpublished dissertation. The George Washington University, 1994.

O'Neil, John. *The Paradox of Success: When Winning at Work Means Losing at Life: A Book of Renewal for Leaders*. New York, NY: Tarcher/Putnam, 1994.

Ornstein, Robert & Paul Ehrlich. *New World New Mind: Moving Toward Conscious Evolution*. New York, NY: Doubleday, 1989.

Osterberg, Rolf. *Corporate Renaissance*. Mill Valley, CA: Nataraj Publishing, 1993.

O'Toole, James. *The Executive's Compass*. New York, NY: Oxford University Press, 1993.

Pagels, Elaine. *The Gnostic Gospels*. New York, NY: Vintage Books, 1989.

Palmer, Parker J. "Leading From Within." Delivered to the Meridian Street United Methodist Church in Indiana on March 23, 1990. Available from Potter's House Book Service, 1658 Columbia Road NW, Washington, DC 20009.

Papert, Seymour. *Mindstorms*. New York, NY: Basic Books, 1980.

Parikh, Jagdish. *Managing your Self. Management by Detached Involvement*. London: Basil Blackwell Publishers, 1991.

Parish, Mary. *Characteristics of Dialogue As a Tool*. Materials available from MVP Associates, 3313 Strawberry Run, Davidsonville, MD 21035.

Parsons, T. R. Bales and E. Shils. *Working Papers In the Theory of Action*. Glencoe, IL: The Free Press, 1953.

Parsons, T. *The Social System*. Glencoe, IL: The Free Press, 1951.

Pearce, Joseph Chilton. *Evolution's End: Claiming the Potential of Our Intelligence*. San Francisco, CA: Harper, 1992.

Peavey, Fran. "Strategic Questioning: An Approach to Creating Personal and Social Change." In her book *By Life's Grace*. Philadelphia: New Society Publishers, 1994.

Pedler, Mike, John Burgoyne & Tom Boydell. *The Learning Company*. London: McGraw-Hill, 1991.

Perry, William G., Jr. *Forms of Intellectual and Ethical Development in the College Years*. New York, NY: Holt, Rinehart and Winston, Inc., 1968.

Popper, Micha. "The Israeli Defence Forces: An Example of Transformational Leadership," *Leadership & Organizational Development Journal,* 1992.

Pór, G. *What is a Corporate Learning Expedition?* Paper distributed at the Collaborative in Social Architecture, Cambridge, MA, June, 1991.

Preece, J. *A Guide to Usability: Human Factors in Computing.* Reading, MA: Addison-Wesley, 1993.

Preece, J., Y. Rogers, H. Sharp, D. Benyon, S. Holland, & T. Carey. *Human-Computer Interaction.* Reading, MA: Addison-Wesley Publishing Company, 1994.

Pritchett, Price and Ron Pound. *High-Velocity Culture Change.* Dallas: Pritchett Publishing Company, 1993.

Progoff, Ira. *At a Journal Workshop.* New York, NY: Dialogue House Library, 1975.

Quinn, Daniel. *Ishmael.* New York, NY: Bantam/Turner, 1992.

Rabb, M. *The Presentation Design Book.* Chapel Hill, NC: Ventana Press, 1993.

Randers, J. "Guidelines for Model Conceptualization" in Randers, Jørgen (ed.). *Elements of the System Dynamics Method.* Portland, OR: Productivity Press, 1980.

Ray, Michael. Paper presented at Ernst & Young's Valuing the Learning Organization Symposium, Vienna, VA, 1992.

Ray, Michael. "The Emerging New Paradigm in Business," *New Traditions in Business.* John Renesch (ed.). San Francisco, CA: Berrett Koehler, 1992.

Rayner, Steven. *Recreating the Workplace.* Essex Junction: Oliver Wright, 1993.

Renesch, John (ed.). *New Traditions in Business: Spirit & Leadership in the 21st Century.* San Francisco, CA: Berrett-Koehler Publishing, 1992.

Renesch, John (ed.). *Leadership in a New Era: Visionary Approaches to the Biggest Crisis of Our Time.* San Francisco, CA: New Leaders Press, 1994.

Revans, R. *Education In A Changing World: The Origins And Growth Of Action Learning.* Unpublished manuscript, 1994.

Richardson, George P., & Alexander L. Pugh. *Introduction to System Dynamics Modeling with DYNAMO.* Cambridge, MA: MIT Press, 1981.

Richmond, Barry, et al. *The ithink™ software and documentation.* Hanover, NH: High Performance Systems, Inc., 1994.

Rilke, Rainier Maria. *Letters to a Young Poet.* New York, NY: Norton & Co., 1954.

Robinson, J. "Managerial Sketches of the Steps of Modeling." In Randers, Jørgen (ed). *Elements of the System Dynamics Method.* Portland, OR: Productivity Press, 1980.

Rocher, G. *Talcott Parsons and American Sociology.* New York, NY: Barnes & Noble, 1975.

Rosen, Robert and Lisa Berger. *The Healthy Company.* New York, NY: The Putnam Publishing Group, 1993.

Rosenbluth, Hal F. and Diane McFerrin Peters. *The Customer Comes Second (And Other Secrets Of Exceptional Service).* New York, NY: William Morrow & Co., 1992.

Rosener, Judy. "Ways Women Lead," *Harvard Business Review,* Nov./Dec. 1990.

Rubin, J. *Handbook of Usability Testing: How to Plan, Design, and Conduct Effective Tests.* New York, NY: John Wiley & Sons, Inc., 1994.

Rubinstein, R. & H. Hersh. *The Human Factor: Designing Computer Systems for People.* Bedford, MA: Digital Press, 1984.

Russell, Peter. *The White Hole in Time: Our Future Evolution and the Meaning of Now.* San Francisco, CA: Harper, 1992.

Ryan, Kathleen D. and Daniel K. Oestreich. *Driving Fear Out of the Workplace.* San Francisco, CA: Jossey-Bass, 1991.

Sakaiya, Taichi. *The Knowledge Value Revolution.* Translated by George Fields and William Marsh. Tokyo and New York: Kodansha, 1991 Originally published in Japanese as as *Chika Kakumei.* Osaka: PHP Kenkyujo, 1985.

Sacks, O. *The Man Who Mistook His Wife for a Hat, and Other Clinical Tales.* New York, NY: Simon & Schuster, 1985.

Sandbulte, Arend. "Lead, Don't Manage," *Industry Week,* Nov. 1, 1993.

Sanford, Carol. "Leadership of Motivation: The Ethics and Practicality of Incentives." In *Leadership in a New Era,* John Renesch (ed.) San Francisco, CA: Sterling & Stone, 1994.

Sanford, Carol. *Systems: A Hierarchy Of Types.* Battle Ground, WA: SpringHill Publications, 1993.

Schein, Edgar H. *Career Dynamics-Matching Individual and Organizational Needs.* Reading, MA: Addison-Wesley, 1978.

Schein, Edgar H. *The Clinical Perspective in Fieldwork.* Newbury Park, CA: Sage Publications, 1987.

Schein, Edgar H. *Organizational Culture and Leadership* (Second edition). San Francisco, CA: Jossey-Bass, 1992

Schein, Edgar H. "On Dialogue, Culture and Organizational Learning," *Organizational Dynamics,* Autumn, 1993.

Schein, Edgar H. "How Can Organizations Learn Faster?" *Sloan Management Review,* Winter, 1993.

Schön, Donald. *Beyond the Stable State.* London: Temple Smith, 1971.

Schön, Donald. *Educating the Reflective Practitioner: Toward a New Design for Teaching and Learning in the Professions.* San Francisco & Oxford: Jossey-Bass, 1990.

Schwandt, D.R. and A.M. Gundlach. *Applying Organizational Learning to the Diagnostic Process.* Presentation at The Academy of Management Annual Meeting, Las Vegas, NV, 1992.

Seagal, Dr. Sandra & David Horne. *Humanity — A Living Technology: An Introduction to Human Dynamics.* To be published, 1995.

Searle, John. *The Re-discovery of the Mind.* Cambridge: MIT Press, 1992.

Senge, Peter M. *The Fifth Discipline: The Art and Practice of the Learning Organization.* New York, NY: Doubleday/Currency.1990.

Senge, Peter M. "Transforming The Practice Of Management," paper presented at the *Systems Thinking in Action Conference,* Nov., 1991; and in *Human Resource Development Quarterly,* San Francisco, CA: Jossey-Bass, 1993.

Senge, Peter M., & Colleen Lannon. "Managerial Microworlds," *Technology Review,* July.1990.

Senge, Peter M., Charlotte Roberts, Richard Ross, Bryan Smith & Art Kleiner. *The Fifth Discipline Fieldbook.* New York, NY: Currency Doubleday, 1994.

Shankman, Albert O. D. Workshop at the Himalayan Institute, Honesdale, PA:.April 28, 1990.

Sharef, Reginald. "QWL Programs Facilitate Change," *Personnel Journal*, Sept. 1990.

Shenson, H. *How to Develop & Promote Successful Seminars & Workshops*. New York, NY: John Wiley & Sons, Inc., 1990.

Shiba, S., A. Graham & D. Walden. *A New American TQM: Four Practical Revolutions in Management*. Portland, OR: Productivity Press, 1993.

Shneiderman, B. *Designing the User Interface: Strategies for Effective Human-Computer Interaction (2nd Edition)*. Reading, MA: Addison-Wesley, 1992.

Silber, K. & M. Stelnicki. "Writing Training Materials," in Craig, Robert (ed.), *Training and Development Handbook: (Third edition) A Guide to Human Resource Development*. New York, NY: McGraw Hill, 1987.

Simpson, Dr. Graham. Integral Health: Beyond the Medical Mystique. To be published, 1995.

Smith, Arthur. "Good Leaders," *Business & Economic Review*, Oct./Dec. 1990.

Smith, B. *Designing a Photograph*. New York, NY: Amphoto, 1985.

Solomon, Robert. *The Passions*. New York, NY: Anchor Press/Doubleday, 1976.

Sommerville, I. *Software Engineering*. Reading, MA: Addison-Wesley, 1992.

Srivastava, Suresh and Associates. *Executive Integrity*. San Francisco, CA: Jossey-Bass, 1988.

Stata, R. "Organizational Learning — The Key to Management Innovation," *Sloan Management Review*, Volume 30 Number 3, 1989.

Sterman, J. "A Skeptic's Guide to Computer Models." In *Foresight and National Decisions*. ed. L. Grant. Lanham, MD: University Press of America, 1988.

Sterman, J. "People Express Management Flight Simulator," Simulation Software and Documentation available from author, MIT Sloan School of Management, Cambridge, MA 02139, 1988.

Sterman, John D. "Deterministic Chaos in Models of Human Behavior: Methodological Issues and Experimental Results," *System Dynamics Review, 4 (1-2)*, 1988.

Sterman, John D. "Modeling Managerial Behavior: Misperceptions of Feedback in a Dynamic Decision Making Experiment," *Management Science, 35(3)*, 1989.

Sternberg, Robert. *The Triarchic Mind: A New Theory of Human Inteligence*. (out of print) New York, NY: Penguin Books, 1988.

Strauss, Anselm L. *Qualitative Analysis for Social Scientist*. Cambridge, MA: Cambridge University Press, 1987.

Tannen, Deborah. *You Just Don't Understand*. New York, NY: William Morrow and Company, 1990.

Tarutz, J. *Technical Editing: The Practical Guide for Editors and Writers*. Reading, MA: Addison-Wesley, 1992.

Thomas, B. *Disney's Art of Animation*. New York, NY: Hyperion, 1991.

Thomas, J. B., S.M. Clark and D.A. Gioia. "Strategic Sensemaking and Organizational Performance: Linkages Among Scanning, Interpretation, Action, and Outcomes," *Academy of Management Journal*, Volume 36, Number 2, 1993.

Thompson, John W. "Corporate Leadership in the 21st Century," *New Traditions in Business*. John Renesch (ed.). San Francisco, CA: Berrett-Koehler, 1992.

Thompson, John W. *The Human Factor: An Inquiry into Communication and Consciousness.* Farmdale, New York, NY: Coleman, 1993.

Tichy, N. "Crotonville: A Staging Ground For Corporate Revolution," *The Executive*, 3, 1989.

Tufte, E. *Envisioning Information.* Cheshire, CT: Graphics Press, 1990.

Tufte, E. *The Visual Display of Quantitative Information.* Cheshire, CT: Graphics Press, 1983.

Underwood, Paula. "When We Open Our Mouths to Speak," *Wildfire*, Volume 3, Number 4, Summer, 1988.

Underwood, Paula. "A Native American Worldview," *Noetic Sciences Review*, Number 15, Summer, 1990.

Underwood, Paula. "We Build In the Sacred Manner," *Wildfire*, Volume 3. Numbers 1 & 2, Winter, 1987.

Underwood, Paula. *Many Circles, Many Paths: A Native American Learning Story.* Georgetown, TX: Tribe of Two Press, Storytellers Edition, Summer, 1994.

Underwood, Paula. *The Walking People: A Native American Oral History.* Austin: Tribe of Two Press, 1993.

Underwood, Paula. *Three Strands in the Braid: A Guide for Enablers of Learning.* Georgetown, TX: A Tribe of Two Press, 1985, 1994.

Underwood, Paula. *Who Speaks for Wolf: A Native American Learning Story.* Georgetown, TX: Tribe of Two Press, 1985, 1991, 1994.

Underwood, Paula. *Winter White and Summer Gold: A Native American Learning Story.* Georgetown, TX: Tribe of Two Press, Storytellers Edition, Summer, 1994.

Vaill, Peter. *Managing as a Performing Art.* San Francisco, CA: Jossey-Bass, 1989.

Van Maaen, John. *Tales of the Field.* Chicago, IL: University of Chicago Press, 1988.

Vogt, Eric E. and Nancy Gottlieb. *An Executive Introduction to Learning Organizations.* Cambridge, MA: MicroMentor, 1993.

Vogt, Eric E. *The Art and Architecture of Powerful Questions.* Cambridge, MA: MicroMentor, 1994.

Wack, Pierre. "Scenarios: Shooting the Rapids," *Harvard Business Review,* Nov./Dec. 1985.

Walsh, J. P. *Managerial and Organizational Cognition: Notes From a Trip Down Memory Lane.* Unpublished Manuscript. Ann Arbor, MI: University of Michigan, 1992.

Walsh, J.P. and G.R. Ungson. "Organizational Memory," *Academy of Management Review,* Volume 16, Number 1, 1991.

Walton, Mary. *Deming Management at Work.* New York, NY: Putnam Publishing, 1990.

Walton, Mary. *The Deming Management Method.* Perigree Books, 1986.

Wardman, Kellie T. *No More Band-Aids for Healthcare Reform.* Cambridge, MA: The Systems Thinker — Pegasus Communications, August, 1992.

Wardman, Kellie T. *Reflections on Learning Organizations .* Cambridge, MA: Pegasus Communications, 1994.

Watkins, Karen E. & Victoria Marsick. *Sculpting the Learning Organization: Lessons in the Art and Science of Systemic Change*: San Francisco, CA: Jossey-Bass, 1993.

Webber, Alan W. "What's So New About the New Economy?" *Harvard Business Review*, Jan./Feb. 1993.

Weick, K.E. "The Nontraditional Quality of Organizational Learning," *Organizational Science,* 2:1, 1991.

Wheatley, Margaret J. *Leadership and the New Science: Learning About Organization from an Orderly Universe.* San Francisco, CA: Berrett-Koehler, 1992.

White, Frank. *The Overview Effect: Space Exploration and Human Evolution.* Boston, MA: Houghton Mifflin, 1987.

Wick, Calhoun W. and Lu Stanton Leon. *The Learning Edge (How Smart Managers and Smart Companies Stay Ahead).* McGraw-Hill, 1993.

Wiklund, M. *Usability in Practice: How Companies Develop User-Friendly Products.* Boston, MA: AP Professional, 1994.

Wilber, K., J. Engler & D.P. Brown. *Transformations In Consciousness: Conventional And Contemplative Perspectives On Development.* Boston: Shambala, New Science Library, 1986.

Wilkins, Alan. *Developing Corporate Character.* San Francisco, CA: Jossey-Bass, 1989.

Wilson, Fiona. "Language, Technology, Gender and Power," *Human Relations,* 1992.

Winograd, Terry & Fernando Flores. *Understanding Computers and Cognition.* Norwood, NJ: Ablex, 1986.

Wittgenstein, Ludwig. *Philosophical Investigations.* New York, NY: Macmillan, 1953.

Wolfe, Dr. Sidney M. *Health Letter.* Washington, DC: Public Citizen Health Research Group, Feb. 1994.

Wood, M., B. Cole, & A. Gealt. *Art of the Western World: From Ancient Greece to Post-Modernism.* New York, NY: Summit Books, 1989.

Zelazny, G. *Say It with Charts: The Executive's Guide to Successful Presentations in the 1990s.* New York, NY: Irwin Professional Publishing, 1985 & 1991.

Zukav, Gary. "Evolution and Business," *The New Paradigm in Business: Emerging Strategies for Leadership and Organizational Change,* Ray and Rinzler (eds.). Tarcher/Perigee, 1993.

Periodicals

The New Leaders:
The Business Newsletter for
Transformative Leadership
(bimonthly newsletter)
New Leaders Press
1668 Lombard Street
San Francisco, CA 94123
800/928-LEAD

New Leaders Update
(a complimentary quarterly newsletter)
New Leaders Press
1668 Lombard Street
San Francisco, CA 94123
800/928-LEAD

The Systems Thinker
(newsletter - 10x/year)
Pegasus Communications
1696 Mass. Ave., Lower Level
Cambridge, MA 02138
617/576-1231

World Business Academy Perspectives
(quarterly journal)
Berrett-Koehler Publishers, Inc.
155 Montgomery St.
San Francisco, CA 94104-4109
800/929-2929

At Work: Stories of Tomorrow's Workplace
(bimonthly newsletter)
Berrett-Koehler Publishers, Inc.
155 Montgomery St.
San Francisco, CA 94104-4109
800/929-2929

Institutes and Centers

The Learning Circle
c/o Rita Cleary
83 Silver Hill Rd
Sudbury, MA 01776
508/443-4735

M.I.T. Organizational Learning Center
30 Memorial Drive
Bldg. E60, 3rd Floor
Cambridge, MA 02142
617/253-1549

The Dialogue Project
c/o M.I.T.
Attn: Dr. William Isaacs, director
30 Memorial Drive
Bldg. E60, 3rd Floor
Cambridge, MA 02142
617/253-2523
FAX: 617/252-1998

Bretton Woods and other gatherings
c/o Sheryl Erickson
11 Sophia Dr.
Uxbridge, MA 01569
508/278-6603

World Business Academy
P.O. Box 21470
Washington, DC 20009
202/822-4022

How to Contact Authors, Co-Authors, and Co-Editors

MARILYNNE ANDERSON
Right Associates
920 - 2nd Ave. #1050
Minneapolis, MN 55403
612/339-7387

SHERRIN BENNETT
Interactive Learning
1505 Bridgeway #121
Sausalito, CA 94965
415/331-4073

SUSAN J. BETHANIS
P.O. Box 2657
Mill Valley, CA 94942
415/383-2124

JUANITA BROWN
Whole Systems Assoc.
166 Homestead Blvd.
Mill Valley, CA 94941
415/381-3368
FAX: 415/388-9262

JUDY BROWN
3907 Calverton Dr.
Hyattsville, MD 20782
301/277-1477

MARY BYRD
Informix Software
4100 Bohannon Dr.
Menlo Park, CA 94025
415/926-6771
e-mail: mbyrd@informix.com

GENE CALVERT
Carpe Diem
1545 18th St. N.W., Suite 212
Washington, DC 20036
202/667-2647

DINESH CHANDRA
Global Quality Associates
567 N. University Dr.
Plantation, FL 33324
305/424-1571

SARITA CHAWLA
Meta Lens
23 Highland Ct.
Larkspur, CA 94939
415/924-8327

DIANE CORY
The Learning Circle
19 Larch Row
Wenham, MA 01984
800/436-4871

ROBERT L. DILWORTH
12400 North Lake Place
Richmond, VA 23284-2020
804/360-8241

ALAIN GAUTHIER
Core Leadership Development
1 Fernhoff Ct.
Oakland, CA 94619
510/530-5500

ALAN K. GRAHAM
Product Development
37 Stoneymead Way
Acton, MA 01720
508/263-8719

BOB GUNS
Probe Consulting Inc.
27790 Sayers Cr.
Maple Ridge B.C. V2X 8X8
Canada
604/462-8757

CHARLES HANDY
73 Putney Hill
London SW15 3NT
U.K.

FRANK HOFFMANN
Rosenbluth International
Travel
2401 Walnut St.
Philadelphia, PA 19103
215/977-4301

ROSABETH MOSS KANTER
Harvard Business School
Boston, MA 02163

DANIEL H. KIM
Pegasus Communications
1696 Mass. Ave.
Cambridge, MA 02138
617/576-1231

FRED KOFMAN
39 Clearwater Rd.
Brookline, MA 02043
617/735-2337

W. BRIAN KREUTZER
Gould-Kreutzer Assoc.
414 Arlington Rd.
Camp Hill, PA 17011
717/761-6629

DAVID P. KREUTZER
Gould-Kreutzer Assoc.
10 Rogers St. Ste. 210
Cambridge, MA 02142
617/577-1430

JOEL & MICHELLE LEVEY
Inner Work Technologies, Inc.
5536 Woodlawn Ave. N.
Seattle, WA 98103
206/632-3551

LISA J. MARSHALL
Syntax Communication Modeling Corp.
1365 Hamilton St. N.W.
Washington, DC 20011
202/829-0795

ROBERT L. MASTEN
Masten Consulting Group
201 Scarlett Dr.
Chesapeake, VA 23320
804/482-9315

SANDRA MOBLEY
The Learning Advantage
4404 S. Pershing Ct.
Arlington, VA 22204-1377
703/979-2133

LINDA E. MORRIS
Ernst & Young
Fairfax Square Tower 2 #8075
Vienna, VA 22182-2709
703/903-5573

KENDALL MURPHY
23 Highland Ct.
Larkspur, CA 94939
415/924-8327

JOHN RENESCH
Sterling & Stone/
New Leaders Press
1668 Lombard St.
San Francisco, CA 94123
415/928-1473

JAYME ROLLS
Rolls & Co. Inc.
1436 20th Street, #2
Santa Monica, CA 90404
310/315-9780

STEPHANIE RYAN
In Care
69 Lincoln St.
Manchester, MA 01944
508/526-9860

CAROL SANFORD
Spring Hill Publications
28036 N.E. 212th Ave.
Battle Ground, WA 98604
206/687-1408

DAVID K. SCHWANDT
The George Washington
University
2134 G St. N.W.
Washington, DC 20052
202/994-8650

PETER M. SENGE
M.I.T.
1 Amherst, E40-294
Cambridge, MA 02139
617/253-1549

BARBARA SHIPKA
P.O. Box 50005
Minneapolis, MN 55405
612/827-3006

JOHN W. THOMPSON
Human Factors Inc.
3301 Kerner Blvd. #200
San Rafael, CA 94901
415/459-6060

PAULA UNDERWOOD
The Past Is Prologue
P.O. Box 216
San Anselmo, CA 94979
415/457-6548

ERIC EDWARDS VOGT
Micromentor, Inc.
44R Brattle St.
Cambridge, MA 02138
617/234-5129

ROBERT WEINTRAUB
IBM Education & Training
500 Columbus Avenue
Thornwood, NY 10594
914/742-5875

BILL WITHERS
Learning Frontiers
2401 Walnut St.
Philadelphia, PA 19103
215/977-4301

JOHN H. WOOD
Center For Developmental
Organizations
20 Aquinas
Lake Oswego, OR 97035
503/635-7914

Index

BOOKS FROM PRODUCTIVITY PRESS

Productivity Press publishes books that empower individuals and companies to achieve excellence in quality, productivity, and the creative involvement of all employees. Through steadfast efforts to support the vision and strategy of continuous improvement, Productivity Press delivers today's leading-edge tools and techniques gathered directly from industrial leaders around the world. Call toll-free 1-800-394-6868 for our free catalog.

Modeling for Learning Organizations

John Morecroft and John Sterman, eds.

An outstanding compilation of articles by top system dynamics thinkers world-wide, offering a "user-friendly" introduction to leading edge methods of organization modeling and answers to many of the questions raised by Peter Senge's best-selling book *The Fifth Discipline*. Part 1 discusses generally how modeling can support management decision making. Parts 2 and 3 offer case studies. Part 4 evaluates the latest software technology for computer simulation modeling.
ISBN 1-56327-060-9 / 426 pages / price $45.00 / Order XMLO-B254

Introduction to Computer Simulation

Nancy Roberts, David Andersen, Ralph Deal, Michael Garet, William Shaffer

Simulation as an aid to solving problems has been a powerful tool for centuries. With the advent of the computer revolution, this tool has come within the reach of virtually everyone. This book is both an introduction to systems thinking—the critical element in problem solving for complex organizations—and a "how to" on building computer simulation models. Primarily developed as a classroom text, it is also a perfect vehicle for professionals in many different arenas (including business, government, and the social sciences) who want to reshape their organizations and their products or services by using system dynamics to solve complex problems. It provides a practical, concrete method for using computer simulation to model complex systems. No computer experience is required.
ISBN 1-56327-052-8 / 570 pages / $35.00 / Order XICS-B254

Fast Focus on TQM
A Concise Guide to Companywide Learning

Derm Barrett

Finally, here's one source for all your TQM questions. Compiled in this concise, easy-to-read handbook are definitions and detailed explanations of over 160 key terms used in TQM. Organized in a simple alphabetical glossary form, the book can be used either as a primer for anyone being introduced to TQM or as a complete reference guide. It helps to align teams, departments, or entire organizations in a common understanding and use of TQM terminology. For anyone entering or currently involved in TQM, this is one resource you must have.
ISBN 1-56327-049-8 / 186 pages / $20.00 / Order FAST-B254

Productivity Press, Inc., Dept. BK, P.O. Box 13390, Portland, OR 97213-0390
Telephone: 1-800-394-6868   Fax: 1-800-394-6286

Feedback Toolkit
16 Tools for Better Communication in the Workplace
Rick Maurer

In companies striving to reduce hierarchy and foster trust and responsible participation, good person-to-person feedback can be as important as sophisticated computer technology in enabling effective teamwork. Feedback is an important map of your situation, a way to tell whether you are "on or off track." Used well, feedback can motivate people to their highest level of performance. Despite its significance, this level of information sharing makes most managers uncomfortable. *Feedback Toolkit* addresses this natural hesitation with an easy-to-grasp 6-step framework and 16 practical and creative approaches for giving and receiving feedback with individuals and groups. Maurer's reality-tested methods in *Feedback Toolkit* are indispensable equipment for managers and teams in every organization.
ISBN 1-56327-056-0 / 109 pages / $15.00 / Order FEED-B254

Handbook for Productivity Measurement and Improvement
William F. Christopher and Carl G. Thor, eds.

An unparalleled resource! In over 100 chapters, nearly 80 front-runners in the quality movement reveal the evolving theory and specific practices of world-class organizations. Spanning a wide variety of industries and business sectors, they discuss quality and productivity in manufacturing, service industries, profit centers, administration, nonprofit and government institutions, health care and education. Contributors include Robert C. Camp, Peter F. Drucker, Jay W. Forrester, Joseph M. Juran, Robert S. Kaplan, John W. Kendrick, Yasuhiro Monden, and Lester C. Thurow. Comprehensive in scope and organized for easy reference, this compendium belongs in every company and academic institution concerned with business and industrial viability.
ISBN 1-56327-007-2 / 1344 pages / $90.00 / Order HPM-B254

The Hunters and the Hunted
A Non-Linear Solution for Reengineering the Workplace
James B. Swartz

Our competitive environment changes rapidly. If you want to survive, you have to stay on top of those changes. Otherwise, you become prey to your competitors. Hunters continuously change and learn; anyone who doesn't becomes the hunted and sooner or later will be devoured. This unusual non-fiction novel provides a veritable crash course in continuous transformation. It offers lessons from real-life companies and introduces many industrial gurus as characters. *The Hunters and the Hunted* doesn't simply tell you how to change; it puts you inside the change process itself.
ISBN 1-56327-043-9 / 582 pages / $45.00 / Order HUNT-B254

Productivity Press, Inc., Dept. BK, P.O. Box 13390, Portland, OR 97213-0390
Telephone: 1-800-394-6868   Fax: 1-800-394-6286

A New American TQM
Four Practical Revolutions in Management
Shoji Shiba, Alan Graham, and David Walden

For TQM to succeed in America, you need to create an American-style "learning organization" with the full commitment and understanding of senior managers and executives. Written expressly for this audience, *A New American TQM* offers a comprehensive and detailed explanation of TQM and how to implement it, based on courses taught at MIT's Sloan School of Management and the Center for Quality Management, a consortium of American companies. Full of case studies and amply illustrated, the book examines major quality tools and how they are being used by the most progressive American companies today.
ISBN 1-56327-032-3 / 606 pages / $50.00 / Order NATQM-B254

The Unshackled Organization
Facing the Challenge of Unpredictability Through Spontaneous Reorganization
Jeffrey Goldstein

Managers should not necessarily try to solve all the internal problems within their organizations; intervention may help in the short term, but in the long run may inhibit true problem-solving change from taking place. And change is the real goal. Through change comes real hope for improvement. Using leading-edge scientific and social theories about change, Goldstein explores how change happens within an organization and reveals that only through "self organization" can natural, lasting change occur. This book is a pragmatic guide for managers, executives, consultants, and other change agents.
ISBN 1-56327-048-X / 208 pages / $25.00 / Order UO-B254

Industrial Dynamics
Jay W. Forrester

A complete presentation of the system dynamics approach to the study of industrial systems, including the managerial viewpoint, classification of models, and advice to managers. The separate functions of management activity (cash flow, orders, materials, personnel, and capital equipment) are integrated by an information network. Critical system variables are revealed and policies for better management indicated.
ISBN 0-915299-88-7 / 464 pages / $50.00 paper / Order XINDDY-B254

WE HAVE MORE THAN 20 BOOKS ON SYSTEM DYNAMICS. CALL FOR A FREE BROCHURE

Productivity Press, Inc., Dept. BK, P.O. Box 13390, Portland, OR 97213-0390
Telephone: 1-800-394-6868   Fax: 1-800-394-6286

The Management Master Series

William F. Christopher, ed.

The Management Master Series offers business managers leading-edge information on the best contemporary management practices. Written by respected authorities, each set deals with a major theme; each of the six books within the set is a short "briefcase book" addressing a specific topic in a concise, to-the-point presentation. These are ideal books for busy managers who want to get the whole message quickly.

Set 1—Great Management Ideas

Management Alert: Don't Reform—Transform!

Michael J. Kami

ISBN 1-56327-064-1, Item # MS1-B254

Vision, Mission, Total Quality
Leadership Tools for Turbulent Times

William F. Christopher

ISBN 1-56327-055-2, Item # MS2-B254

The Power of Strategic Partnering

Eberhard E. Scheuing

ISBN 1-56327-065-X, Item # MS3-B254

New Performance Measures

Brian H. Maskell

1-56327-062-5, Item # MS4-B254

Motivating Superior Performance

Saul W. Gellerman

1-56327-063-3, Item # MS5-B254

Doing and Rewarding
Inside a High-Performance Organization

Carl G. Thor

ISBN 1-56327-061-7, Item # MS6-B254

SET 2—Total Quality

16 Points Strategy for Productivity and Total Quality

William F Christopher and Carl G. Thor

ISBN 1-56327-072-2, Item #MS7-B254

The TQM Paradigm: Key Ideas That Make It Work

Derm Barrett

ISBN 1-56327-073-0, Item #MS8-B254

Productivity Press, Inc., Dept. BK, P.O. Box 13390, Portland, OR 97213-0390
Telephone: 1-800-394-6868   Fax: 1-800-394-6286

Process Management
A Systems Approach to Total Quality
Eugene H. Melan

ISBN 1-56327-074-9, Item #MS9-B254

Practical Benchmarking for Mutual Improvement
Carl G. Thor

ISBN 1-56327-075-7, Item #MS10-B254

Mistake-Proofing
Designing Errors Out
Richard B. Chase and Douglas M. Stewart

ISBN 1-56327-076-5, Item #MS11-B254

Communication, Training, Developing for Quality Performance
Saul G. Gellerman

ISBN 1-56327-077-3, Item #MS12-B254

For additional books in these and other sets, call for a free catalog.

TO ORDER: Write, phone, or fax Productivity Press, Dept. BK, P.O. Box 13390, Portland, OR 97213-0390, phone 1-800-394-6868, fax 1-800-394-6286. Send check or charge to your credit card (American Express, Visa, MasterCard accepted).

U.S. ORDERS: Add $5 shipping for first book, $2 each additional for UPS surface delivery. Add $5 for each AV program containing 1 or 2 tapes; add $12 for each AV program containing 3 or more tapes. We offer attractive quantity discounts for bulk purchases of individual titles; call for more information.

ORDER BY E-MAIL: Order 24 hours a day from anywhere in the world. Our E-mail address is **order@ppress.com**. You can also order directly from our on-line catalog, available on the internet: **http://www.europa.com/productivity/press.html**

INTERNATIONAL ORDERS: Write, phone, or fax for quote and indicate shipping method desired. For international callers, telephone number is 503-235-0600 and fax number is 503-235-0909. Prepayment in U.S. dollars must accompany your order (checks must be drawn on U.S. banks). When quote is returned with payment, your order will be shipped promptly by the method requested.

NOTE: Prices are in U.S. dollars and are subject to change without notice.